Praise for Simon

WHITE H

"In their important, enlightening new book, economist Simon Johnson and lawyer James Kwak point out the absurdities of a budget debate dominated by partisan exaggerations and warnings of pending doom." —*San Francisco Chronicle*

"[Johnson and Kwak] shatter dozens of additional myths about deficit spending. . . . [Johnson and Kwak] thankfully dispel the widespread notion that a national debt totaling trillions of dollars means that a government is too big." —*USA Today*

"A detailed, lucid, sure-to-be controversial account of whether the massive national debt of the U.S. government actually matters. . . . [Johnson and Kwak's] especially valuable insight is that the national debt is a major problem only if it is perceived as a problem. . . . A book to be enjoyed by ideologues and non-ideologues of all stripes because it is not a tract for Republicans, Democrats or any other partisan organization." —*Kirkus Reviews*

"In this powerful book, Johnson and Kwak cut through both the partisanship and the complexities of the debate over America's national debt to give us a clear understanding of why it matters and what to do about it. America's future depends vitally upon bringing our deficits under control while also investing in our growth, and this book tells us how to do both." —Charles Ferguson, director of the Academy Award–winning documentary *Inside Job*

"Full of wisdom and specific recommendations, [*White House Burning*] reminds us that only when citizens understand the seriousness of our predicament will politicians take the necessary steps to strengthen our country. Let's hope this book is a bestseller." —Bill Bradley, former United States senator and cosponsor of the Tax Reform Act of 1986

"By skillfully placing the debt debate in an insightful historical context and providing detailed recommendations, Johnson and Kwak make a major and timely contribution to a national debate that will only get more heated in the years ahead. It's a must-read for those wondering about the relationship between the national debt and America's challenges; the choices that we must make to restore fiscal viability, promote growth, create jobs, and reduce inequality; and the way that polarized politics torpedoes coherent discussion of these complex issues."   —Mohamed A. El-Erian, CEO of PIMCO and prizewinning author of *When Markets Collide*

"Could there be a more important subject today than the national debt? And could there be two smarter, clearer, more incisive writers to tell us about it than Simon Johnson and James Kwak? With precision and common sense, *White House Burning* tells the story of where our debt came from, what it means, and what we can do about it. This is the kind of important, informed, and accessible book a democracy can't do without."   —Noah Feldman, Bemis Professor of International Law, Harvard Law School, and author of *Scorpions: The Battles and Triumphs of FDR's Great Supreme Court Justices*

"As they did in *13 Bankers*, Johnson and Kwak imbed a crucial current policy debate in the history of the United States economy. Their blueprint for resolving the budget problem without trampling on the basic needs of average Americans is must-reading."   —C. Fred Bergsten, director, Peterson Institute for International Economics

"If you are puzzled about how our country's finances got so messed up, look no further. Johnson and Kwak explain, with great lucidity and flair, how the battle lines on debt and taxes have been drawn going back to the founding fathers, and how things got off the rails in the last two decades. And they have good news for you: even if our politicians are incorrigible, our problems are not insoluble."   —Daron Acemoglu, Elizabeth and James Killian Professor of Economics, MIT, and coauthor of *Why Nations Fail: The Origins of Power, Prosperity, and Poverty*

SIMON JOHNSON *and* JAMES KWAK

WHITE HOUSE BURNING

Simon Johnson is the Ronald A. Kurtz Professor of Entrepreneurship at MIT's Sloan School of Management and a senior fellow of the Peterson Institute for International Economics. He was previously the chief economist of the International Monetary Fund. James Kwak is an Associate Professor at the University of Connecticut School of Law. He previously cofounded Guidewire Software.

www.baselinescenario.com

ALSO BY SIMON JOHNSON AND JAMES KWAK

13 Bankers:
The Wall Street Takeover and the Next Financial Meltdown

WHITE HOUSE BURNING

*Our National Debt
and Why It Matters to You*

SIMON JOHNSON *and* JAMES KWAK

VINTAGE BOOKS
A Division of Random House, Inc.
New York

FIRST VINTAGE BOOKS EDITION, FEBRUARY 2013

Copyright © 2012 by Simon Johnson and James Kwak

Portions of this work originally appeared in *Bloomberg View* (March, 2012).

The Library of Congress has cataloged the Pantheon edition as follows:
Johnson, Simon, [date]
White House burning : the founding Fathers, our national debt, and why it
matters to you / Simon Johnson, James Kwak.
p. cm.
Includes index.
1. Debts, Public—United States.
2. Government spending policy—United States.
3 Budget deficit—United States.
I. Kwak, James. II. Title.
HJ8101.J64 2012 336.3'40973—dc23 2012000435

Vintage ISBN: 978-0-307-94764-2

Author photographs © Anthony Armand Placet (Johnson)
and courtesy of the author (Kwak)

Book design by M. Kristen Bearse

www.vintagebooks.com

Printed in the United States of America
10 9 8 7 6 5 4 3 2 1

To Sylvia, Willow, Henry,
Mary, Celia, and Lucie

Contents

WHITE HOUSE BURNING

INTRODUCTION

Nothing is more important in the face of a war than cutting taxes.

—House majority leader Tom DeLay, 2003[1]

On June 1, 1812, President James Madison sent a letter to Congress asking it to consider a declaration of war against Great Britain. The Democratic-Republican majority in Congress was happy to oblige. For the original War Hawks, only military force could avenge repeated British infringements on American sovereignty—"the spectacle of injuries and indignities which have been heaped on our country," in Madison's words.[2] The insults to the United States ranged from seizing American ships on the high seas and impressing their sailors into the Royal Navy to supporting Native American attacks along the Western frontier. Attempts to apply economic pressure had backfired, and diplomacy appeared to be leading nowhere; as Madison said, "Our moderation and conciliation have had no other effect than to encourage perseverance and to enlarge pretensions."[3]

With war approaching, it fell to Treasury Secretary Albert Gallatin to pay for it. Gallatin hoped to finance the war with borrowed money, but he wanted to raise taxes enough to cover the interest on new debt.[4] Without higher taxes, he worried that bond investors would not be willing to lend large amounts of money to a young country fighting with a European superpower. But the War Hawks were ideologically and politically opposed to taxes—particularly the excise (internal trade) taxes that Gallatin wanted to impose. As the party of small government, the Democratic-Republicans believed that higher federal tax revenues constituted a threat to individuals' and states' rights.[5] Perhaps more importantly, they feared that rais-

ing taxes to fight a war could hurt them at the ballot box.[6] Congress
did increase some tariffs (taxes on external trade) in the run-up to
war, but failed to approve the internal taxes that Gallatin had pressed
for, instead authorizing the Treasury Department to borrow money.
But there were not enough investors willing to lend the amount
needed, even before war began, forcing the government to print
paper money.[7] On June 18, 1812, the United States declared war
against Great Britain. Less than a month later, Congress adjourned.

Hampered by Congress's reluctance to raise taxes, the Treasury
Department struggled to pay for soldiers in the field and ships at sea.
In 1813, with the government only weeks away from running out
of money, Gallatin was forced to rely on Philadelphia banker Stephen Girard to underwrite a massive loan—because, at that point,
Girard's credit was better than the government's.[8] The United States
military could win individual victories, but was unable to achieve
any of its major objectives, suffering repeated defeats on the border
with Canada, even with Great Britain distracted by the much larger
war against Napoleon in Europe. Congress finally agreed to impose
excise taxes in 1813,[9] but it was too late to build a world-class military.
After a decade of tight budgets, the U.S. Navy began the war with all
of seventeen ships. The Royal Navy commanded over one thousand
ships; even with many of them committed elsewhere, it was still able
to blockade the Eastern shoreline and raid the coast almost at will.[10]
Chesapeake Bay, the broad waterway leading to both Washington
and Baltimore, was defended by a collection of barges and gunboats
that were outclassed by the British navy and soon trapped in the
Patuxent River.[11] The approach to Washington along the Potomac
River was guarded by Fort Warburton, completed in 1809, about
ten miles downstream from the capital.[12] But when Pierre Charles
L'Enfant, the architect and city planner who had designed the city
of Washington, inspected the fort, he found it severely deficient and
recommended a redesign, more heavy guns, and construction of
a second fort nearby. The secretary of the navy added some more
guns, but there was no money for further improvements.[13]

In August 1814, British forces sailed into the Patuxent, an inlet of
Chesapeake Bay that points toward Washington. They cornered the
overmatched defensive flotilla, forcing the Americans to scuttle their
ships, and landed ground forces in Benedict, Maryland, less than

forty miles from the U.S. capital. The soldiers marched overland from Benedict, defeated an American militia at the Battle of Bladensburg, and eventually reached Washington, where they encountered little resistance. On the night of August 24, they burned the Capitol, the Treasury Building, and the White House*—after eating the dinner that had been set for that evening. Another British squadron sailed up the Potomac and bombarded Fort Warburton, whose defenders quickly abandoned their positions. From there, they continued upriver to capture the city of Alexandria, which was commercially more important than Washington at the time, seizing twenty-one merchant ships and their cargo.[14]

For the Americans, the burning of the White House was the low point of the war, a moment of national humiliation that remains an iconic image in U.S. history. Despite the symbolism, it was not a decisive turning point in the conflict; the two sides negotiated a peace later that year after deciding the war was no longer worth fighting.[15] But the vulnerability of America's capital highlighted the danger of going to war against one of the world's superpowers unprepared. As Admiral George Cockburn supervised the destruction of official Washington, someone called out to him, "If General Washington had been alive, you would not have gotten into this city so easily." "No," Cockburn replied. "If George Washington had been president we should never have thought of coming here."[16] But Washington, who had been forced to fight the Revolutionary War with an under-equipped, underpaid army, knew as well as anyone that any military was only as strong as the treasury that backed it. What the British had, more than anything else, was money—money to outfit and equip hundreds of ships and to fight simultaneous land wars in Europe and North America. By contrast, without a stable source of tax revenue, the United States struggled to attract lenders willing to bet on the country's unproven armed forces. Right up until the end of the war, military operations were hampered by failures to pay troops and contractors.[17]

This deep fiscal crisis was the product of one of the most bitter,

---

* The building was not officially known as the White House until 1901. Although the 1814 fire severely damaged the interior of the building, its external structure survived, and so today's White House is the same building that was burned by the British. The White House, "White House History," available at http://www.whitehouse.gov/about/history.

divisive political struggles in American history. Beginning in 1790, Treasury Secretary Alexander Hamilton pushed through a controversial series of fiscal policies that included restructuring the national debt, federal government assumption of state debts, a national bank, and excise taxes. Opposition to Hamilton's policies led Thomas Jefferson and James Madison to found the Democratic-Republican Party (often known simply as the Republican Party), which faced off against Hamilton's Federalists.* The small-government, anti-tax Republicans swept the elections of 1800, with Jefferson defeating Federalist incumbent president John Adams, and proceeded to reverse some of Hamilton's policies, repealing the excise taxes in 1802. To pay for these tax cuts, the Republicans cut defense spending, which was one reason for the military's unpreparedness in 1812.[18] The elimination of internal taxes also made government revenues dependent on tariffs, which were gutted first by an embargo against Great Britain and then by war. It was this battle over taxes and spending that led to the country's fiscal weakness in 1812.

Ironically, the Republicans, who voted for war but not for the taxes to pay for it, were the political victors of the War of 1812. The Federalists' opposition to the war—which, in some cases, extended to attempts to undermine the Treasury Department's efforts to raise money—made the party appear unpatriotic, and it never again gained power on the national level.[19] In a sense, however, the war also vindicated the principles laid out by Hamilton two decades before. Both Federalists and Republicans had always been "fiscally responsible" in the shallow sense that they believed the country should make required payments on its debts. But there is a deeper meaning of fiscal responsibility: the recognition that if you want something, you have to pay for it, either now or in the future. If a government cannot demonstrate that type of fiscal responsibility—through the willingness and capacity to levy and collect taxes when necessary—it will have trouble borrowing money in a time of crisis. This was missing in the Congress of 1812. As Representative John Randolph (an anti-

---

* The Democratic-Republican Party splintered in the 1820s; one faction became the modern Democratic Party. The Federalist Party dissolved in the 1820s. The modern Republican Party was founded in the 1850s.

war Republican) said sarcastically to his pro-war colleagues, "Go to war without money, without a military, without a navy!"[20] By 1813 and 1814, however, it was Republican majorities in Congress that voted to reinstate and then raise the internal taxes originally imposed by the hated Federalists.[21] Some things, everyone agreed, were worth paying for.

Fast forward to 2011. Once again, Washington is embroiled in a bitter partisan fight over taxes, spending, and debt. This time, unlike two centuries before, it is not primarily about war, although troops are still on the ground in the Middle East. The United States is the world's only true superpower, with the largest military and the largest economy on the planet, and its national survival is not in question. Nor does the Treasury have any trouble borrowing money. The dollar is the backstop currency of the global economy, and Treasury bonds are used in financial markets as the very definition of a safe asset.* Although the national debt is more than $10 trillion,† interest on that debt is barely $200 billion per year—less than 10 percent of the federal government's tax revenues.[22] Investors around the world, seeking safety from economic problems elsewhere, are hungry to lend money to the United States: interest rates on Treasury bonds are at their lowest level in more than half a century.[23]

And yet, on August 2, 2011, political squabbling brought the United States within a few days of defaulting on its debts.[24] Because of the debt ceiling—a legal limit on the total national debt—the Treasury Department could no longer borrow new money and would soon run out of cash to pay all of its bills.[25] Republicans in Congress demanded that any increase in the debt ceiling be accompanied by

---

* A bond is a promise to pay a specified amount of money at some point in the future, so selling a bond is a way of borrowing money. For example, the Treasury might issue a ten-year, $1,000 bond that pays 5 percent interest: that means that the holder of that bond will receive $50 per year and then $1,000 at the end of ten years. If the Treasury sells that bond to an investor for $1,000, then the Treasury is borrowing $1,000 from the investor and the investor is lending $1,000 to the Treasury, at an interest rate of 5 percent.

† Unless otherwise noted, the term "national debt" refers to debt owed by the federal government and held by parties other than the federal government; it does not include obligations of one part of the federal government to another, nor does it include debt owed by state and local governments.

equivalent, dollar-for-dollar reductions in spending;[26] Democrats, led by President Barack Obama, insisted either that the debt ceiling be increased without conditions or that any deal to reduce the deficit also include increased tax revenues. (Both sides declined to mention the fact that they had just months before collaborated on a major tax cut that *increased* the national debt by almost $860 billion.)[27] A minority of influential Republicans even argued that defaulting on the nation's debts would be a good thing, and they were seemingly backed by a plurality of the public, which opposed raising the debt ceiling in the abstract.[28] There the two parties stood until, on August 2, the Senate passed and the president signed a complicated compromise hammered out just two nights before.[29] The agreement cut spending by $900 billion over the next ten years and called on a bipartisan congressional committee to come up with a plan to reduce deficits by an additional $1.2 trillion over the same period. Three months later, just before its deadline, the so-called supercommittee gave up, unable to agree on anything.

This latest battle over taxes and spending was provoked by record federal government budget deficits, which in 2009 and 2010 exceeded $1 trillion for the first and second times in history. These deficits were not the result of war, although a decade of fighting in Afghanistan and Iraq certainly contributed to them. They were primarily due to the 2007–2009 financial crisis, which triggered a severe recession, reducing tax revenues and increasing government spending under existing programs. The second most important cause of those deficits was major tax cuts in 2001 and 2003 that—unlike the 1802 tax cut—were not offset by spending reductions.[30] But the real debate is over future spending.

In 1812, some Republicans like Randolph opposed the war because they did not want higher spending or higher taxes; Treasury Secretary Gallatin, under orders from President Madison to prepare for war, wanted higher taxes to help pay for the higher spending,[31] but the majority of Republicans wanted war without the necessary tax increases. Today, the central debate is over increasing federal government spending on retirement, disability, and health care programs such as Social Security, Medicare, and Medicaid, which threatens to outstrip growth in tax revenues. One possibility, favored by most Republicans, is to scale back those programs to avoid the need for higher taxes. Another possibility is to maintain those spending commitments while raising taxes to pay for them. A compromise position—some spending reductions and some tax increases—is also conceivable. But our highly polarized political system is on the course set by the 1812 Congress: higher spending without higher taxes. This inability to make any fiscally responsible choice is how a dysfunctional political system could cause a true fiscal crisis—in one of the richest, most powerful nations in the history of the world.

In the War of 1812, Congress quickly learned that fighting a war without the money to pay for it was a dangerous proposition, leading to the tax increases of 1813 and 1814. This time, there may be no such wake-up call. The primary forces behind increasing government spending—an aging population and rising health care costs—move slowly but surely, eroding the government's fiscal foundation over decades. This gives politicians ample time to rail against deficits while failing to do anything about them, confident that the true crisis will not arrive on their watch. The specter of national deficits has been a fixture of American politics for most of the three decades since Ronald Reagan won the presidency by promising higher defense spending, lower taxes, and *lower* deficits.[32] Reagan then oversaw what were, at the time, the largest peacetime deficits in history, caused largely by a huge 1981 tax cut,[33] yet suffered no political consequences as a result. The lesson, according to George W. Bush's vice president, Dick Cheney, was that "Reagan proved deficits don't matter."[34] In 2005, Bush attempted to use Social Security's long-term deficit to gain support for reforming the popular retirement program. The president traveled to a Bureau of Public Debt office in West Virginia and dramatically warned, "The retirement security for future generations is sitting in a filing cabinet"; according to his eyewitness account, he said, "There is no trust fund. Just i.o.u.'s that I saw firsthand."[35] Yet his proposal to reform Social Security—diverting some contributions into individual accounts, similar to 401(k) accounts—would have *added* close to a trillion dollars to the national debt over the next decade.[36] Over the past thirty years, inflated rhetoric about the national debt has mainly served as a rhetorical tool that politicians use to argue for unrelated policy objectives, which as often as not increase the debt.

But we should not be too quick to place all the blame on the political class. Politicians, after all, are elected by ordinary people. And ordinary people, at least as measured by opinion polls, are also deeply divided—within themselves. In early 2011, 64 percent of Americans worried a great deal about "federal spending and the budget deficit" (second only to the "economy").[37] In one survey, 95 percent of respondents supported reducing the deficit by cutting government spending (on its own or in conjunction with tax increases). At the same time, however, 78 percent opposed cuts in Medicare spending, 69 percent opposed cuts in Medicaid spending, and 56 percent opposed cuts in military spending.[38]

It is no surprise that people can be illogical. After all, it's not fair to expect most people to know what proportion of federal spending goes to popular programs like Social Security (20 percent) and Medicare (13 percent), or how much of the deficit is due to their favorite tax breaks like the home mortgage interest deduction ($94 billion) or the deferral of taxes on retirement accounts ($142 billion).[39] But the problem goes deeper: many people have no idea what the federal government does. According to a 2008 survey, 44 percent of people who receive Social Security retirement benefits say that they "have not used a government social program." The same goes for 40 percent of Medicare recipients and 43 percent of people who have collected unemployment insurance benefits.[40] Of the people who denied using any government social programs, 94 percent had benefited from at least one.[41] In 2009, when an attendee at a town hall meeting told Republican representative Robert Inglis of South Carolina to "keep your government hands off my Medicare,"[42] many commentators laughed. But the joke is on all of us. People who do not realize that they benefit from the government's largest social programs unsurprisingly think that the government is too big, their taxes should be lower, spending should be lower, and yet their favorite programs should not be touched.

Politicians behave accordingly. So, during the health care debate of 2009, Republicans positioned themselves as defenders of Medicare spending, opposing cuts proposed by the Obama administration (remember, people *like* Medicare). On December 6, Senate majority leader Mitch McConnell of Kentucky issued a press release entitled "Cutting Medicare Is Not What Americans Want." But the next day, responding to a Democratic proposal to allow people of ages fifty-five to sixty-four to buy into Medicare, McConnell played the deficit card with another press release, "Expanding Medicare 'A Plan for Financial Ruin.' "[43] While it is possible to reconcile those two positions, the politics are quite simple: oppose any effort to expand popular government programs on the grounds that they are fiscally unsustainable while simultaneously attacking any effort to make them sustainable by calling it a cut in benefits (or an increase in taxes). In 2011, when House Republicans proposed to convert Medicare from a health insurance plan into a program to help people buy health insurance from private insurers, Democrats attacked them for cutting Medicare. As economist Brad DeLong said, "the political lesson of the past two years is now that you win elections by denouncing the other party's plans to control Medicare spending in the long run . . . sitting back, and waiting for the voters to reward you."[44] This is not an encouraging picture.

As a nation, however, we will make a choice, one way or another. The government budget deficit—the difference between spending and revenues in a single year—will decline in the next few years as the economy eventually recovers, but will then begin to climb again. Each year that the government runs a deficit, it must borrow money (by selling bonds) to make up the difference, and that borrowing adds to the national debt.[45] In other words, the deficit is a *flow*, like the water pouring from a faucet into a bathtub, that is measured over a period of time (typically a year); the national debt is a *stock*, like the water in the bathtub, that is measured at a specific moment (typically at the end of the year).[46] Deficits fluctuate up and down, primarily because of changes in economic conditions, but in the long run it is the national debt that matters; the larger the debt, the more money must be spent on interest payments each year.[47] And since the economy as a whole generates the resources available to pay off the debt, what really matters is the debt as a proportion of the economy, most commonly measured in terms of gross domestic product (GDP)—the total value of all the goods and services produced in the country in a given year.

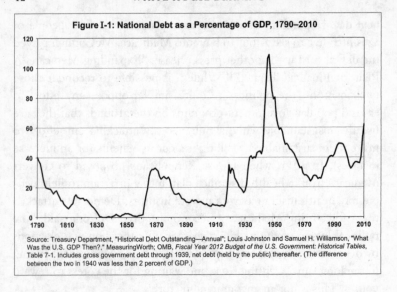

Figure I-1: National Debt as a Percentage of GDP, 1790–2010

Source: Treasury Department, "Historical Debt Outstanding—Annual"; Louis Johnston and Samuel H. Williamson, "What Was the U.S. GDP Then?," MeasuringWorth; OMB, *Fiscal Year 2012 Budget of the U.S. Government: Historical Tables*, Table 7-1. Includes gross government debt through 1939, net debt (held by the public) thereafter. (The difference between the two in 1940 was less than 2 percent of GDP.)

At the end of 2010, the national debt was $9 trillion ($29,000 per person), or 62 percent of GDP ($14.5 trillion)—the highest level ever recorded except during World War II (see Figure I-1). That figure, which reflects the amount owed by the federal government to the public, does not include the "unfunded obligations" of major programs such as Social Security and Medicare—the gap between their future revenues and spending commitments in the long term. While economic growth over the next few years will probably make the debt shrink modestly as a share of GDP, it should resume its upward trend around 2020 as government spending grows faster than tax revenues, which is likely under current policies.[48] Social Security spending will grow because of pure demographics—the retirement of the baby boom coupled with increasing life expectancies—which means the ratio of workers to retirees will go down. Medicare spending will grow even faster because, on top of demographic trends, health care costs are growing much faster than overall inflation.[49] As the debt increases, annual interest payments will grow as well, consuming an increasing proportion of all tax revenues and constraining the government's ability to invest in other priorities ranging from national defense to poverty relief. At some point, if the national debt grows faster than the economy for long enough, bond investors could lose their appetite for Treasury bonds, making it impossible for the government to borrow money at any price—as almost happened in 1813.

The most immediate problem facing our nation is the high level of unemployment that persists years after the peak of the financial crisis, leaving the economy operating significantly below capacity. But our national debt, and the spending and tax policies that underlie its growth, will be a major challenge for at least the rest of the decade, as we figure out how to adapt our government and our society to ongoing demographic trends and rising health care costs. We could end up in a world with low taxes and limited government, where people are largely left to make do as they can, or in a world with high taxes and expansive government services, where people are protected from the risks of unemployment, disability, old age, and poor health. The choices we make during this transition will help determine the nature of American society for generations to come.

Today's trillion-dollar deficits are a direct result of the recent financial crisis. Our previous book, *13 Bankers*, told the story of how an innovative, predatory, and powerful financial sector convinced officials in Washington to look the other way as it nearly wrecked the global economy. That calamity convinced many people across the political spectrum that our financial system was broken—but the subsequent campaign for reform ran aground on the rocks of a monumental lobbying campaign launched by the banks and their allies.[50]

By blowing an enormous hole in the federal budget, the financial crisis has pushed deficits and the national debt to the top of the agenda in Washington. The politics of taxes, spending, and deficits, however, appear even more toxic than the politics of financial reform—in part because they raise fundamental questions about the role of government in society. On one side, people who have long opposed government action—including oversight of the financial system—now see looming deficits as proof that government spending must be slashed. On the other side, the catastrophic failure of financial deregulation, high levels of inequality, and the sorry state of the economy argue for greater government intervention. In addition, any proposal that would actually reduce deficits is sure to face bitter opposition from whatever interest group would pay for it. Listening to the rhetoric in Washington and in the media, it seems as if all sides have dug their defensive fortifications and are willing to fight a long war of attrition to protect their positions, be they low taxes, robust social programs, or prized tax breaks.

This book is our effort to explain how our country got into this situation and what is at stake in these debates. The first three chapters tell the story of the national debt and the economic and political forces that have shaped it over time. The next two chapters describe the factors behind today's deficits, how they are likely to evolve in the future, and why they matter to ordinary people. In the final two chapters, we offer our own thoughts on how to reduce the long-term national debt while preserving the most important services that the federal government provides to all Americans today.

We do not expect all or even most readers to agree with our proposals. But if the American people understand where our national debt came from, the stakes involved, and the tradeoffs involved in reducing the debt, we will be able to choose the future that we want for our government and our society. Until then, our politicians will continue to stagger from one election to the next peddling meaningless and contradictory slogans, full of sound and fury, signifying nothing. There is no need to convince you of that: the evidence is all around you.

One

IMMORTAL CREDIT

[The treasury secretary] ardently wishes to see it incorporated, as a fundamental maxim in the system of public credit of the United States, that the creation of debt should always be accompanied with the means of extinguishment.

—Treasury Secretary Alexander Hamilton, January 1790[1]

On April 30, 1789, when George Washington was inaugurated as the first president of the United States, the country he would lead was a fiscal basket case. Less than six years after the Treaty of Paris ended the American Revolutionary War, the new nation was deeply in debt and already in default. The United States had missed interest payments owed to France for several years in succession, as well as principal payments due in 1787 and 1788.[2] The country's credit was so poor in the 1780s that some claims on the central government could be bought for less than 15 cents on the dollar.[3] In 1790, when Alexander Hamilton, Washington's first treasury secretary, added up the nation's debts, the federal government owed $54 million, almost $12 million to foreigners; on top of that, he estimated individual states had debts that added up to $25 million.[4] To put this in perspective, from 1784 to 1789, the Continental Congress was able to bring in only $4.6 million—and half of that was borrowed money.[5]

These debts were the price of fighting the Revolutionary War—the "price of liberty," in Hamilton's words.[6] In 1776, the North American colonies proclaimed their independence from Great Britain, then one of the most powerful countries in the world. For the next five years, lacking both the authority to collect taxes and the good credit necessary to borrow money, the Continental Congress struggled to keep an army of 10,000 men in the field. The British, by contrast, routinely had 15,000 to 25,000 experienced front-line troops available for battle and had numerical superiority in most confrontations.[7] The British could deploy so many troops because they had the financial resources to mobilize them—or to hire them from other European states, as was the case for the Hessians defeated in the Battle of Trenton.

General Washington, by contrast, struggled to keep the British at bay because there was little money available to mobilize, equip, and pay the Continental Army. The Continental Congress lacked both the power and the infrastructure to levy and collect taxes; without the assured prospect of future income (or even survival), the new government had trouble borrowing money. Most central government payments were made with "continentals"—paper money issued by the government.[8] Benjamin Franklin was initially impressed by this financing solution: "The whole is a mystery even to the politicians, how we have been able to continue a war four years without money, and how we could pay with paper that had no previously fixed fund appropriated specifically to redeem it."[9] But as the government issued more and more paper money with nothing to back it, the currency fell in value, leading Washington to complain in October 1779 that "a wagon load of money will scarcely purchase a wagon load of provisions."[10] Insufficient funds meant that American soldiers had to suffer with little food, poor shoes, and derisory accommodations during harsh winters; in the winter of 1777–1778, 2,500 men died at Valley Forge. Anger over irregular pay in a depreciating currency would later contribute to the Pennsylvania Mutiny of 1783, which prompted Congress to relocate from Philadelphia to Princeton, New Jersey.

The new nation was fortunate, however. France, Britain's traditional enemy, was willing to loan money to the Continental Congress despite the high risk of not being paid back, and the United States was also able to borrow money in Spain and the Netherlands.[11] In addition, the French provided troops and ships that helped tip the military balance, particularly at the decisive Battle of Yorktown in 1781, which helped convince the British that the war was no longer worth fighting. But it was clear that the United States could not truly be independent unless the world's powers were persuaded that the new country could defend itself, which required money. And to raise the money to fight an eighteenth-century war, nothing was more valuable than good credit. This was a lesson that Washington—and Hamilton, his wartime aide[12]—learned firsthand from the British, the masters of the subject.

WAR, DEBT, AND TAXES

During the eighteenth century, Great Britain and France were locked in a struggle for political supremacy in Europe. At first glance, everything seemed to favor France. It had twice as many people as Great Britain (19 million versus 9 million in 1700), an advantage it maintained throughout most of the century. Its army was several times as large (350,000 troops to 75,000 in 1710); even its fleet was larger in the late seventeenth century, although the British navy would take the lead in the eighteenth century.[13] Its overseas possessions were the equal of Great Britain's. Yet throughout the century, Great Britain was more than France's match on the world stage: the two powers fought to a standstill on the Continent, while Great Britain seized most of France's overseas colonies in the Seven Years' War (known in the American colonies as the French and Indian War).

The reason was not economic superiority. In 1700, France's economy was the largest in Europe, nearly twice as big as Great Britain's.[14] The reason was the British government's fiscal superiority: its ability to raise money through both taxation and borrowing. To begin with, Great Britain had a more efficient administrative system for collecting taxes in the form of a modern centralized bureaucracy.[15] In France, taxes were collected by "tax farmers" who leased the right to collect taxes, other officials who bought their positions, and various traditional corporate bodies. Many of these intermediaries took their share of tax proceeds before passing them on to the government (and sometimes more than their share).[16] Still, no country could afford to fight the wars of the eighteenth century solely with tax revenue, and so the crucial factor was a government's ability to borrow money. Here Great Britain had two major advantages. The first was its superior ability to raise taxes, which gave lenders confidence that the loans they advanced during wartime could be paid back by taxes in peacetime.[17] The second, and more important, was that government debts had to be approved by Parliament, which also had the power to raise taxes.

Parliamentary control over spending and taxation was a long-term consequence of the Glorious Revolution of 1688, in which the Catholic King James II was deposed in favor of the Protestant King William III and Queen Mary II. The Revolution led to heightened competition between Whigs (associated with commercial and financial interests) and Tories (representing traditional landowners). William III relied on Whig support to fight on the Continent against King Louis XIV of France; the Tories, by contrast, preferred to withdraw from the Continent and rely on the navy to protect Great Britain.[18] The need for new taxes and borrowing to fight the War of the League of Augsburg (1689–1697) and the War of the Spanish Succession (1702–1713) increased the power of Parliament relative to the monarchy, making fiscal and economic policy more dependent on public support.[19] Parliamentary oversight and the perception that the tax system was basically fair were also major reasons why British society was willing to endure unprecedented levels of taxation.[20]

In the three decades that followed the Glorious Revolution, the British government was able to borrow vast sums of money to fight the French, its national debt growing from £1 million to £54 million.[21] That borrowing was supported by taxes that tripled between the 1670s and 1715.[22] Still, it was only the advent of Whig dominance in 1715 that ensured Great Britain's good credit; a large Whig majority—representing the nation's creditors, among other groups—provided confidence that the government would continue to pay its debts by raising taxes if necessary, allowing it to borrow money at relatively low interest rates.[23] By the time Whig control of Parliament ended in 1760, the idea that servicing the national debt was a crucial priority had become far less controversial.[24] And this was the secret to winning wars in the eighteenth century. As Daniel Defoe (of *Robinson Crusoe* fame) wrote, "Credit makes war, and makes peace; raises armies, fits out navies, fights battles, besieges towns; and, in a word, it is more justly called the sinews of war than the money itself."[25]

France, by contrast, was in a near constant state of financial crisis.[26] The Estates General (a representative assembly that was France's closest approximation to Parliament) had not met since 1614, debts were incurred by the monarchy, and taxes were based on the monarchy's traditional rights and privileges or imposed without consent by the king.[27] The haphazard tax collection system made it difficult to bring in revenues reliably.[28] The sale of offices—bureaucratic or professional positions, sometimes carrying social distinction—was a major source of revenue, but also meant that the government had to pay "interest" in the form of salaries to officeholders.[29] The difficulty of raising adequate revenues through taxation meant that wars periodically led to escalating debts;[30] the government often responded by defaulting or unilaterally rescheduling debt repayments, as occurred in 1715, 1722, 1759, 1763, and 1772.[31] Without the assurance of future revenues to back it up, government debt can quickly become worthless paper. And unlike in Great Britain, creditors had little political power and hence no reason to trust the government to make good on its debts.[32] As a result, France had to pay interest rates that not only were higher than those paid by Britain but also were higher than those paid by the private sector in France.[33]

The difference between the two countries became clear after the American Revolutionary War. At first glance, Great Britain seemed to come out of the war in worse shape, and not just because it lost. Britain had financed the war entirely by new borrowing, and it ended the war with a larger national debt than France (and a much smaller population); in 1782, 70 percent of all British government expenditures went to interest on the debt.[34] (In the United States today, the corresponding figure is 6 percent.)[35] But Britain benefited from lower interest rates, thanks to its good credit, and, more importantly, was able to raise taxes in the 1780s, bringing its debt under control.[36] While France's debt was smaller than Britain's, it was unable to raise taxes due to the weak legitimacy of the monarchy, and so it had to resort to even more borrowing even after the war ended; by 1789, interest payments were consuming 68 percent of all government spending and growing each year.[37] Finally, King Louis XVI was forced to call the Estates General, which convened on May 5, 1789, leading rapidly to the French Revolution and the overthrow of the monarchy. At the time, effective tax rates in Britain were nearly twice as high as in France, leading historian Kathryn Norberg to conclude, "More than any other factor, the inability to tax brought down the French treasury and with it the absolute monarchy."[38]

Even then, some things did not change. The Revolution and the rise of Napoleon Bonaparte led to another twenty years of war, and Great Britain continued to enjoy a vast fiscal advantage, raising more in taxes than France, which helped fund the coalition that would eventually defeat Napoleon.[39] By this time, the Industrial Revolution was well under way in England, and Great Britain would be the dominant world power for the next century.

What was the main difference between Great Britain and France? It wasn't the size of their national debts: at the time of the French Revolution, Great Britain's debt per person was much larger than France's. The difference was politics. In Great Britain, the political system was dominated by elected representatives who supported an activist government and were willing to endorse the taxes necessary to pay for its resulting debts. In France, the government did not have the legitimacy necessary to raise the money to service its smaller debts. And although its tax rates were lower than Britain's, the problem of taxation without representation was an important cause of the Revolution.[40]

LAYING THE FOUNDATIONS

Alexander Hamilton's views on public finance were shaped during the Revolutionary War and largely based on Britain's successful example.[41] He was well aware of the connection between good credit and national power: "'Tis by introducing order into our finances—by restoring public credit—not by gaining battles, that we are finally to gain our object," he wrote in 1781.[42] As treasury secretary, one of his principal goals was ensuring that the United States would be able to raise money in times of national emergency. It was a "plain and undeniable truth," he asserted in 1790, "that loans in times of public danger, especially from foreign war, are found an indispensable resource, even to the wealthiest of [nations]."[43] For Hamilton, this meant reshaping American fiscal policy in the British image.

When Hamilton took office, however, the United States was on course to imitate France, not Great Britain, at least in its fiscal affairs. The country had missed required interest payments for years and seemed to have no realistic prospect of paying its debts. The national government and the states together owed about $79 million—probably about 40 percent of GDP, which would not seem particularly high today.[44] But the economy was very different then, with much more agriculture and much less industry and trade, and the federal government lacked a modern apparatus for collecting taxes, making it difficult to bring in a large amount of revenue.[45] At the time, Hamilton estimated that paying interest in full on the foreign and domestic debt would cost more than $4.5 million.[46] The United States' limited ability to finance the debt raised the prospect of a serious and persistent debt crisis.

These dangerous fiscal straits had been one motivation for the Constitutional Convention of 1787, which created the executive branch of government that Washington and Hamilton now inhabited. Under the prior Articles of Confederation, the central government could spend money but had no power to levy taxes, instead relying on contributions from the states, which often refused to comply.[47] In 1779, John Jay, then president of the Continental Congress, exhorted the states to contribute to the war effort: "Recollect that it is the price of the liberty, the peace and the safety of yourselves and posterity, that now is required."[48] But without an independent executive or judicial branch, the central government had no enforcement powers over the states and could not compel contributions. As superintendent of finance in the early 1780s, Robert Morris tried to raise money for the central government, even using his own personal credit, but was often unable to obtain the necessary cooperation of the individual states.[49] As Davis Rich Dewey wrote in his *Financial History of the United States*, "Morris after all had little real power; he could not overcome the fundamental obstacles in the way of healthy finance; State pride, jealousy, and bickering withstood his appeals to the States to levy taxes."[50]

The lack of a reliable source of revenues was one reason for the central government's persistent weakness. As Sidney Homer and Richard Sylla put it,

In spite of the great potential economic strength of the new country, its financial and political system broke down completely in 1786.
Credit at home and abroad was no longer available. The impossibility
of government without money, credit, or power led to the Constitutional Convention of 1787 and a new nation in 1789.[51]

The convention responded by giving the new Congress power "To
lay and collect Taxes, Duties, Imposts and Excises, to pay the Debts
and provide for the common Defence and general Welfare," as well
as "To borrow Money on the credit of the United States."[52] Still,
however, many politicians—who generally had only a local power
base—feared a strong central government with too much power
to borrow money, increase spending, and expand its influence over
everyday life. For the new constitution to command popular legitimacy, it had to reconcile multiple conflicting interests and balance
the dominant political forces of the time.[53] As a result, the Constitution itself is unclear on how far the federal government's authority reaches. Congress has the power "To make all Laws which shall
be necessary and proper for carrying into Execution the foregoing
Powers"[54]—language that would prompt extensive debate over what
the government can actually do.

   The power of the federal government was the central issue during
President Washington's first term in office, with his two top officials
on opposing sides of the debate. Thomas Jefferson, then secretary
of state, argued for a narrow definition of the government's powers,
particularly in the realm of fiscal policy,[55] while Treasury Secretary
Hamilton asserted that Congress could pass legislation that enabled
the government to further the purposes authorized by the Constitution. In 1787–1788, Hamilton had collaborated with James Madison
and John Jay on the Federalist Papers, a series of articles arguing for
ratification of the Constitution and thus the creation of a relatively
strong central government; Jefferson was U.S. ambassador to France
at the time but was kept informed during the ratification debates
by his ally Madison.[56] During the first years of the new administration, however, both Jefferson and Madison (then a member of the
House of Representatives) increasingly opposed Hamilton, who they
thought was excessively enamored of strong central government.

This split would soon lead to the partisan divide between Hamilton's Federalists and Jefferson and Madison's Democratic-Republicans (or Republicans).

Taxes, spending, and the national debt were at the center of this debate. For Hamilton, prosperity and independence required a strong central government that could mobilize resources quickly in order to cope with national emergencies—first among them war. Rapid access to cash depended on the confidence of the credit market.[57] Sound economic management and political stability were based on and measured by the ability to issue debt at reasonable interest rates. But to borrow money, a government had to have the ability to finance its debts, which required a well-defined revenue stream. In his 1790 "Report on Public Credit," Hamilton concluded,

> Persuaded, as the Secretary is, that the proper funding of the present debt will render it a national blessing, yet he is so far from acceding to the position in the latitude in which it is sometimes laid down, that "public debts are public benefits"—a position inviting to prodigality, and liable to dangerous abuse—that he ardently wishes to see it incorporated, as a fundamental maxim in the system of public credit of the United States, that the creation of debt should always be accompanied with the means of extinguishment. This he regards as the true secret for rendering public credit immortal.[58]

In order to be able to borrow money when necessary, the government would have to prove that it could pay it back.[59]

The nation's huge debts presented the opportunity to put these principles into action. Not only did Hamilton want to restructure the federal government's obligations, but he also wanted the government to assume the debts incurred by the states and pay interest on them as well. Since the government did not have enough cash on hand to do so—it had already missed both principal and interest payments—he proposed to buy back the outstanding debt with new Treasury bonds. The planned debt swap was carefully calibrated. Hamilton proposed multiple classes of bonds, with interest rates ranging from 3 percent to 6 percent. All could be redeemed at the government's option, but there were limits on how much the government could buy back each year.* Holders of debt issued by the Continental Congress or of "state debts incurred for national purposes" could exchange their old debt for new Treasury bonds.[60] This voluntary restructuring (creditors did not have to participate) appealed to the debt holders' self-interest. If the plan succeeded, the government would soon be able to redeem any old debts that were not converted, which meant they would no longer pay interest. Therefore, investors who wanted long-term streams of interest were better off converting their bonds.[61] Of course, issuing new bonds required a way to pay the interest on those bonds. To that end, Hamilton planned to supplement existing tariffs with new excise taxes on liquor, tea, and coffee.[62] He later also proposed to charter a new Bank of the United States, which, while privately owned, would provide liquidity to the bond market and help the government borrow money rapidly in a crisis.

While Hamilton saw the national debt as either a necessary evil or something that was good in itself, Jefferson and Madison were firmly opposed to debt.[63] For them, borrowing and the taxes it necessitated provided the cash that enabled governments to centralize power and to fight wars—both of which were bad. In 1795, Madison wrote,

> Of all the enemies to public liberty, war is perhaps the most to be dreaded, because it comprises and developes [sic] the germ of every other. War is the parent of armies; from these proceed debts and taxes; and armies, and debts, and taxes are the known instruments for bringing the many under the domination of the few.[64]

Jefferson and Madison feared that Hamilton's plan, by creating the machinery to issue debt and collect taxes, would give too much power to the federal government and set the precedent for further borrowing and permanent indebtedness. They particularly objected to the idea of paying off *current* debt holders in full since in some cases speculators had bought debt certificates cheaply from veterans of the Revolutionary War. Madison proposed several alternatives that would have been less favorable to current creditors. In one proposal, the value of each debt certificate would depend not just on its face

---

* Investors generally do not like bonds that can be redeemed by the issuer at any time, because then they might be stuck with cash and no good place to invest it.

value but also on its own idiosyncratic history. But as Madison himself later acknowledged, "the proposition for compromizing [*sic*] the matter between original sufferers and the stockjobbers, after being long agitated, was rejected by a considerable majority, less perhaps from a denial of the justice of the measure, than a supposition of its impracticality."[65]

In Congress, Madison drew the line at federal assumption of state debt. He argued that by essentially bailing out states that were behind on their debt payments, it penalized those—like Virginia, his home state—that had already paid off most of their Revolutionary War debts.[66] By June 1790, the House of Representatives had approved most of Hamilton's fiscal plan, except for assumption of state debt, thanks to Madison's efforts. At the same time, there was an ongoing debate over where the nation's capital city should be located. Finally, Hamilton, Jefferson, and Madison reached a compromise—according to Jefferson, over a private dinner at his house on June 20. Hamilton agreed to push for the banks of the Potomac River as the site of the future capital (and to support a favorable debt settlement for Virginia), while Madison agreed to find enough votes to back the assumption plan, which finally passed on July 26.[67] Madison and Jefferson later opposed the creation of the Bank of the United States, but Hamilton won that battle in Congress and then convinced President Washington not to veto it.[68]

In the end, Hamilton's plan was an economic success. Because the debt swap was attractive to creditors, he was able to restructure the outstanding debt at reasonable interest rates.[69] The new taxes helped bring the budget roughly into balance, making the U.S. government a more attractive credit risk. In 1787, the yield on government debt was in the range of 26–40 percent; investors could buy interest-bearing claims on the government for 15 percent of their face value, a huge discount.* By 1791, the yield on government debt had fallen below 9 percent; while the early data have big gaps, interest rates seem to have remained around 8 percent for the rest of the decade.[70] The newly issued government bonds became an attractive

---

* Bonds typically have a face value and pay interest as a fixed percentage of that face value. When investors begin to worry about whether the issuer can make good on the payments, the market price of the bond falls below face value. As the bond's price falls, its yield—the effective interest rate as a percentage of the price—goes up.

investment in European credit markets, helping attract capital to the United States. Most importantly, the broader credit system functioned again, helping to stimulate sustained economic growth.[71]

Although Hamilton's fiscal system was good for the new federal government, there was still a price to be paid—the taxes that he introduced to service the larger government debt. Popular opposition to those taxes, particularly the tax on whiskey, was fueled by general discontent with the new, more centralized political system ushered in by the Constitution. On an economic level, taxing farmers who produced grain and distilled it into whiskey (or the people who drank the whiskey),[72] in order to pay off old debts at their full face value, seemed like a transfer of wealth from ordinary Americans to the East Coast elites and speculators who held government debt.[73] Farmers on the Western frontier often chose to produce whiskey because it was cheaper than grain to transport to market, so the tax threatened their basic livelihood. Both tariffs and excise taxes are effectively consumption taxes, which tend to be regressive (compared to property or income taxes), although in early America it could be argued that they applied primarily to luxuries.[74] On a political level, the whiskey tax demonstrated the dangers posed by a powerful central government that appeared more concerned with commercial interests and the investor class than with farmers in the West and South. In this context, the federal structure created by the Constitutional Convention seemed to constitute an abandonment of the popular democratic principles that had contributed to the American Revolution.

Opposition to the whiskey tax and to the federal government slowly crystallized in the United States' first serious tax revolt: the Whiskey Rebellion, which gradually grew from protests against Hamilton's proposals in 1790 to armed resistance in 1794, particularly in western Pennsylvania.[75] The rebellion brought together economic grievances against the new taxes and political grievances against a government seen as controlled by economic elites.[76] But a government that was only five years old, which needed tax revenues in order to ensure its fiscal stability (and perhaps its continued existence), saw the rebellion as a test of its determination to enforce the law.[77] After hesitating—in part out of fear that military action would only broaden opposition—President Washington called up a militia and dispatched it to Pennsylvania to put down the rebellion.[78] This show of military force against internal opposition demonstrated that the federal government was serious about exercising its new powers, at least where money was concerned. In the words of historian Howard Zinn, "We see then, in the first years of the Constitution, that some of its provisions—even those paraded most flamboyantly (like the First Amendment)—might be treated lightly. Others (like the power to tax) would be powerfully enforced."[79]

On the one hand, fiscal policy is about ensuring that the government has the resources necessary to address current public priorities and respond to future emergencies. On the other hand, since it involves the crucial questions of who pays taxes and who benefits from government spending, fiscal policy is fundamentally about the distribution of income and wealth. Hamilton's policies were successful at establishing the solvency and creditworthiness of the U.S. government. But the Whiskey Rebellion showed how the distributional implications of taxes and spending can provoke bitter political opposition—something that the United States has seen again and again throughout its history.

ALL TOGETHER NOW

The 1790s were one of the most divisive periods of American political history, with the Hamilton-Jefferson feuds hardening into the split between Federalists and Democratic-Republicans, which saw partisan strife that would seem excessive even today. In 1801, for example, after Federalist president John Adams had lost the 1800 election to Jefferson, Federalist majorities in Congress passed the Judiciary Act—which effectively allowed Adams and his party to pack the federal courts with sympathetic judges. The Republicans responded by repealing the act the next year, tossing the new judges out of office.[80]

The parties were still far apart on fiscal issues, with the Republicans preferring smaller government and lower taxes than the Federalists. Jefferson acknowledged the importance of good credit, writing in 1788, "Though I am an enemy of the system of borrowing, I feel strongly the necessity of preserving the power to borrow.

Without that, we may be overwhelmed by another nation merely by the force of its power to borrow."[81] Madison similarly had used the need for wartime borrowing as a justification for giving the federal government the power to tax.[82] But after taking power in 1801, Jefferson and Republican majorities in Congress set out to overturn key components of the Federalist fiscal program originally designed by Hamilton, preferring to cut taxes and shrink the federal government—which, at the time, consisted mainly of the army and navy. (Unlike in some other countries, however, they did not attempt to renege on debts incurred by the previous government; nor did they attempt to reopen the controversial debates of 1790 over the restructuring of federal and state debt.)[83]

The man that Jefferson and Madison put in charge of the nation's finances was Albert Gallatin, treasury secretary from 1801 to 1814.[84] As Gallatin wrote to Jefferson in 1809, "The reduction of the debt was certainly the principal object in bringing me into office."[85] Gallatin was particularly opposed to maintaining the national debt indefinitely, arguing that "owing a debt cannot contribute more to the welfare, happiness, and real opulence of a people than a private debt contributes to the wealth and prosperity of an individual."[86]

Gallatin was born in Switzerland and immigrated to the United States in 1780 at age nineteen. In 1790 he was elected to the Pennsylvania General Assembly, where he stood out for his grasp of fiscal issues. A fervent opponent of Hamiltonian "big government," he was elected to the Senate in 1793 as a Democratic-Republican, but he was almost immediately removed from office on a technicality by the Federalists.[87] Back in Pennsylvania, Gallatin participated in the Whiskey Rebellion, although he argued consistently for moderation and against unlawful opposition to the government.[88] In 1795 he returned to Congress, this time as a member of the House of Representatives, where he became the Republicans' main public finance expert. Gallatin relentlessly interrogated Federalist treasury secretaries on budget details and helped strengthen congressional oversight of the executive branch, in part through the creation of the House Ways and Means Committee.[89]

As treasury secretary, Gallatin's main objectives were to cut government spending and pay off the national debt. After taking office in 1801, he forecast that revenue the next year would amount to $10.6

million, with most coming from tariffs but $650,000 from the controversial excise taxes. He allocated $7.3 million to debt payments, leaving the rest of the government—including the military—with just over $3 million. From this starting point, Gallatin aimed to pay off the national debt by 1817;[90] at the same time, he hoped to repeal all excise taxes "to strike at the root of the evil and arrest the danger of encroaching taxes, encroaching government, temptations to offensive wars, etc."[91] In 1802, the Republicans repealed the excise taxes while offsetting the tax cuts by reducing spending on the army and navy—scaling back the navy's building program and increasing the federal government's reliance on state militias.[92] Lower spending enabled the Treasury to pay down the national debt: from 1801 to 1812, indebtedness fell by $38 million (despite a large increase to finance the Louisiana Purchase), leaving $45 million outstanding.[93]

Over time, however, both Jefferson and Madison came to appreciate the potential usefulness of debt. Despite his opposition to debt, Jefferson could be a pragmatist, borrowing more than $11 million for the Louisiana Purchase.[94] In this case, issuing debt had obvious benefits: doubling the size of the United States. The War of 1812 showed that borrowing—and the taxes to support it—could also be crucial to national security.

During the Napoleonic Wars at the beginning of the nineteenth century, France and Great Britain each attempted to cut off trade with the other country. Although the United States remained neutral, both countries seized American merchant ships, with the British sometimes forcing their crews into military service. After an adroit move by Napoleon and some belligerent diplomacy by the British, the United States ended up in a confrontation with Great Britain over its policy of excluding American shipping from French ports.[95] Relationships between the two countries were further strained by British support for Native Americans against American settlers in the West and by other resentments left over from the Revolutionary War.

Jefferson's rather dubious response was the Embargo Act of 1807, a self-imposed trade embargo that hurt the American economy more than that of Great Britain. In 1809 this was replaced with the Non-Intercourse Act, which allowed trade with countries other than Great Britain and France. Both acts were difficult to enforce, but by pushing trade out of official view, they directly undermined the main source of Treasury revenues—tariffs. As early as 1807, recognizing the possibility of military conflict, Gallatin recommended that any war be funded through loans, but also that taxes should be sufficient to pay the interest on that new debt. But in 1811 and 1812 Republican War Hawks—including Henry Clay, then speaker of the House of Representatives, and John Calhoun, who would later become vice president—resisted Gallatin's proposals for new excise taxes.[96] In Davis Rich Dewey's words, "In spite, then, of needs which were early apparent, Congress determinedly and definitely turned away from a policy of adequate taxation."[97] In 1811, Congress also voted not to renew the charter of the Bank of the United States, against the wishes of Gallatin and Madison (who had become a supporter of the Bank), leaving the government without a centralized channel for distributing loans shortly before it went to war.[98]

Frustration with what appeared to be repeated British infringements on American sovereignty, both in the Atlantic and on the Western frontier, finally led to a declaration of war in 1812, even though both the military and the Treasury Department were unprepared for the conflict.[99] Total government spending quadrupled from 1811 to 1814, yet revenues—as always, highly dependent on external trade—remained essentially flat.[100] This gap could only be closed by borrowing, but there was relatively little appetite to invest in a country at war with the world's richest country and most powerful navy. Many industrial and commercial leaders in the relatively prosperous Northeast were lukewarm about war with their most important trading partner.[101] The refusal of Congress to authorize new taxes also made it difficult for the Treasury Department to raise new money, especially after two invasions of Canada ended in failure and with the British blockading American ports.[102]

In 1813, it was difficulty finding lenders that forced Gallatin to turn to Stephen Girard for help raising money[103] and finally convinced Congress to reintroduce some of the same internal taxes that the Republicans had eliminated in 1802. The following year, at the urging of Treasury Secretary Alexander Dallas, Congress raised taxes again.[104] Even with these measures, however, the United States had trouble making ends meet. By the end of 1814, the military supply system was breaking down because of a shortage of cash, and Dallas warned that spending in 1815 would be more than three times as high as revenues.[105]

Thanks to some money and to increasing experience, American military fortunes did stabilize beginning in 1813, although another invasion of Canada failed later that year. After the fall of Napoleon in early 1814, however, the British were able to send larger, more experienced armies across the Atlantic. In August, it was veterans of the European wars who sailed up Chesapeake Bay, overwhelmed Washington's meager defenses, and burned the White House.[106] Fortunately for the Americans, the whole campaign was meant primarily as a diversion, and the British soon withdrew.[107]

Although the United States survived the War of 1812, the accompanying fiscal crisis proved the importance of government borrowing and of the infrastructure necessary to raise large sums quickly. By the end of the war, the national debt stood at more than $120 million, a record in nominal terms but probably only about 15 percent of GDP.[108] But, as Hamilton had realized, some amount of debt could be consistent with both political stability and economic prosperity. A given debt level is "sustainable" if lenders think that the government will be able to make required principal and interest payments in the future. In this context, it is the scale of the debt relative to the size of the economy that matters, because a larger economy means a bigger tax base from which government revenues can be drawn. If the economy grows faster than the debt increases—because growth is high, interest rates are low, or the budget is in surplus—then lenders will have confidence in the government's ability to pay and will buy bonds when it needs to borrow.

Maintaining that confidence is crucial to preserving the government's ability to borrow money in a crisis, of which war is the classic example. Confidence in government debt can also provide economic benefits. Both families and companies want to park their savings in a risk-free, interest-bearing asset, of which government debt—at least that issued by certain countries, such as the United States—is the best example. A liquid market for government bonds can also benefit the financial system by providing a risk-free instrument to use as collateral for financial transactions. The ability to issue debt, however, depends on more than just having a large and sound economy. Lenders will believe they are likely to be repaid only if the government has the ability to generate revenues from that economy. The public finance system ultimately rests on the ability to levy and collect sufficient taxes to service the debt. This was a crucial lesson of the War of 1812. As Treasury Secretary Dallas said near the end of the war, the government's fundamental problem was the "inadequacy of our system of taxation to form a foundation of public credit, and the absence from our system of the means which are the best adapted to anticipate, collect, and distribute the public revenue."[109]

The ideas that a government should always pay its debts and that good credit is crucial to national power may seem uncontroversial. But one person's interest payments are another person's taxes, so making those payments requires the political will and the popular legitimacy to raise and collect taxes. This was the fundamental source of Great Britain's power in the eighteenth century (until the Industrial Revolution made it also Europe's economic powerhouse), and Hamilton consciously attempted to mold the United States in the British model. Jefferson, Madison, and Gallatin also believed that debts should be paid, but it was not until the War of 1812 that their party became reconciled to the need for new taxes to finance emergency borrowing. And after the war, in 1816, a Republican Congress chartered the Second Bank of the United States, following the blueprint drawn by Hamilton.

Fiscal prudence and restrained government were certainly part of the American system of public finance established in the late eighteenth and early nineteenth centuries. By today's standards, even Hamilton would probably qualify as a fiscal conservative; the idea that the budget should ordinarily be balanced (barring a national emergency, of which war was the only known example) was virtually unquestioned.[110] (State governments, by contrast, often overborrowed and occasionally defaulted in the early nineteenth century; over time, they have generally imposed constraints on themselves to prevent taking on too much debt.)[111] But the ability to raise taxes when necessary to service and pay down the debt—and, eventually, the government's consistent track record at doing so—was what made it possible to maintain the country's good credit even amid adversity. When it came to public finance, the United States successfully

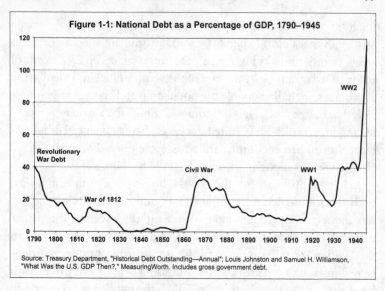

Figure 1-1: National Debt as a Percentage of GDP, 1790–1945

Source: Treasury Department, "Historical Debt Outstanding—Annual"; Louis Johnston and Samuel H. Williamson, "What Was the U.S. GDP Then?," MeasuringWorth. Includes gross government debt.

emulated the model of Great Britain, not that of pre-Revolutionary France.

Because the United States did not face another major war until the 1860s and the federal government played a relatively minor role in economic development, there was no pressing need to borrow large amounts of money. After the War of 1812, high tariffs (imposed in part to protect domestic industry), increased international trade, and dedicated tax revenues made it possible to reduce the national debt to virtually nothing in the mid-1830s under President Andrew Jackson, an enemy of debt in any form. With government spending low, the national debt fluctuated below 3 percent of GDP until 1861 (see Figure 1-1). The issue that had so sharply divided Federalists and Democratic-Republicans in the 1790s slowly faded from the political scene.

STRESS TEST

After decades of seeming irrelevance, the importance of a large credit line became strikingly clear with the onset of the Civil War in 1861. As the first major conflict between industrialized societies, the four-year struggle was by far the most expensive war in American history to that point. Federal (Union) government spending rose to levels twenty times as high as in peacetime, taking up 25 percent of the national economy by the end of the war.[112] The Union had many advantages, including double the population and an even larger edge in industrial production—including 32 times the capacity for producing firearms.[113] The Confederacy was also at a financial disadvantage, with 30 percent of the nation's assets but only 12 percent of the circulating currency and 21 percent of the banking assets.[114]

A bigger problem for the South, however, was that it lacked both the infrastructure to collect taxes and the credibility to borrow money.[115] The Richmond government was forced to print paper money to pay most of its expenses, including military spending. In moderation, printing money can be a reasonable strategy, particularly if inflation pressures are low. But using paper money to finance large amounts of spending—especially if the public has no reason to believe the government will ever stop printing money—is likely to cause inflation as people come to expect the printing presses to run forever. Because there was little reason to believe the Confederacy could ever break its dependence on paper money, printing money triggered a wave of hyperinflation.[116] Prices rose on average by 10 percent per month and, by the end of the war, the price level in the South was 92 times its starting level—a degree of inflation that wreaks havoc with the ordinary functioning of any economy.[117]

The North, by contrast, could increase taxes and issue debt—although even so it struggled to raise enough money to meet the war's unprecedented costs. Salmon P. Chase, President Abraham Lincoln's treasury secretary, recognized the need for new revenues early in the war. Anticipating total spending of $320 million in the 1862 fiscal year (July 1861 through June 1862)—almost eight times total revenues in 1861—he asked for taxes that would cover the interest on wartime borrowing and create a fund to eventually repay that debt. The government increased taxes repeatedly, even levying the first income tax in American history (at a rate of 3 percent on income over $800 per year), eventually collecting over $300 million in 1865. But taxes paid for only about one-fourth of the war's costs.[118]

The solution was borrowing on an unprecedented scale. For the first time, the government tapped into the savings of ordinary

Americans. Jay Cooke became perhaps the first famous investment banker in American history by selling government bonds, in denominations as low as $50, using thousands of subagents and newspaper advertising—the mass media of the time. Through these "bond drives," Cooke successfully sold bonds to about 5 percent of Northern households—in the process vastly expanding the number of people with a direct stake in the national debt.[119] By 1863, the Union was able to close most of its budget gap by selling these long-term bonds.[120] The result was an enormous increase in the national debt, from $65 million in 1860 to almost $2.7 billion (almost 30 percent of GDP) in 1865.[121] Government bond prices reached their lowest point in 1861, when the yield on long-term government debt climbed as high as 6.98 percent—but this was still below the peak yield during the War of 1812.[122]

Despite its superior ability to collect taxes and sell bonds, the Union still faced its share of fiscal emergencies. Early in the war, the Treasury Department was unable to sell bonds fast enough to meet the military's funding needs, forcing Congress to authorize paper currency—the first "greenbacks"—to keep the federal government in operation and pay the troops in the field.[123] As in the South, paper money lost value quickly; while $100 of greenbacks could be bought for $98 in gold in January 1862, by July 1864 they cost only $39 in gold.[124] Relying on printing presses to pay the bills caused high inflation; unlike in the South, however, prices in the North "only" doubled during the course of the war, limiting the damage to the economy.[125] While the Civil War stretched the Union government's capacity to raise money through taxes and borrowing, it did not break, enabling the North to keep its armies in the field long enough to wear down the South. One Confederate leader supposedly went so far as to say, "The Yankees did not whip us in the field. We were whipped in the Treasury Department."[126]

Following the Civil War, the government followed the pattern set in the 1790s and after the War of 1812: high taxes dedicated to paying down the debt. Those taxes were controversial, as always, but they had strong supporters in Congress. The industrial and manufacturing interests that dominated the postwar Republican Party wanted high import tariffs to protect themselves from foreign competition.The tariffs were politically divisive because they increased the prices of consumer goods, disproportionately affecting lower- and middle-income families—especially those in the South and West who did not benefit from protectionism. But the Republican majorities that controlled Congress for most of the late nineteenth century set tariffs significantly higher than was required simply to meet the government's revenue needs, even while eliminating the income tax.[127] As a result, the government ran a consistent budget surplus from the end of the war through 1893, enabling the national debt to fall to less than 10 percent of GDP.

This was also the period when the United States became one of the world's foremost economic powers. American prosperity was based, first and foremost, on a strong system of institutions. Secure private property rights, relatively cheap land, and early industrialization attracted millions of immigrants (although serious economic problems in Ireland, Italy, and other parts of Europe also contributed to the flow of people across the Atlantic). The U.S. population rose from around 2.5 million people when the Revolutionary War began to more than 23 million in 1850 and 76 million in 1900.[128] American entrepreneurs were also at the forefront of technological innovation from the 1840s (if not earlier) and were responsible for the large-scale development of railways and electric power, the application of a myriad of improvements to agriculture and industry, and key breakthroughs in telecommunications. These rapid improvements in productivity, coupled with a historical surge in human capital, gave the United States the world's largest economy, probably at some point in the 1870s.[129]

Industrialization and technology also set in motion a long, gradual change in the role of the government in American society. For example, medical advances made it practical to think about public health investments. The germ theory of disease and the discovery of specific pathogens made apparent the importance of clean water, which justified major expenditures on reservoirs, filtering equipment, and piped water.[130] As vaccines became available, their positive spillover effects—the more people that are vaccinated, the less likely a disease is to spread—created a rationale for public policies to encourage their use. The development of modern medicine provided a basis for regulatory policies to protect the public from fake "patent medicines." Similar forces were at work in many other domains of modern life:

the economic power of the railroads led to their regulation by the Interstate Commerce Commission beginning in 1887, while increasing urban poverty and the high injury rates of nineteenth-century factories led to state workers' compensation laws in the early twentieth century.[131] In the decades following the Civil War, income security—in the form of veterans' pensions—also became a major responsibility of the federal government, accounting for one-third of all spending in 1890.[132] Although many new governmental responsibilities fell to state and local governments, the federal government broadened its mandate as well. For the most part, however, domestic spending remained small relative to the economy (and by today's standards),[133] and could generally be paid for by the high tariffs that Republicans favored for economic reasons. The fiscal consequences of this long-term trend would take decades to become clearly visible.

If population and productivity were the main sources of American economic development, politics and public policy were also important. The early United States had the potential for intense social polarization and even repeated armed conflict of the kind seen in many Latin American countries during the nineteenth and twentieth centuries. Colonies based on European settlement have generally done better over the past two hundred years than those in which Europeans made money primarily by controlling an indigenous population.[134] When the political business model involves attracting new people—for example, to settle in the Western United States—political leaders have a strong incentive to treat ordinary people fairly. But societies based on European settlement did not necessarily produce popular legitimacy and prudent fiscal policies, as evidenced by Argentina, among other countries. Extreme inequality, populist uprisings, and reactionary crackdowns can all produce political instability and undermine sustained economic growth.[135] Endemic political conflict and low levels of legitimacy also make governments more likely to default on their debts. The "original sin" of nineteenth-century defaults can even today make it hard for some Latin American countries to borrow money in their own currency.[136]

The United States, however, did not go down that path. Ours has never been a perfect democracy—slavery, most obviously, would put the lie to that claim. But there was enough consensus among political elites to grant enough rights to enough social groups to ensure that the political system maintained a basic level of popular legitimacy. Governments of different political stripes enjoyed the credibility required to borrow when necessary; growth in the economy and especially in international trade made it possible to collect the taxes necessary to finance that debt. It is a simple formula, but one that few countries mastered.

PAYING FOR TOTAL WAR

The United States' ability to borrow money in a national emergency was never more on display than during the world wars of the first half of the twentieth century. During World War I, federal government spending increased more than twenty-fold, from $700 million in the 1916 fiscal year to more than $18 billion in 1919—more than 20 percent of GDP. Unlike the Revolutionary War, the War of 1812, and the Civil War, however, the government was able to meet its funding needs through taxes and borrowing without risking a fiscal crisis. Congress raised taxes repeatedly before and during the war, increasing revenues from less than $800 million in 1916 to more than $5 billion in 1919.[137] The government's ability to collect revenues had been strengthened by the Sixteenth Amendment, which in 1913 unequivocally gave Congress the power to levy an income tax.* There was considerable controversy over which taxes should be raised. The largest share of new revenues come from corporate taxes and individual income taxes, giving the government a reliable source of revenues that did not depend on the volume of international trade.[138] As usual, the Treasury had to borrow money to fill the gap between spending and tax revenues, but this time its credit remained strong throughout the war, enabling it to sell all of the bonds autho-

---

* In the late nineteenth century, increasing inequality created popular pressure for an income tax, and the Wilson-Gorman Tariff Act of 1894 included such a tax. In *Pollock v. Farmers' Loan & Trust Co.* (1895), however, the Supreme Court held that the specific income tax provisions of the Wilson-Gorman Act were unconstitutional. Dennis S. Ippolito, *Why Budgets Matter: Budget Policy and American Politics* (Pennsylvania State University Press, 2003), p. 87. It was not clear whether another income tax might be constitutional until the issue was settled by the Sixteenth Amendment.

rized by Congress—with the assistance of the Federal Reserve, the country's new central bank, which had been created only in 1913. The national debt grew from $1.2 billion in 1916 to more than $25 billion in 1919, about 30 percent of GDP, but interest rates remained low and inflation was lower than in previous wars.[139]

After the war, in keeping with past practice, the government ran surpluses for the entire decade of the 1920s in an effort to bring down the national debt. Conservative Republicans wanted to roll back the income tax, but were willing to put balanced budgets and debt reduction first.[140] Even Democratic president Franklin D. Roosevelt spoke out in favor of a balanced budget. Criticizing the deficit that appeared at the end of President Herbert Hoover's administration, he said, "It has contributed to the recent collapse of our banking structure. It has accentuated the stagnation of the economic life of our people. It has added to the ranks of the unemployed."[141] In his first budget, Roosevelt cut the pay of government workers by 15 percent and also reduced veterans' pensions.[142]

World War II, however, would require the largest budget deficits in American history. The war demanded centralized activity on an unprecedented scale. In 1938, with war on the horizon, President Roosevelt began spending on rearmament; in 1940, he introduced military conscription and asked Congress for the money to build 60,000 planes each year. But the United States military was still underprepared when the Japanese attacked Pearl Harbor on December 7, 1941.[143] Defense spending rose from less than $2 billion in 1940 to more than $80 billion by 1945.[144] The Manhattan Project alone required a secret $1.6 billion appropriation in 1944.[145] The United States also built much of the weaponry used by its allies—and loaned them the money to pay for it.[146]

Federal government spending, which had already been growing during the Great Depression, soared from $9 billion in 1940 to more than $90 billion in 1944 (more than 40 percent of GDP) as the country shifted virtually its entire economy to war production. Tax revenues rose from less than $7 billion in 1940 to more than $40 billion by 1944 (more than 20 percent of GDP), largely because of major expansions in the individual income tax, which for the first time covered a majority of the workforce, and corporate taxes.[147] Indi-

vidual income taxes, which provided less than 20 percent of government revenues in the 1930s, grew to 45 percent in 1944; they have
remained above 39 percent ever since.[148] As a share of the economy,
both spending and revenues in 1944 set records that still stand today.
Despite these major and politically divisive tax increases, as in previous wars, a majority of government spending was paid for by new
borrowing, this time on an enormous scale; the 1943 budget deficit
of $55 billion exceeded 30 percent of GDP—more than the govern-
ment had ever *spent* in any one year before.[149] As in World War I,
the Treasury Department's fundraising efforts were generally successful: a series of bond drives brought in more than $150 billion at
relatively low interest rates, even as the national debt grew to exceed
100 percent of GDP—three times as high as the peaks following the
Revolutionary War, the Civil War, and World War I.[150] World War II
was fought and won by millions of troops from dozens of countries,
backed by the world's largest economy, but it was paid for by the
credit line that Hamilton had set up in the 1790s.

By the end of the war, however, the forces that would transform
American fiscal policy over the rest of the twentieth century were
already in motion. Although Franklin D. Roosevelt stuck with a relatively traditional view of budgetary policy, the Great Depression
and the New Deal had changed the relationship between the federal
government and the population, most notably with the creation of
Social Security. The Depression had also seen the creation of a new
approach to economic policy, pioneered by John Maynard Keynes,
which would make later politicians much more sanguine about deficit
spending, even during peacetime. Finally, the end of the war saw the
need for a new international economic and monetary system—one
in which the United States, as the dominant superpower of the capitalist world, would necessarily play a central role.

Two

END OF GOLD

The first thing we have to do is to continue to keep confidence abroad in the American dollar. That means we must continue to have a balanced budget here at home in every possible circumstance that we can, because the moment that we have loss of confidence in our own fiscal policies at home, it results in gold flowing out.

—Vice President Richard Nixon, October 13, 1960[1]

Harry Dexter White would never have been mistaken for Alexander Hamilton. An academic who joined the Treasury Department in 1934 and rose to become an assistant secretary, he was one of the world's leading experts on, of all things, the French balance of payments between 1880 and 1913—how France had earned foreign currency for its exports, paid for its imports, and managed any difference between the two.[2] In 1941, however, White was tapped by Henry Morgenthau, Jr., secretary of the treasury under President Franklin Delano Roosevelt, to redesign the global economic system. This was an era of experts, of seemingly colorless men in dark suits (they were mostly men at the time) writing memos to each other and arguing about apparently arcane details that were almost entirely impenetrable to nonexperts—including their political masters. This was a long way from the grand compromises of the Constitutional Convention, the powerful rhetoric of the Federalist Papers, or any of the timeless debates involving Alexander Hamilton and Thomas Jefferson.

It was also a moment of almost unimaginable optimism. Work on planning the postwar world began within a week after the attack on Pearl Harbor; with the Pacific Fleet's battleships sunk or damaged, the premise was still that the United States would soon become the world's predominant market-based power.³ Who today would dare to seriously plan a new international economy, let alone think that it could actually be implemented and work? Yet the ideas produced by White and his colleagues—culminating in the Bretton Woods conference of July 1944, the Articles of Agreement of the International Monetary Fund, and the Bretton Woods system for international payments—ended up reshaping American public finance as profoundly as anything since the debates of the 1780s and 1790s.⁴

The systems created by Hamilton and White both exceeded all reasonable initial expectations. Hamilton's core principles—debt when you need it, taxes to service the debt, and fiscal responsibility as the prevailing ethos—served as the backbone of U.S. fiscal policy from 1790 through 1945, even as the world and the nature of government changed profoundly. The lessons of the Revolutionary War and the War of 1812 stuck with the American political system for a long time. White's impact, however, has been more complicated. Following the devastation of World War II, the Bretton Woods system was wildly successful as the basis for rebuilding world trade during the 1950s and 1960s and for bringing newly independent countries into the global economy. But the system contained the seeds of its own destruction, producing unsustainable trade and capital flow imbalances that could not be easily addressed within the system, leading to its collapse in the early 1970s—a moment that, to many, seemed like the end of the era of American economic predominance. But White's core principle—that the U.S. dollar would be the world's paramount reserve currency, offering a safe haven for all public and private investors—rose like a phoenix from the ashes of his system. The end of Bretton Woods confirmed the 1940s vision of the United States as the world's preeminent economic power while creating the biggest credit line ever—since people and governments around the world wanted to hold American debt. It was not obvious at the time, but once politicians in Washington began to access this line of credit, it made possible a historic increase in the national debt.

To see how this happened, we need to understand how the U.S. dollar—and U.S. government debt denominated in dollars—came to supplant gold as the primary store of value in the international economic system. Gold, of course, is still alive and well as an alternative investment asset whose price springs upward whenever people worry about the ability of governments to keep inflation under control or to service their debts. But the relationship between gold and money has changed dramatically over the past three centuries, both around the world and in the United States, with important consequences for American public finance and the national debt.

PAPER REVOLUTION

What is money? Money is conventionally described as whatever people prefer to use as a store of value, a way to keep accounts, and a means for conducting transactions. A small group of people can informally agree to use anything as a way of keeping track of and settling transactions; throughout history, many transactions within stable communities have been conducted on the basis of credit.[5] In modern history, however, the nature of money has been heavily influenced by government policy.[6] The government decides what is "legal tender"—something that must be accepted as payment of a debt by a creditor (although businesses can reject it in everyday transactions)—and what it will accept as tax payments; both of these choices affect what ordinary people are willing to use and hold as money.[7]

Metal—primarily gold and silver, but also copper, brass, and other alloys—has played an important role in many monetary systems in different historical ages. In some periods, gold and silver were used as the basis for accounts and in international trade, but not as a circulating medium for ordinary transactions; in other periods, governments minted coins with small amounts of precious metals for use as currency.[8] There are good reasons to use gold and silver as money. For something to serve as currency, it has to be relatively rare and relatively hard to produce; otherwise, it would be too easy for ordinary people to find or create, and would lose its value quickly. It also helps if it is durable, so it won't break down into something else, and transportable, so it can be easily traded for goods and services. There are actually very few chemical elements that meet all of these criteria well, and gold is one of them.[9] If there isn't enough gold, however, people will use substitutes; in 1776, for example, some dollar coins were minted from pewter.[10] What applies to ordinary people applies to governments as well. If currency is easy to create at very low cost—for example by stamping numbers on cheap metal or printing numbers on pieces of paper—a government that is short of precious metal will face the temptation to simply manufacture currency to pay its bills.[11] This is not quite as bad as if everyone could print currency in her basement, but large volumes of new paper currency can cause rapid and accelerating inflation as more and more money chases the same amount of goods and services.

Yet sometimes the creation of paper currency may make sense. If there aren't enough coins made from precious metals, you can have the opposite problem: too few coins chasing an increasing amount of goods and services can cause deflation (falling prices). More simply, if there isn't enough currency to go around, it can be hard to transact business.[12] A shortage of metal coin was a chronic problem in the American colonies because the British colonial authorities did not allow either the creation of a local mint or the export of coin from Britain.[13] As a result, the American colonial monetary system was a complicated mélange including a Spanish-Mexican coin, widely circulating in the Caribbean, which became known in North America as the dollar.[14] Necessity also encouraged the proliferation of alternative forms of money, many of which were not conducive to easy calculation:

> Barter was resorted to in the earlier stages of settlement; then certain staple commodities were declared by law to be legal tender in payment of debts. Curious substitutes were employed, such as shells or wampum. Corn, cattle, peltry, furs were monetary media in New England; tobacco and rice in the South. . . . One student, later president of [Harvard] college, settled his bill with "an old cow."[15]

At the same time, the unit of account was British pounds, shillings, and pence, but different colonies set different exchange rates between currencies, with the British authorities also weighing in. None of this worked well and the overall monetary situation was confused, to put it mildly.[16]

In this context, adding to the supply of ready money with some decorative government-authorized paper was not a crazy idea.[17] As an economy develops, the total volume of goods and services grows, which increases the demand for money to finance transactions. Adding more money to the economy can be a good thing, so long as the supply of new money remains under control. Without enough precious metals to mint new coins, paper was the obvious alternative; as long as the paper currency was sufficiently hard to counterfeit, the money supply could remain under government control. And whenever the economy was weak and credit was expensive, meaning that interest rates were high or loans were simply not available, creating money was a tempting alternative.

Benjamin Franklin, a printer by trade, argued for the creation of paper money in 1720s Pennsylvania.[18] The beginning of independent American thinking about money—a series of controversies that is now almost three centuries old—might be traced back to his 1729 essay, "A Modest Enquiry into the Nature and Necessity of a Paper-Currency," written when he was in his early twenties. Franklin argued that it was economic output that mattered, not the supply of precious metals: "The riches of a country are to be valued by the quantity of labor its inhabitants are able to purchase, and not by the quantity of gold and silver they possess."[19] For his efforts, he won a contract to print 40,000 paper pounds, for which he was paid £100, a considerable sum at the time. And that particular issuance of paper money, by increasing the supply of credit, seems to have helped the Pennsylvania economy.[20]

In 1751, however, the British Parliament imposed restrictions on paper currency, prohibiting "any further issue of legal-tender bills of credit by the New England colonies," a restriction that was extended throughout the North American colonies in 1764. Colonial governments were allowed to issue interest-bearing debt (bonds) but not paper that could be used to make payments—legal tender, that is. These restrictions were seen as an imposition on the prerogatives of the colonies and became a bone of contention in the run-up to the American Revolution.[21] It was perhaps fitting, therefore, that the Continental Congress chose to finance the American Revolutionary War with paper money. In June 1775, shortly after fighting began,

Congress ordered the mobilization of the Continental Army and also authorized the issuance of $2 million in "continental bills of credit." Without the power to tax, which was reserved to the states as the true source of sovereign authority, the central government had no other way to pay for the army. Congress also had to rely on the states to authorize its bills as legal tender and to accept them as tax payments.[22]

The distinction between government-issued debt and government-issued currency is easy to state in theory but often confusing in practice, especially in times of political turbulence. Debt pays interest and generally has a maturity date at which the face value must be paid off in full.[23] Currency, on the other hand, does not pay interest. Government debt, unlike government-issued currency, is not legal tender (although people are free to accept government bonds as payment if they choose). The Revolutionary-era bills of credit were currency, despite their name and despite the fact that they were supposed to be redeemed over time, because the states generally passed laws making them legal tender or its equivalent. But, like government debt, their value depended on people's beliefs about the government's solvency: as Congress's fiscal troubles deepened and it printed more and more bills of credit, their value declined (relative to silver and gold coins, collectively known as "specie") and then began to plummet. As the cumulative issuance of bills rose from $2 million to over $200 million, they became worth less and less. The exchange rate between paper dollars and the "Spanish milled dollar" (a silver coin) rose from 1.75 to 1 in March 1778 to 40 to 1 in March 1780, 100 to 1 in January 1781, and over 500 to 1 by May of that year.[24]

For all its adverse side effects, printed money played a major role in funding the Revolution. Government accounts from that period are not well ordered, but of the roughly $66 million in revenue that the national government received from 1775 to 1783, over half came from printing money.[25] As mentioned in chapter 1, like many politicians over the ages, Benjamin Franklin was initially taken with the positive effects of printing money for a good cause: "This currency as we manage it is a wonderful machine. It performs its office when we issue it; it pays and clothes troops, and provides victuals and ammunition; and when we are obliged to issue a quantity excessive, it pays itself off by depreciation."[26] As Franklin realized, this depreciation, or inflation, was effectively a tax on everyone who held paper currency. But this tax soon got out of control. As Philadelphia businessman and writer Pelatiah Webster argued in a contemporary study of Revolutionary finances,

> Paper money polluted the equity of our laws, turned them into engines of oppression, corrupted the justice of our public administration, destroyed the fortunes of thousands who had confidence in it, enervated the trade, husbandry, and manufactures of our country, and went far to destroy the morality of our people.[27]

By the time of the 1787 Constitutional Convention, most politicians understood the disruptive consequences of financing the government by printing too much money.

The birth of the United States was paid for by both a debauched paper currency and large debts that it soon defaulted on. When Alexander Hamilton became treasury secretary in 1789, his job was not just restoring the country's credit by restructuring the debt and imposing new taxes; he also had to clean up the mess that was money in the early United States.

HARD MONEY

Hamilton proposed to base the monetary system on both gold and silver. Gold had advantages including greater stability, he argued, but it would be disruptive to withdraw the large amounts of silver that were already in use.[28] He proposed "ten dollar and one dollar gold pieces, one dollar and ten cent silver pieces, and one cent and one-half cent copper pieces," and the Mint Act of 1792 largely followed his recommendations. As gold and silver were both widely recognized bases for money at the time, this was relatively uncontroversial.[29] This "bimetallic" standard meant that the dollar was defined as either a specific amount of silver or a specific amount of gold. In 1834, Congress set the ratio between the two at 16 to 1, although the market value of gold was slightly lower than 16 times the market value of silver; the California gold rush of the 1840s reduced the relative price of gold further, which meant that the United States was effectively on the gold standard.[30]

Basing the U.S. currency on gold and silver, however, did not mean that what we would now call the money supply was limited to precious metal coins. Currency has always coexisted with various forms of credit—which make it possible to conduct transactions without any currency at all—and a modern financial system makes possible the systematic creation of credit on a large scale. The United States was an early leader in private commercial banking, in part out of necessity.[31] Commerce was essential to the country's economic development, and shipping goods across such a large territory or even overseas required financing: sellers wanted to be paid quickly, while buyers did not want to pay for goods and then wait months before taking delivery. Bills of exchange (a form of commercial credit) were an early answer to this problem, followed by the development of a modern banking system.

Banks solve the problem by creating money. A bank takes in some of its money—whether capital contributed by the bank's owners, deposits, or loans—in the form of government-issued currency (minted gold or silver coins then, printed bills now). When a bank makes a loan, it could give the borrower some of that currency, in which case no money is created. But, more often, the bank creates an account for the borrower and credits that account with the amount of the loan. If you take out a $10,000 home equity loan from your bank today, the bank now has a piece of paper with your signature promising to pay it $10,000 (a bank asset, since it can be sold to someone else for cash); at the same time, your checking account goes up by $10,000 (a bank liability, since you could go in and demand $10,000 in bills). That new money in your checking account was just created by the bank in the very process of extending credit. In the early nineteenth century, the bank might instead have given you "bank notes"—paper, printed for the bank, that was convertible on demand into specie.[32] People were willing to accept bank notes for the same reason people are willing to accept credits to their checking accounts today: they were easier to use in transactions than large amounts of heavy gold and silver coins, and they were widely (though not universally) accepted.[33] In normal times, many people were happy to hold claims on specie, rather than specie itself, so bank notes could serve as a form of money (as could bank deposits).[34]

Although bank notes were convertible to specie on demand, banks did not generally keep enough coins in their vaults to redeem all their notes at the same time. In 1832, for example, the Second Bank of the United States held only $7.0 million in specie, but $21.4 million of its notes were in circulation, while depositors had another $22.8 million in their accounts;[35] most other banks operated along similar lines.[36] In effect, even though the currency of the United States was firmly based on gold and silver, the money supply depended on the amount of risk that private commercial banks wanted to take.[37] This meant, however, that banks were susceptible to financial panics, especially in the lightly regulated environment of early-nineteenth-century America. When depositors or note holders worry about a bank's ability to pay them in hard money, they race to the teller's window to get their money out before anyone else, which can cause even a healthy bank to collapse.[38] Various schemes at the state level attempted to constrain risk taking by individual banks,[39] but bank failures were common in early America, with major panics in 1819, 1837, 1857, 1860, and 1861.[40] One response to a panic was for banks to simply suspend the convertibility of their bank notes into specie, which occurred in both the War of 1812 (after the burning of Washington) and the Civil War.[41] In other words, bank notes were convertible into gold and silver—until they were not.

Some people have long argued that it is government intervention that causes excessive risk taking and financial crises.[42] The panics of the nineteenth century, however, seemed to lend support to the opposite view—that the government could reduce volatility by increasing its involvement in the financial system. Bank runs were not limited to a system based on private bank notes; even after the standardization of bank notes during the Civil War, banking crises reappeared in 1873, 1884, 1890, 1893, and 1907.[43] In 1873, British journalist Walter Bagehot argued that a "lender of last resort" was needed to backstop the financial system in a crisis; otherwise even solvent banks would be vulnerable to damaging runs.[44] In the United States, the Panic of 1907 led directly to the creation in 1913 of the

Federal Reserve System, the nation's first modern central bank. The Federal Reserve had (and still has) the mandate to protect the financial system by lending money to banks in a crisis; over time, it has also gained increasing power over monetary policy.[45]

For centuries, banks have played a central role in the public finance systems of many countries, including the United States. Although their primary role is to pool the savings of many depositors and lend it out to the private sector (businesses and households), banks also have to have safe assets that they can sell quickly when they need cash. Government bonds can serve this purpose admirably—if the government has good credit and there is a large, liquid market for its debt. Banks can invest their excess cash (specie, in the old days) in government bonds, secure in the knowledge that they can sell them quickly at a reasonable price should the need arise; they even earn interest in the meantime. In this case, the bank is pooling individual deposits and lending them to the government, making it easier for the government to borrow money. In the United States, Alexander Hamilton made this possible by restructuring the country's debt and restoring its credit rating, as discussed in the previous chapter, making Treasury bonds a safe asset. He also helped the process along by requiring that investors in the Bank of the United States pay for some of their shares with government bonds.[46]

The federal government relied heavily on private commercial banks to underwrite and distribute loans to the Treasury Department at the beginning of the Civil War.[47] As the war evolved, however, the idea of using banks as a tool to help finance national borrowing took another major step forward. At the time, about 7,000 types of bank notes issued by about 1,500 banks were in circulation (along with more than 5,000 types of counterfeits), hampering commerce and creating volatility in the money supply.[48] To meet its financing needs, the federal government also issued legal tender notes ("greenbacks") that were initially convertible into Treasury bonds but later not convertible into anything.[49] Treasury Secretary Salmon P. Chase used this chaos as an argument for a new banking system in which national banks (chartered by the federal government, not the states) would distribute "treasury notes"—a new, uniform banking currency.[50] The new notes would be backed by government bonds, not by gold or silver coin directly; this meant that national banks would have to buy those bonds (at least $250 million worth, in Chase's estimate) in order to issue the new currency. Thanks in part to patriotic sentiments inspired by the war, Chase's plan was enacted in the National Currency Act of 1863 and the National Bank Act of 1864. Effectively forcing banks to buy and hold government bonds helped finance the Civil War and tied the banks closely to the federal government. Finally, in 1865, Congress imposed a tax on bank notes issued by state banks, driving the notes (but not the banks) out of existence.[51]

It was only in 1879, when greenbacks became convertible into specie, that the country went back onto the gold standard, following the examples of the United Kingdom, Germany, France, and many other countries.[52] In effect, the value of the dollar was fixed at a specific amount of gold. But because the value of most things rises and falls with demand and supply, the real value of the dollar fluctuated depending on economic growth (which increases demand for money) and discoveries of gold (which increase the supply of money). When the world economy grew faster than gold discoveries, gold became more valuable relative to other goods; because the dollar was tied to gold, overall prices fell.[53] Falling prices in the late nineteenth century made it harder for people—particularly farmers with mortgages—to pay off their debts (since the amount of the debt was fixed in nominal terms).[54] But the gold standard and the lack of a central bank meant that there was no way to increase the money supply to prevent deflation. Proponents of "free silver," led by William Jennings Bryan, argued that restoring silver to equal status with gold would expand the money supply, causing inflation and making debts easier to pay back.[55] But Bryan lost the crucial 1896 presidential election to William McKinley, who favored "sound money," and in 1900 the Gold Standard Act reaffirmed the gold-only standard. (By then, the discovery of new goldfields in the American West, Australia, and South Africa was causing the value of gold to fall relative to other goods, so overall prices started rising.)[56]

As international trade increased in the late nineteenth and early twentieth centuries, the gold standard also became the backbone of the international monetary system.[57] Since each major country fixed the value of its currency relative to gold, their exchange rates were fixed relative to each other as well. If a country's imports exceeded its exports, its currency would accumulate in the hands of its trading partners, who could then redeem it for gold—draining the national treasury of gold. Losing gold would reduce the money supply, lowering domestic prices and wages; this would reduce imports and increase exports until the trade deficit was eliminated, stopping the gold outflow. The international gold standard was suspended during World War I, but restoring it was a top priority of politicians after 1918, particularly in the United States and the United Kingdom, and most major countries were back on the gold standard by 1928.[58]

Then, in October 1929, U.S. stock markets collapsed, quickly followed by markets around the world. A credit bubble that had inflated in the 1920s imploded rapidly, leaving households and businesses scrambling to pay off their debts. Families with less money reduced their consumption, slowing down economic activity; debtors were forced to sell assets to raise money, causing prices to fall further; as assets lost value, they became worth less as collateral, reducing overall lending; and falling prices forced more borrowers into default on loans that remained fixed in nominal terms. Banks that had made too many risky loans began to fail, causing the money supply to contract further. A spreading panic prompted numerous bank runs, further weakening the financial system. This malfunctioning U.S. banking system acted as a negative "financial accelerator," crippling the real economy, which slid into the Great Depression.[59]

The Federal Reserve, then less than two decades old, did relatively little to stop the bleeding. The gold standard limited its ability to expand the money supply and increase the flow of credit in the economy. More importantly, under the prevailing orthodoxy of the time, monetary policy was driven by the need to protect gold reserves. The textbook way to increase gold inflows was to tighten the money supply, lowering prices and wages—which only made the economy weaker. President Herbert Hoover had near-religious faith in the gold standard, and Treasury Secretary Andrew Mellon saw no need to deviate from past practice: "Conditions today are neither so critical nor so unprecedented as to justify a lack of faith in our capacity to deal with them in our accustomed way."[60] Initially, as the

American economy contracted, gold flowed from other countries to the United States; in order to stop these gold outflows, central banks around the world raised interest rates, effectively importing the economic slowdown to their own countries. Monetary tightening that began in Germany and the United States in 1928–1929 spread around the world as countries engaged in competitive deflation, creating a vicious cycle.[61] Central banks raced to convert their holdings of foreign currency into gold, reducing the global money supply.[62] High demand for gold increased its price relative to other goods; since the price of gold (in dollars) was fixed, this meant the price of everything else (in dollars) had to fall, making deflation even worse.

In 1931, unable to stop gold from draining out of its reserves, the United Kingdom abandoned the gold standard. In the United States, by contrast, Hoover and Mellon clung to the gold standard and the Federal Reserve even raised interest rates in the midst of the Depression.[63] Franklin D. Roosevelt avoided making a commitment one way or the other before taking office in 1933, but many investors expected the United States to devalue the dollar against gold. Since they expected dollars to fall in value, they exchanged them for gold and other currencies—reducing American gold reserves. At the time, George Harrison, president of the New York Federal Reserve Bank, said that this loss of gold "represents in itself a distrust of the currency and is inspired by talk of the devaluation of the dollar."[64]

When President Roosevelt took office on March 4, 1933, the United States was in the grip of a nationwide financial panic. With banks facing huge demands for cash from their depositors, most states had already declared bank holidays or severely restricted withdrawals, and the financial system was barely working.[65] Roosevelt immediately declared a bank holiday beginning on March 6 and also ordered banks not to export gold—an order that remained in force after the bank holiday was lifted a week later. He quickly pushed through the Emergency Banking Act, which allowed the Treasury Department to demand that all gold in private hands (coin, bullion, or certificates) be exchanged for a nongold form of currency—a power he exercised on April 5, effectively suspending convertibility.[66] Although Roosevelt expressed support for maintaining the gold standard, pressure from Congress for a weaker dollar coalesced around the Agricultural

Adjustment Act, with many representatives from farm states hoping to increase inflation by expanding the money supply.[67] Roosevelt decided he would have to accommodate their demands and accepted an amendment, proposed by Senator Elmer Thomas of Oklahoma, that offered various tools to weaken the dollar, including restoring silver as a base for money and changing the gold value of the dollar.[68]

As fears of devaluation increased, the value of the dollar began to fall relative to foreign currencies and Roosevelt expanded the prohibition on gold exports.[69] At the time, many contracts—including those governing some Treasury bonds—contained gold indexation clauses, which specified that the lender could demand repayment in gold as a form of protection against inflation. On June 5, Congress abrogated all such clauses, eliminating the ability of creditors to demand gold instead of dollars.[70] This was arguably an act of default, since the United States broke an explicit promise to its creditors—the only default since Hamilton restructured the debt in 1790.[71] It was not until January 1934 that Roosevelt officially reset the value of the dollar against gold at $35 per ounce—down from $20.67 per ounce, where it had been since 1834.[72]

Some of Roosevelt's advisers were worried; budget director Lewis Douglas famously remarked, "This is the end of western civilization."[73] But going off gold and abrogating gold indexation clauses did not destroy the government's credit. The market reaction was almost nonexistent: long-term corporate and municipal bond yields fell from April through August 1933, and government bond yields were lower on average in 1933 than in 1932.[74] The convertibility of paper into metal had been suspended often enough under the gold standard that it was not in itself grounds for panic. Most importantly, going off the gold standard and devaluing the dollar almost certainly helped the American economy overcome deflationary pressures and begin to recover from the depths of the Great Depression.[75]

The gold standard had been suspended before without losing its credibility. This time, however, it was blamed for exacerbating the worst economic crisis of the industrial age. While political leaders after World War I had assumed that the gold standard should be restored, there was no such consensus around how to rebuild the international monetary system after World War II. This was the question before the delegates who gathered for the United Nations Monetary and Financial Conference, held in Bretton Woods, New Hampshire, in July 1944.

DOLLAR TRIUMPHANT: 1944–1971

The primary goals of White, Morgenthau, and almost everyone else at Bretton Woods were to rebuild war-torn Europe and prevent another Great Depression. The central question they faced was what kind of money the world would use for international transactions.

White's proposal was to allow both gold and dollars to be used as reserves—the assets that provide backing for a country's money. One problem with gold was that there wasn't enough of it to support an increasing volume of international transactions; another was that a large proportion of gold production was in the Soviet Union (as well as South Africa), and the Western Allies did not want the international monetary system to be subverted by a communist country. The solution was to use dollars as a global reserve currency, since dollars could be created by the Federal Reserve in response to increasing demand. Countries could accumulate and hold dollars as the basis for their money supply rather than competing with each other for scarce gold reserves. Instead of fixing its currency against gold, each country would (roughly) fix its currency against the dollar, facilitating global trade. The United States was also willing to allow other central banks (but not ordinary people) to convert dollars into gold at the rate of $35 per ounce—something no other country was able to do. This provided a measure of stability to the entire system: if the Federal Reserve were to create huge amounts of dollars, other countries could demand to exchange those dollars for gold, draining U.S. gold reserves.

British economist and conference representative John Maynard Keynes, however, had a competing vision. As early as 1941 he had proposed an "international clearing union" for the postwar world;[76] at the conference he argued for, among other things, the creation of an international currency for central banks, known as "bancor," which would be managed by a new international organization.

Keynes wanted nothing to do with gold, which he famously called a "barbarous relic," but he also did not want the dollar to be the predominant reserve currency—in part because he was wary of American preeminence in the international monetary system.[77]

Keynes and the British, however, had to give way to White and the Americans on most points. No international monetary system could succeed without the support of the United States, which had the largest gold reserves and the dollars that other countries would need to import American goods. At the time, the United Kingdom was a large net debtor to other countries, which were likely to sell their pounds in the postwar world.[78] The United States was unwilling to allow an international organization to control an international currency that could be used to buy American goods, and so bancor had little chance of adoption. A monetary system based on the dollar, by contrast, was consistent with American economic interests but also acceptable to other countries. They were reassured by the dollar's convertibility into gold, which in principle gave them a way to switch out of dollars should the United States begin to abuse its control over the global reserve currency.

The Bretton Woods system provided the economic dimension of American hegemony in the postwar Western world. In many respects, it was a resounding success. Fixing exchange rates in dollar terms discouraged countries from engaging in trade wars by devaluing their currencies, promoting stability and facilitating a rapid expansion in international trade. Foreign lending and investment by Americans meant that there was a continual flow of dollars overseas. This helped other countries buy American exports, lubricated international trade (which required dollars), and enabled foreign central banks to accumulate the dollars they needed as reserves.[79] In effect, the United States was operating like a bank to the world under the gold standard, holding gold and issuing the dollars that every country needed to grease the wheels of international commerce. Foreigners were willing to accept and hold dollars because they were widely accepted in international trade, which increased the global money supply.[80] Countries like West Germany and Japan began increasing exports, enabling them to relax import restrictions, which helped spread economic growth to other countries.[81] Western Europe in particular enjoyed growth that seemed miraculous at the time: from

1948 to 1962, GDP per person grew at 6.8 percent per year in West Germany, 5.6 percent in Italy, 3.4 percent in France, and 2.4 percent in the United Kingdom, compared to 1.6 percent in the United States.[82]

Like all aspects of American hegemony, Bretton Woods had its critics. French finance minister (and future president) Valéry Giscard d'Estaing complained about the United States' "exorbitant privilege"—the ability to buy anything it wished with its own currency, since dollars were accepted everywhere.[83] The fact that central banks liked to hold dollars and dollar-denominated assets, such as Treasury bonds, gave the United States the opportunity to finance its deficits by selling debt to foreigners. But at least through the 1950s, the government resisted this temptation.

The massive changes brought on by World War II extended to postwar American fiscal policy. The war, like previous conflicts, brought on huge deficits (over 30 percent of GDP in 1943) and raised the national debt to unprecedented heights (over 108 percent of GDP in 1946).[84] After past wars, the usual pattern had been rapid demilitarization and consistent budget surpluses to pay down the debt. This time, however, the breakdown of the international order after World War I, coupled with the United States' new importance in the world, made isolationism much less appealing. On March 1, 1945, President Roosevelt said to a joint session of Congress, "Twenty-five years ago, American fighting men looked to the statesmen of the world to finish the work of peace for which they fought and suffered. We failed—we failed them then. We cannot fail them again, and expect the world to survive again."[85] America's new role in the world was soon evident in both the 1947 Truman Doctrine—"the policy of the United States to support free peoples who are resisting attempted subjugation by armed minorities or by outside pressures"[86]—and the Marshall Plan, an aid program to promote European reconstruction, named after Secretary of State George Marshall. European countries desperately needed dollars to import goods from the United States and other countries, and the Marshall Plan aimed to fill that gap with up to $17 billion in loans and grants over four years.[87]

If economic aid was expensive, military spending was more expensive still. Although defense spending fell from $83 billion in 1945 to $9 billion in 1948, it immediately began growing again because of the onset of the Cold War, symbolized for Americans by the Berlin Airlift of 1948–1949. Military expenses surged after the outbreak of the Korean War in 1950, reaching $53 billion by 1953, consuming more than two-thirds of total government spending; even after the war ended, defense spending, largely on continued weapons building, continued to account for more than half of the federal budget through the 1950s.[88] But political leaders were willing to pay for the Cold War with taxes rather than with large-scale borrowing, perhaps because, unlike a conventional war, it had no end in sight. Major tax cuts in 1945 and 1948 brought taxes down from wartime levels, but they were soon followed by tax increases, with the top marginal income tax rate rising back up to 91 percent in 1951.[89] Republican president Dwight Eisenhower resisted calls from members of his own party for tax cuts, insisting on the importance of fiscal responsibility; in 1959, he refused to cut taxes to help his vice president, Richard Nixon, win the 1960 presidential election.[90] As a result, the federal budget stayed more or less in balance through the 1950s (see Figure 2-1).

Both the international monetary system and American fiscal policy, however, like so many other things, began to change in the 1960s.

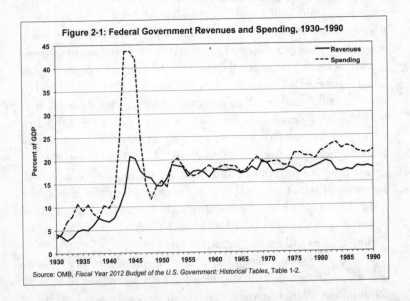

Figure 2-1: Federal Government Revenues and Spending, 1930–1990

Source: OMB, *Fiscal Year 2012 Budget of the U.S. Government: Historical Tables*, Table 1-2.

For one thing, the Bretton Woods system could not last forever, at least not the way it operated through the 1950s. By 1960, foreigners' holdings of dollars exceeded U.S. gold reserves: the United States was like a nineteenth-century bank that had issued more notes than it had gold coins in the vault—and there was no lender of last resort standing behind the United States.[91] In the presidential election that year, both Vice President Nixon and Senator John F. Kennedy took pains to emphasize the importance of maintaining gold reserves and fighting the so-called gold drain.[92] Gold reserves were seen as a crucial element of national strength. As president, Kennedy later said,

> What really matters is the strength of the currency. It is this, not the *force de frappe* [nuclear arsenal], which makes France a factor. Britain has nuclear weapons, but the pound is weak, so everyone pushes it around. Why are people so nice to Spain today? Not because Spain has nuclear weapons but because of all those lovely gold reserves.[93]

At the time, the gold drain was a constraint on monetary and fiscal policy, part of the case for lower budget deficits to maintain confidence in the dollar. Big budget deficits, it was feared, would increase aggregate demand, raising imports and sending more dollars overseas, which would eventually increase gold outflows.

But politicians have to balance many priorities, and President Kennedy was no exception. If gold reserves were important, the Cold War was more important, and Kennedy—who had been elected on a promise to close the "missile gap" with the Soviet Union—chose to increase military spending.[94] Sustaining economic growth was also a top priority, and Kennedy's administration was the first to wholeheartedly embrace deficit spending as a tool for managing the economy. In the 1930s, John Maynard Keynes first made the case for stimulating a slow economy by increasing government spending or cutting taxes, either of which would put money in people's hands, increasing overall demand and boosting economic activity. Although many of President Roosevelt's policies had this effect, he never fully subscribed to the theory. Kennedy's advisers, however, were confident that Keynesian demand management could be used to fine-tune the economy by increasing deficits during slowdowns and reducing them during booms. In 1962, Kennedy began campaigning for a major, deficit-increasing tax cut as a way to increase demand and economic growth, which was eventually enacted in the Revenue Act of 1964. For the first time in American history, a president was arguing that deficits could be a good thing, not an unfortunately necessary response to a military or economic emergency.[95]

Kennedy's vice president and successor, Lyndon Johnson, also found that some things were more important than a balanced budget: faced with the choice between guns and butter, he chose both. Johnson oversaw America's increasingly expensive commitment to the Vietnam War while also expanding domestic social programs to fight poverty. In addition to higher spending on education, infrastructure, and cultural programs, Congress in 1965 created both Medicare and Medicaid, committing the federal government to buy health care for the elderly and the poor. "No longer will older Americans be denied the healing miracle of modern medicine," Johnson declared. "No longer will illness crush and destroy the savings that they have so carefully put away over a lifetime so that they might enjoy dignity in their latter years."[96] At the time, some members of his own party were skeptical about the cost of Medicare. "I'll take care of [the money]," the president responded. "400 million's not going to separate us friends when it's for health."[97]

There was another reason why it was difficult for the United States to slow down the gold drain: the inflation that contributed to gold outflows was also good for the government's balance sheet. Prices have generally risen since 1945—perhaps in part because of the prevailing view among economists that inflation is better than deflation,[98] but mostly because the Bretton Woods system gave central banks more flexibility to manage the money supply. After World War II, the U.S. government was a major debtor and, like any debtor, it benefited from inflation. The government paid down the national debt, which fell from over 108 percent of GDP in 1946 to less than 24 percent in 1974 (see Figure 2-2), much faster than it had after the Revolutionary War, the Civil War, or World War I.[99]

One way to pay down the debt is for the government to run surpluses in its primary budget (not counting interest payments), but those surpluses after World War II were no bigger than after earlier wars. The big difference from previous historical periods was that

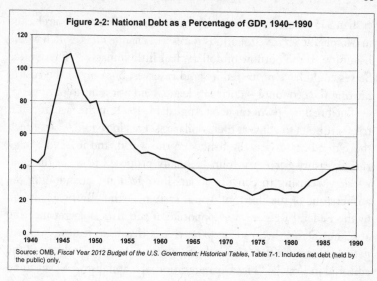

Figure 2-2: National Debt as a Percentage of GDP, 1940–1990

Source: OMB, *Fiscal Year 2012 Budget of the U.S. Government: Historical Tables*, Table 7-1. Includes net debt (held by the public) only.

effective interest rates on the debt were much lower than the growth rate of the economy.[100] Modest but persistent inflation combined with regulation of interest rates meant that real (inflation-adjusted) interest rates were always low and often negative; since creditors' interest payments did not keep up with inflation, part of the debt was inflated away.[101] Low interest rates and rapid economic growth combined to make the debt fall rapidly as a share of the economy. Raising interest rates to slow down the gold drain, by contrast, would probably have increased the government's own interest payments, making the debt harder to pay off.[102]

So while politicians paid lip service to the importance of the nation's gold reserves, the United States continued to send dollars overseas, increasing the ratio of foreign dollar holdings to gold reserves.[103] This produced the "Triffin dilemma," named after economist Robert Triffin: outflows of dollars from the United States were a crucial part of the international monetary system, but those dollars represented liabilities of the U.S. government, which made other countries increasingly nervous about their value.[104] Spending on the Vietnam War helped produce budget deficits throughout most of the late 1960s and also contributed to inflationary pressures, both of which reduced foreign central banks' appetite for dollars. Those banks began to worry about whether they would always be able to cash in $35 for an ounce of gold, prompting a wave of gold purchasing in March 1968.[105] Negotiations to reset exchange rates, which would have slowed the outflow of dollars, had little impact.[106] The United States could have protected its gold reserves, but only at the cost of hurting the economy—a price its leaders did not want to pay.[107]

The breaking point came on August 11, 1971, in the face of countries' requests to convert their dollar reserves into gold.[108] In effect, the United States was the banker to the world, and it faced a bank run. Treasury Secretary John Connally proposed to close the gold window, refusing to convert dollars into gold and abandoning the cornerstone of the Bretton Woods system. Arthur Burns, chairman of the Federal Reserve, was opposed; at the critical secret meeting at Camp David, he argued, "The risk is if you do it now, you will get the blame for the . . . devaluation of the dollar. I could write the editorial in Pravda: 'The Disintegration of Capitalism.' Never mind if it's right or wrong—consider how it will be exploited by the politicians."[109] But on August 15, 1971, President Nixon formally closed the gold window, arguing that "the American dollar must never again be a hostage in the hands of international speculators."[110] Framing the announcement as a New Economic Policy, Nixon added some tax cuts, a reduction in the number of federal employees, a ninety-day wage and price freeze, and a temporary 10 percent surcharge on imports. The era of gold was finally over.

Removing the last link to gold meant putting more power in the hands of central bankers—who are only human, after all. In the words of financial commentator James Grant, "Gold is a hedge against the human animal and an anchor to windward against human history, the tides of which sometimes bear along war, disease, revolution, confiscation and monetary bungling, as well as peace, progress and plenty."[111] Now the anchor was gone.

DEBT WITHOUT LIMIT: 1971–

After Nixon closed the gold window, the dollar was devalued against other currencies, but the new exchange rates could not be maintained against another run on the dollar in 1973. The world abandoned the fixed exchange rate system for a floating rate system in which the value of a currency is set by supply and demand, and the dollar depreciated further, leading *Time* magazine to quip, "Once upon a very recent time, only a banana republic would devalue its money twice within 14 months."[112] But countries still needed reserves, in part to intervene in foreign currency markets, and there was no discernible shift away from the dollar as a reserve currency. In 1977 it still accounted for around 80 percent of total identified foreign exchange reserves,[113] and "dollars held abroad in official reserves" increased by $91.3 billion from 1975 through 1981.[114]

The 1970s were a rocky time for the United States, particularly as inflation increased and the dollar weakened. But predictions that the end of Bretton Woods would mean runaway inflation were not borne out. After becoming chair of the Federal Reserve in 1979, Paul Volcker tightened monetary policy and, at the cost of higher unemployment, managed to squeeze inflation down. The next major test for the United States in the post–Bretton Woods era came in the 1980s. In 1980, Ronald Reagan won the presidential election promising to cut taxes, strengthen national defense, and balance the budget by slashing other government spending.[115] His first major initiative was the Economic Recovery Tax Act of 1981, which cut income tax rates across the board, with the top rate falling from 70 percent to 50 percent. The largest tax cut in history combined with a severe recession in 1981–1982 to reduce government revenues from 19.6 percent of GDP in 1981 to only 17.3 percent in 1984.[116] At the same time, government spending climbed thanks to increases in defense spending, producing what were then the largest peacetime deficits in history—4.8 percent of GDP or higher from 1983 through 1986.[117] Large government deficits combined with large and growing current account deficits* made the United States—both the federal government and the private sector—increasingly reliant on borrowing from other countries.[118]

---

* The current account measures the difference between money earned from the rest of the world (mainly through exports and income on investments in foreign countries) and money paid to the rest of the world (mainly through imports and foreigners' income on investments in this country). In recent American history, the major contributor to current account deficits has been trade deficits (importing more than we export).

Under the Bretton Woods system, this would have been a serious problem. Borrowing from overseas depended on foreign investors' willingness to hold dollars (or dollar-based assets), which required confidence in the value of the dollar; but the more dollars those investors accumulated, the less faith they had that the United States would be able to maintain the gold standard at $35 per ounce, until finally the entire system collapsed. After Bretton Woods, however, every country still needed foreign currency reserves to facilitate international trade and the dollar was still the reserve currency of choice. The large budget deficits of the 1980s helped push up interest rates in the United States, making the dollar more attractive to international investors,[119] and convertibility into gold was no longer an issue to worry about.

At the time, smart observers wondered how long large budget deficits and current account deficits could be sustained. In 1985, Federal Reserve chair Paul Volcker warned,

> Economic analysis and common sense coincide in telling us that the budgetary and trade deficits of the magnitude we are running at a time of growing prosperity are simply unsustainable indefinitely. They imply a dependence on growing foreign borrowing by the United States that, left unchecked, would sooner or later undermine the confidence in our economy essential to a strong currency and prospects for lower interest rates.[120]

But for the time being, at least, the end of Bretton Woods meant that foreigners were willing to hold more dollars, not fewer dollars, since confidence in the dollar was no longer constrained by physical gold reserves. Heated rhetoric about deficits became a constant theme in Washington, producing (among other things) the Gramm-Rudman-Hollings Act of 1985, which attempted to mandate balanced budgets. (It was a failure, because Congress and the president could modify its deficit targets, use accounting gimmicks to meet them, or simply repeal its enforcement provisions if need be.[121]) But in the post–Bretton Woods world of the 1980s, the United States largely escaped any severe consequences of both its budget and current account deficits. In 1990 and 1993, Presidents

George H. W. Bush and Bill Clinton pushed through budgetary legislation that cut spending and increased taxes. As budget deficits fell through the decade and America gained a reputation for stable growth and low inflation, the dollar only became more attractive as a safe store of value.

The new world, however, contained greater risks for many other countries. Increasing financial liberalization—meaning that money could move in and out of countries more easily—heightened the volatility of the international economy. In the 1990s, foreign capital rushed into the newly industrializing countries of East and Southeast Asia, fueling economic booms that caused rapid increases in asset prices and currency values. Cheap money encouraged companies to borrow heavily to invest in risky projects, until the boom could only be sustained through continual infusions of new capital. Then, in 1997, currency traders began betting against the Thai baht, forcing the government to buy baht to defend its value—which required foreign currency reserves. When the government could no longer support the baht, the currency promptly collapsed, taking the over-leveraged economy with it (because domestic companies could no longer repay money they had borrowed in other currencies), and foreign capital rushed out even faster than it had rushed in. The "Asian financial crisis" went on to wreak havoc with the economies of Indonesia, South Korea, and other countries, including even Russia. The globalized economy meant that financial panics could spread around the world rapidly as investors herded out of the same countries they had herded into only a few years before.

The International Monetary Fund (IMF), a product of the Bretton Woods conference, extended emergency loans to several countries during the Asian financial crisis, but the money came with numerous conditions that made the IMF deeply unpopular in certain parts of the world, reinforcing a stigma associated with borrowing from the IMF that had been developing for decades. The lesson, for many emerging market countries, was that they never wanted to have to borrow from the IMF again.[122] Attempts to ensure that the private sector does not borrow too much foreign capital, however, have had limited effectiveness.[123] So central banks around the world have decided to protect themselves by building up large war chests of foreign currency reserves (which they can use to support their currencies and pay foreign debts in a crisis)—particularly U.S. dollars. Some countries—most notably China—also accumulate dollars as a way of suppressing the value of their own currencies.[124] China's huge trade surplus with the United States gives it a surplus of dollars, but if it traded them for yuan on the open market, that would increase the value of the yuan, making it harder to export goods; so instead it invests those dollars in Treasury bonds, bonds of U.S. government agencies, and other dollar-denominated assets. In summary, the instability of the global economy increases demand for safe assets, and there is still nothing safer than U.S. Treasury bonds.

In 1948, after the Bretton Woods system was established, all the international reserves of all the central banks in the world came to $49.5 billion, of which $34.5 billion was gold and $13.4 billion was "foreign exchange," largely dollars. In 1968, after twenty years of global growth, total international reserves had only increased to $73.5 billion, of which $37.8 billion was gold and $29.1 billion was foreign exchange.[125] At the time, if roughly $20 billion out of that $29.1 billion was held in dollars, that would have been just 2 percent of U.S. GDP—too small an amount to have any impact on the ability of the United States to finance its debts.[126]

In 2011, by contrast, total foreign exchange reserves reported to the IMF amounted to more than $7 trillion, and this excludes part of the considerable holdings of China, Saudi Arabia, and Abu Dhabi.[127] The total foreign assets held by central banks and sovereign wealth funds (government investment funds) are probably closer to $10 trillion, of which over 60 percent is in dollars.[128] Since a large proportion of these dollars are invested in Treasury securities—the classic central bank reserve asset—foreign governments have become a major source of financing for the U.S. national debt, which reached $10.1 trillion in September 2011.[129] Foreigners in general, including private households and companies as well as central banks and other government agencies, own about $5 trillion of Treasury bonds.[130]

In today's unstable world, this enormous international appetite for safe dollar assets has given the U.S. government the largest credit line in economic history.[131] Even when a financial crisis that originated in the United States created record peacetime deficits in

2009 and 2010, surging demand for safe assets pushed interest rates on Treasury bonds to historically low levels.[132] Under the Bretton Woods system, the capacity of the world to buy American bonds was limited by American gold reserves; today it is limited only by market demand, which has turned out to be much more forgiving. As long as people around the world think that the U.S. economy will continue to grow and that government policy will remain generally responsible, they are willing to buy and hold dollar assets.

Markets, however, can turn against you. The dollar's status as the world's effective reserve currency is not written into any treaty that has been ratified by the community of nations. Instead, it depends on the belief that the United States will not mismanage the dollar to the point where it will lose a lot of its value—and on the fact that the dollar has no serious competitor at the moment, especially with the eurozone beset by multiple sovereign debt crises. Beliefs can change, or other currencies can become more attractive, or countries like China might decide they don't need quite so many reserves as they have now. And then the central bankers and sovereign wealth fund managers of the world might decide they don't need as many dollars, making it harder for the U.S. government to finance its budget deficits. The fact that so many countries have been willing to buy Treasury bonds because of the need for safe reserves, rather than the pursuit of high interest rates, has benefited the United States enormously. But it also means they could abandon Treasuries for noneconomic reasons, reducing the government's access to credit.

The end of Bretton Woods and the increase in the federal government's borrowing capacity do not tell the whole story, however. Ever since Ronald Reagan, American politicians have relentlessly inveighed against deficits and claimed the high ground of fiscal responsibility—yet the government has run deficits almost every year, culminating in the trillion-dollar deficits of recent years. Never before has there been such a combination of balanced budget rhetoric and deep deficits. What happened?

Three

DEFICITS DON'T MATTER

I am the leader, the insider-revolutionary in this country. . . . If you're writing the history of modern conservatism, I'm at least in one of the chapters.

—House minority whip Newt Gingrich, 1992[1]

"The federal budget is structurally unbalanced. This imbalance will do increasing damage to the economy in the future and is unsustainable in the long term. . . . Failure to reverse these trends in fiscal policy and the composition of federal spending will doom future generations to a stagnating standard of living, damage U.S. competitiveness and influence in the world, and hamper our ability to address pressing national needs."[2] Within three decades, the annual budget deficit will rise to 20 percent of GNP.[3] Because the political system is incapable of solving the deficit problem, "the United States could suddenly find itself a second-class citizen in the world economy, subject to the same strictures as Nigeria."[4] Unless we take decisive steps, the debt will continue to escalate, until the world's greatest superpower becomes a "fiscal Brazil."[5] The year is 1992.

The 1990s began with our first modern deficit crisis. The massive 1981 tax cut did not, as some advocates predicted, increase tax revenues.[6] Instead, it contributed to the record peacetime deficits of the 1980s. Even repeated tax increases and the economic expansion of the 1980s could not keep pace with federal spending, and by the early 1990s it seemed as if large deficits were here to stay. The 1991–1993 deficits all exceeded $250 billion, which was a lot of money back then—almost 5 percent of GDP in 1992, a level exceeded in peacetime only in the mid-1980s. Entitlement spending was on the march, promising to consume a growing share of the budget. The Gramm-Rudman-Hollings Balanced Budget Act had proven no match for Congress's ability to game the system with phony projections and technical gimmicks. The decline of America was a major theme among commentators, with one group claiming that large deficits were the cause of our economic and geopolitical deterioration.[7]

Yet the 1990s ended with the largest federal budget surpluses in half a century. In the 2000 presidential election, George W. Bush and Al Gore fought over what to do with trillions of dollars of projected surpluses. Political attitudes inside the White House changed by 180 degrees, with Vice President Dick Cheney famously saying, "Reagan proved deficits don't matter."[8] A decade later, of course, and we are back where we started, with Washington panicked about deficits and the optimism of the new millennium replaced by a resurgence of the theme of America in decline.

The 1990s seemed to show that our political system could bring deficits under control, at least in good economic times. But in the story of American fiscal policy, the 1990s were a crucial turning point that saw the final breakdown of the fragile political consensus that fiscal responsibility mattered. Just as the Democratic Party came under the leadership of a moderate president who put balanced budgets ahead of increased spending on social programs, a conservative revolution that had been brewing for decades finally took control of the Republican Party. Bitter opposition to President Clinton united and strengthened conservatives inside and outside Washington, giving the antigovernment, antitax movement a populist image that today we call the Tea Party. The growing strength of this modern tax revolt meant that when Republicans recaptured control of Washington in 2001, they restored business as usual—large and seemingly permanent deficits—through massive tax cuts that were never matched by spending reductions. When deficits climbed even higher in the wake of the financial crisis of 2007–2009, Republican politicians—backed by a resurgence in conservative antipathy toward Washington—insisted on shrinking the government and cutting taxes further. At the same time, the retirement of the leading edge of the baby boom generation now means that spending promises made under Democratic presidents decades ago are finally coming due. With the federal government's popular legitimacy increasingly under attack and Congress incapable of raising taxes to pay for its past crises and future spending commitments, the fiscal foundation of the United States is beginning to crumble, making the country a little less like eighteenth-century Great Britain and a little more like eighteenth-century France.

LONG MARCH OF THE TAX REVOLT

Conservatism is a storied political philosophy, its modern form dating back to Edmund Burke, the great Irish critic of the French Revolution. The French Revolution attempted to remake all of society and mankind at the same time. Like many other revolutions, it spawned chaos, bloodshed, and autocracy. For Burke, individual liberty and good government were rooted in the institutions that each generation inherited from its forefathers; overthrowing those institutions in the hope of creating a better future from abstract principles was both foolish and dangerous. But from the beginning, conservatism did not merely seek to preserve the status quo. Burke and his successors have always been activists and counterrevolutionaries, developing new ideas and rallying cries to beat back reform movements and reimpose traditional hierarchies in a modern form.[9]

In the seemingly stable America that developed after World War II, conservatism was a relatively weak political force. Although conservatives today may want to roll back the accomplishments of the Franklin D. Roosevelt administration and even the Progressive reformers of the early twentieth century, the postwar Republican Party was largely reconciled to the New Deal; many corporate executives accepted Social Security as a permanent fixture—in part because it helped offset the costs of their own pension plans.[10] As Republican president Dwight Eisenhower wrote in 1954,

> Should any political party attempt to abolish social security, unemployment insurance, and eliminate labor laws and farm programs, you would not hear of that party again in our political history. There is a tiny splinter group, of course, that believes you can do these things. . . . Their number is negligible and they are stupid.[11]

There were business leaders who sought to build a conservative movement that could one day topple the liberal welfare state, but they had relatively little influence in the party, except for Barry Goldwater's nomination for president in 1964—which ended in a crushing defeat to President Lyndon Johnson.[12] The apogee of the regulatory state arrived under Republican president Richard Nixon, who oversaw (though perhaps reluctantly) the creation of the Environmental Protection Agency and the Occupational Safety and Health Administration, among other liberal initiatives.

At the same time, however, powerful forces, including the civil rights movement, the 1960s counterculture, women's liberation, and the expansion of government welfare and regulatory programs, were provoking a backlash on the right. Faced with a seemingly omnipresent enemy, the free market conservatism nurtured by some members of the business community in the postwar period reemerged as the most important ideology and the major storyline in American politics over the past forty years. From the Reagan Revolution to the Tea Party, the new conservatives have portrayed themselves as an embattled revolutionary vanguard, fighting against a dominant liberal elite that threatens their basic freedoms.[13] In 1964, Ronald Reagan said, "Our natural, unalienable rights are now considered to be a dispensation of government, and freedom has never been so fragile, so close to slipping from our grasp as it is at this moment." In 1971, soon-to-be Supreme Court justice Lewis Powell wrote, "What now concerns us is quite new in the history of America. We are not dealing with sporadic or isolated attacks from a relatively few extremists. . . . The assault on the enterprise system is broadly based and consistently pursued."[14] The modern conservative movement was born out of the struggle against this apparent menace.

Contemporary American conservatism has many important themes: the "traditional values" often associated with evangelical Christianity; economic and philosophical libertarianism; a pro-business antipathy toward government regulation; a generally hawkish position on national security issues; and an anticrime, "law and order" ethos. But the strand with the greatest impact on fiscal policy and the national debt has been a tax revolt that has been growing for over thirty years, since the days when taxes really were high: in the 1970s, the top federal income tax rate was 70 percent, and that was already down from 91 percent in most of the 1950s.[15] The modern antitax movement is often traced back to the 1978 passage of Proposition 13 in California, which cut property taxes in half overnight. Proposition 13 has been widely seen as the product of a populist, grassroots protest movement (although it received major support from associations of real estate agents and apartment owners).[16] But at the same time that local activists were pushing for lower taxes on the state level, the editorial page of *The Wall Street Journal* was popularizing what came to be known as supply-side economics, often associated with economist Arthur Laffer: the theory that cutting taxes would motivate people to work, save, and invest more, leading to higher economic growth and even higher tax revenues. The idea that tax cuts could cure all of our nation's economic woes—and social problems such as drug abuse and divorce, according to *Wall Street Journal* writer Jude Wanniski—won the attention of Republican representative (and presidential hopeful) Jack Kemp and was endorsed by the Republican National Committee in 1978.[17]

Ronald Reagan brought together the two major strands of the antitax movement and pushed them to the top of the national agenda. Back in 1973, as governor of California, he had backed Proposition 1, which (unsuccessfully) aimed to reduce state income taxes, limit the state's total income tax revenues, and require two-thirds votes in the legislature to increase taxes.[18] And during the 1980 presidential campaign, Reagan signed on to Kemp's version of supply-side economics, which was the foundation of the 1981 tax cut.[19] Tax cuts were a natural part of the new president's overall worldview. The enemy was government (in his first inaugural address he said, "In this present crisis, government is not the solution to the problem; government is the problem"),[20] and the weapon to bring government under control was tax cuts. In theory, the plan was to cut taxes, cut spending, and balance the federal budget at a much lower level. In practice, things did not work out that neatly—which is why Reagan, despite his symbolic importance to the conservative antitax movement, was ultimately only a transitional figure.

The main architect of Reagan's plan to reshape the federal government was David Stockman, his first head of the Office of Management and Budget. Stockman entered the administration believing that it was possible to cut taxes and slash spending enough to balance the budget—and that the economy would take off as a result.[21] Tax cuts, by reducing the flow of money to Washington, would "put a tightening noose around the size of government," forcing Congress to cut spending drastically.[22] At the same time, by increasing the incentives to work and to invest, they would stimulate economic growth. As a tax cutter, however, Stockman had one major weakness: he actually thought the budget *should* be balanced, as opposed to more extreme supply-siders who said that deficits didn't matter.[23] When deficit projections skyrocketed through 1981 and political realities showed how hard it was to cut spending, he argued for undoing at least part of Reagan's signature tax cut.[24] (Martin Feldstein, who became chair of Reagan's Council of Economic Advisers in 1982, also argued that higher taxes would be necessary to reduce deficits.)[25] Although Stockman lost the battle within the White House, enough Democrats and moderate Republicans in Congress thought that deficits mattered to raise taxes modestly in 1982, 1983, 1984, 1986, and 1987 (though nowhere near enough to make up for the 1981 tax cut), with the consent of the avowedly antitax president.[26] Reagan and congressional leaders also agreed on the Tax Reform Act of 1986, which reduced the top income tax rate from 50 percent to 28 percent, yet eliminated enough loopholes to slightly increase tax revenues. Although the antitax movement was gaining strength, the Republican Party's center of gravity still lay with moderates like Senate majority leader Bob Dole, who believed in fiscal responsibility.[27]

The experience of the Reagan years showed that a conservative president alone could not roll back the federal government to its pre–New Deal size. It seemed impossible to get Congress to agree to large spending cuts—which was not surprising, since many spending programs were extremely popular—and a lingering sense of fiscal responsibility stood in the way of continued tax cuts. The result, as Stockman wrote in 1986, was "a fiscal and political disorder that was probably beyond correction."[28] When it came to cutting taxes, however, the next generation of Republican leaders was made of sterner stuff.

The central battle within the party was over deficits and taxes, between moderates like Dole who thought balanced budgets were more important than cutting taxes and radicals who put slashing taxes and spending before all else.[29] The radicals were led by Newt Gingrich, perhaps the central figure in the transformation of conservatism from an ideology into a dominant political force. Gingrich was elected to the House of Representatives in 1978, but instead of currying favor with the moderate Republican leadership, he assembled a group of combative, hard-line conservatives who set out to discredit the Democratic majority and push the Republican minority into increasingly confrontational positions. Gingrich personally led a successful campaign against Democratic House speaker Jim Wright, who eventually resigned amid evidence of ethics violations. Gingrich's allies cultivated controversies that embarrassed both Democrats and Republicans, such as a scandal over the House bank;[30] discrediting Congress as a whole could only help the conservative revolutionaries aiming to take it over.

While Gingrich was upsetting the congressional balance of power, he was also building up a new generation of conservative legislators who could seize power for themselves. His political organization, GOPAC, harvested money from rich donors and used it to recruit and train conservative candidates. (Current House speaker John Boehner decided to run for Congress after listening to audiotapes that GOPAC sent to potential recruits.)[31] Gingrich found that hard-line stances were good for business: beginning in the mid-1980s, while just the leader of a minority within a minority, Gingrich was able to raise more money than Bob Michel, the Republican minority leader.[32] Gingrich fought against any proposals to raise taxes, bringing him into direct conflict with Dole and traditional party leaders.[33] But his instinct was that rigid orthodoxy, not accommodation, would ultimately bring the conservatives to power, and the first Bush presidency proved him right.

George H. W. Bush campaigned in 1988 as the heir to the legacy of Ronald Reagan. He promised to come up with a plan to balance the budget while also promising not to raise taxes, famously vowing to the Republican National Convention, "The Congress will push me to raise taxes and I'll say no. And they'll push, and I'll say no, and they'll push again, and I'll say, to them, 'Read my lips: no new taxes.' "[34] In 1990, however, facing increasing deficits, rising costs to rescue the banking system from the savings and loan crisis, and a weakening economy, Bush agreed with Democratic negotiators on a deal that included one dollar in tax increases for every two dollars in spending cuts.[35] Gingrich refused to go along, taking a stand for low taxes against "those with the traditional view that reducing the deficit is more important," and successfully turned a majority of House Republicans against the compromise, helping ensure its defeat.[36] This forced the president to reopen negotiations and ultimately pass a new deal with mainly Democratic votes—meaning that the final bill shifted even further toward Democratic priorities.[37] But victory over the president burnished the House conservatives' antitax credentials and showed how difficult they could make life for moderates.

The final Omnibus Budget Reconciliation Act of 1990 reduced deficits by a projected $500 billion over five years, mainly by placing caps on discretionary spending* but partly by raising taxes on the wealthy.[38] In addition, the 1990 agreement created the pay-as-you-go (PAYGO) rule, which required that spending increases or tax reductions in one part of the budget had to be offset with lower spending or higher taxes in another part of the budget.[39] The tax increase, PAYGO rule, and spending caps helped reduce deficits later in the decade.[40] By then, however, George H. W. Bush was gone, the casualty of a sluggish economy and his decision to renege on his most famous campaign pledge, which cost him the loyalty of the conservative base.[41] The 1990 battle showed that the balance of power within his party had shifted away from the fiscally responsible moderates and toward the antitax radicals led by Gingrich—a lesson that was not lost on Bush's heir, George W. Bush.

RISING TIDE

If George H. W. Bush was good for the Gingrich radicals, the election of Bill Clinton was even better—because it gave conservatives someone to rally against. While it was fine to criticize government

---

* Discretionary spending is spending that is subject to annual appropriations bills passed by Congress. Mandatory spending, by contrast, is required by law and does not require annual congressional action.

social programs, it was harder to demonize the entire federal government so long as it was led by a Republican. But any scruples vanished when the Democrats swept the 1992 elections, unleashing a tidal wave of antigovernment sentiment eagerly cheered on by Republican leaders. As Republican National Committee official Don Fierce said, "Washington is financially and morally bankrupt and because of that it is the glue that binds economic and social conservatives. These are people that love their country but hate their federal government. Where is the evil empire? The evil empire is in Washington."[42] The antigovernment coalition that emerged in the first years of the Clinton presidency united diverse interest groups, ranging from the National Rifle Association to the National Federation of Independent Business to the Christian Coalition, behind a platform of limited government and low taxes, with tactics and rhetoric that would be familiar to Tea Party activists today. That coalition was fertilized and tended by Gingrich, party organizations like the Republican National Committee, and inside-the-Beltway allies like Grover Norquist and his organization, Americans for Tax Reform.[43]

President Clinton's budget and tax policies only provided more fodder for antitax conservatives. During the presidential campaign—in which Ross Perot won 19 percent of the popular vote, in part by vowing to balance the budget—Clinton promised to reduce the deficit while expanding domestic spending.[44] After winning the election, however, he had to face the reality of still rising deficits coupled with a sluggish economy.[45] On January 7, 1993, Clinton assembled his economic team in Little Rock, Arkansas.[46] His advisers argued that persistent deficits were hurting the economy. According to their analysis, bond investors, skeptical that Washington could bring the deficit under control and afraid that the government would eventually resort to printing money, were demanding high interest rates on Treasury bonds.[47] High interest rates were making it harder for households and businesses to borrow money, constraining consumption and investment and hurting economic growth.* Several of Clinton's advisers argued that reducing the deficit would increase

---

* Since households and businesses are riskier bets than the U.S. government, they generally pay higher interest rates.

investors' confidence, lowering interest rates for everyone and stimulating the economy.[48] According to legend, Clinton's response was: "You mean to tell me that the success of the program and my reelection hinges on the Federal Reserve and a bunch of fucking bond traders?"[49] But he sided with the "deficit hawks," deciding that the highest priority was to satisfy bond investors. The new president proposed to reduce the deficit through a combination of spending cuts and tax increases, abandoning most of his domestic spending priorities. Republicans eagerly attacked the tax increases, hoping to defeat the president and brand the Democrats as the party of high taxes, and Clinton was forced to pass his plan entirely with Democratic votes.[50]

The Omnibus Budget Reconciliation Act of 1993 reduced projected deficits by $433 billion over five years, roughly half through higher taxes that fell mainly on the wealthy, with the top income tax rate rising to 39.6 percent.[51] In the medium term, Clinton's bet on deficit reduction paid off, as higher taxes and lower spending helped balance the budget later in the decade without hurting (and possibly helping) the economic boom of the 1990s.[52] That lower spending was made possible by the end of the Cold War, which allowed defense expenditures to fall from 6.2 percent of GDP in 1986 to 3.0 percent in 1999.[53] But in the short term, the 1993 tax increases, along with the failure of health care reform in 1994, only strengthened Gingrich's hand by underlining the difference between Democrats and the new, resolutely antitax Republicans.

Republican victory in the 1994 elections proved Gingrich right: radical conservatism was the key to control of Congress. As the new speaker of the House, he had an apparent mandate to take on the president. His stated goal was to lower taxes and balance the budget by dramatically rolling back domestic spending, and he was backed by a large class of Republican freshmen that largely shared his views.[54] The result was the 1995 budget war and the United States' first brush with potential default in recent history. In early November, the Republican majorities passed two bills that would keep the government functioning and allow it to borrow more money, but also cut spending on social programs and require a balanced budget by 2002. President Clinton vetoed both bills, prompting a government shutdown until the parties came to a temporary compromise.[55] Later that month, the Republicans passed a budget combining major spending cuts, largely in entitlement programs, with tax cuts for the wealthy.[56] Clinton vetoed that bill, too, and the government shut down again in December. With polls showing that the public largely blamed Republicans for the impasse, Dole (then Senate majority leader) and Gingrich finally agreed to reopen the government, and the eventual budget was little changed from previous years. Although the 1995 confrontation ended in a Democratic victory, it was a sign of things to come: a battle where Republicans used deficits to press for both spending cuts *and* tax cuts—and were willing to play chicken with a government default.

Although Gingrich lost the battle against Clinton, what mattered in the long run was his overwhelming victory within the Republican Party. He upended the seniority system, reserving prized committee chairs and assignments for members who backed the conservative agenda—and who were willing to raise the most money for the party. He and his allies, including Majority Leader Dick Armey and Majority Whip Tom DeLay, used their personal control over large streams of money to ensure loyalty and bolster their own power. This system helped uncompromising conservatives with connections to major donors win and hold leadership positions in Congress.[57] DeLay, along with Grover Norquist, launched the K Street Project, which pressured lobbying firms to donate to Republicans and hire only Republicans as lobbyists, increasing the conservatives' access to cash and strengthening their relationships with big business.[58] Political scientist Thomas Ferguson has argued that these organizational changes created a machine in which hard-line stances paid off in campaign donations and personal influence, heightening polarization within Congress and ensuring that the Republican Party would not slide back toward moderation.[59] The Democrats were quick to copy Gingrich's new system and even set specific fundraising requirements for committee and subcommittee chairs and for members of "power committees."[60]

This was the final victory of Gingrich over onetime moderates like Bob Dole and even earlier revolutionaries like David Stockman, who had balked at the prospect of huge deficits. The new leadership embraced the idea of balanced budgets, but what they really cared about was cutting taxes and slashing the federal government; deficits only mattered as a tool to help cut spending. As Armey said, "Balancing the budget in my mind is the attention-getting device that enables me to reduce the size of government. . . . If you're anxious about the deficit, then let me use your anxiety to cut the size of the government."[61] This "starve the beast" strategy dates back at least to the late 1970s, when conservative icons Milton Friedman and Irving Kristol argued that cutting taxes now was the only way to create enough pressure—through higher deficits—to cut spending in the future. Reagan endorsed the strategy, adopting the homey metaphor of cutting off Congress's allowance in order to break its spending habit, but he lacked either the votes or the will to prevent multiple tax increases.[62] It was up to Gingrich and his allies to supply the votes and the discipline necessary to make the Republicans an unwavering force against tax increases.

This anti-Washington, antitax strategy was headed out of Washington, of all places. Besides the Republican House leadership, Grover Norquist, head of Americans for Tax Reform (ATR), also provided organizational discipline.[63] Norquist has been consistently candid about his objectives, most famously saying, "My goal is to cut government in half in twenty-five years, to get it down to the size where we can drown it in the bathtub."[64] He is equally open about the fact that he cares only about reducing government spending, not the deficit. In 2011, as Congress debated raising the debt ceiling, he said, "Anyone who says we have a deficit problem is either a Democrat who wants to raise taxes or a Republican who's dimwitted and doesn't understand what he's talking about."[65] And his plan to cut spending in the long term was not to propose bills that actually cut spending, which would be unpopular, but instead to cut taxes at every opportunity.

In 1986, Norquist hit upon the idea of the Taxpayer Protection Pledge: a promise by politicians that they would not vote to raise taxes.[66] In the beginning, some traditional moderate Republicans ignored the pledge—including Dole, whose refusal to sign may have cost him the 1988 presidential nomination.[67] Still, Norquist was able to sign up 110 House representatives within the first year.[68] As Gingrich's organizational tactics shifted his party to the right, signing the pledge became a mandatory step for any Republican seeking election to Congress for the first time.[69] (Even Dole signed it in 1995, as he was preparing to run for president again.)[70] By 2001, when George W. Bush took office, the pledge itself had become a major factor in budgetary politics, with the signatures of 210 members of the House of Representatives (a near majority).[71] In the current (2011–2012) Congress, the pledge has been signed by 238 representatives—an absolute majority of the House of Representatives—and 41 senators.[72]

The pledge matters in part because of the power wielded by Norquist, one of the movement's consummate power brokers. In 1993, he began organizing his now legendary Wednesday morning meetings, bringing together conservative leaders and strategists to oppose the Clinton administration and drive the Democrats from power. Norquist connected his loose network of right-wing operatives and activists with Gingrich's band of insiders, helping the Republicans take control of Congress in 1994. After the Republican victory, the Wednesday meetings became a central forum for the conservative establishment, where politicians, party operatives, lobbyists, and organizers shared information, built networks, and plotted strategy.[73] Norquist later helped convince conservative leaders and activists to rally behind George W. Bush in the lead-up to the 2000 Republican primaries, and the new president sent representatives to the Wednesday meetings after his election.[74] Today, with no Republican in the White House to serve as the party's leader, Norquist is if anything even more powerful: "I don't know of anyone outside of government who has had this kind of influence on politics before," wrote historian Alan Brinkley.[75]

Republican politicians listen to what Norquist has to say—and they don't break the pledge. After the 1994 victory, when moderate Republicans protested the size of the tax cuts proposed by the House leadership, Norquist launched a direct mail attack on one of the group's leaders in his home district, forcing the moderates to back down;[76] during the 2011 debt ceiling crisis, even his definition of what constituted a "tax increase" became a major factor in negotiations.[77] And Norquist is only one of the conservative leaders who enforce the contemporary antitax orthodoxy. As political scientists Jacob Hacker and Paul Pierson have described, conservatives have been able to maintain control of the Republican agenda because of the ability of a small group of power brokers to reward loyalty and punish opposition—most dramatically by supporting primary challenges against Republicans they deem insufficiently conservative.[78] For example, Senator Arlen Specter barely survived a primary challenge from Pat Toomey in 2004; rather than run against Toomey (who had spent the intervening years as president of the antitax Club for Growth) in 2010, he switched to the Democratic Party. (Toomey won the Republican nomination and the Senate seat.) By building alliances across key conservative constituencies, the power brokers have been able to enforce strict party discipline on a number of important issues, including the antitax pledge.

Effective inside-the-Beltway organization is one reason why the conservative tax revolt has been successful. The other is that Norquist's call for smaller government and lower taxes resonates among the grass roots of the conservative movement—at least when a Democrat is president. By 2010, only 11 percent of self-identified conservative Republicans (and only 7 percent of Tea Party supporters) said that they could trust the government most of the time.[79] At the same time, 59 percent of conservative Republicans said they were frustrated with the federal government, and another 32 percent said they were angry (along with 43 percent of Tea Party supporters); 47 percent thought that the federal government posed a major threat to their personal rights and freedoms (57 percent for Tea Party supporters).[80] To some extent, partisan disaffection with the federal government reflects who is in the White House. But the long-term trend is one of increasing resentment of Washington among conservatives. For example, only 28 percent of conservative Republicans considered the federal government a major threat to their personal rights in 1995, two years into the Clinton administration and one year after the battle over health care reform; by 2010, this group had grown to 47 percent.[81]

It's not as if millions of people woke up in the morning and independently decided that they didn't like the federal government. Nor, in fact, has the country become more conservative overall during the past forty years, as shown by opinion surveys that ask the same questions over long periods of time. The proportion of people identifying as liberal, moderate, or conservative has remained remarkably stable since the 1970s, although there has been a modest uptick in the number of conservatives since 2008.[82] More specific questions, such as whether the government should increase or decrease both services and spending, also yield no visible trends.[83] Instead, increasing antipathy toward Washington among existing conservatives was largely fostered by conservative strategists, organizers, and consultants in a multimedia campaign stretching over four decades.

In 1965, Richard Viguerie founded American Target Advertising, the first modern political direct mail firm.[84] Viguerie pioneered the use of direct mail in politics, building up huge mailing lists of conservative households and using antiliberal, antigovernment mailings to mine those lists for money for conservative groups. The purpose of political direct mail is not just to raise money, but also to communicate with and expand one's base of sympathizers, and conservative operatives and consultants became experts at the form.[85] Direct mail gave conservative organizations an alternative channel to the mainstream Republican Party, and they used it to spread the gospel of smaller government and lower taxes directly to tens of millions of households.

In the 1980s and 1990s, talk radio and then cable news gave the conservative vanguard an even more powerful medium for broadcasting its message.[86] Rush Limbaugh has been the top-rated talk radio host for the past two decades;[87] in 2011, seven of the top eight talk radio shows featured conservative hosts.[88] Fox News has been the dominant cable news channel since 2002.[89] House Republican leaders were quick to realize the potential of talk radio and pioneered the use of "blast faxes" to spread their key messages to talk show hosts around the country.[90] Like direct mail, conservative radio and television have consistently reminded their audiences that the federal government is too big, too wasteful, and a threat to their personal freedoms—whether those are the freedom to own guns, the freedom to worship in the manner they choose, or the freedom to run their businesses the way they want to.

This is not to say that there is some vast conspiracy behind the modern conservative media. The rise of direct mail and talk radio was a simple market phenomenon: political and media entrepreneurs finding and catering to an audience that had been underserved by traditional media and the traditional political establishment. Nor do conservative leaders and media figures always talk from the same script. There are major ideological and policy differences within the movement, such as the split between libertarians and traditional "family values" conservatives over gay rights. And the conservative positions being blasted through the mail and over the airwaves have certainly rung true to millions of ordinary people. Many Americans have legitimately developed their own grudges toward the federal government—whether small business owners struggling to comply with regulations, retired people caught in an argument with the Social Security Administration over benefits, or homeowners watching the government bail out major banks while allowing those same banks to foreclose on their houses. Liberal groups have also launched their own media outlets, although with decidedly less success.

For forty years, however, the conservative media have broadcast and amplified the message that the federal government is the enemy. The National Rifle Association sees the government as out to take people's guns away: in 1995, a direct mail letter signed by NRA executive vice president Wayne LaPierre referred to agents of the Bureau of Alcohol, Tobacco, and Firearms as "jackbooted Government thugs" and claimed that federal agents "harass, intimidate, even murder law-abiding citizens."[91] Business groups see the government as a jealous, meddling bureaucracy that imposes costly regulations for no good reason: in the wake of the financial crisis, the U.S. Chamber of Commerce ran issue ads warning that the proposed Consumer Financial Protection Agency would affect "even the local butcher,"[92] and in 2010 the Chamber spent over $50 million on political advertisements overwhelmingly supporting Republican candidates.[93] Christian conservatives see an activist, liberal federal judiciary as a threat to traditional values, most importantly because of the 1973 Supreme Court decision in *Roe v. Wade* legalizing abortion.[94] The common denominator of these messages is not that we need better government, but that we need less government. And all conservative groups can agree that the federal government should have less money to carry out its sordid affairs—which conveniently means lower taxes.

These overlapping media campaigns further damage popular impressions of the federal government, ultimately reducing its legitimacy. People are less willing to pay taxes to a government they do not believe in, which strengthens antitax groups and increases the pressure on politicians to hold the line against higher taxes. The strategy of reducing taxes whenever possible and never raising taxes makes it harder for the government to balance its budget. When deficits go up, as they do in any economic slowdown, they just become more evidence of government waste and incompetence: in 2011, the Republican-led House Budget Committee blamed both government deficits and the recent financial crisis on "mismanagement and over-spending," overlooking both the major tax cuts of the second Bush administration and the culpability of the financial sector.[95] The conservative base, seeing deficits (and the inability to do anything about them) as further evidence of incompetence in Washington, hardens its stance against taxes and further tilts the Republican Party toward its right wing.

The impressive successes of the conservative movement in general, and the tax revolt in particular, can create the impression that America as a whole is becoming more conservative and more opposed to taxes. But, as mentioned above, Americans' positions on broad ideological issues have remained relatively stable over the past forty years—even as Congress and political elites have become increasingly polarized.[96] The achievement of the tax revolt has not been convincing all Americans that taxes are too high; for the past decade, a majority of Americans have consistently said that their income taxes are fair.[97] Rather, its achievement has been strengthening that belief among conservatives and developing the organizations, tools, and funding sources to enforce antitax positions among Republican politicians. In the 1980s, conservatives had one of their own in the White House, but no way to enforce the antitax agenda within the Republican Party, let alone Congress as a whole. By 1995, cutting taxes and shrinking the federal government were orthodoxy among the Republican majorities in Congress. All they needed, they thought, was control of the White House.

BRIEF SHINING SURPLUS

The deficits of the 1990s evaporated before they could be used to slash government spending. Economic growth, along with the 1990 and 1993 deficit reduction bills, settled the issue. By 1997, the deficit had fallen for four consecutive years, eliminating the argument that major sacrifices were necessary. This allowed President Clinton and Republican leaders to negotiate a plan in 1997 that balanced the budget by 2002 while cutting taxes modestly.[98] The long boom of the 1990s did the rest of the job, balancing the budget in 1998 (four years early) and creating a $236 billion surplus in 2000. George H. W. Bush and Bill Clinton showed that it was still barely possible to pass bills that raised taxes, cut spending, and reduced the national debt. The deficit dragon, it seemed, had been slain, making way for a debate about what to do with projected budget surpluses. At the 2000 Republican National Convention, George W. Bush said,

> Today, our high taxes fund a surplus. Some say that growing federal surplus means Washington has more money to spend. But they've got it backwards. The surplus is not the government's money: the surplus is the people's money. . . . Now is the time to reform the tax code and share some of the surplus with the people who pay the bills.[99]

At the Democratic National Convention, by contrast, Al Gore said, "We will balance the budget every year and dedicate the budget surplus first to saving Social Security," promising to put "both Social Security and Medicare in an iron-clad lockbox where the politicians can't touch them."[100] The world, it seemed, had been turned upside down.

Victory over the deficit—and a spreading belief that America had entered a new era of prosperity, thanks to the miracle of technology—also removed the political pressure to do anything about the long-term growth of entitlement spending. That spending was growing nonetheless, driven by the brute force of population. In 1946, as the United States demobilized in the wake of World War II, the annual birthrate jumped from 20 to 24 per 1,000 people. It stayed above 24 through 1959 and above 21 through 1964, the conventional end of the baby boom.[101] In 1992, when Bill Clinton became the first baby boomer to be elected president, the oldest members of his generation were forty-six; today, they are beginning to collect Social Security and Medicare benefits. At the same time, people are living longer: life expectancy at age 65 has increased by more than three years since 1970.[102] It was never any secret what an aging population would do to the federal budget. In 1992, the annual report of the Social Security trust funds projected that they would be exhausted in 2036*—a forecast that remains remarkably accurate today.[103] At the same time, the Congressional Budget Office (CBO) warned about a "boom in health care spending," which was growing three times as fast as the overall economy. Only 7 percent of the federal budget in 1970, health care was over 13 percent of the budget in 1990 and projected to grow to 28 percent by 2002.[104]

The combined impact of an aging population and rising health care costs was clear for anyone to see. In 1996, with deficits declining for their fourth consecutive year, the CBO warned, "The shortfalls projected for future years are so large that they could put an end to the upward trend in living standards that the nation has long enjoyed."[105] Even in 2000, with surpluses expected for the next decade, growing entitlement spending was projected to cause the national debt to skyrocket sometime between 2030 and 2060, depending on how the surpluses would be used.[106]

The fact is that most of the surplus was created by the same demographic trends that would produce future deficits. In 2000, the baby boom generation was entering its peak earnings years, so payroll tax revenues were high, but had not started retiring, so benefit payments were low. As a result, Social Security ran an aggregate surplus of $312 billion in 1998 through 2001—more than half of the government's total surplus of $559 billion in the same period.[107] The forces that

---

* When Social Security payroll taxes exceed benefit payments, the surplus is deposited in the Social Security trust funds (which invest the money in interest-bearing Treasury bonds). When benefit payments exceed payroll taxes, money from the trust funds (including interest on those bonds) is used to make up the difference. When the trust funds are exhausted, benefit payments will be limited to incoming payroll taxes under current law.

created these surpluses would just as surely create much larger deficits once the baby boomers started to retire. In that light, the government in the 1998–2001 period was like a person who can balance her budget but knows she isn't putting aside enough for retirement. But the political system fixated on the word "surplus"—Democrats because they could claim it as an achievement, Republicans because it was a justification for tax cuts. The effect was that people, for the most part, stopped worrying about the long-term budgetary picture.[108]

Even including the trust funds, the surpluses were the product of a short-term perspective. A budget shows a surplus if revenues exceed spending in a given year, regardless of what will happen in the future. Businesses also use annual results (income statements) to measure their profitability. But for their retirement plans, they have to calculate their future obligations to their employees and make sure their pension funds will have enough money to keep those promises.[109] Like a business, the federal government has ongoing operations, such as national defense, but it also runs some huge insurance plans called Social Security and Medicare. Evaluated over the long term, those plans were already deeply in the red. In early 2000, at the peak of the budget surpluses, the Social Security trust funds faced a long-term deficit worth about $3 trillion at the time.[110] Although Medicare's long-term financial condition is much harder to estimate because of uncertainty about health care costs, by 2000 no one could doubt that it was worse off than Social Security.[111]

In short, the federal government's long-term unfunded obligations already loomed over the 1998–2001 surpluses. This is not to say that the deficit reduction of the 1990s was meaningless. The federal government ended the decade in a position where it could have closed Social Security's funding gap without major sacrifices and might even have been able to tackle the larger problem presented by Medicare. But that was not to be—because of the political shifts of the 1990s. On the Democratic side, President Clinton's decision to focus on deficit reduction and ultimately balance the budget marked a major shift in party priorities away from domestic spending programs. As he said in 1995, "If I'm going to get heard on anything else, I first have to show a balanced budget. Once I do that, I can talk about progressive programs. But if I don't show a balanced budget, they'll never listen to me about progressive programs."[112] (Liberals objected that he never got around to the progressive programs.) But while the New Democrats were promising to put fiscal responsibility first, Gingrich, Armey, DeLay, and especially Norquist were locking the Republicans into the position that only tax cuts mattered and deficits could always be dealt with later.

TAX CUTS FOR ALL SEASONS

The election of George W. Bush gave the conservatives their chance, with control of the White House and both branches of Congress.[113] Deficits were off the agenda. Instead, as the new president was inaugurated in January 2001, the CBO was projecting trillions of dollars in surpluses over the next decade, including a 2010 surplus of $796 billion.[114] The actual 2010 deficit was almost $1.3 trillion—a difference of over $2 trillion.

True to his campaign pledges to the conservative base, the first major item on President Bush's agenda was large income tax cuts. Originally justified as a way of returning budget surpluses to the people, the tax cuts were repositioned as a way to stimulate a weakening economy—an example of touting tax cuts as the appropriate response to any situation. Politically, the challenge was that the public did not particularly want the Bush tax cuts: while tax cuts in the abstract garnered weak majority support, large majorities favored higher domestic spending over tax cuts and also preferred focusing tax cuts on "middle income Americans."[115] And with only fifty Republican senators, the administration had little margin for error. But here the antitax network came into play. Norquist in particular helped rally interest groups ranging from Christian conservatives to business organizations behind Bush's tax cut plan, putting pressure on moderates in both parties.[116] Ultimately, the strategy worked, and the 2001 tax cut passed with a decent majority of 58 votes in the Senate.[117]

The Economic Growth and Tax Relief Reconciliation Act of 2001 (EGTRRA) was the third-largest tax cut in modern history.[118] It lowered tax rates for nearly everyone who paid income tax (with the top rate falling from 39.6 percent to 35 percent), increased deductions and exemptions for high-income households, made it easier to shield retirement savings from taxes, increased family tax credits, and eventually repealed the estate tax.[119] The advertised impact of the tax cuts was $1.3 trillion over ten years, but their true size was significantly greater. In order to avoid the threat of a filibuster in the Senate, the tax cuts were passed through the budget reconciliation process,* which meant that they could not permanently increase deficits, and so all of the tax cuts were scheduled to expire by the end of 2010.[120] In order to reduce the total ten-year cost of the tax cuts—to make them easier to pass—several of them were deferred, with over 70 percent of the total tax reduction coming after 2006.[121] By 2010, when most of the tax cuts would be in effect, they were officially expected to cost $176 billion (1.1 percent of GDP), not counting the additional interest payments they would require.[122] But the real impact of the 2001 tax cuts would be even bigger, because they increased the number of households exposed to the alternative minimum tax (AMT); since Congress can be counted on to "patch" the AMT to shield middle-class households,† this meant that future patches would have to be even bigger.[123]

The complicated phase-ins made the impact of the 2001 tax cuts much larger in 2010 than in 2001—and President Bush's goal was to make them permanent at the 2010 level. The 2010 sunset provision made it possible to argue that allowing the tax cuts to expire would amount to a tax increase. As early as 2004, when Congress began extending provisions of the 2001 tax cuts, Representative Jim

---

* By Senate rules, most measures require sixty votes in order to end debate and move to a vote; a filibuster allows forty-one senators to prevent a vote. The budget reconciliation process, originally created by the Congressional Budget and Impoundment Control Act of 1974 to expedite budgetary legislation, provides an exception to this rule for bills that change revenue and mandatory spending laws. Allen Schick, *The Federal Budget: Politics, Policy, Process*, 3rd. ed. (Brookings Institution Press, 2007), pp. 142–47.

† The AMT is an alternative tax system originally designed to ensure that the very wealthy paid at least some tax; it does this by disallowing many common tax deductions for high-income taxpayers. Because the AMT is not indexed for inflation, it would affect a growing number of middle-class households as time passes. Therefore, Congress regularly "patches" the AMT (raising the thresholds to account for inflation), but only for a few years at a time.

McCrery argued, "Anyone voting 'no' is voting for a tax increase for the American people, especially the middle class."[124] When 2010 rolled around, Republicans reliably attacked, as a tax increase, any proposal to let any of the tax cuts expire; aided by a financial crisis and a major recession, which created an economic argument against "raising" taxes, the tax cuts were extended through 2012 with the support of a Democratic president and Democratic majorities in Congress. The 2001 tax cuts had became a Trojan horse that threatened to make a permanent, structural change in the tax system.[125]

By 2003, the surplus was gone, the victim of the 2001 tax cut and an economic slowdown.[126] But President Bush repeated the 2001 strategy: large tax cuts justified as an economic stimulus and passed through the reconciliation process, their total size masked by phase-outs, with intense pressure from conservative groups to keep Republican legislators in line. In addition to Americans for Tax Reform, the Club for Growth attacked moderate Republicans who wavered.[127] This time, the Jobs and Growth Tax Relief Reconciliation Act of 2003 (JGTRRA) lowered the tax rate on capital gains (profits on the sale of investments) and dividends (payments made by corporations to their stockholders) to a maximum of 15 percent; it also accelerated several of the 2001 tax cuts so they kicked in sooner than originally scheduled. The official ten-year cost was $350 billion, but again that figure relied on early phase-outs that few people expected to occur.[128] (Not surprisingly, the major 2003 tax cuts were later extended through 2010 by the Tax Increase Prevention and Reconciliation Act of 2005.)[129]

While most households that paid income taxes saw their taxes go down in 2001 and 2003, the biggest beneficiaries by any measure were the wealthy. When fully phased in, 67 percent of the tax cuts passed during the Bush administration went to the richest 20 percent of households; 15 percent of the benefits went to the richest 0.1 percent of households.[130] Households making between $40,000 and $50,000 saw an average 2010 tax reduction of $962, but households making more than $1 million got an average of $168,052.[131] And this is not just because the rich pay more taxes to begin with. The richer you are, the larger the percentage increase in your after-tax income (8.2 percent for the wealthiest one-thousandth of all households, but only 2.6 percent for the median family) and the more percentage points shaved off your effective federal tax rate.[132]

One major reason for the unequal distribution of the tax cuts is that they focused on the income tax, while most people pay more in payroll taxes—the taxes on wages that are dedicated to Social Security and Medicare—which were unaffected by the tax cuts.[133] Another is that the 2003 tax cut primarily benefited people who earn taxable income from investments rather than income from labor—that is, the rich.[134] It is true that most taxpaying households did see their taxes go down, but those same households have to pay for the tax cuts in the form of reduced government services, lower future benefits, or higher future taxes; seen as a complete package, it's likely that most households were made worse off.[135] The sharp decrease in taxes for the very rich also contributed to increasing income inequality, as the top 1 percent of all households saw their share of the entire population's income rise steeply from 2002.[136]

The Bush tax cuts certainly weakened the federal government's financial situation. Total government revenues fell from 20.6 of GDP in 2000 to 16.1 percent in 2004, the lowest level in more than half a century. (See Figure 3-1.) That decline was due in part to the stock market collapse of 2000 and the brief recession of 2001. A bet-

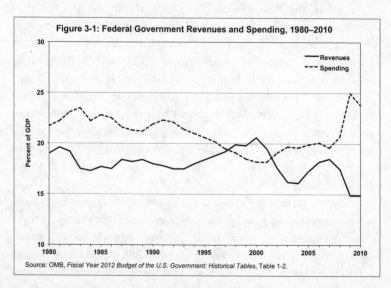

Figure 3-1: Federal Government Revenues and Spending, 1980–2010

Source: OMB, *Fiscal Year 2012 Budget of the U.S. Government: Historical Tables*, Table 1-2.

ter comparison is that during the 1991–2000 economic expansion (the period between two recessions), revenues averaged 18.9 percent of GDP; during the 2001–2007 expansion, they averaged only 17.3 percent—a difference worth about $200 billion a year.[137] Supporters have argued that the tax cuts actually increased tax revenues by stimulating economic growth. In 2007, President Bush claimed, "It is also a fact that our tax cuts have fueled robust economic growth and record revenues."[138] But there are two problems with this claim. One is that real economic growth was not particularly robust, averaging only 2.7 percent per year during the 2001–2007 expansion, as compared to 3.7 percent during the 1990s expansion (when tax rates were higher).[139] The other is that multiple economic analyses have shown that the economic growth caused by a tax cut can at best offset a portion of the revenues lost by that tax cut.[140] In addition, while a tax cut may increase growth in the short term (because people will have more money to spend), a tax cut that increases deficits tends to reduce economic growth in the long term (because more government borrowing increases interest rates for everyone), according to a study by the congressional Joint Committee on Taxation (issued in 2006, when Republicans controlled both the House and the Senate).[141]

Together, the Bush tax cuts (including the higher interest payments they caused) added about $270 billion to the 2010 deficit.[142] Over the past decade, their cumulative effect has been to increase the national debt by close to $3 trillion.[143] They are not the primary reason why the national debt is so much bigger today than expected in 2001: tax cuts take second place to economic weakness, in particular the severe recession triggered by the financial crisis.[144] But of the conscious policy choices of the current century, the tax cuts (and their extension in December 2010) made the single largest contribution to today's budget deficits and to the recent growth in the national debt.[145]

In the conservative playbook, the reason to cut taxes is not just to put more money in people's pockets, but more importantly to force the government to shrink. If the Bush administration had cut spending to match the tax cuts, then the national debt would be far smaller today. But instead, the administration increased spending, which grew from 18.2 percent of GDP in 2001 to 20.7 percent of GDP in 2008.[146] Half of this increase was due to defense spending, largely because of the Afghanistan and Iraq wars, which so far have cost well over $1 trillion.[147] Democrats often blame the Iraq War on the Bush administration, which mounted a concerted campaign to build public support for the war. On the other hand, the congressional resolution authorizing the invasion was backed by a majority of Democrats in the Senate and a near majority in the House.[148]

In any case, what mattered for the federal budget was how we chose to pay for those wars: increased borrowing. President Lyndon Johnson resisted raising taxes to fight the Vietnam War because he was afraid higher taxes would undermine support for his domestic initiatives;[149] President Bush resisted raising taxes to fight the Iraq War because tax cuts *were* his major domestic initiatives. Instead, Bush introduced his 2003 tax cut in January,[150] while he was building international support for the invasion, and it was passed in May, two months after the war began. The administration reconciled war with tax cuts in part by downplaying the costs of the war. When Lawrence Lindsey, director of the president's National Economic Council, estimated that the upper bound on the war's costs would be $100–200 billion (which, he added, was "nothing"), he was shot down by Mitch Daniels, director of the Office of Management and Budget, and Lindsey soon left the administration.[151] Secretary of Defense Donald Rumsfeld claimed the cost would be no more than $50–60 billion.[152] Tom DeLay, by then House majority leader, said, "Nothing is more important in the face of a war than cutting taxes"—going even further than the original War Hawks of 1812, who merely declined to find a way to pay for the war they had just declared.[153]

While many conservatives were happy to spend more on national defense, where they really wanted to cut spending was in the major entitlement programs: Social Security and Medicare. When asked what his ideal policies were, Norquist said,

> The first would be personalizing Social Security, privatizing Social Security, instead of having the state take 12 percent of your income and then promising to pay you something if you make it to 65 or 67.

Instead, they should let you put that money into a 401(k), and then you would control it.[154]

Structural Medicare reform had already been one of Gingrich's major goals in the 1995 budget fight.[155] By the Bush years, it was clear that current Social Security and Medicare policies would lead to large long-term deficits. But even here, President Bush's policies only increased long-term entitlement spending. In 2003, the president and his congressional allies *added* a new prescription drug program to Medicare—at the request of elderly people struggling with rising drug prices—without finding a way to pay for its benefits in full. The new program was officially estimated to cost $395 billion over ten years;[156] Medicare's chief actuary estimated it would cost $500–600 billion, but was ordered by the program's administrator, a political appointee, not to provide his estimates in response to congressional requests.[157] In any case, the prescription drug benefit has made Medicare's future funding problems much larger: today, almost one-third of Medicare's long-term deficit is due to the prescription drug program.[158] After the 2004 elections, President Bush also made reforming Social Security a top priority. He proposed allowing people to divert part of their payroll taxes into individual accounts that they would control and keep; but since those accounts would have reduced the amount of money available to pay current benefits, the government would have had to borrow up to $1 trillion over the next ten years, adding to the national debt.[159] Because of widespread opposition, Social Security privatization never came close to a vote.

The tax policies of the Bush administration were a lopsided victory for the tax revolt—a victory that produced vast increases in government deficits and the national debt. The 2004 deficit reached $413 billion (3.5 percent of GDP); modest economic growth reduced the deficit to $161 billion in 2007 (1.2 percent), but it would have been significantly larger without a Social Security surplus that could not last once the baby boom generation began retiring.[160] Even before the financial crisis, the outlook for 2010 had shifted from the $796 billion surplus projected in 2001 to a $241 billion deficit.[161] (See Figure 3-2.) And it was clear that demographic trends would soon turn against the federal government.[162]

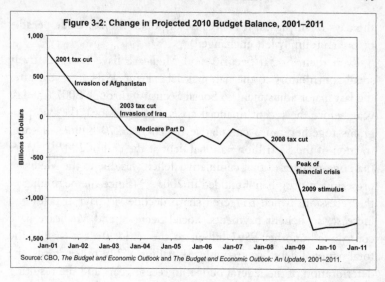

Figure 3-2: Change in Projected 2010 Budget Balance, 2001–2011

Source: CBO, *The Budget and Economic Outlook* and *The Budget and Economic Outlook: An Update*, 2001–2011.

Focusing on the politics of taxes rather than the politics of spending may seem simply a matter of framing. Arguably, if increases in the national debt can be blamed on one side's insistence on tax cuts, they could as easily be blamed on the other side's insistence on spending increases. More concretely, Republicans may claim that the growth of the national debt is the fault of higher spending on Social Security and Medicare, not tax cuts. When considering the recent history of deficits and the debt, however, this is a false equivalence. In politics, there is a major difference between action that changes policy and inaction that simply preserves existing policy. The national debt was on a certain course in 2001, and it was the policies of the tax revolt that shifted it to a different course with higher deficits. Republicans invested heavily and successfully in tax cuts that were meant to be permanent. Democrats, by contrast, made no significant efforts to expand spending on the major social insurance or welfare programs: Social Security has gone untouched, and while the Obama health care reform bill of 2010 increased certain types of health care spending, on balance it reduced future deficits rather than increasing them.[163] (The only recent entitlement expansion that significantly increased deficits was the Medicare prescription drug bill of 2003.) Insofar as Social Security and Medicare spending has increased since the days of surpluses, it is because of policy choices made decades before and simply left unchanged.

Even then, Social Security and Medicare have been relatively small contributors to the national debt. From 1984 (the year after the last major adjustment to Social Security) through 2007 (the last year before the recent financial crisis and recession), the two programs together ran a cumulative deficit of $270 billion—a small fraction of the $5 trillion national debt at the end of 2007.[164] More than one-quarter of that cumulative deficit was due to the Medicare prescription drug benefit added in 2003.[165] (Since the beginning of the recession, which triggered sharp declines in payroll taxes and increases in benefit payments, Social Security and Medicare have contributed another $597 billion to the national debt—while the total national debt has grown by $4 trillion.)[166] In other words, the deterioration of the federal budget in recent years and the resulting increase in the national debt are not the fault of Social Security and Medicare. Growing spending on these programs is a major factor in the future growth of the national debt (as we discuss in the next chapter), but not in the story of how we got to where we are today.

Despite the tax cuts of the Bush years, few people in 2007 thought that budget deficits amounted to a national emergency. Foreign investors' growing appetite for Treasury bonds ensured that significant budget deficits could be financed easily. The national debt was only 36 percent of GDP, right around the average for the previous fifty years.[167] As of January 2008, the CBO's baseline projection was for the national debt to fall to 23 percent of GDP by 2018 (assuming that all of the Bush tax cuts would expire on schedule).[168] The next president, it seemed, would inherit a significant long-term deficit problem, but not a crisis.

BIG BAD BANKERS

Less than five years later, however, deficits are the order of the day, every day. The political agenda has been rewritten by successive trillion-dollar deficits—deficits generated by the most severe financial crisis the world economy has seen in over seventy years.

The story of the financial crisis of 2007–2009 has been told many times.[169] In brief, the end of the twentieth century saw a transformation of the financial services industry and the rapid growth of complex new financial products, from subprime loans with creative payment terms to new investment vehicles built out of highly customized credit derivatives. Major financial institutions shifted their emphasis from traditional, low-margin businesses to riskier, more profitable businesses such as issuing and trading exotic new securities. Pressure from Wall Street and a rising tide of money from the financial sector, coupled with the pro-business agenda of both Republican and Democratic administrations, led to the deregulation of traditional financial markets and the nonregulation of new financial markets, allowing the banks to innovate rapidly and take on more and more risk in pursuit of higher profits. Demand from Wall Street for certain types of loans, such as subprime mortgages and commercial real estate loans, made it too easy for households, businesses, and financial institutions to take on huge amounts of debt—adding to features of the tax code, such as the mortgage interest deduction, that already encouraged borrowing. The result was the largest housing bubble in American history and parallel bubbles in many other types of assets.

In 2006, housing prices started falling; by 2007, it was clear that many of the securities that Wall Street had been churning out were next to worthless; and in 2008, it turned out that most of the world's largest financial institutions were still holding huge piles of these toxic assets and could go bankrupt quickly. In September 2008, panic froze the world's financial markets, threatening a collapse of the global economy. Governments and central banks around the world reacted by bailing out their banking systems, preventing a complete meltdown of the financial system, but the economic damage was severe. In the United States, a moderate recession became the worst downturn since the Great Depression, costing almost nine million jobs.[170] The unemployment rate, which had averaged around 5 percent over the previous decade, jumped to over 10 percent in 2009 and remains stubbornly high today.[171] As of mid-2011, the U.S. economy was producing less than at the end of 2007.[172] In one of history's ironies, the economy was blown up not by the government debt that politicians had inveighed against for decades, but by private sector debt that banks had been manufacturing as fast as they could—and it was the federal government that had to pick up the pieces.

This "Great Recession" caused tax revenues to plummet as households and businesses made less money. Federal government revenues fell from $2.6 trillion in 2007 to $2.1 trillion in 2009, constituting the smallest share of the national economy since 1950.[173] At the same time, spending went up under preexisting policies as more people claimed unemployment insurance, qualified for needs-based programs such as Medicaid, or began taking Social Security benefits early. Government responses to the financial crisis and recession also cost money. Although most of the Treasury Department's investments in financial institutions through the controversial Troubled Asset Relief Program (TARP) were paid back, the bailout of Fannie Mae and Freddie Mac—private entities that the government counted on to support the housing market, but that collapsed along with housing prices—cost over $100 billion by 2011.[174]

Both the Bush and Obama administrations also pushed through stimulus programs, hoping they would encourage households to spend more and help revive the economy. The Economic Stimulus Act of 2008 cut taxes by $150 billion that year.[175] A year later, with the financial crisis at its peak and the economy in much worse shape, President Obama and congressional Democrats passed the American Recovery and Reinvestment Act, which cut taxes by another $288 billion while increasing spending by nearly $500 billion, mainly in 2009 and 2010.[176] Passed with zero Republican votes in the House and only three in the Senate, the "Obama stimulus" would become the focus of Republican attacks describing it as wasteful government spending that failed to create jobs. Most private economic analysts, however, found that it helped cushion the impact of the recession and keep unemployment from climbing even higher—which was perhaps the most that could have been hoped for, given the severity of the financial crisis.[177]

The recession and the stimulus bills passed in response created the largest peacetime deficits in history, well over $1 trillion in 2009 (10 percent of GDP) and 2010 (almost 9 percent of GDP). The recession's long-term impact on the nation's finances was even more striking. By the summer of 2009, the idea that the national debt would melt away thanks to economic growth was a distant memory. Instead, large deficits continued as far as the eye could see (long after the stimulus packages would expire), with the CBO now projecting that the debt in 2018 would exceed $13 trillion (67 percent of GDP)[178]—an increase of $8 trillion over the pre-crisis, January 2003 forecast (see Figure 3-3). The financial crisis increased the projected national debt by 44 percent of GDP—something that only a major war had been able to do in the past. Yet the interest rates on government debt only went down (from 4.6 percent on ten-year Treasuries in 2007 to 3.2 percent in 2009) as investors looked for safe harbor in a global financial storm.[179]

Conservatives seized on these large deficits, charging that excessive government spending, symbolized by the Obama stimulus bill, and onerous government regulation were the cause of continuing economic weakness. With unemployment remaining well above 9 percent throughout 2010, Republicans claimed that the stimulus had failed (some Democrats, by contrast, countered that the stimulus had not been big enough) and that it was time instead to shrink government further. Arguing that more spending would only increase deficits, Republicans made it impossible for Democrats to pass a second stimulus bill. But both parties agreed to extend the Bush tax

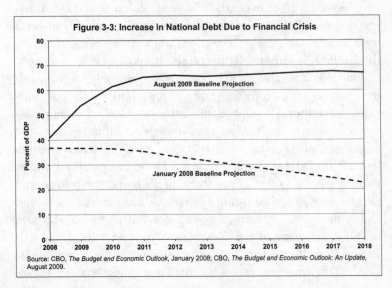

Figure 3-3: Increase in National Debt Due to Financial Crisis

Source: CBO, *The Budget and Economic Outlook*, January 2008; CBO, *The Budget and Economic Outlook: An Update*, August 2009.

cuts (arguably making them now the Bush-Obama tax cuts) on the grounds that this would help the economy—even though it would *increase* deficits.

More profoundly, the financial crisis and the recession strengthened resentment toward the federal government, which was seen—with at least some justice—as having bailed out wealthy, politically connected bankers while failing to help ordinary Americans, particularly homeowners facing foreclosure in the wake of the housing bust. Increasing economic insecurity mixed with widespread suspicion among conservatives that President Obama favored a larger, more intrusive government (symbolized by his health care reform plan, often labeled "Obamacare"), adding to the antigovernment sentiment that had been stoked for decades. The resulting backlash against Washington was a major contributor to the emergence of the Tea Party movement, which demanded lower taxes, lower spending, and strict limits on the federal government—the same list of demands as in 1994. Although the Tea Party is more a movement than a political party, one of its central principles is opposition to taxes. Its name refers to the 1773 Boston Tea Party, a protest by American colonists against taxation without representation, and one of its first nationwide events was a series of demonstrations on "Tax Day," April 15, 2009. In contrast to insider antitax groups like Americans for Tax Reform and the Club for Growth, which had small memberships but strong connections and large amounts of money, the Tea Party seemed to give the tax revolt a popular base of support.

The prominence of the Tea Party is due not only to grassroots mobilization but also to financial and organizational support provided by traditional Republican power brokers like Dick Armey, conservative billionaires with an antigovernment, antitax agenda, and established media outlets, especially Fox News.[180] Detailed research into the Tea Party by political scientists David Campbell and Robert Putnam also shows that its members are not new entrants to politics hurt by the economic downturn or radicalized by recent events, but largely the white, Christian, socially conservative activists who have been the backbone of the conservative movement for decades.[181] In other words, the Tea Party is to a significant degree the public face and the conscious product of the same antigovernment movement that Newt Gingrich led to power in the 1990s. But whatever its provenance, the Tea Party has succeeded in making overt hostility toward government and taxes a powerful force in Washington.

In the country as a whole, unfavorable opinions of the Tea Party outnumber favorable ones.[182] But this matters less than the fact that Republicans, and especially the conservatives who are highly represented in primary elections, generally support Tea Party positions by large margins.[183] This has pushed Republican politicians even further to the right on taxes and spending for fear of being attacked by Tea Party candidates in primary campaigns. In 2010, candidates affiliated with the Tea Party defeated Republican incumbents or establishment candidates in Senate primaries in Alaska, Delaware, Florida, Kentucky, Nevada, and Utah. In the general elections, the Tea Party helped Republicans win a majority in the House of Representatives, and it ensured that the new Republican members were more conservative than the incumbents.[184]

Since the Republicans won the 2010 elections, with the aid of the Tea Party, Washington has been preoccupied with spending cuts. On the surface, the debate is about deficits and the national debt. But the success of the tax revolt and the power of Grover Norquist's antitax pledge mean that the Republicans who control the House of Representatives refuse to consider tax increases.[185] The power of the antitax coalition makes it almost impossible for congressional Republicans to concede to any tax increases; and because it is almost impossible for them to compromise, they have the upper hand in any negotiation.

This political dynamic has been clearly visible since the 2010 elections. First there was the matter of the Bush tax cuts, which were scheduled to expire at the end of the year. President Obama favored extending only the tax cuts for the "middle class"—households making up to $250,000 per year—on the grounds that higher taxes would make the economic slowdown worse. Republican leaders demanded the extension of all of the Bush tax cuts on the same grounds. Ultimately the only thing the parties could agree on was tax cuts, so they compromised by giving each side the tax cuts it wanted, with the Bush tax cuts extended through 2012 and a new payroll tax cut for 2011, at a total cost of $860 billion over just two years.[186]

Then there was the debt ceiling showdown of 2011. The debt ceiling is an archaic historical artifact (enacted in 1917 to avoid the need for congressional approval every time the Treasury has to borrow money) and a contemporary absurdity: a limit on total government borrowing set by Congress, even though Congress's tax and spending bills determine how much borrowing is needed.[187] Yet with the Treasury Department about to run out of cash, many of the same politicians who had just months before added $860 billion to the national debt refused to increase the debt ceiling without a deficit reduction agreement. Republicans insisted on reducing the deficit solely through spending cuts, while Democrats insisted on including tax increases. Negotiations over a deal that could have reduced deficits by over $4 trillion over ten years collapsed when House Speaker Boehner walked out over President Obama's insistence on "raising taxes."[188] Another plan put forward by the "Gang of Six," a bipartisan group of senators, which would have reduced deficits by $3.7 trillion, was shot down in the House because it included increases in tax revenues (even though it would have reduced income tax rates for both households and corporations).[189]

At the eleventh hour, all sides agreed on the Budget Control Act of 2011, a complicated deal that cut spending by $900 billion over ten years and promised to reduce deficits by at least another $1.2 trillion later—either through a deficit reduction plan hammered out by a bipartisan committee and approved by Congress or through automatic spending cuts. On November 21, 2011, however, the "supercommittee" reported that it could not come to an agreement. Anticipating that failure, some congressmen had already started planning to undo the automatic spending cuts.[190] Even with the automatic cuts, $2.1 trillion would take only a modest bite out of the next decade's deficits, which at the time of the agreement were expected to total anywhere from $6.7 trillion (if the Bush tax cuts were allowed to expire) to $11.5 trillion (if all tax cuts were extended).[191] A larger agreement was impossible because the two sides could find little to agree on—no tax increases, no significant entitlement cuts, and no economic stimulus.[192]

The House Republicans did not break any rules, and they did not play the game of politics unfairly. They wanted lower spending; the debt ceiling gave them political leverage, and they used it. There's no rule of negotiation that says you have to meet your opponent halfway. As Norman Ornstein of the American Enterprise Institute, a conservative think tank, said, "If you hold one-half of one-third of the reins of power in Washington, and are willing to use and maintain that kind of discipline even if you will bring the entire temple down around your own head, there is a pretty good chance that you are going to get your way."[193] The fact that keeping taxes and spending low was more important to House Republicans than actually reducing the deficit was a policy choice that they were entitled to make—and one that their electoral base largely supported. The debt ceiling standoff does show, however, how far the tax revolt has come since the days of Ronald Reagan. And it shows how difficult it will be to solve our long-term deficit problems in our current political environment.

Four

WHAT DOES THE FEDERAL GOVERNMENT DO?

It's clearly a budget. It's got a lot of numbers in it.

—George W. Bush, 2000[1]

In August 2011, just weeks after the debt ceiling standoff ended with an agreement to cut government spending by more than $2 trillion over ten years, Hurricane Irene took aim at the East Coast of the United States. Tens of millions of people from Miami to Boston nervously watched forecast models that predicted hurricane-force winds sweeping across the North Carolina coastline and up the Atlantic seaboard before dumping torrential rains directly on New York City and New England. New York mayor Michael Bloomberg took the unprecedented steps of evacuating parts of lower Manhattan and shutting down the subway system. Even though the hurricane weakened slightly before striking New York, it was still one of the most expensive storms in U.S. history.[2]

How did people know where Hurricane Irene was going to strike, how strong it would be, and what kind of damage it could do? Hurricane warnings are issued by the National Weather Service (NWS), which gathers meteorological information across the country and around the world, including radar and satellite data. The National Hurricane Center (NHC) tracks all tropical storms that originate in the North Atlantic Ocean and develops computer models that predict how strong they will be and where they will turn. The NHC's Storm Surge Unit forecasts how high sea levels will rise; local governments rely on these forecasts when deciding whether to evacuate low-lying regions. The "Hurricane Hunter" pilots who fly into hurricanes to gather data are from the Air Force Reserve and the

National Oceanic and Atmospheric Administration. The data generated by the National Weather Service (NWS) are used (sometimes along with privately gathered data) to produce the forecasts trumpeted by private media outlets such as the Weather Channel, AccuWeather, and local news stations around the country. Finally, money to help communities recover from hurricanes and other natural disasters is routinely appropriated by Congress and distributed by the Federal Emergency Management Agency.

This is one of the things people expect the government to do: protect them from risks that are beyond their individual control. In 2005, Senator (and later presidential hopeful) Rick Santorum, an outspoken free market advocate, sponsored a bill that would have prevented the National Weather Service from providing the public with weather forecasts that might compete with private companies; but even he still insisted that the NWS should continue gathering data and providing it to those private companies.[3] In other words, the government shouldn't compete with the private sector, but should still fly planes into hurricanes so the private sector can make money. When House majority leader Eric Cantor said that emergency appropriations in the wake of Hurricane Irene should be offset by spending cuts, he was criticized by Republican governors Bob McDonnell of Virginia and Chris Christie of New Jersey, both members of the party's conservative wing, for putting spending cuts ahead of emergency aid.[4]

Flying planes into hurricanes, developing weather forecast models, and everything else the federal government does costs money. But for most of the past half-century, the government has been spending more than it brings in. In 2010, the most recent year for which official figures are available, the federal government deficit was $1.3 trillion—the difference between $3.5 trillion of spending and $2.2 trillion of revenues.[5] Spending, at almost 24 percent of GDP, was at the second-highest level (after 2009) since 1946; revenues, at less than 15 percent, were at the lowest level (tied with 2009) since 1950. The national debt—the total amount the government has borrowed to fill budget gaps over the years—was more than $10 trillion at the end of 2011 and growing rapidly. Dealing with the national debt will be one of our country's major challenges for this

decade. But before we can talk about what (if anything) to do about
the national debt, we need to understand what those numbers mean.

Before digging into the numbers, there are a couple of important
points to remember. The first is the difference between the annual
budget deficit and the national debt. The deficit is the gap between
the government's spending and tax revenues in a given year, which it
makes up by borrowing money. The debt is the total amount owed
by the government at a specific moment, so it represents the accumulation of all previous years' deficits.

Second, when making comparisons across time, it is important
to measure both deficits and the debt against the overall size of the
economy, which is typically represented by gross domestic product
(GDP): the total value of all goods and services produced in a given
year. Paying off the debt, or just making interest payments on the
debt, means allocating some of our national income to that purpose.
The more income we generate as a society, the easier it is to support
a given amount of debt.

WHERE DOES THE MONEY GO?

Today, most Americans think that the federal budget deficit is primarily due to "spending too much money on federal programs that
are not needed or wasteful" and that the deficit should be reduced
mainly through spending cuts—in the abstract.[6] At the same time,
however, majorities oppose spending cuts not just to Social Security and Medicare, but to national defense, homeland security, anti-
poverty programs, education, aid to farmers, and even the arts and
sciences. The *only* thing that a majority believes should be cut is foreign aid.[7] That's because Americans typically think that foreign aid
accounts for 25 percent of the federal budget; in fact, the correct
figure is closer to 1 percent.[8] So when people consider what the government actually does, it's not clear that they still think it spends too
much.

What does it mean to spend "too much money," anyway? In the
short term, the government does not have a hard budget limit: it
can either borrow money (if the bond markets are receptive) or raise

taxes (if it has the political will). Whether it spends too much really depends on what it is spending that money on.

In 2010, $196 billion went to pay **interest on the national debt,** which was $7.5 trillion at the end of 2009. Assuming that we do not want to default on our debt, those interest payments are the price that must be paid for deficits incurred in the past, regardless of current policy decisions. Subtracting off that $196 billion from total spending, **primary (noninterest) spending** was $3.3 trillion. The **primary deficit,** which measures the impact of current policies, excluding interest to pay for past deficits, was $1.1 trillion.

That $3.3 trillion in spending is divided into discretionary and mandatory spending.[9] **Discretionary spending** is money allocated by Congress in specific appropriations bills that must be passed each year. This includes spending on defense; on most federal agencies such as the FBI, the Federal Aviation Administration, and the National Weather Service; and on various programs in areas such as veterans' health care, education, and housing. Theoretically, in any year, Congress could decide to appropriate no money for, say, the Pentagon, in which case it would soon run out of money to pay soldiers, refuel airplanes, or buy new equipment. In practice, however, appropriations in one year are usually adjusted up or down from whatever the appropriations were in the preceding year. **Mandatory spending,** by contrast, does not require annual action by Congress.[10] In this case, an existing law, such as the Social Security Act, requires the federal government to spend money unless that law is specifically amended or repealed. Most mandatory spending goes to programs such as Social Security, Medicare, Medicaid, and food stamps. The laws establishing these programs require that money be spent for all people who are entitled to benefits because they meet certain eligibility criteria (hence the common label of "entitlement programs"). This means that when more people qualify—for example, when a recession makes more people eligible for Medicaid—spending must go up.

Mandatory spending dominates the federal budget (see Figure 4-1). In 2010, it came to $1.9 trillion, or 59 percent of primary spending. The large majority of mandatory spending goes to Social Security ($701 billion), Medicare ($446 billion), and Medicaid ($273 billion),

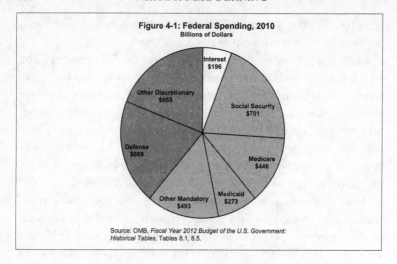

Figure 4-1: Federal Spending, 2010
Billions of Dollars

Interest $196

Social Security $701

Medicare $446

Medicaid $273

Other Mandatory $493

Defense $689

Other Discretionary $658

Source: OMB, *Fiscal Year 2012 Budget of the U.S. Government: Historical Tables*, Tables 8.1, 8.5.

which together account for almost one-half of all primary spending. This is the outcome of the long-term trends discussed in chapter 3: as the population ages and health care costs increase, mandatory spending goes up, even if these programs are not becoming more generous. Since 1962, mandatory spending has grown from 28 percent to 59 percent of total primary spending;[11] by 2021, under conservative assumptions, it will be over two-thirds of primary spending.[12] This matters because if you want to balance the budget through spending cuts, mandatory spending is hard to cut. Procedurally, Congress has to take action to pass a law that reduces benefits, rather than simply appropriating less money for some program. More importantly, Social Security, Medicare, and Medicaid are popular programs. Most Americans currently benefit from or will someday benefit from Social Security and Medicare. A majority of Americans say that Medicaid is important to their families, which may seem surprising for a program dedicated to the poor—until you realize that it served 68 million people in 2010.[13] This is in part because Medicaid, unlike Medicare, pays for long-term care (although beneficiaries must first exhaust all of their assets)—relieving many middle-class, working-age people from having to pay for their parents' care. In other words, most federal spending is spending that people like, and that will grow year after year under current law.

While mandatory spending largely goes to pay for individual benefits such as retirement income and health care, most of what we typically think of as government *activity*—national defense, border security, aviation safety, the FBI, hurricane planes, disaster relief, highways and bridges, regulation, research and education, national parks, and so on—is paid for by discretionary spending. In 2010, more than half of all discretionary spending ($689 billion) went to **national defense.** Everything else, conventionally called **nondefense discretionary spending,** amounted to $658 billion. While mandatory spending has been steadily growing over the past half-century, discretionary spending has been falling from over 12 percent of GDP in the 1960s to just 7 percent in the decade before the financial crisis (see Figure 4-2).[14] (It climbed to more than 9 percent of GDP in 2010 because of additional spending under the 2009 stimulus bill, but is falling again now that most stimulus programs have run out.) Most of this long-term decline has been due to major reductions in defense spending since the Cold War—from more than 10 percent of GDP in the 1950s (even after the Korean War) to 3 percent after the collapse of the Soviet Union.[15] (Defense spending climbed again, to almost 5 percent of GDP in 2010, because of the Afghanistan and

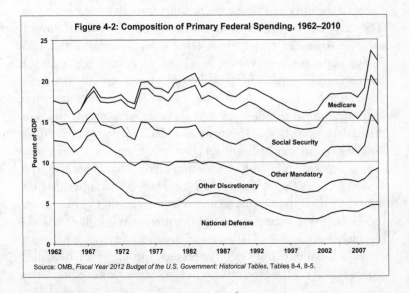

Figure 4-2: Composition of Primary Federal Spending, 1962–2010

Source: OMB, *Fiscal Year 2012 Budget of the U.S. Government: Historical Tables*, Tables 8-4, 8-5.

Iraq wars.) Nondefense discretionary spending has been relatively stable at around 4 percent of GDP over the past fifty years, growing slightly in the 1970s before falling back thanks to the cutbacks of the Reagan and Clinton eras. (Because it includes neither popular entitlement programs nor national security, nondefense discretionary spending is also the category that is most often singled out for budget cuts; the month before Hurricane Irene, the House Appropriations Committee voted to cut the Hurricane Hunters' budget by 40 percent—a savings of $17 million.)[16]

In other words, most of the federal government has been getting smaller, not larger, over the past half-century. Not counting Social Security (and Medicare, which didn't exist yet), primary spending averaged 15 percent of GDP in the 1950s. In 2007, before the recession began, primary spending other than those two programs was just 11 percent of GDP. In other words, except for Social Security and Medicare, the government has been steadily shrinking. The government's civilian workforce, which fluctuated between 0.9 percent and 1.1 percent of the population from 1954 to 1991, was only 0.7 percent of the population in 2010.[17] Seen in this light, President Eisenhower, not President Obama, presided over a large and expensive federal government.

Social Security and Medicare, of course, are large and expensive. They represent a profound transformation in the role of government in American society. While the federal government spends less money and employs fewer people for everything else it does, it has become an important insurance provider to virtually the entire population.[18] The government has always played an important role in protecting Americans from risks that they were unable to insure themselves against; Social Security and Medicare marked the expansion of that risk management function into the areas of retirement income security and health care for the elderly.[19] Social Security, created in 1935 at the height of the New Deal, protects people from not saving enough for retirement, losing their savings to bad investments, outliving their money, and the premature death of a working spouse through its Old-Age and Survivors Insurance program; through Disability Insurance, it protects people from becoming unable to work. Medicare, created in 1965 at the height of the Great

Society, protects people from becoming uninsurable due to poor health, from long-term health care inflation, and from needing to pay for expensive health care in old age.

These programs are the two largest examples of social insurance in the United States. They provide *insurance* because people pay for protection from outcomes that may or may not occur; we don't know who among us will live to be one hundred, but Social Security protects all of us from completely running out of money before we die. They are *social* insurance because they pool risk across most or all of society; although largely funded by individual contributions that resemble insurance premiums, their financing and benefit structure partially reflect the idea that everyone should be able to participate and that the total burden should be shared fairly. With Social Security, you make mandatory contributions while you work; when you retire or become disabled, you receive benefits based on the amount that you contributed. With Medicare, you make mandatory contributions while you work and also pay insurance premiums in old age; in exchange, Medicare pays for most of your health care costs after you turn sixty-five.[20] As of 2010, 54 million people received Social Security benefits and 47 million were enrolled in Medicare; 157 million people paid Social Security payroll taxes and (along with their spouses) could expect to receive benefits in the future.[21]

Unlike traditional government activities, social insurance programs pay concrete, individual benefits to just about everyone. This makes them the opposite of public goods like national defense and environmental protection, which we all benefit from and whose benefits cannot be divided up by individuals for themselves. Social Security and Medicare, by contrast, pay cash directly to you or to your health care providers. Because these programs pay individual benefits that people value—guaranteed retirement income or health care—they substitute for insurance that otherwise most of us would want to buy anyway. Without Social Security, people would want to save more for retirement, which means they would pay money to asset management firms instead of to the government. Without Medicare, people would try to buy health insurance from private insurers; but depending on their age and health status, they might not be able to buy insurance at any price. In other words, if we cut Medicare, our taxes will go down, but most of us will go right out and spend most of that money, or more, on health insurance—assuming that we can.

Over the past half-century, then, federal spending has gone up largely because the government's insurance operations have grown. Those operations exist because, as our society has become richer, we value insurance more, and we expect to get it from the one entity large and creditworthy enough to provide it—the federal government. In recent decades, spending on social insurance programs has grown mainly because of increasing life expectancy and increasing health care costs, not because the programs themselves have become more generous. The 2003 expansion of Medicare to cover prescription drugs did increase Medicare spending. On the Social Security side, however, the biggest policy change in the past thirty years, the Social Security Amendments of 1983 (a compromise between President Reagan and Democratic House speaker Tip O'Neill), actually reduced spending growth, primarily by gradually raising the full retirement age and making some benefits taxable.[22] (Social Security benefits generally are quite modest: in 2011, the average annual benefit was only about $13,000.)[23]

This means that the biggest factor behind the long-term growth of federal spending is not reckless, wasteful spending by politicians and bureaucrats in Washington—whether warmongers or environmental zealots, depending on your perspective—but demographic and economic trends that are largely beyond anyone's control. We can argue about whether the government should be providing old age insurance, disability insurance, and health insurance (and we will, in chapter 6). Less insurance would mean a smaller federal budget. But to a large extent, it would simply transfer the burden of saving for retirement and paying for health insurance back from the government to individuals, making some people better off (mainly the rich, but also the heirs of people who die young) and some people worse off (certainly the poor and the long-lived, but arguably much of the middle class as well).[24]

The growth of Social Security and Medicare also means that it would be difficult if not impossible to balance the budget by cutting spending outside of these two popular programs—despite the widespread belief that unneeded or wasteful spending is the cause

of the deficit. Many people think that there is too much government regulation and want to get rid of agencies like the Consumer
Financial Protection Bureau; others think the government has no
place in the cultural sphere and want to get rid of the National
Endowment for the Arts. Again, we can argue about whether those
agencies are worth their costs, but that's not where the money is:
the CFPB's budget is about $300 million and the NEA's is about
$150 million—each less than one-hundredth of 1 percent of total
federal spending.[25] In 2010, by contrast, Social Security, Medicare,
and interest on the debt cost over $1.3 trillion, while tax revenues
were less than $2.2 trillion. Balancing the budget at that level of taxes
would have required cutting all other federal spending—national
defense, immigration control, federal courts and the federal prison
system, Medicaid, food stamps, student loans, everything—by over
60 percent.

Social Security and Medicare are also the most visible examples
of a major shift in the nature of government spending over the
past half-century. In the 1950s, payments for individuals (such as
Social Security checks or, today, Medicare reimbursements) made
up barely one-fifth of total federal spending. Today, they account
for more than three-fifths. Cutting federal spending means taking
money directly out of people's pockets; there just isn't enough governmental waste and bureaucratic empire building to make a big
difference. Any spending cuts that significantly reduce deficits over
the long term would directly affect tens of millions of people, making them politically difficult to enact; the other option, tax increases,
is at least as unpopular. But the idea that we can balance the budget
solely by eliminating unspecified "bad" government programs is a
fantasy.

HOW BIG IS THE GOVERNMENT?

Add it all up, and many Americans believe that federal spending is
out of control. At over 23 percent of GDP, total spending in 2009
and 2010 was the highest since 1946, when the country was demo-
bilizing after World War II. But by international standards, our

government is relatively cheap. Over the past decade, total government spending in the United States, including state and local governments, was 37 percent of GDP—the second-lowest figure among the twenty-seven advanced economies (according to the International Monetary Fund) in Europe or North America.[26] We may not get value for our money, but our government does not spend a lot compared to its peers. And in the long term, federal spending has not been growing—at least not yet. In the postwar period, spending peaked in the 1980s, when it averaged 22 percent of GDP, largely thanks to the Reagan defense buildup. In the 2000s, after the end of the Cold War but before the 2007–2009 recession, it averaged only 19 percent. The problem is that in the next few years, the retirement of the baby boom generation will trigger a long climb in mandatory spending that will be difficult to match with cutbacks in discretionary spending.

Higher spending obviously means that the budget can only be balanced through higher taxes. But to many people it means something more: that the government is too big. This is a core tenet of the tax revolt, which is focused not on balancing the budget, but on cutting government spending. Grover Norquist has been repeating this to anyone who will listen; in a 2011 interview, he said, "The way we could screw up the pending Republican [success] in 2012 . . . is to lose focus on spending and get distracted on chasing the deficit."[27] As government spending increases, the thinking goes, so does its influence over the private sector, hurting economic growth and reducing personal liberty.

This line of argument is based on a couple of big assumptions and a basic fallacy. The first assumption is that government actions invariably reduce liberty. But the opposite is often the case. As economist Bruce Bartlett pointed out, the countries with the lowest taxes and the smallest governments are often very poor precisely because their governments fail to protect property rights, enforce the rule of law, and provide basic public goods such as transportation infrastructure. Meanwhile Denmark, where total government spending is well over 50 percent of GDP, provides more economic freedom than the United States, according to the Heritage Foundation and *The Wall Street Journal*.[28] The idea that government reduces liberty also depends on a peculiarly narrow conception of liberty. According to this viewpoint, the Americans with Disabilities Act infringes on the liberty of business owners, who now (in certain circumstances) must make accommodations for people with disabilities. But that same law enhances the liberty of disabled people, who now have greater opportunities to work, attend cultural or sporting events, and otherwise lead fulfilling lives. Medicare may force people to pay a payroll tax during their working careers, but it also assures them of a basic level of health care in retirement, with all the additional opportunities that depend on having decent health. As Franklin D. Roosevelt said in 1941, freedom from want is also a kind of freedom.[29]

The second assumption is that shifting responsibility from the government to the private sector is always a good thing. But spending cuts usually come with a price. If we eliminate funding for the Hurricane Hunters, someone will have to fly planes into hurricanes, unless we want to live with less hurricane data and more uncertainty about when and where they will strike. That someone could be private weather services like the Weather Channel and AccuWeather, but they can't do it for free; instead, their costs would get absorbed by shareholders or passed on to customers. It is possible that private competition could eventually provide hurricane data with higher quality and at a lower cost than the government can, although that's by no means certain. We can debate what services should be provided by the private sector rather than the government. But in any case, someone has to pay.

The same thing goes for insurance. In some areas, like auto insurance, the private sector seems to do a decent job of meeting people's needs (although, even here, we rely on state governments to make sure high-risk drivers can get insurance). In other areas, however, private insurance markets often fail to provide coverage to many people who want or need it, at least in the absence of government encouragement. At the beginning of the twentieth century, for example, most workers had little or no insurance against workplace injuries. In response, most states adopted workers' compensation laws that ensured benefits to injured employees; these laws were even supported by some employers, who preferred the cost certainty of workers' compensation insurance to the risk of losing a lawsuit and having to pay a large damage award.[30] Today the most glaring failure is the individual market for health insurance (where people buy insurance for themselves instead of getting it through their employers or a government program), which has left fifty million people without coverage.[31] And for some risks, only the government is a credible insurer, because it is the only institution with the ability to absorb large, unexpected costs if necessary. (This is why many private insurance markets, including auto, home, life, and workers' compensation insurance, are backstopped by state guaranty funds.) Throughout American history, both businesses and individuals have seen the government as the "ultimate risk manager," in the words of historian David Moss, in part because it has the power to raise taxes, ensuring that it can make good on its promises.[32] Shrinking government insurance programs is one way to reduce government spending, but either many of us will have to pay private insurers for the same insurance—or we won't be able to buy it at all.

The fallacy is the idea that total government spending is an accurate measure of the size of government. The best definition of a big government is one that has a large influence on society: in economic terms, it causes major changes in people's choices and in the allocation of resources. But the number of dollars collected and spent by the government doesn't tell you how much it interferes in the private sector in any meaningful sense.[33] To begin with, most government policies can be accomplished at least three different ways: spending, tax credits (provisions that let you reduce your taxes), and regulation. For example, let's say politicians in Washington want to help poor people afford rental housing. Among other things, they can build and manage public housing projects; they can give tax credits to developers who build affordable housing; or they can write a regulation saying that a certain percentage of all new housing units must be rented at affordable rates. The first increases the amount of cash flowing in and out of the government; the second decreases it; and the third leaves it the same. Yet all increase the impact of government on society.

The discovery that government policies can be pursued through tax loopholes has led to the extraordinary proliferation of what are known as "tax expenditures"—laws that use the tax code as a means of distributing money to people.[34] Tax expenditures allow individuals or companies to reduce their taxes if they do certain things that the law is trying to promote. For example, if you take out a loan to buy a house, you can take a tax deduction for the interest on your mortgage, which will save homeowners a total of $94 billion in 2012—ostensibly promoting homeownership.[35] Alternatively, the government could have eliminated the tax deduction (increasing tax revenues by $94 billion) and instead mailed $94 billion in checks to homeowners, which would have had essentially the same effect for all parties involved. That, however, would count as higher taxes, which are politically unpopular. Tax expenditures allow politicians to pursue their policy objectives (or provide favors to important interest groups) while lowering taxes, which accounts for their tremendous popularity in Washington: today, no matter how you count them, they amount to over a trillion dollars in "spending."[36] Much of that money goes to the wealthy, both because they have more to deduct (bigger houses and bigger mortgages) and because they pay income tax at higher rates, so deductions are worth more to them.[37]

Like other subsidy programs, tax expenditures can have perverse effects on people's economic incentives. The mortgage interest deduction encourages people to buy bigger houses and borrow more money, which increases household indebtedness, increases the risk of default and foreclosure, and makes the economy more vulnerable to the collapse of a housing bubble. Similarly, the fact that businesses can deduct interest payments on their debt but cannot deduct dividends paid to shareholders encourages them to take on more debt.[38] Since tax expenditures influence the choices that people and companies make, they both reduce the amount of revenue flowing into the Treasury Department, increasing deficits, and increase the influence of the federal government on society, making government bigger. Yet tax expenditures only contribute to many Americans' confusion about just what it is that government does. People who benefit from traditional programs run by government agencies, such as unemployment insurance or Social Security, are more likely to feel that government has helped to provide them with opportunities. By contrast, people who benefit from government subsidies in the form of tax breaks, such as the mortgage interest deduction or tax-preferred educational savings accounts, are actually *less likely* to believe that the government has increased their opportunities.[39]

Even ignoring tax expenditures, the total cost of a program has little to do with its real size. For example, which has a bigger impact on society, Social Security or the Environmental Protection Agency? Social Security cost $701 billion in 2010; the EPA, only $11 billion. But the EPA writes regulations that affect virtually every major business in the country, forcing them to incur costs not counted in the federal budget, with the goal of protecting all Americans from harmful toxins in the air they breathe and the water they drink. Social Security shifts income from your working years to your retirement years—perhaps more income than you would shift otherwise—and insures you against outliving your savings. There's no meaningful way to say that one has more of an impact on the country than the other, even though Social Security "costs" more than sixty times as much as the EPA.

In the end, we can debate whether the EPA should regulate business more or less, and we can debate whether Social Security should shift more or less income between our working years and our retirement years. But if there is an optimal balance between private sector activity and government intervention, it cannot be fully measured in dollars. When it comes to social insurance programs, the real question is how much risk we want to shoulder ourselves and how much we want to pool with our fellow citizens, with the government acting as the administrator. The total dollar level of government spending is a red herring.

HOW DO WE PAY FOR ALL THAT?

The more money the federal government spends, the more money it has to come up with, one way or another. In 2010, the federal government collected $2.2 trillion in revenues, the vast majority of that from taxes. The much maligned **individual income tax** (for which returns are due on April 15) was the largest source of government revenues, accounting for $899 billion, or 42 percent of the total. Each household has to pay a percentage of its income, ranging from

0 percent for the first few thousand dollars it earns to 35 percent for income that exceeds several hundred thousand dollars per year.* (Because of various exemptions, deductions, and tax credits—as well as basic poverty—almost half of all households pay no federal income tax at all.)[40] This structure means that the individual income tax is progressive: rich people generally pay a higher percentage of their income than poor people.

Today, 40 percent of Americans say they are "angry" about the level of federal income taxes they pay.[41] (To be fair, that was in a poll taken in early April 2011, and other polls consistently show support for some tax increases, especially to reduce budget deficits.)[42] Yet individual income taxes have only fallen over the past thirty years, from 8.5 percent of GDP in the 1980s and 8.4 percent in the 1990s to 7.4 percent since the 2001 tax cut and 6.2 percent in 2010—the lowest level since 1950.[43] Even if we ignore the recent recession (which lowered income taxes, since people have been making less money), individual income taxes were significantly lower as a share of the economy during the 2001–2007 economic expansion than during the 1991–2000 expansion, largely thanks to the Bush tax cuts.[44]

As individual income taxes have been falling, the government has come to depend more on **social insurance contributions,** which brought in $865 billion in 2010, or 40 percent of total revenues. The vast majority of this money comes from the dedicated payroll taxes for Social Security and Medicare, which are levied only on income from work, not income from investments.[45] Under current law, 12.4 percent of each person's wages goes to the Social Security trust funds.† That money is used to pay benefits currently owed to retirees and disabled people; in previous years, when payroll taxes exceeded benefit payments, the surpluses were invested in Treasury bonds,

* These are marginal tax rates, meaning that even if you are in the 35 percent tax bracket, you pay 35 percent only on income above a certain threshold, now around $400,000. The current tax brackets were set by the 2001 tax cut; if it is allowed to expire, the top marginal rate will go back up to 39.6 percent. Technically speaking, there is no 0 percent tax bracket, since taxes start at 10 percent on any taxable income. In practice, the personal exemptions and the standard deduction ensure that some of your income is not taxable.
† Technically speaking, the employee pays half of each payroll tax and the employer pays the other half. In addition, the December 2010 tax cut lowered the Social Security payroll tax by 2 percentage points for 2011 (since extended through February 2012).

meaning that they were lent to the rest of the federal government. Another 2.9 percent of wage income goes to another trust fund that pays for the Medicare Hospital Insurance program (Part A). Medicare's Medical Insurance and Prescription Drug Coverage programs (Parts B and D), however, are *not* funded by the payroll tax; instead, they are paid for by beneficiaries' premiums and copayments and by money from general government revenues (that is, other taxes). Together, the payroll tax, premiums, and copayments barely cover half of Medicare's total expenses, which means that the program is heavily subsidized by the rest of the federal government.

The Social Security tax is only collected on each person's wage income up to a cap, which was $106,800 in 2011 (and is indexed to inflation), while the Medicare payroll tax is collected on all wage income.[46] This means that payroll taxes on the whole are regressive: poor and middle-income people pay a higher percentage of their income than rich people.* As social insurance contributions have grown (due to rising tax rates), from 2 percent of GDP in the 1950s to more than 6 percent in the first decade of the 2000s (see Figure 4-3), an increasing share of government revenues has come from regressive rather than progressive taxes, shifting the overall tax burden onto lower-income people.[47]

The third major source of federal revenues is the **corporate income tax,** which in 2010 brought in $191 billion, or 9 percent of total revenues. Businesses routinely complain that the United States has one of the highest corporate tax rates in the world, with a federal tax rate of 35 percent; including state corporate taxes, we have the second-highest tax *rate* among all advanced economies.[48] But the effective tax rates that U.S. corporations actually pay have been falling for decades as powerful business interests successfully lobby for tax loopholes and companies become more aggressive at taking advantage of those loopholes.[49] Figuring out ways to book profits in overseas subsidiaries where corporate tax rates are lower has become a lucrative pastime for many companies from General

---

* Someone who makes $50,000 a year ordinarily pays 15.3 percent of her salary, or $7,650, in payroll taxes. Someone who makes $200,000 a year, however, pays $19,043 in payroll taxes because of the cap on the Social Security tax; this works out to a tax rate of only 9.5 percent.

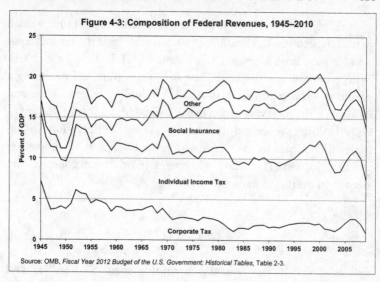

Figure 4-3: Composition of Federal Revenues, 1945–2010

Source: OMB, *Fiscal Year 2012 Budget of the U.S. Government: Historical Tables*, Table 2-3.

Electric to Google, which have claimed billions of dollars in tax benefits.[50] While the corporate tax amounted to 4.8 percent of GDP in the 1950s and 3.8 percent in the 1960s, it fell to 1.9 percent by the first decade of the 2000s and only 1.3 percent in 2010.[51] Including state taxes, corporate taxes in the United States are among the lowest as a share of GDP in the industrialized world.[52]

Tax loopholes not only reduce government revenues but also lead large companies to expend time and money on activities that serve no purpose other than reducing their taxes. They also put smaller companies, unable to afford expensive lawyers and accountants, at a competitive disadvantage. Our low effective corporate tax rates have led to calls from liberals for corporations to pay higher taxes, but it is important to remember that companies are not real people. If they did pay higher taxes, it is hard to identify how that burden would be spread across employees (as lower wages), shareholders (as lower profits), or other capital owners (as lower rates of return).[53]

In addition to individual income taxes, social insurance taxes, and corporate income taxes, the federal government brought in another $208 billion in 2010 from sources such as alcohol, tobacco, and gasoline taxes, customs duties, and estate taxes. From any perspective, the total revenues of $2.2 trillion (less than 15 percent of GDP) were remarkably low. Not since 1950 were total federal taxes such a small part of the economy as in 2009–2010. Leaving aside the recent recession, federal taxes averaged 17 percent of GDP during the 2001–2007 economic expansion; the last time taxes were so low during a period of growth was in 1958–1960.[54] Including federal, state, and local taxes, the total tax burden in the United States was 24 percent of GDP in 2009, the second-lowest level among the thirty-four industrialized countries in the Organisation for Economic Co-operation and Development (OECD).[55] Compared to other rich countries, we are not an overtaxed nation.

IT GETS WORSE

In total, in 2010 the federal government spent $3.5 trillion and brought in $2.2 trillion, producing a $1.3 trillion deficit. Our recent deficits have been big by any measure: the largest ever in dollar terms, the largest peacetime deficits ever as a share of the economy, and among the largest in the industrialized world.[56] Repeated trillion-dollar deficits have also been a major factor (along with more urgent sovereign debt crises in Europe) in shifting political debate in Washington away from unemployment and economic growth and toward the deficit and spending cuts. But are those deficits really worth all the attention?

Large deficits clearly increase the national debt. If tax revenues are not enough to cover spending, the federal government has to make up the difference by borrowing money. If a country has a history of not paying back its debts, it may not be able to find anyone willing to lend it money, which has been a big problem for many national governments throughout history. But this has not been a problem for the United States, thanks to a relatively strong record of fiscal responsibility dating back to Hamilton and Gallatin and, more recently, the dollar's status as the world's reserve currency. Throughout recent history, the federal government has always been able to borrow money by selling Treasury bonds. Every year that there is a deficit, the government has to borrow more money, adding to the national debt; the larger the deficit, the larger the increase in the debt.[57]

If the Treasury Department never had to pay interest (and could always borrow as much as it needed), the national debt would not matter very much. Like most borrowers, however, the federal government usually has to pay interest on the money it borrows, even if it pays less interest than just about anyone else. This is a major reason why the national debt matters. In 2010, interest rates were historically low—partly because the stagnant economy meant that few households and businesses were borrowing money and partly because nervous investors around the world wanted the safety of Treasury bonds. The federal government had to pay only $196 billion in interest as the national debt grew from $7.5 trillion (at the beginning of 2010) to $9.0 trillion (at its end), an average interest rate of about 2.4 percent. But under ordinary economic conditions, interest rates are closer to 5 percent.[58] At that rate, each additional trillion dollars in borrowing means an additional $50 billion in interest payments every year, indefinitely. That is not necessarily a bad thing: as we discuss in the next chapter, if the money is invested in something that generates more than $50 billion of value to society each year, then the borrowing makes sense—just as it makes sense for a business to borrow money to make profitable investments. If instead the money is simply distributed to people as transfer payments, it is harder to justify as an investment, but it can still make sense on other economic grounds. In any case, however, a larger national debt means more money that must be set aside from each year's tax revenues to pay interest on the debt, leaving less for current spending obligations and new investment priorities. By the end of the decade, interest payments alone will probably consume close to 3 percent of GDP.[59]

The impact of a trillion-dollar deficit on the national debt is real, and will continue to be felt for years to come. Beyond that, however, the large annual deficit numbers we have seen recently can be misleading. In fact, they both overstate and understate America's real debt problem.

The recent deficit numbers overstate the debt problem because they have been temporarily inflated by the financial crisis, the resulting recession, and the government's responses. Deficits *automatically* go up when the economy is weak. A recession means that individuals and companies are making less money, so they pay less in taxes; it also means that more people qualify for safety net and social insurance programs such as Medicaid, food stamps, and unemployment insurance, so government spending goes up. Under these conditions, the government should let the deficit go up instead of trying to balance the budget. The Hoover administration's efforts to balance the budget no matter what (which was standard operating procedure at the time) were one of the factors that prolonged and deepened the Great Depression, and the Roosevelt administration's attempt to balance the budget in 1937 also triggered a severe recession.[60] In addition, many (though not all) economists think that the government should take additional steps to boost the economy during a recession; whether spending or tax cuts, these policies will increase the deficit further. Conversely, when the economy recovers, tax revenues go back up, spending on the safety net falls, and stimulus programs end, reducing deficits.

One way to measure our fundamental deficit problem is to look at the structural deficit—what the deficit would be if the economy were operating at full capacity. In 2010, over one-quarter of the total annual deficit was due solely to the automatic drop in revenues caused by the economic crisis and the automatic increase in spending that helped mitigate the crisis.[61] More than one-third was due to the 2009 stimulus bill, which has since largely faded away.[62] Without the financial crisis, in other words, the deficit would have been only $490 billion, or 3.4 percent of GDP: not pretty, but not a front-page national emergency, either. This is not to say that trillion-dollar deficits can simply be ignored. For one thing, all that money does get added to the national debt, which means that we will have to pay interest on it indefinitely. But the recent record deficits in themselves do not necessarily indicate a fundamental problem with current policies.

At the same time, the current deficit numbers understate the future debt problem. The biggest problem with focusing on the annual deficit is that it ignores the future—even when we have a decent idea about what will happen. We already saw this problem at the end of the 1990s, when the annual budget went into surplus even as the government's long-term financial health was continuing to deteriorate because of demographics and rising health care costs.

Today we face the same problem—only we have gotten older and health care has been getting more expensive for more than a decade. We need a long-term picture that takes into account future spending and tax revenues, insofar as they can be predicted. And this picture looks considerably worse than it did a decade ago.[63]

A few words of caution are in order before entering the realm of budgetary projections. Like most analysts (and politicians), we begin with the projections issued by the Congressional Budget Office (CBO). The CBO periodically issues "baseline" projections, which forecast spending and revenues in detail over the next ten years, as well as long-term projections, which go out twenty-five years or more (with less detail). Since no one can see the future, these projections will always be wrong, for two sets of reasons.

The first is economic uncertainty. Any budget projection depends on a forecast of how the economy will perform. Over the long term, economic growth depends largely on productivity—what amount of goods and services can be produced with a given amount of labor and capital investment. If the economy does worse than expected, deficits will be bigger; if productivity growth takes off and the economy booms, deficits will be smaller.

The second is political uncertainty. Forecasts require assumptions about how policy will change (or not) in the future, which are likely to be wrong. For example, it is common to assume that the Social Security payroll tax and Social Security benefits will remain the same indefinitely, even though that leads to an apparent contradiction: at some point, the Social Security trust funds will not have enough money to pay benefits in full. This is why long-term projections sometimes produce what seem like nonsensical results. In that case, they are less predictions of what will happen than an indication that current policies are unsustainable. In addition, the CBO baseline forecast generally must assume that current law will not be changed—for example, that tax cuts will expire when scheduled, even if political factors make that unlikely.[64] For this reason, it is common practice to adjust the official CBO baseline when attempting to predict what is most likely to occur.

With those warnings, we are ready to peer into the future. And over the next ten years, despite the rhetoric swirling around Wash-

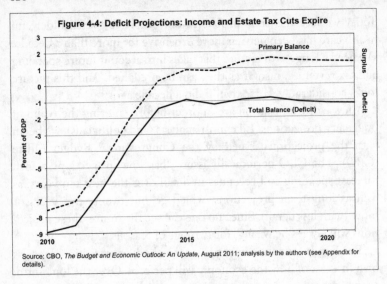

Figure 4-4: Deficit Projections: Income and Estate Tax Cuts Expire

Source: CBO, *The Budget and Economic Outlook: An Update*, August 2011; analysis by the authors (see Appendix for details).

ington and on the campaign trail, we do not see a deficit crisis. Figure 4-4 shows one possible path for the federal government's primary balance (excluding interest on the debt) and the total deficit (including interest).* From 2017 through 2021, the federal budget shows a primary *surplus* between 1 percent and 2 percent of GDP. Because the national debt has already grown so large, the government has to pay over 2 percent of GDP in interest each year, producing deficits around 1 percent of GDP.[65] This is not an ideal situation, since our accumulated debts will cost us hundreds of billions of dollars per year in interest payments. In addition, discretionary spending will fall to its lowest level since the Hoover administration because of the spending caps agreed to in the 2011 debt ceiling compromise. But

* We begin with the CBO's official baseline projection and make three adjustments, all among the CBO's "alternative policy assumptions": (1) we assume that deployments for Iraq, Afghanistan, and similar operations will decline as planned; (2) we assume that Medicare payment rates will be maintained rather than being allowed to fall by 30 percent, as would occur under current law; and (3) we assume that the income threshold for the alternative minimum tax will continue to be increased to account for inflation. CBO, *The Budget and Economic Outlook: An Update*, August 2011, Tables 1-4, 1-8, pp. 4–5, 26–27. The CBO baseline assumes $1.2 trillion in deficit reduction over ten years due to the actions of the "supercommittee" created by the Budget Control Act. The committee failed to reach an agreement, but instead the act requires $1.2 trillion in automatic spending cuts. For further details, see the Appendix.

an annual deficit of 1 percent of GDP would be well below the average for the fifty years before the financial crisis and would be easily sustainable given even mediocre economic growth.[66]

This relatively rosy picture comes with one big caveat: it assumes that the income and estate tax cuts of 2001 and 2003 are allowed to expire on schedule, as dictated by current law.[67] If, instead, these tax cuts are made permanent, we will be in the world shown in Figure 4-5: a primary deficit indefinitely, interest costs over 3 percent of GDP, and deficits close to 4 percent of GDP and rising.[68] In other words, over the next ten years, we do not have a deficit crisis so much as a tax cut crisis. And if you are worried about deficits over the next ten years, you should tell your representatives to let the Bush tax cuts expire. (Alternatively, if you think the tax cuts should not expire because that would increase unemployment, then what we really have is an unemployment crisis.)

In the short term, then, the deficit picture is better than what reading the headlines would lead you to believe. In the long term, though, the picture becomes murkier. On the one hand, the further out a forecast tries to go, the more likely it is to be wrong. On the other hand, the fundamental forces behind our long-term budget problems are simple. Our population is aging, turning more and more Social

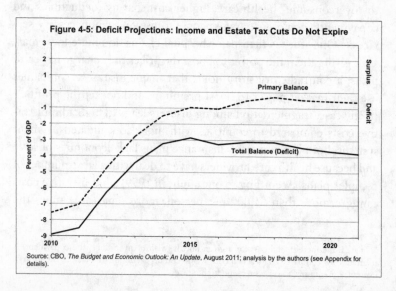

Figure 4-5: Deficit Projections: Income and Estate Tax Cuts Do Not Expire

Source: CBO, *The Budget and Economic Outlook: An Update*, August 2011; analysis by the authors (see Appendix for details).

Security and Medicare contributors into beneficiaries. The increase in Medicare enrollees means that the government is responsible for a growing share of national health care spending. This is a problem for two reasons: first, we already spend much more on health care than any other comparable country; and second, health care costs are growing faster than the economy, meaning that spending on government health programs will grow faster than tax revenues.

The United States pays almost twice as much per person on health care as the typical industrialized country, yet our actual outcomes are mediocre at best; for example, our life expectancy is three years worse than you would expect given our general prosperity.[69] There are many explanations for why our health care is so expensive and not particularly good. One is that our insurance system gives providers (doctors, hospitals, and so on) the incentive to order too many tests and conduct too many procedures, since they will be reimbursed for them whether or not they are needed or effective.[70] This system encourages doctors to become specialists, who provide more expensive care (and make more money), rather than primary care physicians, who are relatively less expensive and are crucial to integrating care effectively. Another, related explanation is that since individuals bear only a small part of the costs of their treatment,* they tend to "overconsume" health care; higher cost sharing (deductibles and copayments) could encourage people to use fewer unnecessary services.[71] One story is that major hospital chains dominate local markets, giving them the power to boost the prices they charge to health plans; a contradictory story holds that major insurance companies use their market power to boost premiums and pocket the profits.[72] In any case, fragmentation among insurers leads to high administrative costs compared to countries with more consolidated payment systems, both because many insurance plans lack economies of scale and because health care providers have to deal with a large number of complex plans. According to one study, in 1999, administrative costs came to more than $1,000 per person, more than three times the

---

* That is, the incremental cost for a given doctor's visit or procedure (the copayment) is relatively low compared to its actual cost; we do end up paying the full cost in the form of insurance premiums, lower wages, and higher taxes.

level in Canada; while there may be several reasons for that differ-ence, billing- and insurance-related expenses account for more than 20 percent of health care spending that is paid for through private insurers.[73] High income inequality in the United States means that we have to pay our doctors (at least specialists) more than in other countries (because they would otherwise become hedge fund man-agers).[74] Another argument is that large medical malpractice awards drive up malpractice insurance costs (which get bundled into the price of health care) and motivate doctors to engage in "defensive medicine"—ordering unnecessary tests and conducting unnecessary procedures to shield themselves from lawsuits.

Whatever the reason, health care in the United States is expen-sive, and the aging of the population means that the federal gov-ernment will have to buy more and more of it. This problem is compounded by the fact that health care spending has been growing faster than inflation and faster than the economy for decades, even after accounting for demographic shifts, and there is little reason for it to slow down. The most common explanation of rising health care costs is increasing spending on medical technology: medical innovation generates new procedures, devices, and drugs that can help patients, but at an ever-increasing price.[75] Rising incomes have also contributed to higher spending by increasing demand for health care.[76] Again, it's not clear that our increasing spending on health care is buying us very much in the way of health. From 1990 to 2007, life expectancy at birth increased from 75.3 to 77.9 years; this gain of 2.6 years was the second-lowest among the thirty-four countries in the OECD (even though we were only in the middle of the pack in 1990).[77]

In the future, average incomes are likely to continue rising (although perhaps not median incomes), and there is no reason to believe the pace of medical innovation will slow. The Affordable Care Act of 2010 (the Obama health care reform bill) does contain several measures designed to reduce the growth rate of government health care spending, ranging from formulas that limit the growth of Medicare payment rates to pilot programs trying out new ways of paying for health care. There is considerable debate about how effective these provisions will be (and debate about whether the entire thing should be repealed), but in any case health care costs are still likely to grow faster than the economy in the long term.[78]

As health care becomes a larger and larger part of the economy and of federal government spending, it will become increasingly difficult to balance the budget. In 2011, federal spending on health care, including Medicare, Medicaid, and the Children's Health Insurance Program, came to 5.6 percent of GDP; by 2035, it is likely to be around 10 percent of GDP, more than half of that because of Medicare.[79] It is true that health care costs cannot grow faster than the economy forever, but in the absence of structural change in the health care industry, there is also little reason to expect their growth to slow down dramatically.[80] In addition, half of the projected growth in government health care spending over that period is due simply to the aging of the population and not to the assumption that health care costs grow faster than the economy.[81]

Alongside growing health care costs, Social Security, which reduced federal deficits over the past decade (because payroll tax revenues exceeded benefit payments), will instead start contributing to the overall budget deficit.[82] The main factor pushing Social Security into the red is the aging of the population and the resulting decrease in the ratio of workers (who make contributions) to retirees (who collect benefits). The other factor is increasing income inequality. Because the payroll tax is only levied on earnings up to a cap, the more money the very rich make, the more income escapes the payroll tax. This is exactly what has happened: 10 percent of wage earnings were not subject to the payroll tax in 1983, but that figure climbed to 16 percent by 2010 and is expected to continue rising to 17 percent by 2020.[83] Because of these factors, in 2010 Social Security payroll taxes for the first time were not enough to pay benefits, and that gap will only grow as the baby boom generation retires, the ratio of workers to retirees falls, and life expectancy increases.[84] If both payroll taxes and promised benefits remain unchanged, the gap between the two will climb to 1.4 percent of GDP by 2035.[85]

The fundamental problem is that government spending on Social Security and health care will grow faster than tax revenues. In our "optimistic" scenario, where all the recent tax cuts expire and the rest of the government (other than Social Security and health care) remains at the early 1930s levels mandated by the 2011 debt ceiling agreement, the deficit will grow to 5 percent of GDP around 2030 and continue upward. (The national debt will be 68 percent of GDP in 2030 and rising, as shown in Figure 4-6.) If, instead, the income and estate tax cuts are extended, the deficit will be over 8 percent of GDP in 2030 (with the national debt at 103 percent of GDP) and climbing rapidly.[86] In the latter scenario, the economy will not be able to grow fast enough to keep pace with both rising interest payments on the debt and rising primary deficits—meaning that the debt will only continue to grow.[87] Before we reach that point, however, something will have to give; the only question is what.

If the short-term deficit problem is due to tax cuts, the long-term deficit problem is largely due to health care. If the tax cuts were allowed to expire and, in addition, government health care spending could magically be kept at 2021 levels, there would be no long-term deficit problem. In that case, government spending other than interest payments would be about 20 percent of GDP in 2030, revenues would be about 21 percent (assuming Congress simply did nothing except index the alternative minimum tax to inflation), and the primary budget would show a slowly growing surplus.[88] There is no magic wand, however, that can freeze health care spending. So the

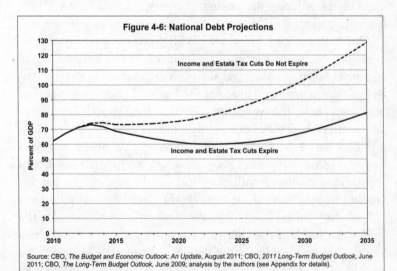

Figure 4-6: National Debt Projections

Income and Estate Tax Cuts Do Not Expire

Income and Estate Tax Cuts Expire

Percent of GDP

Source: CBO, *The Budget and Economic Outlook: An Update,* August 2011; CBO, *2011 Long-Term Budget Outlook,* June 2011; CBO, *The Long-Term Budget Outlook,* June 2009; analysis by the authors (see Appendix for details).

federal government does have a long-term deficit crisis—but it is the product of a national health care crisis.

As the largest buyer of health care in the economy, the government has some influence on overall health care prices, but that influence is limited. Congress can dictate how much Medicare will pay doctors for a given medical procedure, but Congress cannot force doctors to accept Medicare patients; so for Medicare to be a viable health insurance plan, it must pay something reasonably close to the market price.[89] While the cost of Medicare and Medicaid has been growing over the past few decades, the cost of health care that is not paid for by the government has been growing as fast or faster because it is subject to the same pressures: technological innovation and rising incomes.[90] And without structural change, there is no reason to expect private health care costs to start falling. In 1985, health care spending accounted for one-tenth of the national economy; in 2009, it was about one-sixth; and by 2035, it is likely to be more than one-quarter.[91] This means that Americans will have to devote a larger and larger share of their incomes to paying for health care, whether they pay for it in the form of lower wages (for employer-paid health insurance), higher premiums and copayments (for all types of health insurance), or higher taxes (for government-paid health insurance)—reducing the amount of money available for everything else.

Our health care problems are broader than our deficit problems. The long-term deficit could be eliminated, if you were willing to eliminate Medicare, Medicaid, the Children's Health Insurance Program, and government subsidies for buying health insurance. But that would only shift costs onto individual families and, in all likelihood, increase total health care spending. In 2011 the House Budget Committee, chaired by Representative Paul Ryan, proposed converting Medicare into a program where beneficiaries buy health insurance on their own with subsidies from the government; but this would only *increase* total spending on the same health care by 41 to 67 percent.[92] Such a solution makes sense only if we care about the budgetary health of the United States government but not the real health (and financial health) of the people it serves. Our goal must be finding a way to prevent the federal budget deficit from spiraling out of control without abandoning the elderly and the poor to pay for health care on their own—just as health care becomes harder and harder to pay for.

NO FREE LUNCH

Looking at the projections, balancing the long-term federal budget may seem like a hopeless task. But from an economic standpoint, it is certainly possible. The best solution would be one that reduces the long-term growth of health care costs for everyone, including the government. There's no law of nature that says we have to pay so much for health care. The Affordable Care Act was a first step in the right direction, but few people expect it to solve the problem completely.

Even without an effective solution to health care costs, however, we should still be able to afford everything that the federal government does—if we want to. The United States is one of the richest countries in the world.[93] And, as mentioned before, we pay less in taxes than most rich, industrialized countries. If we really want to balance the federal budget, there is no *economic* reason why we can't raise taxes enough to keep pace with growing health care spending. As long as health care is becoming more expensive, we all pay real money for it, one way or another. It is true that, at some point, higher tax rates can harm economic growth by reducing people's incentive to work. But the highest tax rate today is lower than at any point since World War II except the 1986–1993 period, and there are many other ways around that problem, such as closing tax loopholes or broadening the tax base (which we discuss later).[94]

Now, you may not want to pay more taxes. Instead of paying higher taxes, you may prefer receiving lower Social Security and Medicare benefits—in effect, betting that you don't need as much insurance as the government currently provides. That is also a reasonable solution to the long-term deficit. The bottom line is that the only way to reduce the deficit is raising taxes, reducing spending, or some combination of the two. From an economic standpoint, any of these approaches will work. We have plenty of money; we just have to decide how we want to allocate it between individual bank accounts and social insurance programs.

In a low-tax/low-benefit world, your bank account is a little bigger (if you make enough money to pay taxes), but you face more risk of running out of money in retirement or not being able to afford health care; in a high-tax/high-benefit world, your bank account is a little smaller, but you face less risk. Since rich people are better able to self-insure, they gain less by pooling their risk with other people, so they might be better off in a low-tax/low-benefit world; poor people cannot self-insure, so they gain the most from risk pooling, and they will be better off in a high-tax/high-benefit world.[95] Compared to current policy, reducing benefits so we can keep our low tax rates is a form of redistribution from the poor to the rich; raising taxes so we can maintain today's benefit levels is a form of redistribution from the rich to the poor (assuming that the tax increases are progressive). But again, either way will work. All we need to do is decide, as a country, what we want from our government.

This is fundamentally a political decision, which is why solving the long-term deficit problem seems so hard. Today, Republicans are dug in against tax increases and are demanding benefit cuts in the name of fiscal discipline (and, thanks to the antitax pledge, have even managed to sink their ships behind them, eliminating the possibility of retreat[96]). Democrats, led by President Obama, have shown the willingness to combine tax increases with benefit cuts, but are adamantly opposed to a solution that only includes benefit cuts. As long as this political stalemate continues, the national debt will continue to grow.

Five

WHY WORRY

It is important to stress that at present, liquidity concerns aside; all of the Irish banks are profitable and well capitalised.

—Merrill Lynch, September 28, 2008[1]

Alexander Hamilton may have won the policy debates of the 1790s, but Thomas Jefferson had the last word when it came to the popular understanding of the national debt. In 1816, he wrote, "I, however, place economy among the first and most important republican virtues, and public debt as the greatest of the dangers to be feared."[2] For Jefferson, national debt threatened to corrupt the basic principles of republican government.[3] That moralistic attitude—not dispassionate analysis of the costs and benefits of borrowing—has shaped public rhetoric about the federal government's finances for most of American history.[4] Politicians still talk about budget deficits as if they are bad in and of themselves, some kind of moral blight afflicting the American people or a stain on the American flag—so self-evidently evil that no further discussion is required.

But the deficit and the debt are just numbers. A national debt over $10 trillion may be more than $30,000 per person in the country, but no one is coming after you for your share of that money. The real question is: why should we care about the national debt?

THE GOVERNMENT IS LIKE A FAMILY

There is one thing that both Democrats and Republicans have been able to agree on. On July 2, 2011, during the negotiations over raising the debt ceiling, President Obama said in his weekly address,

"Government has to start living within its means, just like families do."[5] He was echoing what John Boehner, then the Republican minority leader in the House, had said two years before: "American families are tightening their belts. But they don't see government tightening its belt."[6] In 2011, Rand Paul, a newly elected senator from Kentucky, published a book titled *The Tea Party Goes to Washington*; its cover showed the Capitol with a belt tied tightly around its midsection.[7]

The comparison between the government and a family is appealingly simple. It implies that the government has to bring in enough income to cover its spending, and if it doesn't have enough income, it has to reduce its spending; in other words, it has to balance its budget. There is something to this basic point. If the government borrows money to run a deficit today, it has to pay back that money (with interest) tomorrow. The national debt never has to be completely paid off, because the government lives indefinitely, and hence there is no final reckoning. Still, the need to pay interest means that some portion of the government's income must be dedicated to paying for past deficits, and, under ordinary circumstances, a government cannot run primary deficits (not counting interest payments) forever.[8] Similarly, the more money that a family borrows, the more of its future income will be taken up by interest payments. But this analogy has two deep flaws. First, the government isn't like a family in some extremely important ways. Second, even if the government were like a family, that still wouldn't mean that balancing the budget is always a good idea.

Most obviously, the federal government has the power to levy and collect taxes. This gives it considerably more control over its income than an ordinary family has. But it doesn't have to raise taxes now: the simple fact that it can raise taxes in the future means that the government can run a deficit this year and plan to make it up later. (A family could make the same plan, but it would be betting on future income that might not materialize.) This was Great Britain's strength in the eighteenth century, which Alexander Hamilton set out to imitate. Raising taxes in the future can have harmful effects, particularly if those taxes create major distortions in the economy, so deficit spending is not free.[9] But it certainly gives the government considerably more financial flexibility than the average family.

In addition to the power to tax, the federal government also has the power to print money. In theory, a sovereign government—one that does not have to answer to a higher level of government—could finance its budget deficit and avoid borrowing by simply printing money. The problem is that printing money can lead to higher inflation—as happened in the North and especially in the South during the Civil War—and if a government gets a reputation for printing money to pay its bills, inflation can get out of control quickly. This is why, despite widespread belief to the contrary, the federal government does not print money and put it in its own wallet.[10] Instead, money is "printed" by Federal Reserve banks, which use it to buy securities (usually Treasury bills) on the open market. The Federal Reserve does not take orders directly from the president or Congress, which prevents politicians from creating money whenever they want more of it. Instead, the primary purpose of the Fed's operations is to maintain interest rates and the money supply at the levels it thinks are best for the economy.[11]

Even if the government were like an ordinary family, what would that mean? Families often spend more than they earn in a given year and make up the difference by borrowing: they run "deficits" to pay for houses, cars, college tuition, medical emergencies, and many other things. There is no ironclad law that says that a family can't borrow money, or that it's a bad idea to borrow money. Sometimes going into debt makes financial sense, as is often the case with student loans. On average, the higher earning potential you get from a college degree more than compensates for the interest you have to pay on your loans (especially since that interest is artificially low, at least for federally guaranteed loans). Sometimes you have no choice, like in the case of a medical emergency: it makes sense to go into debt, get healthy, and try to pay the debt back later—just like it makes sense for a country to go into debt to fight a war, end the war on acceptable terms, and pay down the debt later. Sometimes it's just a bad idea all around, like borrowing money from a loan shark to gamble at a casino.

The same goes for businesses. Ross Perot won 19 percent of the popular vote in the 1992 presidential election by promising to use his business expertise to balance the budget. In 2011, presidential candidate Mitt Romney also claimed his business experience taught him how to balance budgets.[12] But what many people don't realize is that debt is a routine part of business. In this context, the government is more like a family business than like a simple family. In a family business, it makes sense to borrow money if you can invest it in a worthwhile project, such as opening a new retail location. This is even more true if some family members are unemployed, because then the new investment can also provide them with work, making both the family business and the family members better off. (It can also make sense to provide retirement benefits to grandparents who have retired from the family business, rather than kicking them out on the street.) What's true for family businesses is equally true for big business. Put together, the companies in the S&P 500* have much more debt than equity, which means that most of their assets are funded by borrowed money. They regularly borrow huge amounts of money to invest in new projects, or even just to buy back stock from their existing investors in a piece of financial engineering. And no one expects these companies to ever pay off all of their debt; if they did, investors would criticize them for not having *enough* debt.[13] What businesses are good at—and governments are often not good at—is figuring out when they can borrow money at low interest rates and invest it to earn higher returns.

So even though the government isn't like a family or like a business, there is an important lesson to be learned from this analogy. Borrowing money isn't necessarily a bad thing. What makes it good or bad is what you spend it on. For a government, it's usually a good idea to borrow money to pay for productive investments. What's a "productive investment" is a valid question. For example, roads and bridges are often considered good investments because they help the economy—but not the famous "Bridge to Nowhere."[14] And even if roads are good investments, people disagree about whether the government or the private sector should build them.

There's one more problem with the government-as-family analogy. The government isn't supposed to act like a family: that's the point of having a government. The government exists to solve problems that families and businesses can't handle on their own, like

---

* The S&P 500 is a stock market index that includes 500 of the largest companies in the United States.

national defense; to do that, it pools resources from those families and businesses. In the economic sphere, this means that the government should take action to cushion the impact of economic downturns. In a recession, families have less money and consume less, causing businesses to produce less and delay investments, reducing the number of jobs and forcing families to "tighten their belts" even more. This downward spiral can continue for years, especially if the government also "tightens its belt" by trying to balance the budget despite lower tax revenues, as occurred at the beginning of the Great Depression. Government spending should go up, if only because more people qualify for welfare and other entitlement programs, and tax revenues should go down, if only because people's incomes are lower; this will require larger deficits and more borrowing.[15] One of the purposes of having a government is to take actions that are good for society as a whole but that families and businesses won't make on their own, which in this case implies higher deficits. (The corollary is that the government should raise taxes or cut spending during a boom—something governments have never been good at doing.)

THE GOVERNMENT IS BROKE

It's fine to say that families, businesses, and governments should all borrow money when they can invest it productively. But what about when you can't come up with the cash to make your monthly payments, you've hit your credit limit, and you can't borrow any more money? After taking over the leadership of the House of Representatives in early 2011, John Boehner said, discussing the prospect that spending cuts would lead to job losses in the federal government, "If some of those jobs are lost in this, so be it. We're broke."[16] In introducing their budget proposal that spring, the House Budget Committee, led by Representative Paul Ryan, claimed that the nation was "on the brink of bankruptcy."[17] Representative and presidential candidate Ron Paul went further, saying, "The fundamentals show this country is bankrupt."[18]

This sounds serious. Being broke generally means that you don't have enough cash on hand to make your debt payments, which means you have to default. Default can mean bad things, like losing your house or, in some cases, having your wages garnished. And there is often a hard limit on how far a family can go into debt. If you lose your job and a medical emergency wipes out your savings, at some point no one will let you borrow any more money, and you will have to declare bankruptcy.

The rules are different for sovereign governments, however. If you take out a mortgage, there are laws that govern what happens if you don't pay, and the bank can go to court to enforce those laws; declaring bankruptcy gives you some protection from your creditors, but also gives a court the power to distribute your assets. Because there is no international government, there are no equivalent laws for sovereign government debt.[19] So even if a government is unable or unwilling to raise enough taxes to make its debt payments, it has other options. For one thing, an advanced industrial nation like the United States often borrows most or all of the money it needs in its own currency: the Treasury Department sells bonds in exchange for U.S. dollars, and when the bonds mature it redeems them with U.S. dollars. One option, used many times in the past in various countries, is for the government simply to create more of its own currency and use that to pay off its debt.

In addition to raising taxes or printing money, a sovereign government has a third option for dealing with its debt: it can renege. A Treasury bond is just a promise to pay by the federal government, and governments break their promises all the time. The U.S. government's promise not to renege on its debt is a special kind of promise—one that has rarely been broken, and that financial markets around the world assume will not be broken—but not all governments' promises have that status.[20] In the modern world, it is unusual for a government to simply default and turn its back on its creditors, because then it will have little or no access to credit. More often, they *restructure* their debt: they extend the maturity (giving themselves more time to pay it off), lower the interest rate, pay it off with new bonds instead of cash, or do some combination of all three. The terms might be unilaterally dictated by the government, but more often they are negotiated with its creditors. Ultimately, as in many negotiations, it's a question of power.[21] No one can legally compel a government to pay debts it doesn't want to pay. But if the government needs more cash, or just the credit necessary to finance international trade, it can't simply walk away from its creditors; it has to negotiate a deal that they find acceptable. So while governments do sometimes default on their debts, they have considerably more control over the outcome than a family or a business.

This doesn't mean that default is an easy way out. A government default is equivalent to a tax on bondholders; since it makes them immediately poorer, it will hurt the domestic economy (unless all the bondholders are foreigners[22]). A default or even a successful restructuring will make investors less willing to buy that government's bonds, and therefore it will have to pay higher interest rates in the future—which will often raise interest rates for private borrowers. After a default, investors are more likely to lend money in a currency that the government cannot control. So, for example, the United Kingdom might not be able to borrow money by selling bonds denominated in pounds, and might instead have to issue bonds denominated in U.S. dollars or in euros. But once again, this is a choice. Governments deciding whether or not to default or restructure have to weigh the short-term benefits of lower debt payments against the short-term costs of economic disruption and the long-term costs of higher interest rates.

In any case, a government can only get to this point if it loses the ability to borrow money on acceptable terms. Otherwise, it could always make its current debt payments by borrowing more money, just like businesses roll over their debt by issuing new debt. And for this reason, the United States is far from going broke. For all of our long-term fiscal problems, the federal government still has just about the best credit in the world, with both short- and long-term interest rates at historic lows in 2011. Even after Treasury bonds were downgraded by Standard & Poor's in August 2011, the markets responded by driving interest rates even further down to record low levels.[23]

There is some evidence that, if we do nothing about our long-term deficits, interest rates will eventually go up, making it more expensive for the government to borrow money.[24] But even in that case, any decisions we make about paying our debts will be based on economic factors—whether it would be better to borrow money at high interest rates, raise taxes, or restructure our debt—not on whether or not we can come up with the cash. The only thing that could plausibly cause the United States to default would be a refusal by Congress to raise the debt ceiling. Then, no matter how many investors want to buy Treasury bonds, the Treasury Department would be unable to increase its total borrowing. At that point, the government would have to start running a balanced budget immediately or default on its debt payments.[25] But apart from a failure to raise the debt ceiling—the fiscal equivalent of shooting ourselves in the foot—bankruptcy is one thing the federal government does not have to worry about today.

OUR GRANDCHILDREN WILL PAY

Inaugurating his bipartisan fiscal commission in 2010, President Obama said, "We have an obligation to future generations to address our long-term, structural deficits, which threaten to hobble our economy and leave our children and grandchildren with a mountain of debt."[26] The idea that growing deficits are unfair to future generations is another one on which Democrats and Republicans can agree. In 2010, Republican presidential candidate Mitt Romney wrote, "I cannot fathom the argument that it's fine to spend more than we earn year after year. Passing on ever-increasing debt to our children is not just bad policy, it is morally wrong."[27] Now this sounds like a compelling argument: high deficits today mean that we are spending money that our grandchildren will have to pay back.

There is something to this idea, but not as much as one might think. First of all, the simple fact that our government runs a deficit today does not by itself make us any richer or our grandchildren any poorer. The material well-being of a society depends on the total volume of goods and services that are available for consumption. When the government borrows money, it is not reaching into the distant future and eating apple pies that otherwise our grandchildren would get to eat. Instead, it is borrowing money from people who are alive today—people who prefer to invest their money in government bonds rather than eating more apple pie.

To simplify things, imagine for a moment that the United States is a closed economy—one that has no interactions with the outside world. The federal government needs cash to pay for whatever it does—building roads, managing national parks, protecting the country from asteroids, and so on. One way to do this is taxing everyone. But there's another option: selling bonds to people who have cash left over after consuming all they want. In two generations, the government decides to pay off its debt. To do that, it raises taxes and pays the additional cash to the bondholders' grandchildren (who have since inherited the Treasury bonds). We have deferred the taxes from now to our grandchildren, but as a whole their generation hasn't lost anything. The transfer of cash among our grandchildren—from taxpayers to bondholders—leaves them, as a group, no better or worse off than before. (And that transfer just balances the transfer in our generation, where the bondholders' cash pays for services that we all enjoy or for public investments that benefit future generations.)

Although this picture captures the basics, it's too simplistic in a few ways. One is that whether future generations are better or worse off depends on what the government does with the money it borrows. If the government spends money on something, how it pays for it doesn't matter to our grandchildren (as a whole). But what it spends the money on does matter. Our descendants' prosperity depends on the economy that we leave to them, which depends on the investments that we make between now and then. From an economic perspective, families have two choices for what to do with their money: consumption or saving. Savings flow through the financial system to businesses, which invest it in equipment, factories, and other things that are required for higher production. So as a generation, we can either consume our income, making us happier now, or we can invest it, increasing the economic growth that will eventually benefit our grandchildren.

When the government borrows money, this can reduce the amount of money available for businesses to invest. But the government doesn't just take that money out to a big field and burn it: it spends it on the priorities set by the political system. If it makes productive investments, the economy as a whole will benefit and all of our grandchildren will be a little better off. If instead it spends the money on "consumption"—for example, buying health care for people—this can reduce the amount of investment by our generation, making all of our grandchildren a little worse off. In this context, government spending on health care sounds bad for future generations, because borrowing is used to finance consumption today rather than investment for tomorrow. But this has to be weighed against the policy reasons for government health care programs, which can foster a healthier, more productive workforce and provide valuable insurance benefits to the population as a whole. In short, what the government spends its money on matters more than how it finances that spending.

The other issue is that the United States is not a closed economy. When the government sells bonds, the buyers aren't just Americans, but also investors around the world—who are more than happy to buy Treasuries, since they are widely considered the safest assets available. But this means that if our grandchildren want to pay down the national debt, they will have to transfer money overseas to the grandchildren of the non-Americans who are buying Treasury bonds today. (In practice, most of the buying is done by foreign governments and institutions, but that doesn't make a difference here.) That looks like it's making us richer and our descendants poorer: we can borrow money from overseas and eat more apple pie today, while they will have to ration apple pie so they can pay off our debts. But things aren't necessarily so bad. Businesses borrow money from "outsiders" all the time, meaning they have to dedicate some of their future profits to paying back their bondholders, but no one thinks that makes it a bad idea. Government borrowing from abroad to finance investment can be good for our grandchildren; borrowing from abroad to finance consumption, by contrast, shifts the burden of paying for that consumption to them.* In addition, because the

---

* There is one theory, called "Ricardian equivalence" after the economist David Ricardo but most closely associated with the economist Robert Barro, that says that even in this case our grandchildren are no worse off. According to that theory, if the government borrows money for consumption today, each person will anticipate that taxes will have to go up in the future to pay back that borrowing. Therefore, people in aggregate will reduce private consumption by the same amount that the government increases public consumption; they will save the extra money, passing it down to their grandchildren to pay the eventual taxes. By the same logic, attempts to stimulate the economy will necessarily fail, since people will automatically increase saving to compensate for tax cuts or spending increases. Most economists are skeptical that people actually behave this way; in any case, the effect is likely to only partially offset current fiscal policy. Barro presented the modern theory of Ricardian equivalence in Robert J. Barro, "Are Government Bonds Net Wealth?," *Journal of Political Economy* 82, no. 6 (1974): 1095–1117. For an overview and conventional assessment of

government can sell bonds to foreign investors, every extra dollar of government borrowing does not automatically mean a dollar less in private sector investment. Finally, although foreign holdings of debt issued by Americans (including households, businesses, and governments) represent money that will have to be sent overseas in the future, total foreign investments in the United States are almost matched by American investments in other countries; our rising debts to foreigners simply reflect, in part, the globalization of the world economy.[28]

Still, we cannot be confident that the federal government is investing the money that it raises overseas in projects that will increase long-term productivity—in particular, we know that a large proportion of government spending consists of transfers to the elderly—so current deficits could force our grandchildren to pay higher taxes without giving them any commensurate economic benefits. Economists Laurence Kotlikoff, Alan Auerbach, and Jagadeesh Gokhale developed a way of calculating how the costs and benefits of fiscal policy are spread over generations.[29] This technique, called "generational accounting," predicts that if current policies continue indefinitely and the national debt must be paid down someday, future generations will have to pay much higher taxes or receive much lower transfers than people who are alive today.[30] But generational accounting involves a couple of major complications. First, like any economic calculation that involves long periods of time, it requires us to place a weight (discount rate) on cash flows that will occur in the distant future, and its results depend heavily on that weight.[31] Second, the tax differential between current generations and unborn generations results in part from the extreme assumption that the burden of policy change will fall entirely on the latter and not on the former.

Even if borrowing money from overseas to finance Social Security and Medicare spending does impose a burden on future gen-

Ricardian equivalence, see Douglas W. Elmendorf and N. Gregory Mankiw, "Government Debt," chapter 25 in John B. Taylor and Michael Woodford, eds., *Handbook of Macroeconomics*, vol. 1 (Elsevier, 1999), pp. 1640–59. For a recent overview of empirical studies, see Oliver Röhn, "New Evidence on the Private Saving Offset and Ricardian Equivalence," OECD Economics Department Working Paper 762, May 6, 2010, pp. 5–6.

erations, that doesn't necessarily make transfers to the elderly a bad thing. Since Social Security and Medicare are self-funded systems (to different degrees), the "problem" could be framed not as excessive spending today but as insufficient payroll taxes in the past (when current beneficiaries were working). Policies that reduce transfers to the elderly also affect the young and the unborn: for example, without Medicare, working-age adults would have to spend more money taking care of their parents, leaving less to spend on their children. More generally, there is nothing intrinsically wrong with a system that transfers income from the young to the old, even if it may not be the best thing for economic growth (since investments in the young will have a greater impact on future productivity).[32]

This is especially true since, as a group, our grandchildren are likely to be richer than we are, just as we are richer than our grandparents were.[33] A society's standard of living is determined by the total volume of goods and services it can produce per person. The secret to a higher standard of living is productivity: if the average worker can produce more each year than the year before, then there will be more goods and services for everyone. Labor productivity has risen consistently since the nineteenth century;[34] productivity has quadrupled, growing at an average rate of 2.3 percent per year, since the Bureau of Labor Statistics began collecting data in 1947.[35] Over a fifty-year period—about two generations—productivity should roughly triple, which should more than compensate for the fact that a growing proportion of the population will be retired.

Rising productivity, of course, doesn't mean that everyone will become more productive, or that wages will grow as fast as productivity. (In fact, median wages have been stagnant for the past decade or longer.) Our grandchildren may face problems of inequality, just as we do today. Higher borrowing from overseas today means that our grandchildren will have to send a larger share of their output overseas in the form of interest payments, which will partly offset the benefits of higher productivity. So the growth rate of the American standard of living could be lower in the future than it has been in the past.[36]

How much our grandchildren should have relative to us is ultimately a moral question, and one without a clear answer. Assuming that we want them to be better off than we are, a large national debt is one thing we should worry about, but far from the only thing. We should also worry about leaving them a productive economy and a healthy planet to live on, which means investing in the physical, environmental, and educational infrastructure that they will inherit. Simply invoking the interests of future generations does not provide easy answers to any of our fiscal policy questions.

DEBT HURTS ECONOMIC GROWTH

Back in 1993, when President Clinton decided to make deficit reduction his top economic priority, he feared that high government deficits were harming economic growth. Lower deficits, he argued, would make the economy grow faster, helping to balance the budget and providing more money for the social programs he promised during his campaign. The boom of the 1990s seems to support this argument, but economic cycles have so many possible causes that it is impossible to prove that the 1993 budget act led directly to higher growth.

The impact of deficits on the economy is a controversial and complex topic, largely because different people claim that deficits have *opposing* effects on the economy. Some people (often but not always Democrats) argue that deficit spending in a recession will increase growth by injecting more money into the economy and thereby stimulating economic activity. Other people (often but not always Republicans) argue that when the government borrows large amounts of money, it forces up interest rates for everyone, hampering economic growth. The problem is that both schools of thought are correct; which effect will win out depends on the circumstances.

In a recession, it is generally true that increasing government spending or cutting taxes increases short-term economic growth. As the economy slows down, households reduce their consumption and businesses lay off workers, pushing the economy into a vicious cycle: in the 2007–2009 recession, consumption fell by more than 3 percent, and businesses responded by eliminating almost nine million jobs.[37] In these circumstances, higher government spending or lower taxes will put more money in people's bank accounts, encouraging them to spend more and thereby motivating businesses to invest and hire more, reversing the vicious cycle. This was the goal of the stimulus packages passed in 2008 and 2009 under the Bush and Obama administrations; without the 2009 stimulus, businesses would probably have eliminated an additional one to three million jobs.[38] Higher spending and lower taxes both mean larger deficits, but if the economy returns to its full potential as soon as possible, economic growth will bring the higher tax revenues that will make it possible to balance the budget. (By the same logic, lower spending or higher taxes—which are necessary to reduce a budget deficit—can reduce economic growth.)

Considered on their own, however, all other things being equal, deficits can hurt economic growth. Deficits mean that the Treasury Department must sell its bonds in the financial markets, where they compete with all other bonds, which represent companies building factories, families buying houses, college students paying their tuition, and so on. More government borrowing means more demand for bond investors' money, so the price of that money—the interest rate on loans—goes up, at least in theory. Therefore, as government deficits increase, bond investors will want higher interest rates from the Treasury Department and from all the other people and companies trying to borrow money. Higher interest rates make it harder for companies to build factories, families to buy houses, and students to go to college—all things that tend to be good for the economy. This phenomenon, known as "crowding out," can result in lower growth.

To recap, then, budget deficits can hurt economic growth—but the things that create deficits (higher spending and lower taxes) can help economic growth.* This is not very helpful as a guide to policy, but it is helpful to politicians, who can pick whichever side of the issue is convenient at the time. In 1993, both President Clinton's Democratic economists and the Republican chair of the Federal Reserve, Alan Greenspan, agreed that deficit-produced high inter-

---

* According to Ricardian equivalence, however, neither will have any effect. Increased spending or lower taxes don't matter because households will increase their saving in anticipation of higher taxes in the future; higher government borrowing doesn't matter because that increased saving means there is more money available in the bond market.

est rates were the major constraint on the economy, and therefore they made deficit reduction their top priority.[39] In the economic slowdown of 2001, when deficits were no longer a political issue, President George W. Bush argued for cutting taxes as a way to boost economic growth.

Today, however, when deficits are high *and* economic growth is slow, many people debate which policy is better: increasing spending and cutting taxes to stimulate the economy at the cost of increasing the deficit, or cutting spending and increasing taxes to reduce the deficit at the cost of hurting economic growth. Although the conventional wisdom is that deficit cutting will only make a slowdown worse, it is theoretically possible that, in some circumstances, a "fiscal contraction" can help produce growth.[40] Much of the policy debate for the past two years has been about precisely this issue. Democrats today usually argue that slow growth calls for more economic stimulus, especially with unemployment well above the levels that could cause inflation to accelerate;[41] Republicans today usually argue that high deficits are weighing on the economy and must be slashed, preferably through spending cuts. (These positions are not set in stone, however: in 1984, Democratic presidential candidate Walter Mondale argued that large deficits were raising interest rates, reducing investment, and crippling economic growth—although he thought that higher taxes would be the solution.)[42]

Fortunately, there is a way to judge this debate: looking at the numbers. If high deficits are harming the economy, as was believed in the early 1990s, that should be showing up in higher interest rates demanded by the "bond market vigilantes." Yet interest rates have remained stubbornly low, averaging barely over 3 percent in 2011—and showing no relationship to increases in the national debt (see Figure 5-1).[43] These rates have also been far lower than in the periods following previous recessions.[44] Low interest rates generally mean that the financial markets are more worried about low economic growth than about high deficits. In effect, the bond market has been encouraging the federal government to borrow more money by lending it so cheaply.[45]

That isn't quite the end of the story, however. Even if large deficits are not showing up in high interest rates today, the theory of crowding out says that they will show up eventually. Today's low interest

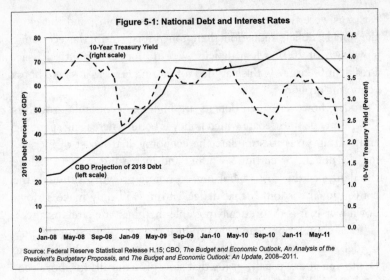

Figure 5-1: National Debt and Interest Rates

Source: Federal Reserve Statistical Release H.15; CBO, *The Budget and Economic Outlook, An Analysis of the President's Budgetary Proposals*, and *The Budget and Economic Outlook: An Update, 2008–2011*.

rates are partly due to economic weakness itself: as long as consumers aren't buying a lot, businesses won't make new investments, which means less demand for money and therefore lower interest rates. As the economy recovers, interest rates should go up, and if the federal government continues to borrow large amounts of money, that could push interest rates up even faster. In 2011, Macroeconomic Advisers, a leading economic consulting firm cofounded by former Federal Reserve governor Laurence Meyer, projected that interest rates on ten-year Treasury notes would rise to 8.75 percent by 2021 because of concerns about deficits.[46] But reducing the deficit still might not increase economic growth. Macroeconomic Advisers estimated that the deficit reduction plan proposed by the bipartisan National Commission on Fiscal Responsibility and Reform (established by President Obama in 2012) would *reduce* economic growth, increasing unemployment by almost 2 percentage points. In the short term at least, the economic benefits of reducing the deficit would be outweighed by the costs.

In the long term, we can't be sure at what point the national debt imposes a significant drag on the economy. A recent paper by economists Carmen Reinhart and Kenneth Rogoff has been widely cited as evidence that bad things will happen if the national debt exceeds 90 percent of GDP.[47] They show that growth rates tend to be somewhat lower (about 1 percentage point) for countries with debt over that threshold than for countries with debt below it.[48] But while this may be a reasonable warning sign, it is hard to know what it means for the United States because even their findings for advanced economies are the averages over sixty years of twenty different countries—nineteen of which did not enjoy the particular benefits of issuing the world's reserve currency.[49] (Reinhart and Rogoff also find no evidence that higher debt levels will cause higher inflation.)[50]

In general, higher interest rates and resulting lower growth are a valid reason to worry about the national debt. If we do nothing about our long-term deficits, they could have real economic consequences before the end of this decade. But that does not mean that we have to slash government spending or raise taxes *right now*, when the economy is weak, unemployment is high, and interest rates are low. From a purely economic standpoint, the best policy is to stimulate the economy (and increase the deficit) now while simultaneously committing to deficit-reducing policies that will kick in later, when sustained growth has resumed.*[51] Politically, however, such an agreement is almost impossible to imagine because it requires Congress to do two seemingly contradictory things at the same time—and counts on Congress not to undo the painful part of the deal (deficit reduction) after the painless part (stimulus) has already happened. Given our current political system, it is likely that we will have to make tougher choices.

NO ONE WILL LEND US MONEY

From the time Greece adopted the euro as its currency in 2001, its economy boomed. As a member of the eurozone, its credit was considered almost as good as Germany's, despite a national debt hovering around 100 percent of GDP.[52] The government and the private

---

* Another argument for deficit reduction later is that then the Federal Reserve will be able to counteract the contractionary (antigrowth) effects of deficit reduction through expansionary (pro-growth) monetary policy—that is, lowering interest rates. That would be very difficult today because the interest rate that the Federal Reserve controls directly—the rate at which banks borrow money from each other for short periods of time—is close to zero, and therefore cannot be lowered any further.

sector were both able to borrow money cheaply, allowing the country to grow much faster than Europe as a whole through 2007; that growth prevented debt levels from climbing too much relative to the economy. Then, in 2008, the global financial crisis sent the world into recession. The Greek government responded with unpopular budget cuts, fueling street riots. In 2009, a new government came to power and announced that the annual budget deficit would be 12.7 percent of GDP—over twice as high as claimed by the previous government.* (It eventually turned out to be over 15 percent.) With growing deficits and the economy still shrinking, bond investors began to worry that they might never get their money back: interest rates soared, making it harder for the government to borrow the money it needed to pay off debts that were coming due. A default would have meant steep losses for the financial institutions that held Greek debt and could have triggered another financial panic, especially since Greece was considered a leading indicator of what might happen in other struggling European countries such as Portugal, Ireland, Spain, and Italy. To prevent this potential nightmare scenario, in May 2010 the European Union and the International Monetary Fund came to the rescue with an emergency loan package that required Greece to cut spending and raise taxes even further, generating more popular unrest. But with the deficit still above 10 percent of GDP, the national debt rising, unemployment over 14 percent, and no solution in sight, the bond market again became skeptical about Greece's prospects. Interest rates spiked above 25 percent in 2011, forcing the country to enact even more "austerity" measures and ask for another emergency bailout.[53]

This is a "fiscal crisis." Instead of large government debts slowly weighing down the economy through higher interest rates, everything goes bad all of a sudden: investors stop lending money, the government can't sell new bonds to pay off its old ones, and it either

---

* *Der Spiegel* reported in 2010 that the Greek government had earlier used derivative transactions with the investment bank Goldman Sachs to hide the true size of its budget deficits and comply with the requirements for membership in the eurozone. Beat Balzli, "How Goldman Sachs Helped Greece to Mask Its True Debt," *Der Spiegel*, February 8, 2010. See also Tracy Alloway, "Goldman's Trojan Currency Swap," Alphaville (blog), *Financial Times*, February 9, 2010.

defaults or gets bailed out by an international organization, usually the International Monetary Fund. In either case, unable to borrow easily, the government must slash spending and raise taxes simply to continue functioning.

A fiscal crisis is what happens when investor psychology reaches a tipping point. The experience of the past two decades has shown us that stock markets and housing markets can swing up or down rapidly based on changes in investor sentiment; the same holds true for bond markets. For years, the market can look on serenely as Greece runs large deficits on top of an already large national debt, confident that a booming economy will solve all problems. Then one day something happens—growth projections (which are never particularly stable) get revised downward, interest rate projections get revised upward, the deficit gets revised upward, the government fails to pass a measure that investors were counting on, or something else—and suddenly no one wants to buy Greek bonds. Bond rating agencies that had blindly recommended Greek debt during the preceding boom now start downgrading it. Rising interest rates exacerbate fears of default, making rates rise even faster.

But that's Greece. Could it happen here?

The problem with the theory of fiscal crises, like any tipping point theory, is that it is impossible to disprove. During the recent financial crisis, every time someone warned that interest rates were about to go up, they remained historically low.[54] But no matter how many times you cry wolf, a wolf could still show up. Greece, after all, is suffering from an acute fiscal crisis that is dramatically lowering living standards for its citizens and putting the eurozone itself in jeopardy. As a matter of logic, the United States is not immune to fiscal crises: at some point, if the debt is big enough, the deficit is high enough, and the chances of reducing the deficit appear slim enough, we could go the way of Greece. It probably isn't anytime soon. But no one knows when it could happen.

No one knows because there is no other country in the world quite like the United States—and there never has been one, either, for several reasons. Two centuries of fiscal responsibility count for something. So do a generally healthy economy and the ability to borrow money in our own currency (which means that, unlike Greece, we have the option of devaluing the dollar to make the debt easier to pay off[55]). But what really matter are our unique status as the world's safe haven in a financial storm and the dollar's unique status as the world's reserve currency.

For a moment at the peak of the recent economic boom, there were rumblings that the dollar might be losing its privileged place in the international economy. In 2007, superstar rapper Jay-Z released a music video in which he flashed wads of 500-euro bills, and rumors circulated that supermodel Gisele Bündchen was insisting that she be paid in euros.[56] But the ensuing financial crisis showed that the world was not yet ready to move on from the dollar. In uncertain economic times, it's dollars that people want: not euros, with Europe facing a succession of sovereign debt crises that could split the eurozone apart; not yen, with Japan entering its third decade of slow growth and with government debt at the highest levels in the industrialized world; and not yuan, with an autocratic government in power in China. In general, wealthy governments and central banks store their rainy-day money in U.S. dollar assets. And every time the world's financial markets wobble, investors dump their risky assets and buy U.S. Treasury bonds—never more so than in the panic of 2008–2009, when the price of everything else went down and the price of Treasuries went up so high that investors were actually paying the U.S. government to hold their money for them.[57] The concentration of U.S. debt holdings among central banks does come with a risk, however. Today, Treasury interest rates are heavily influenced by a relatively small group of investors who care much more about safety than about their economic returns. So if these central banks decide that the United States is no longer particularly safe, interest rates could rise quickly—faster than if our bonds were held only by "ordinary" investors.

As long as the dollar is the dominant global safe haven, however, it's hard to envision the United States experiencing a severe, sudden fiscal crisis at our current debt levels. There may be some debt threshold where investor sentiment is likely to turn against Treasury bonds rapidly—but it is probably higher than for other countries. Things would have to go badly before investors would pull the plug on the United States, and they would have to go worse than anywhere else. Most major shocks that would severely damage the American economy would also hurt the other contenders for reserve currency status; the financial crisis, for example, started in the United States but rapidly spread to the rest of the world, and demand for Treasuries went up as a result. To lose our privileged position quickly, we would probably have to fumble it away—for example by failing to increase the debt ceiling and then defaulting on our debts (and even that might not do it[58]).

Like all good things, however, our current status will not last forever. Empires rise and fall, whether military or economic. As emerging market countries mature, they may shift toward more domestic investments, reducing overall demand for dollars.[59] Someday, perhaps, China will become the world's safe haven, although that would require major changes in both its political and economic systems. Confidence in the euro is currently falling, not rising, but another possibility is that the ongoing European sovereign debt crisis will force fiscally weaker countries out of the eurozone, leaving a smaller nucleus centered on Germany; this new euro could then be a serious competitor for reserve currency status. Perhaps the most likely possibility is that we will enter a multipolar monetary world where central banks and government investment funds hold different mixes of dollars, euros, and yuan, depending on who their major trading partners are. In that case, the dollar would still be an important international currency, but demand for dollar assets would be lower than it is today.[60] This is unlikely to happen in the next three years, in part because it is difficult for central banks and international markets to shift away from dollars.[61] But it could happen in the next thirty, at which point our unique fiscal buffer could melt away. Over the next few decades, we may very well become more like an ordinary rich country—one that could have trouble adding continual deficits to already high debt levels. That should give us time to put our fiscal house in order before we become vulnerable to a Greek-style crisis.

Or does it?

NO ONE WILL SEE IT COMING

When 2007 began, Ireland was booming. Its economy had been growing at an average of 7 percent per year for a decade, making it one of the richest countries in Europe. Newfound prosperity fueled a surge in housing construction that helped keep the economy expanding; at its peak, construction employed one in five Irish workers. Irish banks grew rapidly during the boom, gathering deposits from around the world and lending most of them to Irish developers and homebuyers. Rapid economic growth reduced the national debt from over 90 percent of GDP in the early 1990s to just 12 percent by 2007.[62]

But then housing prices began to fall, American investment banks started to fail, the global financial markets froze up, and suddenly Ireland's now massive banks were unable to roll over their debt. As Ireland plunged into recession—the economy would shrink by 10 percent—the Irish government decided to guarantee the banks' liabilities (relying in part on a Merrill Lynch memo insisting that the banks were sound),[63] effectively shifting their debts onto the backs of the government and its taxpayers. Government debt soared to more than 60 percent of GDP by 2010 as the banks' financial condition deteriorated, requiring a steady drip of government money.[64] With a stagnant economy and unemployment over 13 percent, Ireland could no longer grow its way out of its economic problems. In November 2010, the Irish government had to request a bailout package from other European countries and the International Monetary Fund. But government debt continued to grow—to more than 90 percent of GDP in 2011—leading the rating agency Moody's to downgrade Ireland's credit rating to junk bond status amid fears that yet another bailout would be necessary.[65]

According to our conservative scenario (in which the income and estate tax cuts are made permanent), the U.S. national debt should grow from close to 70 percent of GDP today to around 76 percent of GDP in 2021.[66] For the reasons described in the previous section, we think that these debt levels are unlikely to trigger a severe fiscal crisis during this period. But Ireland's national debt was only *12 percent* of GDP as recently as 2007. The moral of the Irish story is that bad things can happen quickly.

All projections about future deficits and debt depend heavily on assumptions—about government policy, about economic conditions, and about the state of the world. We believe the Congressional Budget Office generally does a good job of coming up with reasonable forecasts of policy decisions and economic trends (and its forecasts are consistent with and as accurate as those of private sector forecasters), but no one can see the future.[67] This creates two types of risks. The first is that economic growth will be lower than expected. For example, at the peak of budgetary optimism in May 2001, when politicians were talking about surpluses for decades, the economy had already entered a moderate slowdown that was lowering tax revenues and reducing surpluses. The second type of risk is that something completely unexpected can happen. In May 2001, no one could see two specific things: the terrorist attacks of September 11, 2001, which helped tip the slowing economy into a mild recession,[68] led directly to a buildup in national security spending and the Afghanistan War, and led indirectly to the Iraq War; and the financial meltdown of 2007–2009, which triggered the worst economic crisis since the Great Depression. September 11 (with the political decisions that followed it) and especially the financial crisis together added trillions of dollars to the national debt.

Every economic projection involves uncertainty, and if growth is below expectations, deficits will be larger. But forecasts may be too low as often as they are too high; forecasts in the mid-1980s tended to overestimate future growth, while those in the mid-1990s tended to underestimate it.[69] But the second type of risk—large, unexpected shocks—seems to be heavily weighted toward the downside, at least as far as the federal budget is concerned. We have seen the impact of unforeseen terrorist attacks, wars that turned out to be far more expensive than promised, and a near collapse of the global financial system; by the middle of 2011, the U.S. economy was still not as big as it was at the end of 2007.[70] Most of the other surprises that could significantly affect the federal budget also seem to be of the nasty variety: pandemic, natural catastrophe, or nuclear meltdown. The biggest positive "surprise" in recent memory was the rapid collapse of the Soviet bloc at the end of the 1980s, which allowed both the George H. W. Bush and Clinton administrations to reduce defense spending. This "peace dividend," however, is unlikely to be repeated, since current projections already assume the planned drawdown of forces in Iraq and Afghanistan. In short, this second category of risk is asymmetric: if something is going to suddenly shift the national debt one way or the other, it is more likely to go up than to go down.

The fact that bad things can happen has two major implications. First, a major shock can cause a rapid jump in the national debt, bringing a country that much closer to a fiscal crisis, as happened in Ireland. Second, in order to cope with a major shock, a country may need to rapidly increase spending, cut taxes, or take on additional debts. In 2008–2009, the United States government was able to prevent the financial system from completely collapsing because it could commit trillions of dollars to back up major financial institutions and protect them from running out of money.[71] The government was also able to deploy close to $1 trillion in new spending and tax cuts that helped limit the severity and duration of the recession.[72] The federal government was able to take these extraordinary measures for two reasons. First, it had "fiscal space": there was still a wide gap between the national debt and the level at which lenders might get nervous and stop buying Treasury bonds.[73] Without sufficient fiscal space, the government might not have been able to bail out the financial system, and the crisis could have triggered a lasting worldwide depression. Second, the government had barely enough political legitimacy to use that fiscal space: despite the support of President Bush, both presidential candidates, and leaders of both parties, the Troubled Asset Relief Program required two votes (and a plunge in the stock market when the first vote failed) to get through Congress.

Fiscal space matters because you need it as a buffer against the sudden debt increase caused by a crisis and because having that space helps you fight that crisis. This is an idea that Alexander Hamilton would have recognized, although he was more familiar with eighteenth-century wars than with twenty-first-century financial panics. It was brought home to the United Kingdom during the 1956 Suez Canal crisis, when it was forced to withdraw its troops from Egypt—in order to gain needed United States support for an emergency loan from the International Monetary Fund. The final decline of the world's largest empire, it turned out, was marked by a speculative run on the British pound—because pounds were no longer the world's reserve currency.[74]

Unfortunately, it's impossible to know how much fiscal space you have at a given moment. Market sentiments can change rapidly, so you may not realize you are running out of fiscal space until you have none left. A government may be able to borrow at low rates up until a nasty surprise—recession, financial crisis, or discovery that the previous government fudged the numbers—makes interest rates skyrocket.[75] Greece, for example, could borrow money at an interest rate of less than 5 percent as late as November 2009; a year later, it had to pay more than 11 percent; and in 2011 interest rates went above 25 percent.[76] Fiscal space also depends on political factors: whether or not the government is willing to raise taxes in the future to pay off the additional debts it needs to incur now. Since there's no way to know how a government will behave in the future, a country's past behavior—how willing it has been to pay down debt in the past—affects how much investors trust it today. According to an estimate by IMF economists, based on past experience, the United States probably could withstand a shock that increased the national debt by 50 percent of GDP, but probably could not withstand a shock that increased the debt by 100 percent of GDP—at least not without something changing significantly.[77]

Still, 50 percent of U.S. GDP is a lot of money—more than $7 trillion. Do we need to worry? We do know one thing that can add that much to the national debt in a hurry: a financial crisis. As discussed in chapter 3, the recent financial crisis caused our projected national debt level to increase by almost 50 percent of GDP in less than two years.[78] This is a major reason why serious reform of our financial system should be an urgent national priority. With all the rhetoric about the national debt spinning in Washington, you would hope that politicians would at least focus on preventing a repeat of the events that triggered the current debt crisis. But instead, despite some worthwhile provisions, the Dodd-Frank Wall Street Reform and Consumer Protection Act of 2010 left largely intact the highly concentrated, highly leveraged, highly unstable financial system that failed in 2008.[79] Since the 2010 elections, the new Republican majority in the House of Representatives has been working to weaken financial regulation further, cutting the budgets of key regulatory agencies in the name of saving money (even though, in at least one case, the savings go directly to financial institutions, not to reducing the deficit[80]) and thereby increasing the chances of a financial melt-down that could add trillions of dollars to the debt.

A financial crisis is not the only thing that could go wrong. There is the centuries-old cause of budget deficits: war.[81] The Iraq and Afghanistan wars have directly added well over $1 trillion to the national debt in war-related appropriations and interest payments on the additional debt.[82] And Iraq, by historical standards, was a relatively small war, mainly fought with fewer than 200,000 soldiers at any one time. By comparison, over 500,000 soldiers were deployed to Vietnam in 1968–1969, and over 300,000 to Korea in 1951–1953 (although military equipment and health care were much less expensive back then).[83] The national debt will constrain our ability to use military force against overseas threats, whether real or imagined.

Lack of fiscal space and vulnerability to a major shock are serious problems. How much we should worry about them, however, is a difficult question because we don't know how much fiscal space we have—and we don't know how likely we are to suffer a major shock. All other things being equal, more fiscal space is always better, but other things are never equal. When it comes to budgetary policy, it's difficult to balance unpleasant options today—higher taxes or lower spending on services or transfers that people value—against threats that are difficult to quantify and that may not materialize. That doesn't mean that there is a magic quantity of fiscal space that we have to have, but it is another reason why, over the long term, it is important to bring down our government deficits and national debt. Right now, with Europe undergoing its own sovereign debt crises, a slow economy in the United States keeping interest rates low, and no good alternative to the U.S. dollar as a global reserve currency, we could probably cope with a major crisis. Any constraint on the ability of the government to respond to a crisis is likely to be imposed by political forces in Congress, not by the markets. But we should not assume that we will have that capacity forever.

WHAT THE DEBT MEANS TO YOU

Today, with high unemployment and stagnant wages, many families are worried about balancing their own household budgets. Compared to the day-to-day challenges of paying for housing, food, clothing, electricity, education, and health care, the federal government's finances are a distant and unfathomable abstraction. American citizens can be forgiven for not knowing where budget deficits come from and why they matter.

In ordinary times, the national debt has only an indirect, invisible effect on most people's lives: growing debt and continued government borrowing can produce higher interest rates, slowing down economic growth and ultimately making all of us worse off. But there are several ways that the national debt could have a direct impact on the living standards of middle-class Americans.

One possibility is that our political system will stumble along for another decade or two, with deficits growing under the weight of serial tax cuts, demographic shifts, growing health care costs, and government inaction. At the same time, Europe straightens out its debt problems; China not only continues growing but also becomes more democratic and transparent, making it an attractive place for countries to invest their excess cash; and those newly wealthy emerging market countries begin consuming more and saving less, reducing their foreign investments. The Treasury Department needs to borrow more and more money, but faces a global bond market that has less and less appetite for its bonds. As interest rates climb, investors quickly become nervous about the federal government's ability to redeem its rapidly growing pile of outstanding debt; they demand higher interest rates, which spiral up further, and suddenly there is no one willing to lend new money. The Federal Reserve could print new money to pay off the debt, but that would fuel high inflation (and make it harder for us to borrow money in the future). Alternatively, the United States would need an emergency loan, but those loans typically come with strict conditions. One way or another, we would be forced into steep tax increases and spending cuts that would depress the economy, causing a painful contraction in living standards. The result could be widespread unemployment and poverty. This is what Greece is going through today, and it could happen here—though it would take some time for us to reach that point.

Things could also unravel faster. Imagine the financial crisis of 2018, when our largest megabanks, their balance sheets leveraged to the hilt with securities backed by real estate or commodities or whatever the latest bubble is made up of, are suddenly unable to roll over their debt and the global financial system teeters on the edge of collapse. In 2008, it was essentially the enormous credit lines of the United States and some European countries that saved the financial system and the global economy: no one doubted that the Federal Reserve and the Treasury could absorb hundreds of billions of dollars of losses if necessary to keep the system functioning. In 2018, with the national debt twice as high as in 2008 and still growing rapidly (and with Europe still recovering from a decade of sovereign debt crises), investors might have their doubts. More likely, if the current mood continues, Congress will be unwilling to sign a blank check and the government will be unable to bail out the financial system—at least not until things got much worse than they did in 2008. Deficit hysteria in 2011 was almost enough for Congress to force the government into default rather than raise the debt ceiling. By 2018, with a much larger national debt, it will probably be enough for Congress to gamble with a financial crisis rather than bail out the bankers again. Without an immediate, forceful response, the next financial crisis could produce mass chaos and another depression.

Finally, we don't have to wait until 2018. The national debt is already having serious consequences for ordinary people—not direct economic consequences such as higher interest rates, but political consequences. Like it or not, the vast majority of Americans depend in part on the federal government for their basic livelihood, either now or in the future. Most obviously, we rely on Social Security and Medicare to maintain our income and pay for our health care in retirement. It's not just seniors who depend on these programs. If Medicare did not exist, for example, all of us would have to save much more money to pay for health care in old age—and even then we might not be able to buy health insurance, at any price—in addition to supporting our elderly relatives. One in four people rely on Medicaid or the Children's Health Insurance Program for health care.[84] Without the trillion-dollar deficits produced by the recent financial crisis, these popular programs would not be under siege in Washington as they are today. Political posturing over deficits has also made it impossible for the government to do anything to bring down unemployment, which remains at high levels years after the worst of the financial crisis; it has made it difficult to enact even the most minimal policies to help struggling families and preserve valuable human capital, such as extending unemployment insurance benefits for the millions of people who have been out of work for more than six months; and it has even been mobilized for ideological purposes such as cutting off federal funding for Planned Parenthood and crippling enforcement of new financial regulations. In all these ways, deficits are already, through the workings of the political system, taking their toll on ordinary people.

What could a couple decades of this kind of politics look like? Every time growth goes down and deficits go up, we'll cut spending on government services and make modest reductions to Social Security and Medicare benefits. Growth will return as the business cycle turns up, deficits will come down for a few years, and the national debt will fall off the political agenda. But then deficits will come back because of a recession or because of demographic and health care trends. Then we'll repeat the process, cutting spending some more. Each time, services and social insurance programs that lower- and middle-income people depend on will bear the brunt of the spending cuts, eroding away our already modest social safety net. Since many government programs, broadly speaking, distribute money from the rich (who pay more in taxes) to the poor (who benefit more from social insurance), these periodic rounds of deficit cutting will have the net effect of reversing this flow, shifting resources back toward the rich and increasing inequality above its already historic levels. A few rounds of this and the United States will look like a stereotypical Latin American country, with the super-rich living on private islands in the Caribbean, a comfortable professional class that holds the desirable jobs, and a large, struggling lower class.

America does face a long-term debt problem. Today, the specter of the national debt is a blunt instrument that is used to block needed investments and chip away at the modest programs that benefit the poor and the middle class. As long as we face the prospect of significant long-term deficits, our political system will continue to be dominated by hysteria, demagoguery, and delusion. Given the current balance of political power, the most likely outcome is that government deficits will be invoked to slash spending that ordinary people depend on—while continued tax cuts ensure that the deficits never go away. In other words, if we don't solve our debt problem the right way, it is certain to be solved the wrong way. Our challenge is to defuse our national debt crisis in a way that is credible and fair, that maintains our ability to make vital productive investments, that preserves the services that most people value and depend on, and that encourages economic growth for decades to come. It is to that challenge that we now turn.

Six

ARGUING FIRST PRINCIPLES

My friends and I have been coddled long enough by a billionaire-friendly Congress. It's time for our government to get serious about shared sacrifice.

—Warren Buffett, 2011[1]

During the debt ceiling showdown of 2011, Republicans, locked in by the antitax pledge they signed to protect their right flanks, insisted on reducing the deficit entirely through spending cuts. As House Speaker John Boehner said, "With the exception of tax hikes . . . everything is on the table."[2] The Democratic position was that the deficit should be reduced through a combination of spending cuts and tax increases, with President Obama even willing to endorse a package that included $5 in spending cuts for every $1 in tax increases, despite the grumbling of liberals in Congress.[3] Half of the Democrats in the House of Representatives voted against the final bill to increase the debt ceiling, largely out of frustration that it only included spending cuts.[4]

The debt ceiling agreement created a joint congressional "super-committee" to come up with a deficit reduction plan. The members appointed by Republican leaders included Senators Pat Toomey, who previously headed the antitax Club for Growth, and Jon Kyl, who had walked out of debt ceiling negotiations over the issue of tax increases.[5] (All six Republican members signed the antitax pledge.) The supercommittee failed, largely because the two sides again could not agree on the balance between tax increases and spending cuts.

At times, it seemed as if the only thing that mattered to politicians in Washington was one number: the ratio of tax increases to spending cuts. Republicans wanted the ratio to be zero; Democrats wanted it to be 1 to 1, or perhaps 1 to 2, but at least something bigger than zero. The Democrats' position was closer to the preferences of the public, but that leaves aside the bigger question: whether the ratio has any real meaning.[6] As discussed in chapter 4, the distinction between taxes and spending is ambiguous to begin with, since the federal government "spends" hundreds of billions of dollars in the form of tax loopholes. More importantly, the category of "lower spending" could include anything from lower Social Security benefits to fewer fighter planes for the armed forces; the category of "higher tax revenues" could include anything from eliminating the child tax credit to higher tax rates for multimillion-dollar estates. Instead of focusing on the ratio of tax increases to spending cuts, we first have to figure out what we are trying to achieve. Only then can we make specific policy choices.

Any long-term deficit reduction strategy should be based on a few core principles. It should promote long-run economic growth: budget debates boil down to how we allocate scarce resources, and policies that generate more of those resources will ultimately make us better off. It should be fair: if sacrifices are necessary, they should be broadly shared, not concentrated on any one group of people—especially not those who are least able to afford them. And, where possible, it should offer solutions to the major challenges that we face as a society: there is no point in solving our budget problems if, in doing so, we increase our exposure to severe risks, whether insufficient retirement savings, nuclear terrorism, or climate change. These principles may sound appealing to everyone, but different people have different ideas about what promotes economic growth, what fairness means, and what major challenges we face. This chapter spells out what we think they mean and what they imply for government policy.

Our national debt problem will be solved, one way or another. After all, even default is a solution, though probably the worst possible one. How we solve that problem will shape the role of government in twenty-first-century America and the society that our children and grandchildren will live in. We could have a minimal federal government that protects our borders, runs the federal court system, and largely leaves people and companies to their own devices, regulated only by state and local governments. We could have a social-democratic welfare state, where the government ensures that everyone can meet her basic needs, including subsistence, housing, health care, and education, from cradle to grave. Or we could have something in between. Ultimately, any major deficit reduction strategy implies a vision of society. This is all the more reason why any discussion of the national debt must begin with basic principles, not just a list of numbers.

ECONOMIC GROWTH AND EFFICIENCY

We live in a capitalist society, where our collective prosperity depends on the individual decisions made by all the people around us. As Adam Smith described in 1776, when people pursue their own self-interest, they collectively and inadvertently increase the wealth of society as a whole, each person "led by an invisible hand to promote an end which was no part of his intention."[7] When capitalism works, it is because the individual incentives that people face in their everyday lives are well aligned with the overall interests of society: people go to work because they value working (including both their wages and their job satisfaction) more than free time; companies produce goods and services because they can sell them for more than they cost to produce; people buy those goods and services because they value them more than alternative things they could do with their money; and on and on, markets produce more and more of the things that we want. The invisible hand—the ability of independent, self-interested people, interacting through market transactions, to produce outcomes that are beneficial for everyone—is the fundamental principle of modern economics.

This means that most of modern economics is devoted to identifying and explaining the many situations where pure free market systems fail to produce socially beneficial outcomes. The limits of the free market are one of the major conceptual reasons why we need governments. Without some kind of coordinated public policy, the free market would not produce enough public goods such as national defense or clean air, since you cannot sell national defense or clean air to people in a market. In practice, governments also seem to be necessary to ensure certain basic things like property rights, which are an important element of a sound economy. While we need governments, they also introduce distortions into the economy: they change people's behavior from what it would have been otherwise. In theory, that is the point of having a government: for example, since people undervalue the public health benefits of vaccines, we want policies that change their behavior. But public policies are rarely perfect. It is difficult to figure out what the right amount of environmental regulation is, let alone write a set of rules that optimally balances industry costs and public benefits. In the private sector, if a company makes poor products at high cost, there is good reason to believe it will be forced out of business by a competitor that makes better products at lower cost; this is one reason why free markets are supposed to result in better outcomes for everyone. But this dynamic is missing in the public sector, where most institutions are monopolies: neither Congress nor the EPA faces any real competition. Instead, governmental actors are subject to political forces, which even in a reasonably functioning democracy like the United States cannot be trusted to deliver optimal results for society.[8]

In principle, the government should adopt policies that generate social benefits (national defense, clean air) while minimizing the adverse side effects of those policies. In some cases, adverse side effects cannot be escaped. For example, the government needs tax revenues in order to function, and all practical tax systems have some distorting effect on the economy. Higher taxes on wage income make some people less inclined to work because they earn less per hour; but higher taxes also make some other people more inclined to work because they now need to work more hours to meet their financial needs.[9] Increasing taxes on investment income may make people less inclined to save their money (and earn investment returns) and more inclined to use it for current consumption instead.[10] Sometimes these distortions can be justified on other valid grounds: taxes on cigarettes reduce smoking, improving people's health. More often these distortions are justified on other, more questionable grounds: tariffs on imported goods can protect domestic manufacturers, preserving jobs, but at the cost of increasing prices for consumers (and provoking other countries to retaliate by raising taxes on our exports, hurting domestic manufacturers). As a general approximation, if you raise taxes on something, you will get less of it; if you cut taxes, you will get more of it.

The basic principles of a sound tax system—one that raises sufficient revenue with a minimum of economic distortions—are simple. The tax base—the transactions or assets that are being taxed—should be as broad as possible, which allows tax rates to be as low as possible. Gaps in the tax base create an incentive for people to modify their activity to fit into those gaps: if we only tax income from work on weekdays, then suddenly everyone will shift to working as much as possible on Saturdays and Sundays. A smaller tax base also requires higher tax rates to collect the same amount of revenue, and higher tax rates create larger distortions.[11] In addition, the tax system should itself be simple. A more complicated system not only increases administrative and compliance costs for everyone but also creates opportunities for legal or illegal tax evasion. For example, Google funnels its revenues from European operations through a subsidiary in Ireland, a subsidiary in the Netherlands, and another Irish subsidiary located in Bermuda in order to legally avoid billions of dollars in taxes—not only lowering government tax revenues but also diverting large amounts of money to lawyers and accountants whose main business is tax shelters.[12] These principles imply that the best way to raise tax revenues is to close loopholes, which will both broaden the tax base and make the tax code simpler.

But don't taxes always reduce economic growth and cost jobs? This is the backbone of the Republican position that the deficit should be reduced solely through spending cuts, not tax increases. There is a bit of truth to this argument: in the short term, higher taxes, by reducing the amount of money in people's pockets, lower spending and decrease economic activity. But spending cuts have the exact same short-term effect because they also reduce the amount of money in people's pockets. So if the goal is to reduce the deficit, tax increases are no worse or better than spending cuts in the short term—and there is some evidence that spending changes affect the economy more than tax changes.[13]

The core of the antitax argument, popularly known as supply-side

economics, is that higher taxes, especially on the rich and especially
on investment income, will have the long-term effect of hurting economic growth by reducing the incentives to work and to invest. This
is a difficult claim to evaluate empirically because it is hard to separate tax policy from other factors that affect economic growth, but it
appears weak. In the high-tax 1947–1986 period, when the top marginal tax rate ranged from 50 percent to 91 percent, annual real GDP
growth averaged 3.5 percent; in the low-tax 1987–2007 period, when
the top rate ranged from 28 percent to 44 percent, GDP growth averaged 3.0 percent.[14] Detailed empirical studies have generally found
that higher income tax rates do reduce the amount of taxable income
that people generate, but this effect is relatively small—and most of
it occurs not because people work less, but because they engage in
other behavior to avoid paying taxes.[15] Capital gains tax rates have
not ranged as widely as rates on ordinary income, but since 1947, in
years where the top capital gains rate has been 25 percent or higher,
GDP growth has averaged 3.4 percent; in years where the rate has
been less than 25 percent, growth has averaged 3.2 percent (excluding the recent recession).[16] Changes in capital gains taxes do affect
when people choose to sell their assets and realize taxable gains,
but they seem to have little if any impact on actual savings rates.[17]
Finally, the theoretical arguments for low taxes on the rich and on
investment income only hold up if those low taxes do not increase
government deficits. If lower taxes are instead financed by higher
government borrowing, they can hurt economic growth, primarily
because that additional government borrowing makes it harder for
companies to borrow money to finance their investments.[18]

Government spending programs (including tax expenditures,
which function like spending through the tax code) also introduce
potentially damaging distortions into the economy. In general, the
government spends money on things that politicians think are good
for society or for special interests they rely upon to get reelected.[19]
In the first case, politicians can be wrong; in the second, it's unlikely
that favors for special interests will turn out to be good for the country as a whole. As a result, both the federal budget and the tax code
are riddled with line items that favor one interest group or another,
including direct cash payments to farmers, subsidies to produce eth-

anol and mix it into gasoline (and a special tariff to protect domestic ethanol from foreign competitors), energy subsidies for both fossil fuels and renewable energy sources, and weapons programs that even the Pentagon doesn't want.[20] It doesn't make sense to get rid of all targeted spending that directly or indirectly benefits some interest group, since that's largely how the government does what we expect it to do. Furthermore, what looks like a special interest handout to one person can look like sound public policy to another. But as a general principle, payments and subsidies that create economic distortions should be focused on problems that markets fail to solve on their own. For example, being healthy benefits people other than you (because if you are sick, you are more likely to make other people sick), so some investments in public health make sense; and markets will not magically provide food to people who lack the money to pay for it, so some safety net programs such as food stamps make sense.

A solution to our deficit problems should also increase the efficiency and transparency of government operations and the federal budget, which will help us allocate our scarce resources more effectively. Right now most people have very little idea what the government does and how it is funded. This makes it easy for congressional representatives to pad legislation with those notorious "earmarks"—provisions to pay for specific projects in their home districts. In general, the more people are confused about the taxes they pay, the benefits they receive, and the relationship between the two, the more likely they are to question the legitimacy of the government and demand their taxes back—even while insisting on keeping their own particular handouts.[21] To some extent, this is an unavoidable problem, given the breadth and complexity of the modern federal government. But the government is needlessly complicated, with responsibility for similar activities spread among multiple overlapping bureaucracies and congressional committees; for example, derivatives regulation is divided between the Securities and Exchange Commission and the Commodity Futures Trading Commission. The Government Accountability Office has identified dozens of areas of duplication or fragmentation that could potentially yield tens of billions of dollars in savings.[22] Simplifying the tax code and the federal bureaucracy could help reduce the deficit, make the government more efficient, and make the budget easier for everyone to understand, increasing the prospects for sound policies in the future.

FAIRNESS

We may all agree that the burden of reducing our long-term deficits should be distributed fairly, but that leaves open the eternal question: what is fair? One plausible interpretation of fairness is that the burden should be distributed equally among all people, so Warren Buffett's taxes should go up by the same amount that your grandmother's Social Security benefits go down. Most people, however, would not consider this to be fair (including Warren Buffett[23]). Nor is it practical: in 2010, the budget deficit came to over $4,000 per person, meaning that to balance the budget each family of four would have had to contribute more than $16,000.

Another way to determine how the burden of deficit reduction should be distributed is to ask people. For example, when people were asked about five ways of reducing the national debt, the most popular option was increasing taxes on the wealthy, while the two least popular were reducing spending on Social Security and Medicare and reducing spending on defense.[24] Numerous polls consistently show that significant majorities of Americans support higher taxes on the wealthy as a means of reducing budget deficits, while generally opposing cuts to broad-based social insurance programs.[25] This implies that most people think that the rich should pay more in the form of higher taxes, while ordinary people should not pay more in the form of lower benefits. But even if that's what most people want, that doesn't necessarily make it fair: most obviously, people could simply be responding in their own self-interest.

There is a more fundamental way of describing the requirements of fairness. Today, when we express our preferences between different public policies, we know who we are—rich or poor, employed or unemployed, old or young, sick or healthy—and therefore we know whether we will benefit from those policies or not. What if we didn't know whether we individually stood to gain or lose? What choices would we make then? In his book *A Theory of Justice*, the philosopher John Rawls argues that a group of people situated behind this hypothetical "veil of ignorance" would agree on two basic principles. First, everyone should enjoy the broadest set of basic liberties that could be enjoyed by everyone. And second, inequalities that do exist should be "to the greatest benefit of the least advantaged" and subject to equality of opportunity.[26] Rawls's argument has been the subject of extensive debate. But the takeaway is that government policy should be measured not just by how it affects specific haves and have-nots in today's society, but by how it affects people who *don't know* whether they will be haves or have-nots.

In that context, both fairness and overall welfare require policies that benefit the have-nots. The question isn't just whether cutting Medicare benefits hurts the unhealthy more or less than it helps the healthy (by allowing them to pay lower taxes and premiums). The question is whether cutting Medicare benefits helps or hurts someone who doesn't yet know whether she will turn out to be healthy or unhealthy. This is not just a hypothetical question. Most of us know something about our current situation and our future prospects, but this knowledge is dwarfed by what we do not know: how valuable our job skills will be in the future; how long we will be able to work; how much support our parents will need; whether our children will be healthy; whether we will be healthy or unhealthy in old age (or before); how long we will live after retirement; how our investments will perform; and how well our children will make out in a future that we can hardly predict.

Scholars Michael Norton and Dan Ariely recently attempted to approximate the veil of ignorance in a study of beliefs about inequality. They asked people to choose what the distribution of wealth in society should be, assuming that they would then be randomly placed at some point along that distribution. Americans overwhelmingly preferred the wealth distribution of Sweden to the much more unequal distribution in the United States. In other words, putting aside their own individual situations, most people think there should be much less material inequality than there is today.[27] A significant and stable plurality of Americans even favors federal government action to help close the income gap between rich and poor.[28] Inequality is a broader problem than the federal budget deficit, and the goal of reducing the deficit is not simply to reduce inequality. But a strategy to reduce the deficit should not increase inequality, and many Americans think that asking the rich to shoulder a larger share of the burden is not only in their individual interests but also fundamentally fair. This is one reason why we have a progressive income tax system, in which rich people pay a larger share of their income than poor people. Progressive taxation both appeals to our basic sense of fairness and increases overall welfare. In general, an additional dollar of income provides more benefit to a poor person than to a rich person, so up to a point raising taxes on the rich in order to reduce taxes on the poor makes society as a whole better off. Economists Peter Diamond and Emmanuel Saez have estimated that overall welfare would be increased by raising marginal tax rates on the very rich to 54 percent in order to reduce taxes for lower-income households.[29]

Progressive taxation is one policy that might be popular behind the veil of ignorance (and is popular in front of it as well). Another is government-sponsored insurance. A central reason for our long-term budget imbalance is the government's major social insurance programs, Social Security and Medicare. Other government health care programs, such as Medicaid and the Children's Health Insurance Program, also provide insurance to large numbers of Americans. One obvious way to reduce the long-term deficit is for the government to provide less insurance. This was the essence of President George W. Bush's proposal to introduce individual accounts into Social Security. It was also a key feature of Representative Paul Ryan's 2011 proposal to convert Medicare into a voucher program; vouchers would increase in value at a predetermined rate, shifting the risk of higher health care inflation from the government to individuals.[30] And Republican presidential candidate Mitt Romney has suggested replacing unemployment insurance with unemployment savings accounts that people would contribute to while working and draw on when unemployed.[31] These approaches all have one thing in common: they reduce the element of risk sharing that is common to all insurance. With private Social Security accounts, the risk of outliving your retirement savings would no longer be spread across the population, since people who die young would leave their accounts to their heirs. With Medicare vouchers, the risk of poor health would remain with individuals in the form of higher premiums and out-of-pocket costs.[32] With unemployment accounts, the risk of unemployment would no longer be spread across all workers; instead, each person's ability to withstand unemployment would depend solely on the amount of money she accumulated while working.

Insurance, however, is something that people want and need when they don't yet know how their lives are going to turn out. We may want to live in a market society where the people with the most talent, ambition, and luck make the most money. But we also want to know that if things don't turn out right, possibly through sheer bad luck, we won't be kicked out on the street and turned away from the doctor's office. Human beings, in general, are risk-averse—we worry more about bad things happening than we enjoy the prospect of good things happening—and therefore we value programs that reduce uncertainty. That's why we want insurance (at least until we've made enough money to know that we don't need it anymore). And that's why insurance can provide overall social benefits even if it only seems to move money around. If one thousand homeowners put money into a fund that will rebuild the few houses that eventually burn down, they all benefit. After those houses burn down, the insurance payments look like redistribution; but when the homeowners decided to create the fund in the first place, they didn't know which of them would need the money, and buying insurance made them all better off.

When it comes to society-wide, long-term risks, there is only one institution that is big enough and credible enough to provide real insurance: the federal government, with its ability to raise taxes in the future to pay for unanticipated expenses, whether caused by soaring health care costs or collapsing financial systems. Private companies are pretty good at insuring short-term risks that are reasonably predictable, like auto accidents. But the federal government has a distinct advantage in insuring against severe catastrophes: If the financial system goes down, why would private insurers' assets be safe? If terrorism suddenly becomes more prevalent, why would private insurers be able to price the risk appropriately? The government is also better at insuring against risks that will materialize far in the future: if a private company sells you insurance that isn't supposed to pay out for several decades, there is a good chance that it will misprice the risk—so it won't be around when you need it.[33]

Insurance is a primary way that the government implements the basic principle of fairness that people recognize when not thinking about their own interests—the idea that we should be protected from misfortune that we cannot foresee. No one entering the workforce today knows how much health care she will need in retirement or how much it will cost, nor can she buy a policy from an insurance company that will guarantee her coverage that begins in forty-five years and lasts until she dies. Fairness demands that we spread these risks across society as a whole, which is why we have social insurance programs today. Reducing the national debt by dismantling those programs would leave the future have-nots—who could be any of us today—with no place to turn.

DO NO HARM

The national debt is not the only problem our country faces. Arguably the national debt is not itself a problem: its potential economic consequences are the problem, and those consequences haven't appeared yet. At the same time, the United States does face some very real and very serious challenges. A solution to our long-term deficits should help overcome those challenges, or at least not intensify them.

The most likely threat to our national security is the possibility that rogue states or terrorist groups could gain access to weapons of mass destruction and use them against us.[34] The possibility of war against another major power seems to be less of a threat—in part because there is no comparable military power, as we currently spend six times as much on our armed forces as any other country.[35] Since we already have the world's dominant military, reducing the risk we face from rogue states and terrorist groups will probably depend mainly on diplomacy, public relations, intelligence, and special operations—not the expensive conventional armed forces we built up to fight the Soviet Union. These are not major line items in the federal budget, with the exception of intelligence spending, which has grown rapidly over the past decade, reaching $80 billion in 2010.[36] For example, despite periodic warnings abut the threat of nuclear weapons, programs that help other countries protect their nuclear materials and weapons consume only one five-hundredth of total national security spending.[37] The spending we need to protect ourselves from terrorist attacks should not prevent us from bringing the national debt under control in the long term.

Other national challenges, however, are directly relevant to fiscal policy. Rising health care costs are a threat both to the federal budget and to the traditional American promise of widespread prosperity. Fifty million people today do not have health insurance—almost one in six Americans.[38] This is one reason why, on many measures of public health, the United States does badly compared to other industrialized countries; out of thirty-four advanced economies, for example, we have the fourth-highest rate of infant mortality.[39] Poor health makes for a less productive workforce: the United States is one of the least healthy countries in the advanced industrialized world when both premature death and disability are taken into account.[40] Having to pay more for health care means that American businesses are also increasingly squeezed by rising health care costs over which they have little control. As of 2004, health care costs contributed $1,525 to the price of each General Motors vehicle—more than seven times as much as for Toyota.[41] This makes it harder for American exporters to compete globally and more attractive for them to shift their operations overseas. As health care consumes a growing share of the national economy, the rate of growth of the rest of the economy will have to fall.

Health care costs are obviously a major cause of the federal government's long-term deficits, but reducing government spending in a way that simply shifts the costs onto the private sector—or that makes the problem worse—is not a real solution for the American people. As the largest buyer of health care in the economy, the federal government has some influence on both prices and utilization patterns. Government tax policy, such as the exemption of employer-provided health benefits from taxation, also helps shape the private market. Ideally, the government should use its leverage to reduce its own deficits and to reduce costs for the private sector at the same time.

Rising health care costs are also complicating the transition to an aging society faced by many wealthy countries that have experienced post–World War II baby booms, declining birthrates, and increasing life expectancy.[42] In the United States, because of the retirement of the first baby boomers and the recent recession, Social Security payroll taxes are no longer able to cover program benefits. But while the federal deficit could be reduced simply by cutting Social Security benefits, this is not a real solution because many middle-aged Americans are financially unprepared for old age. In 2009, only 63 percent of households that were close to retirement had any retirement accounts; of those households, the median value of those accounts was only $86,000.[43] Against this backdrop, sharp cuts to Social Security—the largest source of income for most retired Americans—would only further erode families' already fragile retirement security.[44] Instead, policies to bring down federal government deficits should seek to increase saving by or on behalf of people who are still in their working careers.

The most menacing long-term threat, though the least predictable, is climate change, which is likely to accelerate over this century as higher concentrations of greenhouse gases in the atmosphere create new pressures on the global ecosystem.[45] A comprehensive approach to limiting the effects of climate change is far beyond the scope of this book, but fiscal policy can help address this major challenge. One reason for high levels of greenhouse gas emissions is that companies and individuals do not bear the full costs of the energy they produce and consume.[46] A coal-fired power plant has to pay for its coal, but not for the emergency room visits by children who suffer asthma attacks due to air pollution;[47] customers of the power plant have to pay for their electricity, but not to protect coastal cities from rising sea levels decades in the future. A plan that forces buyers and sellers of energy to recognize these costs, by taxing carbon emissions or by auctioning emission permits to companies that produce energy, could both raise additional government revenue and help cool the planet.

This is by no means a complete list of the important priorities we face as a nation. The important thing to remember is that the purpose of a government is to improve the lives of its citizens, not to balance its budget. Paying off the national debt but giving up on the government's traditional duty to protect ordinary people from the most important threats to their basic welfare is a fool's bargain. Instead, reshaping the federal budget for the next few decades is an opportunity to focus our scarce resources on the problems that most require concerted action and the areas where the government can have the greatest positive impact on society.

WITH ALL DELIBERATE SPEED

As Alexander Hamilton recognized over two centuries ago, there can be good reasons to have a national debt. One of his original motivations—tying the fortunes of the investor class to the fortunes of the federal government—may not seem especially important today. Treasury bonds, however, still serve a crucial role in global markets as the universally accepted collateral for financial transactions. A liquid market for government debt also makes it easier for the government to borrow large amounts of money quickly should the need arise. More importantly, there is no compelling economic reason why the debt needs to be entirely eliminated. Paying down debt is the exact opposite of borrowing: it means spending money now in order to save on interest payments in the future. Just as borrowing only makes sense if money today will give you benefits that outweigh the cost of the future interest payments, paying down debt only makes sense if lower interest payments in the future outweigh the cost of the money today.

A sovereign government needs to keep its national debt at a level where it can borrow money at reasonable interest rates and where it has the fiscal space to respond to major crises in the future. This means that the national debt must be stable as a proportion of the economy, or it must be likely to stabilize at some level. If investors believe that the national debt will continue to climb indefinitely, they are unlikely to lend money at anything like a reasonable interest rate, at least not for long time periods.[48]

The big question is at what level the national debt should be stabilized, and here there is no magical right answer. As discussed in chapter 5, economists Carmen Reinhart and Kenneth Rogoff have suggested that a national debt above 90 percent of GDP is associated with lower economic growth, but we find it unlikely that this rule applies closely to the United States—at least as long as the U.S. dollar remains the dominant global reserve currency. But this unique status will not last forever, and we think its life expectancy is probably measured in decades, not centuries or years. Someday, the United States will become an ordinary rich country, at least as far as our capacity to attract investments is concerned. At that point, we think that a useful target would be stabilizing the national debt at 50 percent of GDP.

This target does not result from any master formula, but from a combination of practical considerations and comparative observations. It is close to the debt level that appears to be naturally stable for most countries, according to research by IMF economists based on different nations' historical track records.[49] This level of debt would probably also provide just enough fiscal space for the federal government to cope with a shock that, like the 2007–2009 financial crisis, could add another 50 percent of GDP to the national debt. In that case, our national debt would be 100 percent of GDP, which recent experience implies is on the border of the danger zone. The financial crisis and recession are likely to push four countries' national debt levels above 100 percent of GDP; three of those countries—Greece, Ireland, and Italy—are enduring sovereign debt crises to varying degrees. (The fourth, Japan, has been able to maintain high levels of government debt because it has a high household savings rate and there is little competition from private sector businesses to borrow money.)[50]

While our recommendation might seem to err on the side of safety, a national debt equal to 50 percent of GDP is still large by historical standards. Before the financial crisis, the national debt last exceeded that level in 1956, when it was falling rapidly from World War II levels; the average for the entire postwar period (from the record year of 1946 through the crisis-swollen year of 2010) was 44 percent of GDP.[51] While future growth rates are hard to forecast, they are likely to be slightly lower than during the post–World

War II decades because the overall workforce is growing more slowly, making it harder to sustain the same level of debt. Our target of 50 percent of GDP is based on the assumption that at some point the U.S. dollar will no longer be the unique global reserve currency, which will make it harder to finance the national debt than it has been in the past. Given the difficulty of predicting the future and the potentially very high costs of a fiscal crisis, we also think it is right to err on the side of safety—just as we should be taking action now to slow the rate of climate change precisely because its costs could be catastrophically high. Finally, as we show in the next chapter, it is possible to stabilize the national debt at 50 percent of GDP without the need for severe benefit cuts or debilitating tax increases. If painful austerity measures were necessary, then perhaps this target would not be worth aiming for—but that is not the case.

The next question is *when* we need to stabilize the national debt. Again, this question does not have a simple answer, because no one knows when the United States will lose its privileged position in world financial markets. In our opinion, we should aim to bring the national debt down to a sustainable level by 2030 because it is entirely possible that a shift in the financial balance of power could be well under way by then. In theory, sooner is better than later, but there is virtually no plausible scenario in which the national debt will be lower than 60 percent of GDP by the end of this decade. The Congressional Budget Office's most recent baseline forecast, which assumes that all of the previous decade's tax cuts are allowed to expire on schedule, predicts that the debt will be 62 percent of GDP in 2020.[52] In addition, the U.S. economy is still recovering from the effects of the financial crisis, which has so far cost us four years of lost growth. Attempting to reduce the deficit even faster than required by current law could hurt the economy in the short term.

Ideally, new policies to reduce the deficit should be largely deferred until after the economy is growing strongly again, which may still be years away.[53] Many of those policies should be phased in over several years, so that they do not fully take effect until the late 2010s or early 2020s. Then those policies will have several years to bring the national debt down to our target level by 2030, or at least to demonstrate that the debt is on course to stabilize at the target level. This is far from an exact science, since changes in economic conditions can cause deficits to swing wildly one way or another, but the strategy is simple. We have a long-term problem, and it requires a long-term solution. Our potential budget imbalances are so large that any policy changes must be phased in over a long period of time. And while we should begin making those changes soon, we should not do so at the risk of making the longest period of economic stagnation in more than seventy years even longer.

If our goal is to stabilize the debt at 50 percent of GDP by 2030, what does that mean for annual budgets? Under current policies, as described in chapter 4, if the Bush tax cuts expire on schedule, the national debt in 2030 will be close to 70 percent of GDP and rising.[54] To meet our long-term goal, we would need to reduce our annual budget deficits by 3 percent of GDP by the early 2020s.[55] In that case, as shown in Figure 6-1, the national debt would fall to 40 percent of GDP in 2030 and continue falling for several more years.[56] (Note that this would not completely balance the budget in the 2030s, but would reduce annual deficits sufficiently to keep the debt under control for several decades.) The national debt would not reach current levels until the 2060s. Given the limited value of forecasts that try to reach so far into the future, and all the things that

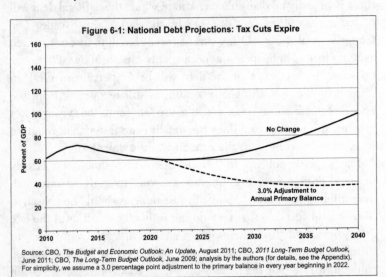

Figure 6-1: National Debt Projections: Tax Cuts Expire

Source: CBO, *The Budget and Economic Outlook: An Update*, August 2011; CBO, *2011 Long-Term Budget Outlook*, June 2011; CBO, *The Long-Term Budget Outlook*, June 2009; analysis by the authors (for details, see the Appendix). For simplicity, we assume a 3.0 percentage point adjustment to the primary balance in every year beginning in 2022.

can happen between now and then, we think now is not the time to worry about the deficit crisis of 2070.

If all the Bush tax cuts are made permanent, however, and other current policies continue, the national debt in 2030 will be over 100 percent of GDP and growing rapidly. To prevent that outcome and meet our target, we would need to reduce our annual deficits by 5.5 percent of GDP by the early 2020s, as shown in Figure 6-2— a much more difficult task. In that case, the national debt would still be 53 percent of GDP in 2030, but it would decline to 50 percent only two years later. In this scenario, the national debt would continue falling for another decade and would not reach current levels until the 2060s.

Fortunately, there are many options available to increase tax revenues or reduce spending. In the next chapter, we describe several options, including those that we prefer. Other people may prefer a different mix of policy choices. Ultimately, however, our political system will only make *any* of these choices if our elected leaders actually want to keep deficits under control. We are living in a curious moment: deficits have become highly visible, but the politicians who talk about deficits the most are primarily interested in using them to reduce government spending or to score points against their oppo-

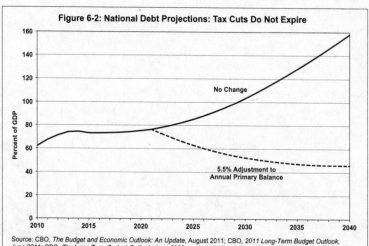

Figure 6-2: National Debt Projections: Tax Cuts Do Not Expire

Source: CBO, *The Budget and Economic Outlook: An Update*, August 2011; CBO, *2011 Long-Term Budget Outlook*, June 2011; CBO, *The Long-Term Budget Outlook*, June 2009; analysis by the authors (for details, see the Appendix). For simplicity, we assume a 5.5 percentage point adjustment to the primary balance in every year beginning in 2022.

nents. Fiscal responsibility, though waved as a flag on both sides of the political aisle, does not have much of a constituency compared to either cutting taxes or protecting Social Security and Medicare. In the long term, either the voting public will ensure that the national debt is brought down to a sustainable level, or bond investors will do it for us, as they are doing to Greece and Ireland. One way is much better than the other.

Seven

WHERE DO WE GO FROM HERE?

A billion here, a billion there, and soon you're talking real money.

—Attributed to Senator Everett Dirksen (1896–1969)[1]

A specter is haunting the Western world: the specter of austerity. New governments in Greece, Ireland, Italy, Portugal, and the United Kingdom have all solemnly invoked large government deficits to justify harsh measures including both sharp tax increases and major cutbacks in public spending. Austerity has an appealing narrative resonance: after years of living beyond our means, it is now time to face facts, assume our responsibilities, and make sacrifices—or else we will go the way of the Roman Empire.

It makes a good story—but that doesn't make it true, at least not everywhere. We take the national debt seriously (seriously enough to write hundreds of pages about it). The federal government does need to fill a hole in its long-term budget that ranges from 3.0 percent to 5.5 percent of GDP (depending on the fate of the Bush tax cuts). But we can fill that hole without gutting our major social insurance programs, without eliminating the meager safety net for the poor, and without raising taxes to the levels that prevailed from World War II until the 1970s. We can bring the national debt under control in a way that encourages economic growth, preserves the essential services and programs that many Americans depend on, and spreads the burden of lower spending or higher taxes fairly across the population. This chapter shows how.

Of course, we are not under the illusion that our proposals will magically break open the logjam of American deficit politics. The problem is not a shortage of deficit reduction plans; indeed, the past few years have seen a bumper crop of such plans, many with more illustrious sponsors.[2] We do not expect all readers to agree with us on how the deficit should be reduced; even those who share our views about the historical causes of our current and future deficits will have different visions for our society and the place of the federal government. Our goal is simply to show that we can achieve a sustainable level of national debt while maintaining a government that plays the crucial role we expect from it today—protecting all of us from major risks to our welfare today and investing in a more prosperous future.

TAX CUTS

The first important question is what to do with the tax cuts that are due to expire under current law, most notably the income and estate tax reductions originally passed under President Bush in 2001 and 2003.* They are big: extending the income and estate tax cuts alone will increase the 2021 deficit by almost 3 percent of GDP and increase the 2021 national debt from 60 percent to 76 percent of GDP.[3] As discussed in the previous chapter, extending them would also increase our long-term budget gap (the amount by which annual deficits must be reduced) from 3.0 percent to 5.5 percent of GDP. The tax cuts also represent a unique opportunity to reduce the deficit in our difficult political climate. Because they are already scheduled to expire under current law, Congress simply has to do nothing. Given how hard it is for Democrats and Republicans to agree on any spending cuts or tax increases, it is hard to imagine Congress enacting *anything* that would reduce the national debt by 16 percentage points within a decade. When it comes to expiring tax cuts, gridlock can help reduce deficits.

In addition, letting the tax cuts expire is good policy. The major provisions of the 2001 and 2003 tax cuts, as extended in 2010, are:

---

* In this chapter, we assume that the alternative minimum tax (AMT) will effectively be indexed to inflation to protect large numbers of middle-class households from having to pay it. We consider this much more of a political certainty than the extension of the other recent tax cuts such as the reduction in income tax rates and the lower rates for capital gains and dividends.

- Reductions in all income tax rates, with the highest rate falling from 39.6 percent to 35 percent;
- Reductions in tax rates on long-term capital gains, with the highest rate falling from 20 percent to 15 percent;
- Taxation of stock dividends at lower rates (rather than at ordinary income tax rates);
- Elimination of existing rules that reduced the ability of high-income taxpayers to lower their taxes through personal exemptions or itemized deductions;[4]
- Increases in the child and dependent care tax credits;
- Gradual repeal of the estate tax; in 2010, Congress reinstated the tax on estates over $5 million (up from $1 million in 2001).

In addition to extending the 2001 and 2003 income and estate tax cuts (through 2012), the December 2010 tax act also reduced the Social Security payroll tax by 2 percentage points (through 2011, later extended through February 2012) and extended some tax cuts introduced in the 2009 stimulus bill.

The main problem with the Bush tax cuts is that, in addition to vastly increasing government deficits, they constituted a major transfer from the federal government to the rich (relative to preexisting policy). As described in chapter 3, a large majority of the tax cuts went to the richest 20 percent of households, with the greatest benefits for the very richest families, both in dollar and percentage terms. If the federal government were simply throwing money away, this might have been defensible since most households got some tax cuts (but not households that are only subject to payroll taxes). But most federal spending is payments on behalf of individuals (Social Security checks, Medicare or Medicaid reimbursements, Pell Grants, and so on), which clearly benefit real people; the difficulty of getting Congress to agree to cut *any* spending demonstrates that most other spending must benefit someone. Since the biggest chunk of government spending is on insurance programs for all working Americans, tax cuts that favor the wealthy must eventually translate into lower benefits for the middle class—unless they are paid for by future tax increases aimed primarily at the wealthy. There is a reasonable argument to be made that both taxes and spending are too high and therefore both should be reduced. But that argument implies that taxes and spending should be reduced at the same time; it does not justify a permanent reduction in taxes on the rich that will be paid for through unspecified future spending cuts that must largely be borne by the poor and the middle class.[5] In short, the income and estate tax cuts were bad policy a decade ago, and extending them is simply making bad policy permanent.

The Bush tax cuts had another rationale, which was that lower taxes would increase the incentives to work and to save, boosting economic growth in the long term. But there is little evidence that they had the impact claimed by their supporters. Growth following the tax cuts was lower than in the "high-tax" 1990s, even before the recession caused by the recent financial crisis.[6] It is difficult or impossible to isolate the impact of the tax cuts from everything else that has happened since 2001, but there is a basic reason to be skeptical that they have helped the economy in the long term: although lower taxes can boost growth by increasing incentives, lower taxes that are paid for through larger deficits mean *reduced* saving, higher interest rates, and slower growth. In the words of two economists at the Brookings Institution:

> Several studies have quantified the various effects noted above in different ways and used different models, yet all have come to the same conclusion: Making the tax cuts permanent is likely to reduce, not increase, national income in the long term unless the reduction in revenues is matched by an equal reduction in government consumption.[7]

In 2010, Congressional Budget Office analysis also indicated that extending the tax cuts would increase economic growth in the short term but decrease it in the long term (because higher government borrowing would crowd out private investment), making the economy smaller in 2020 than it would have been otherwise.[8] Again, there is a valid argument that tax cuts coupled with spending reductions could be good for the economy—but that argument does not apply to extending the Bush tax cuts on their own.

The last argument against extending the income and estate tax cuts is that you shouldn't raise taxes when the economy is weak. This is a reasonable argument. Since unemployment is still likely to be high at the end of 2012, it would be better to extend some of the tax cuts until the economy is recovering and then let them expire, perhaps even by passing a law that left them in place until the economy hit certain benchmarks. In practice, however, Republicans in Congress are highly unlikely to agree to any plan to phase out the tax cuts; and each time a tax cut is extended, the more it seems like a permanent feature of the tax code, and the harder it is to eliminate. Ideally we would let the tax cuts expire and use some of the new revenues to finance explicit, short-term stimulus measures that have more impact on employment and have little chance of becoming permanent (such as spending programs or one-time tax rebates).[9] But politically speaking, this is even more unlikely. In these circumstances, where the only realistic choices are no tax cuts or permanent tax cuts, we think the right choice is no tax cuts. While this could hurt growth in the short run, it should make the economy larger over the next decade.[10] More importantly, this is the single biggest step we can take toward assuring the revenues necessary to pay for Social Security, Medicare, and the other insurance programs that the middle class needs in the long term.

Unfortunately, it is highly likely that most or all of the income and estate tax cuts will be made permanent. President Obama wants to extend all of the tax cuts for households making less than $250,000—which accounts for the large majority of their dollar value.[11] Republicans have long wanted to make all of the tax cuts permanent, and Grover Norquist has said that any deal that extends only some of the tax cuts would count as a tax increase and hence would violate the Taxpayer Protection Pledge.[12] With unanimous agreement among the principals that most of the tax cuts should be made permanent, even the power of gridlock will probably be insufficient to prevent their extension. For this reason, the rest of this chapter assumes that all of the income and estate tax cuts will be made permanent. (If that does not happen, then our long-term deficit problem will be correspondingly smaller, and fewer of our other recommendations will be necessary.)

In addition to the major tax cuts introduced under President George W. Bush and extended under President Obama, many other tax breaks are scheduled to expire over the next decade, ranging from the "Depreciation Classification for Certain Race Horses" to the

"Partial Expensing of Certain Refinery Property." Most of these are relatively small; the largest are a bonus depreciation provision (which allows businesses to deduct the cost of their investments faster) and a tax break that helps companies shield foreign income from U.S. taxation.[13] If they are all extended (in addition to the income and estate tax cuts), they will together add 0.5 percent of GDP to the 2021 deficit and increase the 2021 national debt to 80 percent of GDP.[14] As a general rule, we think that all of these tax provisions should expire. A temporary tax break should exist if Congress originally thought it was only needed for a certain period of time; in that case, it should be extended only if Congress decides that its original rationale is still valid. If a tax break really is good long-term policy, it should be individually justified and made permanent, even if it needs sixty votes in the Senate. In this case, as opposed to the income tax cuts, we think it is reasonably likely that many other tax breaks will be allowed to expire; for example, the largest individual line item is the bonus depreciation provision, which has historically been justified as an economic stimulus measure and should be allowed to lapse when the economy recovers.[15]

SOCIAL SECURITY

Social Security is the primary source of retirement income for most Americans. Because the ratio of workers (who make payroll tax contributions) to retirees (who collect benefits) is falling, the system will run increasing deficits in the future, reaching 1.3 percent of GDP around 2030, when most of the baby boomers will have retired. The deficit will then fluctuate around that level for several decades before slowly rising due to increasing life expectancy.[16] Over the next seventy-five years (the period over which Social Security's finances are conventionally measured), the cumulative deficit—the gap between the payroll taxes we pay and the benefits we are supposed to get—is equivalent to 2.2 percent of taxable payroll (the total amount of earnings subject to the payroll tax).[17]

The solution long sought by conservatives and proposed by President George W. Bush is to privatize Social Security, making it essentially like a 401(k) plan, where at least some of each person's contributions would go into her own individual account. From the budgetary perspective, the main benefit of privatization is that it eventually eliminates the government's long-term obligations. At some point, what retirees get will depend solely on their savings decisions and investment returns, just as with a 401(k) plan. The federal government will just be an administrator, and so there cannot be a Social Security deficit.

The problem with privatization is that it dismantles Social Security as we know it today. The whole point of Social Security is to provide guaranteed income in retirement and protect people against a wide range of risks—disability, having a spouse die young, living too long, poor investment returns—by shifting those risks to the population as a whole, via the federal government. Individual accounts do not protect people against any of these risks unless they are layered over with additional features (mandatory contributions, mandatory annuities, minimum benefits, disability benefits, and so on) that turn them back into traditional Social Security. By making Social Security more like the rest of our retirement "system"—tax-advantaged accounts, such as 401(k)s, that people can use (or not) to save for retirement—privatization would most likely leave many more Americans unprepared for retirement. A much simpler solution to the long-term Social Security deficit is to acknowledge that payroll taxes won't be enough to cover benefits in the long term and either increase the former or reduce the latter.

There are many ways that this could be done.[18] We favor a combination of four policy changes: increasing the cap on earnings that are subject to the payroll tax, indexing the full benefit age to life expectancy, broadening the system to include all newly hired state and local government employees, and increasing the payroll tax rate. The payroll tax is currently 12.4 percent of earnings, but is only assessed on the first $106,800, an amount that is adjusted for inflation. When the cap was set in 1983, it covered 90 percent of all wage earnings in the country. Since then, however, the proportion of earnings that escape the payroll tax has increased from 10 percent to 16 percent, primarily because of increasing inequality.[19] (Since rich people make more than $106,800, as the rich earn a larger share of total income, more income escapes taxation.) The cap should be increased so that it includes 90 percent of all wage earnings, as in 1983, and should be indexed at that level. This would reduce the program's seventy-five-year deficit by 0.5 percent of taxable pay-roll.[20] Maintaining a cap on taxable earnings means that the payroll tax is slightly regressive, but the program as a whole is modestly progressive today (because the progressive benefit formula outweighs the regressive payroll tax), and would be more progressive with the higher cap that we propose.[21]

Social Security's normal retirement age—the age at which you can begin drawing full benefits—is sixty-six for people retiring now, but will slowly increase to sixty-seven for people born in 1960 or later. (You can begin taking benefits as early as age sixty-two, but your monthly benefits will be lower.)* Greater life expectancy, by increasing the ratio of retirees to workers, is one of the contributors to Social Security's long-term deficits; at the same time, because it increases the amount of time that people collect benefits, it also makes Social Security more valuable to retirees. If the normal retirement age is indexed to rise as life expectancy increases (beginning with a full retirement age of sixty-seven for people born in 1960), the ratio of retirees to workers can be kept roughly stable except for fluctuations in births and immigration. Over time, the full retirement age would increase by one year about every twenty-five years; on average, that means that each person would be expected to work about one year longer than her parents.[22] This change would reduce the seventy-five-year deficit by 0.6 percent of taxable payroll.[23]

Social Security currently does not cover more than six million employees of state and local governments that previously opted out of the system.[24] These employees do not pay payroll taxes and will not receive retirement benefits (at least not for the years they spend as government employees). The system should be expanded to cover all newly hired government employees. This would give them access to a highly dependable pension system, which is particularly important given the current political and financial pressures on state pen-

---

* We are not proposing an increase in the early benefit age, so people will still be able to begin collecting benefits at sixty-two. Given the way early benefits are calculated, however, those benefits would be smaller than if the normal retirement age were left unchanged from current law.

sion systems. Social Security can coexist with another retirement plan (as is the case for every private sector employee who has a traditional pension or a 401(k) plan), so state and local governments could elect to preserve or scale back their existing retirement plans for new hires. Broadening Social Security coverage would improve the system's finances because most newly hired employees would make contributions for many years before beginning to receive benefits. This change would reduce the seventy-five-year deficit by about 0.2 percent of taxable payroll.[25]

Finally, increasing the payroll tax rate by 1 percentage point, from 12.4 percent to 13.4 percent, would reduce Social Security's seventy-five-year deficit by another 1.0 percent of taxable payroll.[26] We favor increasing the tax rate (gradually, over several years) rather than reducing benefits because Social Security benefits are already quite modest, averaging around $13,000 per year.[27] Given how little many households have saved for old age, this is not the time to weaken the one component of our retirement system that seems to be working reasonably well.[28] Together, these four reforms would bring Social Security's finances roughly into balance for the next seventy-five years.[29] Beginning in the 2020s, they would also reduce annual federal budget deficits by about 0.9 percent of GDP.*[30] They are not a permanent solution, since they would leave the program with a modest deficit after the seventy-five-year horizon, but given all the things that can happen between now and the 2080s, we think additional tax increases or benefit reductions would be premature at this point.[31]

HEALTH CARE

Our expensive yet mediocre health care is one of the major problems facing Americans today. Many businesses struggle with the rising

---

* In general, we estimate for the impact of a deficit reduction proposal at the time when the proposal is fully phased in. We draw on various sources for our estimates (indicated in the endnotes). Our GDP estimates (for the denominator) are from the CBO. CBO, *The Budget and Economic Outlook: An Update*, August 2011, Table 1-2, pp. 4–5. For estimates based on years prior to 2011, we use GDP figures from OMB, *Fiscal Year 2012 Budget of the U.S. Government: Historical Tables*, Table 1.2.

costs of their employee health plans, which force them to charge higher prices to customers, clamp down on wages, drop their health benefits, or shift jobs overseas. Cutbacks in employer-sponsored health plans, combined with the high price of buying health insurance directly from insurers, have left fifty million Americans without any type of coverage.[32] Even families with insurance are highly vulnerable to medical emergencies: illness or injury is a significant factor in more than half of all bankruptcies, and in more than three-quarters of these cases, the person suffering the illness or injury had health insurance at the time.[33] Health care spending continues to rise, even after accounting for inflation, demographic shifts, and increasing prosperity. Because the federal government is committed to buying health care for about one hundred million people, including the elderly, the poor, veterans, and federal employees, the cost is expected to take up a larger and larger share of the federal budget, growing from 5.6 percent of GDP in 2010 to 10.3 percent in 2035.[34]

This spending can be reduced in two ways: reducing health care costs overall and reducing the government's share of that spending. The former is clearly better for society as a whole, if it can be done without significantly hurting health outcomes. Otherwise, reducing the government's obligations simply shifts costs onto businesses and households, leaving everyone no better off in the short run.[35] The problem is that it is by no means clear how to hold down growth in health care costs. There is ample evidence that we could spend less without becoming any less healthy—other countries obtain comparable or better outcomes for much less money, and high-spending regions within the United States do not achieve better outcomes than low-spending regions[36]—but how to get there is open to debate: simply spending less could reduce valuable care as much as unnecessary care.[37] A growing body of comparative effectiveness research is helping to identify which procedures are likely to help and which are not. For example, aggressive treatment of people with advanced terminal illnesses not only is expensive but also results in more people spending their last days in the intensive care unit and dying in the hospital; palliative care programs, which focus on relieving suffering and improving quality of life, can save money, increase patients' comfort, and at least in some cases help people live longer.[38] But even with this research, there is no easy way in our current, fragmented system to induce providers to stop conducting unnecessary procedures or to hold them accountable for patient outcomes.

Most other developed countries, by contrast, have universal health insurance systems, which come in several different forms. At one extreme are countries like England, where health care is provided by the National Health Service and financed by taxes (with a small private insurance sector providing supplemental insurance). Then there are countries like Canada and France, where health care services are delivered by both the public and private sectors, but universal health insurance is provided by provincial governments or government-regulated insurance funds and financed by taxes; in both cases, private insurers also offer supplemental health insurance plans. Finally there are "managed competition" systems in countries like the Netherlands and Switzerland, where everyone is required to buy health insurance from private insurers, but the insurance market is tightly regulated to ensure access to basic plans.[39]

A universal, government-sponsored health insurance plan is one way to control costs over the long term. If everyone is enrolled in a single basic insurance plan—which could be funded by premiums, deductibles, and copayments in addition to taxes (like Medicare today)—that plan would have the power to set payment rates for services and medications. This would make it possible to limit future spending growth without sacrificing access to care. Unlike today, when doctors and hospitals are free to turn Medicaid and Medicare patients away if those programs don't pay them enough, a universal health plan would be the only payer for many services, ensuring that providers would accept its payment rates. (Private insurance companies could offer supplemental insurance plans providing additional benefits not included in the basic plan.)[40] Varying levels of copayments could be used to guide people toward preventive care and away from procedures with questionable benefits. Universal insurance would require higher payroll taxes than we pay for Medicare today, but those higher taxes would replace the amount we currently pay in health insurance premiums. Over the long term, such a plan could reduce total health care spending—the number that really matters to our wallets—because the universal plan could control how much it pays for services.

A universal health plan would have other benefits. Over time, it could adopt payment practices that increase accountability among providers, such as bundled payments for a given episode of care (as opposed to paying for each service individually) or a system of bonuses and penalties based on quality measures. It would also separate health insurance from employment, ensuring that people do not lose their coverage when they leave their jobs—which is often when they need it most.[41] Of course, nothing comes for free: if the government sets payment rates too low, hospitals will go out of business and fewer people will want to be doctors, which could reduce the overall supply of health care services.[42] The experience of other countries, however, shows that it is possible to have lower costs and better outcomes with a universal, government-sponsored health plan. In any case, this would at least allow us to make conscious trade-offs between spending and outcomes through our democratic system; today, instead, virtually everyone agrees that spending is growing too fast, but we have no good way of doing anything about it.

Universal, government-sponsored health insurance is probably a political impossibility, at least today. President Obama's health care reform plan, which relies entirely on the private insurance market, barely made it through Congress with zero Republican votes and would certainly not be passed today. This means that we will have to find other ways to slow the growth of health care spending and close the federal government's long-term budget gap. The best way to reduce spending is probably to shift toward new health care delivery models that make providers accountable for both costs and quality; this will give them the incentive to improve coordination, apply the lessons of comparative effectiveness research, and focus on outcomes rather than simply maximizing their revenues by supplying unnecessary services.[43] The Affordable Care Act of 2010 attempted to give the system a nudge in this direction, but no one knows what it will take to turn the enormous ship of U.S. health care spending in a new direction.

In this uncertain environment, we need to take additional steps to reduce the government's health care deficit. The first place to look is the tax break for employer-sponsored health plans, which are currently excluded from the income tax and from payroll taxes— even though they are valuable compensation received by employees.

Not only will the employer health plan exclusion cost the Treasury Department almost $300 billion in 2012, or 1.9 percent of GDP, but it also contributes to the problem of high health care costs.*[44] Because of the exclusion, it is cheaper for companies to pay their employees in health benefits than in wages; this means that they buy more generous health plans than they would without the tax break. This distortion increases demand for health insurance and probably increases health care spending modestly.[45] It locks people into their current jobs, making it harder and riskier to switch employers and cutting them off from health coverage when they lose their jobs involuntarily. And it is poorly targeted, since rich people are more likely to have employer-sponsored health plans to begin with and the exclusion is worth more to people in high tax brackets: more than 40 percent of the tax break goes to families in the top quintile by income, and less than 2 percent to families in the bottom quintile.[46]

For these reasons, the employer health plan exclusion should be phased out,[†] as in the bipartisan Healthy Americans Act proposed by Senators Ron Wyden and Bob Bennett (but never seriously considered).[47] One concern is that this would accelerate the decline of employer-sponsored health plans, which are still the way that a majority of Americans get health insurance. The Affordable Care Act, however, created a system of state-based exchanges where insurers offer plans meeting basic minimum standards; these insurance plans must be available to anyone, cannot be priced based on preexisting conditions, and cannot be taken away.[48] In addition, the Affordable Care Act subsidizes insurance purchased on an exchange by low- and middle-income families.[49] We also recommend spending half of the proceeds from eliminating the current tax break on cash rebates to low- and middle-income workers (delivered either through the income tax or the payroll tax system). Roughly speaking, half of the tax break currently enjoyed by high-income workers

---

* Unless otherwise noted, estimates of revenue losses from tax expenditures are static estimates.

† This could be done by placing a cap on the amount of health benefits that can be excluded from income for tax purposes (which would differ for individual and family coverage) and letting that cap fall over time. Alternatively, the Obama health care reform bill introduced an excise tax on plans above a threshold that will increase with inflation; that threshold could instead fall to zero over time.

would go to reduce deficits, while the other half would be shared among all low- and middle-income workers, not just those fortunate enough to get health care from their employers. It's difficult to estimate how much revenues would increase under this plan, but we expect it would be between 0.6 percent and 0.9 percent of GDP.[50]

There are other ways to lower government health care spending without reducing beneficiaries' access to care. The most significant is equalizing the treatment of prescription drugs by Medicare and Medicaid. Today, pharmaceutical companies must pay minimum rebates to the government for drugs purchased through Medicaid; as a result, it receives significantly larger discounts than Medicare for the same drugs.[51] Various other inefficiencies in these programs could be eliminated: Medicare currently overpays teaching hospitals for the incremental costs of training doctors; Medicare overpays for some types of rehabilitation and other medical care in long-term settings; and Medicaid can reduce spending on durable medical equipment by adopting Medicare's practices. But the savings available from these types of reforms are relatively small: minimum prescription drug rebates for Medicare would save 0.1 percent of GDP, and additional cost-saving measures proposed by the Obama administration in 2011 would save another 0.1 percent.[52]

The last way to reduce the long-term health care deficit is to increase Medicare revenues, either from current beneficiaries, through higher premiums, deductibles, and copayments, or from future beneficiaries, through payroll taxes.[53] We favor a balanced approach that does not concentrate the burden of health care inflation either on current workers or on the elderly; looked at from an alternative perspective, most of us will work for part of our lives and be old for part of our lives, but it is better to spread the burden across both periods than to impose it only in one. First, we recommend gradually increasing Medicare Part B premiums so that they cover 30 percent of the program's costs instead of only 25 percent, as under current law. This would work out to an increase of about $240 per beneficiary per year in today's dollars, and would increase revenues by 0.1 percent of GDP in the long term.[54] This premium increase is slightly progressive: low-income beneficiaries are protected by a provision of Medicaid, while a growing number of high-income beneficiaries pay higher premiums under current law. We think this is preferable to raising revenues through higher deductibles and copayments, which will concentrate the burden on people with poor health who are already incurring greater out-of-pocket expenses for health care.

Second, we recommend raising the Medicare payroll tax, which currently funds the Hospital Insurance program (Part A).[55] For most people, the payroll tax rate has remained at 2.9 percent since 1986, a period during which health care spending has grown by two-thirds as a share of the economy.[56] That payroll tax is perhaps the best bargain on the planet: it buys you guaranteed hospital insurance from the day you turn sixty-five, no matter how healthy or unhealthy you are, until the day you die—at a tax rate that hasn't changed in a quarter-century.[57] We recommend gradually increasing the payroll tax by 1 percentage point, to 3.9 percent—still far less than the increase in health care costs since 1986. This means that someone making $50,000 a year would pay up to $500 more per year in taxes (depending on how the employer's share of the tax is distributed), and total payroll tax revenues would increase by 0.5 percent of GDP.[58]

This is not a pretty picture, with higher payroll taxes for current workers and higher premiums for beneficiaries. The better solution is to change the way health care is delivered, so that we spend less and get better care. Medicare itself is far from a perfect system; in particular, it epitomizes the fee-for-service model (in which providers are paid by the procedure, regardless of results) that produces high costs and mediocre outcomes. We should continue to implement reforms to government health care programs that increase accountability and promote patient-centered care. But we cannot simply assume that they will solve all our problems, nor do we know how long it will take to bring costs under control. In the meantime, we need to be prepared for a world in which health care costs continue to grow faster than the rest of the economy. Our proposals are one way to pay for those higher costs without forcing people to go without needed care. The alternatives—higher cost sharing at the moment that people need services, arbitrary caps on government spending that ignore whether people get the care they need, or health insurance vouchers that are not indexed to actual costs—are all mechanisms that save the government money by forcing families to pay more out of their own pockets.

NATIONAL DEFENSE

Along with Social Security and health care, the third major component of the federal budget is defense spending. We spend a lot on national defense: $689 billion in 2010, more than in any year since World War II after accounting for inflation; 4.7 percent of GDP, more than in any year since 1992, when the military was shrinking after the Cold War; 20 percent of all federal spending; and 43 percent of all military spending in the world, almost six times that of any other country.[59] Even excluding current operations in Iraq and Afghanistan, real defense spending is higher than it was during the Cold War, when we had a military superpower as a mortal enemy.[60] Nor is it clear that our current defense spending—which pays for over five thousand nuclear warheads and a navy that is larger than the next thirteen combined (eleven of which belong to our allies or partners), among other things—buys us the security we need today.[61] Since 2001, our primary enemies have been terrorist groups that someday may gain access to nuclear or other weapons of mass destruction. Perhaps someday, when China has built multiple aircraft carrier groups, we will need the eleven we currently have (no other country has more than one carrier group). But that day is not today.

At a high level, it should be possible to gradually reduce overall defense spending to 1999–2001 levels (3.0 percent of GDP) or lower without significantly increasing our national security risks. As Lawrence Korb, an assistant defense secretary under President Reagan, has pointed out, it was essentially this relatively inexpensive military that rapidly drove both the Taliban and Saddam Hussein from power.[62] The budget submitted by President Obama in 2011 already projected that defense spending would fall to around 3 percent of GDP by 2021.[63] Analysts from across the political spectrum have also agreed on various specific steps that could be taken to reduce defense spending. For example, the left-leaning Center for American Progress, the bipartisan Sustainable Defense Task Force, and conservative Republican senator Tom Coburn have all endorsed several spending reductions such as decreasing the number of aircraft carrier groups, limiting procurement of the F-35 and V-22, lowering troop levels in Europe and Asia, shrinking the nuclear arsenal, and reforming the Defense Department's health care system—steps that together would reduce spending by hundreds of billions of dollars over the next decade.[64] The decade following the September 11 attacks also saw the expansion of a vast, overlapping, poorly coordinated, and expensive intelligence apparatus, with a total cost exceeding $80 billion each year (most of which is outside the military budget).[65] With operations split across more than 1,200 government organizations and 1,900 private contractors, it is likely that eliminating redundant operations could both reduce spending and actually increase our security by improving communication among agencies—although organizational complexity and secrecy present high barriers to greater efficiency.[66]

We do not count any military or intelligence savings toward our long-term deficit reduction goals because we expect that these or similar cuts will be necessary to comply with the caps placed on discretionary spending by the Budget Control Act of 2011.* These savings opportunities, however, imply that our current high levels of defense spending can be brought down as required without materially compromising our national security.

ENERGY

One of the major challenges we face as a country is the need to transition away from fossil fuels and toward new energy sources. Over the long term, the price of fossil fuels is likely to increase as we exhaust more easily accessed deposits of oil, coal, and natural gas, and especially as developing countries such as China and India increase their

---

* The Budget Control Act placed caps on appropriations for discretionary spending in future years, leaving it up to future Congresses to decide how to reduce that spending. There is no specific cap for defense spending, but assuming that defense and nondefense spending fall by the same proportion, defense spending would have to fall to 2.7 percent of GDP by 2021. CBO, *The Budget and Economic Outlook: An Update*, August 2011, p. 21.

energy consumption. At the same time, fossil fuels impose significant costs on society, including air pollution (and its harmful health effects), dependence on various undemocratic or otherwise unsavory regimes around the world, and long-term climate change. Yet our current energy "strategy"—a hodgepodge of subsidies and tax breaks for renewable energy sources, biofuels such as ethanol, and fossil fuels—is unlikely to ensure long-term energy independence or to significantly reduce emissions of harmful pollutants and greenhouse gases.

The basic problem is that the total societal costs of using fossil fuels are not reflected in their prices; because they are too cheap by this standard, we use too much. The textbook solution is to impose taxes on fossil fuels (and other sources of greenhouse gas emissions) that reflect the additional costs they impose on society. Ordinarily we think taxes introduce distortions into the economy, changing the way resources are allocated. In this case, taxes can reduce distortions, making the economy more efficient. A "carbon tax" would be assessed on each ton of carbon dioxide (or its equivalent in other greenhouse gases) from the major sources of emissions—primarily combustion of oil, natural gas, and coal for electricity generation, transportation, industrial and commercial operations, and residences.[67] Properly designed, this tax could be applied to approximately 90 percent of all U.S. emissions.[68] Over time, it would induce companies and households to become more efficient at producing and using energy, thus reducing emissions.

Ideally, the tax per ton of carbon dioxide should be equivalent to the total societal cost of that ton of carbon dioxide—which is notoriously hard to estimate because it depends on complex climate models, estimates of the monetary cost of climate change, and discount rates (how much we care today about bad things that will happen in the future).[69] An alternative approach is to estimate the tax rate necessary to lower greenhouse gas emissions to a level that reduces the risk of major climate impacts.[70] Policy analysts have suggested that the price should be around $20 per ton of carbon dioxide and should rise from there (to encourage progressive reductions in emissions).[71] To put this in perspective, $20 per ton of carbon dioxide emissions works out to an additional 18 cents per gallon of gasoline—a price increase that is not insignificant, but that is small compared to recent swings in gas prices caused by volatility in oil prices.[72] A carbon tax at that level would generate revenues beginning at 0.6–0.8 percent of GDP and rising by an additional 0.1 percentage point by the early 2020s.[73]

A major problem with a carbon tax is that it is regressive. Although rich people consume more energy than poor people (they typically have larger houses with higher heating costs, for example), poor people have to devote a larger share of their income to energy (because everyone needs a basic amount of heat, electricity, and transportation).[74] The point of a carbon tax, however, is to counteract the social costs of greenhouse gas emissions while raising additional revenue to reduce deficits—not to change the distribution of income in society. Therefore, the carbon tax should ideally be made "distribution neutral": that is, it should increase everyone's total taxes by the same percentage amount.[75] This can be done by modifying income tax rates (raising them at the high end and lowering them at the low end) to neutralize the regressive impact of a carbon tax.[76] As an alternative, if raising income tax rates turns out to be politically impossible, up to one-half of the carbon tax revenues should be spent in the form of cash rebates to low-income households to cushion the impact of the tax.

A carbon tax could be implemented in two different ways. One is a direct tax on carbon, where, for example, each refinery has to pay the tax on each gallon of gasoline it produces. (That tax would be passed on to drivers at the pump.) The other is setting a cap on total emissions and auctioning off the right to emit greenhouse gases; in that case, each refinery would have to buy enough emission permits to cover the gasoline it produces, so in the end there would effectively be a tax on each ton of emissions. There has been extensive debate about which system is better; to simplify, one side argues that a direct tax is more efficient, the other that an emissions cap is more politically feasible.[77] In practice, however, most of the features of one approach can be replicated in the other, depending on the details of how each is implemented.[78] In our opinion, either approach would be a vast improvement over the current situation, both for economic incentives and for the federal budget.

Finally, a carbon tax would account for the greenhouse gases emitted by our cars, but not for all of the other social costs created by driving, which produces congestion, accidents, and local air pollution. In order to account for these externalities—costs to society that are not reflected in the cost of driving itself—taxes on gasoline would have to be about $1 per gallon, double their current level, or even higher.[79] Increasing the federal gasoline tax by 50 cents per gallon would benefit society by encouraging people to drive less, reducing congestion, accidents, and air pollution, and would also increase tax revenues by about 0.3 percent of GDP.[80] Alternatively, the gasoline tax could be made variable—higher when oil prices are low and lower when oil prices are high—in order to reduce volatility in gasoline prices.[81] In any case, a gasoline tax is regressive for the same reasons a carbon tax is regressive, and so we recommend either modifying income tax rates to make it distribution neutral or spending up to half of the additional proceeds as rebates to lower-income households.

FINANCE

Our current deficit problems are largely the product of our financial sector. As discussed in chapter 3, the financial crisis of 2007–2009 and ensuing recession increased projected national debt levels by almost 50 percent of GDP. Subtracting 50 percent of GDP has a major impact on any projection of future national debt. If there were no financial crisis and the Bush tax cuts were allowed to expire, our long-term deficit problems would be small and manageable; even if the Bush tax cuts were extended, the long-term national debt would look uncomfortably large, but nothing like it seems today. In addition, the risk of another financial crisis—and the need for fiscal space to respond to such a crisis—is a major reason to worry about our current situation. For these reasons, policies that reduce the risk and impact on taxpayers of a financial crisis are crucial to our long-term fiscal health—even leaving aside any desire to make the financial sector pay for all the trouble it has caused.

We have previously argued that the most direct way to reduce the riskiness, concentration, excessive size, and political power of the financial sector is to impose hard limits on the size of financial institutions.[82] A version of our proposal, however, was voted down in the Senate and appears even less likely to succeed today.[83] There are many other ways that excessive risk taking in the financial sector can be curbed, such as increasing capital requirements for large financial institutions—those most likely to be bailed out in a crisis, and hence those most likely to take the most risks.[84] Here we focus on ideas that can both reduce the incentives for financial institutions to engage in socially destructive behavior—like taking risks that only make sense because of the prospect of a government bailout—and raise additional revenues to reduce the deficit.

The first is a fee imposed on large financial institutions to compensate for the likely costs of future government rescues.[85] Since our largest banks are even larger than they were in 2007, they are even more "too big to fail," and it is virtually certain that they will require government support in a future crisis. That support should be given on less generous terms than during the recent crisis, but it will cost real money all the same. These too-big-to-fail institutions should have to pay a fee today based on their size and riskiness; for example, the more highly leveraged a bank, and hence the more vulnerable it is, the more it should have to pay. A fee that increases with leverage will also help counteract existing incentives for companies to take on too much debt. If properly designed, it will discourage financial institutions from taking on too much risk, which will reduce the threat they pose to the financial system. If designed solely to correct for the implicit government subsidy enjoyed by too-big-to-fail financial institutions, this fee could bring in close to 0.1 percent of GDP per year.[86] In addition, it will improve our long-term fiscal situation by helping to protect future taxpayers from the consequences of future financial crises, which are virtually inevitable.

The second idea is a financial activities tax aimed at curbing excessive risk taking in the financial sector.[87] Many financial institutions are highly leveraged (they have large amounts of debt relative to the money invested by shareholders), which gives them the incentive to engage in risky behavior: if things go well, shareholders and managers get to keep the profits, but if things go badly, some of the losses will be borne by creditors. These types of risks are like greenhouse gas emissions: good for the banks that take them but bad for society as a whole.[88] In theory, the solution is to tax risk taking to the point that the financial sector will only produce the amount of risk that is optimal for society—but in isolation it is difficult or impossible to identify which risks are good and which are bad. One solution to this problem is to impose an additional tax on high profits earned by financial institutions, which will make highly risky strategies less attractive and thereby reduce risk taking. Such a tax would be assessed only on unusually high compensation (the difference between what highly paid employees make in the financial sector and what people with similar skills and experience make in other sectors) and on unusually high profits (above a level reflecting ordinary or even moderately high returns to capital). According to an estimate by economists at the IMF, this tax base would range between 0.7 percent and 2.8 percent of GDP, so a tax at a 10 percent rate could raise 0.1–0.3 percent of GDP.[89] The major purpose of this tax, however, is not to reduce deficits, but to shift incentives in the financial sector away from levels of risk taking that are, on balance, bad for society. Together, these policies will help make the financial system safer and provide at least some of the funds necessary to cope with the next crisis.

THE SMALL STUFF

The federal government spends money on a myriad of other programs ranging from educational grants to housing subsidies to medical and space research. We do not have the space (or the expertise) to review all of these programs in detail, but there are certainly places where the government could spend less money and increase economic efficiency.

Fannie Mae and Freddie Mac are a classic (though complicated) example of a government program that distorts market outcomes. Before the recent financial crisis, Fannie and Freddie were "government-sponsored enterprises"—private companies subject to specific congressional mandates to support the housing market. They did this by buying mortgages from lenders, guaranteeing mortgages against default, and issuing securities backed by mortgages, all of which made it easier for banks and other lenders to make new housing loans. Because Fannie and Freddie were highly exposed to the mortgage market, they both failed when housing prices collapsed and were taken over by the government in 2008; they continue to buy and guarantee mortgages and to issue mortgage-backed securities. Currently, they charge less for guarantees than the private sector would charge; they do this in order to subsidize mortgages and keep the housing market going, and they can get away with it because, as wards of the federal government, they can borrow money cheaply. This policy lowers the cost of borrowing, encouraging families to go more deeply into debt; because it makes it easier to take out a big mortgage, it also inflates the price of houses.

Although Fannie and Freddie were relatively modest contributors to the financial frenzy that created the housing bubble, the experience of the last decade should have demonstrated the dangers of government policies that promote homeownership by subsidizing debt.[90] We think that Fannie and Freddie should gradually raise their guarantee fees to levels competitive with those of the private sector, which will increase their revenues and improve their long-term financial position while reducing this distortion in the price of mortgages.[91] We also recommend gradually lowering the limits on the mortgages that Fannie and Freddie are allowed to buy or guarantee, which will reduce government housing subsidies further, particularly for people who buy more expensive houses.[92]

Another complicated spending program that distorts economic decisions is our system of agricultural subsidies. In 2010, the Department of Agriculture distributed over $15 billion in subsidies through several overlapping programs.[93] Direct payments give people cash based on how much their land used to produce (whether or not it is still used as farmland); counter-cyclical payments pay farmers when crop prices fall below a target, effectively locking in a minimum price; marketing loans also guarantee a minimum price while allowing farmers to benefit if prices are higher than the target; crop insurance protects them from losses due to natural causes, with premiums heavily subsidized by the government; and in addition to crop insurance, the government also makes direct disaster payments to farmers affected by bad weather and other natural phenomena.[94]

These policies encourage overproduction of subsidized crops

such as corn and soybeans (since the government absorbs the risk
that prices will be low)—which is one reason why the American diet
includes so much high-fructose corn syrup.[95] Government subsidies
also help American companies export corn, cotton, and other crops
cheaply, undercutting farmers in developing countries.[96] In 2005, the
World Trade Organization ruled against the United States in a case
brought by Brazil challenging U.S. cotton subsidies; in response, the
federal government is now paying over $100 million per year in sub-
sidies to *Brazilian* cotton growers.[97] While farm subsidies are often
portrayed as a way to protect small family farms, an increasing share
of the money goes to the largest farms (and another chunk goes to
people who don't farm at all).[98] In this context, farm subsidies could
be dramatically scaled back, leaving unsubsidized insurance markets and commodity derivatives to protect most farmers from natural disasters and extreme price swings.[99] If preserving small family
farms is an important policy goal, then the government could provide them with subsidized crop insurance and assistance in hedging
transactions.

A more coherent energy policy, as described above, would also
allow the government to cut back on transportation subsidies. For
example, the federal budget currently allocates about $4 billion per
year on subsidies to intercity rail service and another $2 billion
per year to subsidies for building mass transit systems.[100] While
long-distance and mass transit train systems would help reduce air
pollution, slow the rate of climate change, and ease congestion on
roads, both a carbon tax and a higher gasoline tax should make them
more competitive compared to driving and flying, thus reducing
the need for subsidies. The federal government also subsidizes air
travel in various ways. For example, new fees introduced after September 11, 2001, cover less than half of federal spending on aviation
security, and corporate and personal aircraft do not pay their share
of air traffic control expenses.[101]

Although the potential benefits are often exaggerated, the federal
government could also save money simply by making its operations
more efficient. For example, the government currently spends about
$540 billion per year on goods and services. In 2009, about $170
billion in spending commitments were made in noncompetitive con-

tracts, and additional billions were spent in "competitive" contracts where only one bid was received. In some cases, this is unavoidable in the short term, because there may be only one qualified supplier for a given specialized product or service. The Government Accountability Office, however, has identified cases where federal agencies could use competitive processes to reduce costs.[102] The federal government could also follow the lead of many large corporations in centralizing procurement decisions in order to increase its buying power and obtain lower prices.[103]

Market forces should be able to produce a reasonable amount of home mortgages or corn. By contrast, a free market on its own will not produce enough public goods, such as education and basic research, because they generate benefits for society that are not captured by the people who pay for them (think of all the people who have benefited from the Internet, which was originally a Defense Department research project). For this reason we do not recommend withdrawing federal spending on education, although there may be ways to reduce waste and increase efficiency in the way that spending is delivered. Our future prosperity will depend on the productivity of our workforce, which largely depends on our educational system. Now, when our students rank twenty-fifth out of thirty-four OECD countries in math performance, is not the time to reduce government support for education.[104] We also do not recommend cutbacks in safety net programs such as the National School Lunch Program, the Supplemental Nutrition Assistance Program (food stamps), or Temporary Assistance for Needy Families. More than 15 percent of Americans live below the poverty line (about $22,000 for a family of four), the highest level since 1993;[105] in 2009, 15 percent couldn't afford to buy enough food, the highest level since the Census Bureau began collecting this information in the late 1990s.[106] Although providing basic subsistence to poor people may violate some theoretical norm of economic efficiency, we believe it falls well within the government's responsibility to protect its citizens from extreme misery and insecurity.

Domestic spending (other than Social Security and health care) is fragmented across many departments, agencies, and programs, of which we have only touched on a few. The cutbacks to Fannie Mae and Freddie Mac and to agricultural subsidies described above together would reduce spending by about 0.1 percent of GDP.[107] Spending cuts in areas such as transportation subsidies and through greater procurement efficiency will be necessary to bring discretionary spending down to the levels required by the Budget Control Act of 2011; since our projections already assume that Congress complies with that law, we do not count these spending cuts toward our long-term deficit reduction target.[108]

TAX EXPENDITURES

One of the major achievements of the Reagan administration was the Tax Reform Act of 1986, which simplified the tax code by eliminating a host of loopholes. Since then, however, Congress has steadily created new tax breaks, which reduce tax revenues, increase administrative costs, and give rise to complicated tax avoidance behavior—effort and expenses that serve no purpose other than reducing taxes. Many of these exemptions, deductions, or other loopholes are tax expenditures—the equivalent of government spending programs, since people receive cash (in the form of lower taxes) for engaging in certain activities (such as taking out mortgages). These tax expenditures, broadly defined, reduce federal tax revenue by about $1.2 trillion, or 7 percent of GDP.[109]

Eliminating or reducing tax expenditures presents a rare "win-win" opportunity: it increases revenues (reducing the deficit) without increasing tax rates, preserving the incentives to work and to save; and it increases economic efficiency by reducing government influence on individuals' decisions—a point argued by Martin Feldstein, a chair of the Council of Economic Advisers under President Reagan.[110] Some of the higher revenues could theoretically be set aside to lower tax rates, as suggested by some proponents of comprehensive tax reform or a "flat tax." This would only be prudent, however, if the Bush tax cuts were allowed to expire; otherwise the revenues from eliminating tax breaks will be needed to reduce long-term deficits.[111] In some cases, tax expenditures encourage behavior that may be beneficial for society—such as saving for retirement—so they need to be considered one at a time. Because there are far too many questionable tax provisions to review in this section, we only discuss a few proposals that will have the largest impact on both tax revenues and economic efficiency.

The single largest tax expenditure is the exclusion for employer-sponsored health benefits; as discussed above, we believe this exclusion should be phased out. The second largest is the deduction for mortgage interest on residences (and vacation homes, for the lucky). This deduction, which will lower tax revenues by about $99 billion in 2012, is the poster child for everything that is wrong with tax expenditures.[112] By reducing the real cost of a mortgage, it encourages people to borrow more money to buy bigger houses, contributing to the excessive household debt that helped produce the financial crisis. Because the value of the deduction depends on the size of your loan and the tax bracket you are in, it disproportionately benefits the wealthy.[113] The mortgage interest deduction does a bad job at its supposed objective of encouraging homeownership because the people who are most likely to be on the fence between owning and renting—low- to middle-income families—gain the least from it.[114] (In particular, if you don't have enough other deductions to make itemization worthwhile, you get nothing from the mortgage interest deduction.) Finally, in the wake of the housing bubble and financial crisis, it's less apparent than ever that using government policies to increase homeownership is a good idea to begin with.

For these reasons, we would prefer that the mortgage interest deduction did not exist. Unfortunately, eliminating it now could cause a severe economic shock: without it, families will not be able to pay as much for houses, and the value of all houses will fall, making it harder for homeowners to refinance and increasing foreclosure rates. Therefore, we recommend partially phasing out the deduction over several years and then letting it fade away over several decades. Today, the deduction is available on $1.1 million of mortgage debt. We would reduce that limit to $1 million in 2014 and gradually reduce it to $400,000 by 2020; since less than 10 percent of existing homes in the United States sell for more than $500,000 today, the vast majority of homes should not suffer immediate price declines.[115] This would increase tax revenues by about 0.2 percent of GDP in 2020, and by 0.3 percent in 2030.[116]

Another poorly designed subsidy hidden in the tax code is the exemption for interest on state and local bonds, which will cost the

Treasury $50 billion in 2012.[117] This is a transfer from the federal government to state and local governments because the tax exemption means that investors will accept lower rates of interest on their bonds. For technical reasons, however, about one-third of the subsidy winds up in the hands of the investors who buy these bonds.[118] If the tax exemption were replaced by a direct subsidy to the issuers of state and local bonds, the federal government could provide the same amount of assistance for only two-thirds of the cost. This change would increase tax revenues by about 0.1 percent of GDP, beginning later this decade.[119]

The federal government also helps state and local governments through the deduction for state and local taxes, which will reduce revenues by $74 billion in 2012.[120] The deduction means that the Treasury Department is essentially paying part of your state and local taxes, making it easier for state and local governments to raise money. This is an inefficient subsidy because, on a per capita basis, more money goes to states and towns that have higher taxes, and more money goes to states and towns that have more rich people (since this tax break only benefits people who itemize their deductions, and these people tend to be wealthier than others). In particular, this deduction benefits towns with expensive houses much more than towns with inexpensive houses because the former collect much more in property taxes than the latter. We recommend phasing out this deduction entirely and converting half of the new revenues into grants to states and localities; state and local governments could then decide whether to use the grants to lower taxes or increase services. After accounting for the grants, eliminating this tax break would increase revenues by about 0.2 percent of GDP.[121]

Not only does the federal government subsidize state and local governments, but it also subsidizes nonprofit organizations through the tax deduction for charitable contributions. If you are in the 35 percent tax bracket, out of every dollar you donate, the government is actually paying 35 cents. This tax deduction is occasionally defended as a way of patching our meager social safety net, but homeless shelters and soup kitchens compete for donations with the Metropolitan Opera, Harvard University, and even politically oriented think tanks.[122] In effect, the federal government spends $53 billion (in

2012) on nonprofit organizations—but lets rich people (the ones who make most of the contributions) decide who gets the money. There are many ways to scale back this subsidy that would have a small impact on nonprofit organizations. For example, only allowing the deduction for total donations above 2 percent of adjusted gross income (a policy applied to some other deductions) would increase tax revenues by 0.1 percent of GDP but reduce total charitable contributions by only 1 percent. Put another way, the federal government (meaning future taxpayers) would gain five times as much as charities would lose.[123]

Another large tax expenditure is preferential tax rates on income from investments, including capital gains (profits from selling assets for more than they cost) and dividends (payments made by corporations to their shareholders). Taxation of investment income is a complex problem that has occupied lawyers and economists for decades because it has no perfect solution. Taxing capital gains distorts economic choices by discouraging people from selling assets they would otherwise want to sell.[124] Because corporations already pay tax on their profits, taxing dividends on the individual level constitutes double taxation. One argument for a lower (but not zero) tax rate on capital gains is that some of the "gains" are really due to inflation, not real investment returns. But a lower rate on capital gains encourages people to engage in expensive tax avoidance strategies to convert ordinary income into capital gains. In addition, effective taxes on capital gains are already artificially low (even if they are taxed at the same rate as other income) since people can defer them indefinitely by waiting to sell their assets.[125]

The main economic argument for a lower tax rate on capital gains is that it encourages saving (by increasing the after-tax return on saving), which in turn encourages investment and economic growth. As discussed in chapter 6, however, the empirical evidence that higher taxes on capital gains reduce savings and economic growth is weak. The case for lower capital gains taxes becomes even weaker when they have the effect of increasing deficits, because any increase in private saving is offset by an increase in government borrowing. We have had a lower tax rate on capital gains than on ordinary income for most of the history of the income tax, but the 15 percent rate set by the 2003 tax cut is remarkably low; from the 1930s until 2003, the maximum capital gains rate never fell below 20 percent.[126] And the benefits of lower taxes on investments are highly skewed toward the wealthy: 96 percent of the total benefits are claimed by households making more than $100,000 per year, with 67 percent of the benefits going to households making more than $1 million per year.[127]

Given the large deficits we face today and in the foreseeable future, it makes sense to increase capital gains tax rates in order to reduce government borrowing; any reduction in personal saving is likely to be at least offset by the increase in government saving.[128] We propose increasing the maximum rate on capital gains and dividends to 28 percent, the level that applied from the Tax Reform Act of 1986 until the 1997 tax cut[129] and slightly above the median level for the entire post–World War II period (25 percent).[130] In the short term, a higher capital gains tax rate could make people less willing to sell their assets, reducing tax revenues. In the long run, however, a permanent change in tax rates should have little impact on actual asset sales, since most assets are sold eventually.[131] Leaving aside short-term fluctuations, this change should increase tax revenues by about 0.3 percent of GDP.[132]

Another problem with the current taxation of capital gains is called "stepped-up basis" at death. If you die and leave your assets to your heirs, no one ever pays tax on any appreciation that occurred during your lifetime. This reduces tax revenues and exacerbates the "lock-in" problem: people who would otherwise sell assets have a powerful incentive to hold on to them until they die. We do not see why families should pay lower taxes on investment profits simply because they can afford to pass assets from one generation to the next. One rationale for stepped-up basis was that it may be hard for heirs to figure out how much the deceased person originally paid for an asset, but today this should be an easily solvable problem, at least for the financial assets and real estate that produce a large portion of capital gains. This tax expenditure will cost the Treasury Department $61 billion in 2012; eliminating it should increase tax revenues by about 0.5 percent of GDP.[133] We also propose to scale back another capital gains tax break that exempts profits from the sale of a house. The amount of profit exempted from taxes should be gradually reduced from $500,000 (for couples) to $100,000. This would still protect most middle-income families from having to pay taxes on gains that are due solely to inflation while reducing the subsidy given to the rich. We estimate that reducing this tax expenditure would increase tax revenues by another 0.1 percent of GDP.[134]

Not all tax expenditures are equally bad. The various tax preferences for pension plans and retirement accounts (401(k) plans, IRAs, and so on) together cost $147 billion, but these provisions are designed to encourage saving in general and retirement saving in particular—both things that Americans currently do not do enough of. Other commonly cited tax expenditures, such as the child tax credit and the earned income tax credit, are more like features that modify the distribution of the income tax based on ability to pay than like covert spending programs.[135] But besides the examples discussed above, there are plenty of other tax expenditures of questionable value, such as the tax exemption for life insurance products.

Since some tax expenditures are better than others, we prefer to review them on their individual "merits." Politically, however, this may be impossible because each one benefits a particular interest group that will defend it tooth and nail: the mortgage and real estate industries for the mortgage interest deduction, the life insurance industry for the life insurance exemption, and so on. Other people and groups have proposed across-the-board solutions. President Obama's bipartisan National Commission on Fiscal Responsibility and Reform recommended simply eliminating all tax expenditures or, alternatively, eliminating all of them except the earned income tax credit, the child tax credit, and reduced versions of a few other popular tax breaks.[136] Eliminating all tax expenditures would increase revenues by something on the order of 7 percent of GDP, solving our deficit problems for several decades in a single stroke, and would generally be progressive, since the rich benefit more from tax expenditures overall. But it could also cause severe economic disruptions as housing prices fall, retirement savings rates fall, low-income families lose the earned income tax credit, and nonprofit organizations are forced to contract.

Another nearly comprehensive approach that would have a less drastic impact on the economy is limiting the amount by which any family can benefit from tax deductions. Martin Feldstein, Daniel

Feenberg, and Maya MacGuineas have estimated that capping benefits from tax expenditures at 2 percent of each household's income would have increased tax revenues by $278 billion in 2011, or 1.8 percent of GDP.*[137] This proposal would increase revenues and reduce distortions, but would hit all tax expenditures equally, regardless of their redeeming features. In addition, it would constitute a flat tax increase, since all income groups would see their taxes go up by roughly the same percentage of their income;[138] so while it might make up much of the revenue lost in the Bush tax cuts, the overall tax system would end up being much less progressive than before 2001. A more progressive alternative is limiting the percentage by which deductions can be used to reduce taxes. Today, a $1,000 deduction is worth $350 to someone in the top (35 percent) tax bracket but only $100 to someone in the lowest (10 percent) bracket. Limiting the value of itemized deductions to 15 percent of the deduction amount, regardless of tax bracket, would increase tax revenues by 0.7 percent of GDP per year;[139] this change would only affect people who are not in the lowest tax bracket and who itemize their deductions, so it would be somewhat progressive. It would also avoid the need to debate the merits of individual tax expenditures (but, unfortunately, would not affect several tax expenditures that do not appear as deductions, such as lower tax rates on capital gains).

Through some combination of these proposals, individual income tax expenditures (other than the employer health plan exclusion) could be reduced by 1–2 percent of GDP while maintaining existing incentives to work and save and avoiding a severe economic shock. Much larger revenue increases are possible if we are willing to eliminate tax expenditures that encourage saving (such as tax preferences for retirement accounts) or to undergo short-term economic risks (such as by completely eliminating the mortgage interest deduction).

The corporate income tax offers fewer opportunities to raise revenue while reducing distortions because business tax expenditures in aggregate are much smaller than individual tax expenditures. Still, the tax code includes over $30 billion worth of tax breaks targeted

---

* The increase in tax revenues would have been only $138 billion, or 0.9 percent of GDP, not counting the employer health plan exclusion, which we discussed above.

at particular industries such as energy (both fossil fuels and renew-ables), timber, agriculture, or manufacturers.[140] Eliminating all of these tax expenditures would increase revenues by about 0.2 percent of GDP without raising tax rates, while reducing economic distor-tions created by government policies that favor one industry over another industry or one group of companies over another group. There are other, more fundamental problems with our corporate tax system: among other things, it encourages companies to take on more debt and to leave their earnings overseas for as long as pos-sible. But while solutions to these problems are desirable on other grounds, they are unlikely to raise additional tax revenues and help solve our long-term budgetary problems.[141]

CONSUMPTION AND SAVING

American families do not save a lot of money. The household savings rate—the percentage of after-tax income that is not consumed in purchases of goods and services—averaged 9.6 percent in the 1970s and then declined steadily from the early 1980s until the peak of the housing bubble in 2005–2006, falling as low as 1.5 percent.[142] This long-term decline in savings probably has multiple causes. Many middle-class families, which have seen stagnant wages for most of the past three decades, became increasingly reliant on credit to main-tain or improve their standard of living; while inflation has been low since the 1990s, the rising prices of health care and education forced many families to take on additional debt; financial innovations, such as the exotic mortgages that fueled the housing bubble, made it eas-ier for people to borrow money out of proportion to their income; and the bubble itself, by making people richer on paper, encouraged them to consume more and worry less about saving.[143] Low savings and high debts hurt our economy in several ways. The vast increase in household debt not only helped inflate the recent housing bubble but also made many families acutely vulnerable to the ensuing crash, deepening the recession; insufficient savings mean that many people are not adequately prepared for retirement (making them that much more dependent on Social Security and Medicare); and less household saving means that less money is available for productive invest-ment by businesses, which can hurt long-term economic growth and increases our reliance on borrowing from overseas.

The benefits of encouraging savings, or at least not discouraging savings, are one reason why many experts have suggested shifting from an income tax system (where we pay tax on money when we make it) partially or entirely to a consumption tax system (where we pay tax on money when we spend it).[144] The basic reason is that an income tax encourages people to spend their money today rather than saving it for tomorrow, while a consumption tax does not affect decisions about when to spend.[145] Of course, adding a new consump-tion tax without reducing other taxes would not increase household savings. But the conundrum we face is that if the Bush income tax cuts are made permanent, we will need to either increase tax reve-nues somehow or scale back the social insurance system for the mid-dle class. If we have to raise additional tax revenues, we should do so in a way that is efficient—that distorts economic choices as little as possible—and that best supports long-term growth.

These considerations imply that some of our long-term budget gap should be filled through a value-added tax (VAT), a type of con-sumption tax that is currently used (typically alongside an income tax) by every developed country except the United States.[146] A value-added tax does not affect companies' decisions about how to do business, and, unlike an income tax, does not discourage people from saving. Because it is applied to a very broad tax base—almost all final sales of goods and services to consumers—a relatively low tax rate can generate large amounts of revenue. For example, a VAT of 5 percent with only a small number of exclusions (education, government-paid health care, charitable services, and government services) could bring in 1.7 percent of GDP in revenues.[147]

The major problem with a value-added tax is that it is regressive: households with lower incomes pay a larger share of their incomes because high-income households tend to save more and consume less. This discrepancy can be dramatic, with bottom-quintile house-holds paying an effective tax rate five times as high as top-quintile households (although other ways of measuring the distribution of the tax burden yield different results).[148] As with a carbon tax, our preferred solution is to adjust the income tax to make the introduction of a VAT distribution neutral—increasing income tax rates at the high end and lowering them at the low end (and expanding tax credits to benefit households that pay no income tax) so that each income group sees its taxes go up by the same percentage. (Households that rely primarily on Social Security would be protected from a VAT—which will create a one-time increase in prices when it is introduced—by the fact that Social Security benefits are indexed for inflation.) Alternatively, one-half of the proceeds of a value-added tax could be used to cushion the impact of the tax on low-income households, in the form of either lower income or payroll taxes or cash rebates. (In this case, we could still reduce the deficit by 1.7 percent of GDP simply by doubling the tax rate.)

Introducing a value-added tax, along with our earlier recommendations to scale back tax expenditures, would reduce the long-term budget deficit while minimizing the distortions introduced by our tax system. It would not, however, do much to make the tax code less complicated and more efficient in general—something tax experts have been recommending for a long time. The central task at hand, however, is dealing with our growing national debt, and while comprehensive tax reform has its own merits, we do not believe it should stand in the way of reducing the federal government's long-term budget deficits.

In addition to a value-added tax, there are more direct ways to increase the household savings rate, particularly by encouraging people to save more in their current retirement accounts (401(k)s, IRAs, and so on). The problems with these defined contribution plans (so named because participants put aside a specific amount of money, but don't know how much they will be able to withdraw in retirement) are well known: many people don't sign up in the first place; those who do don't save enough and don't increase their contributions as their earnings increase; some of their contributions get withdrawn early and never make it to retirement; and even the money that does stay in the account gets eroded by unnecessary asset management fees. These are all reasons why, despite the popular belief that a 401(k) is the ticket to a comfortable old age, the median household that was close to retirement only had $86,000 in its retirement accounts as of 2009.[149] Recent research has shown that simply changing the default options for retirement plans can increase savings rates dramatically: for example, if employees are automatically enrolled but can opt out, participation rates will be much higher than if they are not enrolled but can opt in—even though the two situations present the exact same choices.[150]

Many large companies have voluntarily switched to automatic 401(k) enrollment, but there are many other ways to increase retirement savings. In addition to requiring automatic enrollment for retirement plans, Congress could mandate other default options: for example, plans could be required to automatically increase each participant's savings rate over time, although individuals could opt out of those increases.[151] In these cases, participants still have freedom of choice, but they are likely to save more—something that most Americans admit they should be doing anyway.[152] The government could also change plan rules to make it harder for people to take early withdrawals (while still allowing them to borrow from their accounts), which would increase the amount of money actually available for retirement. Although these policies would not directly reduce government budget deficits, they could significantly boost private savings rates, which would have two important effects. First, it would increase the pool of savings available for government borrowing—which could be especially important if countries such as China begin reducing their savings rates. Second, higher household savings could, in the long term, make people better prepared for retirement; only then would it be possible to reduce spending on Social Security and Medicare without causing a major increase in poverty among the elderly.

SUMMARY

This is not an exhaustive list of the ways that we can reduce spending or increase tax revenues while promoting economic efficiency, correcting for negative externalities such as pollution and climate change, and increasing fairness in the distribution of burdens and benefits; such a list would require an encyclopedia, not a chapter. In addition, there are other sensible things we can do that do not affect the federal budget directly but that will improve the government's financial position over the long term. One is encouraging legal immigration, since more workers are good for Social Security's and Medicare's finances—unless they are undocumented. Another is investments that improve the long-term productive capacity of our economy—ranging from basic scientific research to early childhood education (which could produce a more highly skilled workforce and make it easier for new parents to continue working)—which will increase the tax base and shrink the national debt as a share of GDP. This is not the place to debate which policies can best foster innovation and productivity, but ideally we should reduce our projected deficits by enough so that the federal government will have the capacity to make productivity-enhancing investments.

The recommendations in this chapter show one way to reduce our long-term deficits and bring the national debt down to a reasonable level without major changes in the social insurance programs that most Americans rely on today or will rely on in the future. The idea that fiscal responsibility requires large cuts in spending on Social Security and Medicare is simply not true. As discussed earlier, assuming that the Bush-era income and estate tax cuts are made permanent, we will need to reduce deficits by 5.5 percent of GDP over the long term in order to stabilize the national debt at 50 percent of GDP around 2030. The proposals summarized in Table 7-1 would together reduce deficits by about 6 percent of GDP and make only small changes to Social Security and Medicare benefits. Closer inspection of other tax expenditures and spending programs would certainly yield additional savings, although we have touched on many of the largest opportunities.

Our recommendations do not reduce federal spending simply by shifting that spending to households. In addition to bringing the national debt under control, our proposals eliminate economic distortions and directly address some of the most pressing problems facing our society—the kinds of problems that government exists to solve. These polices would eliminate some of the incentives for increased borrowing that helped produce the recent housing bubble; reduce taxpayer subsidies for homeownership; make large financial institutions pay for the effective government guarantee that they enjoy today; reduce excessive risk taking in the financial sector; reduce unnecessary, market-distorting agricultural subsidies; get the government out of the business of picking winners and losers among

Table 7-1: Long-Term Deficit Reduction Proposals

	Average Impact on Deficits in 2020s (percent of GDP)
Social Security	
Increase earnings cap on payroll taxes	0.3%
Index retirement age	0.1%
Cover newly hired state and local government employees	0.1%
Increase payroll tax by 1 percentage point	0.4%
Health Care	
Phase out employer health plan exclusion (rebate one-half of proceeds)	0.6–0.9%
Require minimum rebates for pharmaceuticals purchased through Medicare	0.1%
Increase Medicare Part B premium to 30 percent of costs	0.1%
Increase Medicare payroll tax by 1 percentage point	0.5%
Energy	
Introduce carbon tax (rebate one-half of proceeds)	0.4%
Increase gasoline tax (rebate one-half of proceeds)	0.2%
Finance	
Charge "too-big-to-fail" financial institutions for anticipated rescue costs	0.1%
Tax excessive risk taking in financial sector	0.1–0.3%
Other Domestic Spending	
Mandatory spending reductions (Fannie Mae/Freddie Mac, farm subsidies)	0.1%
Individual Tax Expenditures	
Reduce mortgage interest deduction	0.3%
Replace exemption for interest on state and local bonds with a direct subsidy	0.1%
Phase out deduction for state and local taxes (convert one-half of proceeds into direct subsidies)	0.2%
Add floor to allowable charitable contributions	0.1%
Increase maximum capital gains and dividends tax rate to 28 percent	0.3%

Eliminate step-up of capital gains at death	0.5%
Reduce capital gains exemption for sale of house	0.1%
Alternative Proposals (cannot be simply added to those above)	
Eliminate all tax expenditures	~7%
Cap tax expenditures at 2 percent of household income	0.9–1.8%
Limit value of deductions to 15 percent	0.7%
Business Tax Expenditures	
Eliminate business tax expenditures	0.2%
Consumption Tax	
Introduce value-added tax (at 5 percent tax rate, rebate one-half of proceeds)	0.9%
Total (excluding alternative individual tax expenditure proposals)	**5.8–6.3%**

This table excludes reductions in discretionary spending because those are already required to meet the spending caps set in the Budget Control Act of 2011.

different industries; reduce greenhouse gas emissions and accelerate the necessary transition to alternative energy sources; and encourage Americans to save rather than consume. In addition, they would scale back tax breaks that largely benefit wealthy families and replace them with transparent spending programs that benefit all people equally.

Because there is no such thing as a free lunch, our proposals largely fill the long-term budget gap by increasing tax revenues. People who evaluate the federal government solely by the dollar value of taxes and spending will object that our proposals amount to "big government." As we explained in chapter 4, however, this is a misleading measure of the true impact of government on the private sector. A large portion of those higher tax revenues comes from cutting back on tax expenditures, which are really spending programs hidden in the tax code. From an economic standpoint, this has the same effect as reducing spending (and the impact of government), not increasing taxes. Another chunk of revenues comes from taxes that correct for well-known problems created by the energy and finance sectors. These taxes, by forcing people and companies to bear the full societal costs of their actions, are necessary in order for markets to function properly. Finally, increases in the payroll taxes for Social Security and Medicare reflect the increasing value of those programs to participants. Medicare, for example, is a health plan that all of us buy from the federal government, and as health care becomes more expensive, the value of that plan goes up. More generally, because we maintain Social Security and Medicare in roughly their current form, the government's role in both retirement saving and health care for the elderly will remain essentially the same. The number of dollars involved will go up not because the government becomes more active, but because there will be more elderly people and health care will be a larger share of the economy.

These proposals raise the amount of taxes paid by the rich, because high-income families benefit the most from the tax expenditures that we target. Our plan will have a much smaller impact on their incentives to work and to save. The top marginal income tax rate will go up by only 1 percentage point (because of our proposal to increase the Medicare payroll tax rate);[153] assuming that the Bush income tax cuts are made permanent, the top marginal rate would still be considerably lower than it was under President Clinton. Our plan also leaves the tax rates on capital gains and dividends at the levels set by the Tax Reform Act of 1986.

The cumulative impact on the middle class is more problematic. Although tax expenditures such as the mortgage interest deduction benefit the rich more than the middle class, they do benefit the middle class as well (ignoring the long-term impact of higher deficits). Higher payroll taxes will also reduce the disposable income of all working families. And the rebates that we propose to cushion the impact of several of our recommendations will not fully protect the middle class from paying higher taxes. This is not an ideal solution. But if the goal is to increase tax rates on the rich, the easiest way to do that is to let the Bush income and estate tax cuts expire; it is far easier for Congress to do nothing than to pass a bill that increases tax rates. Failing that, we think the most important priority for the middle class is preserving Social Security, Medicare, and Medicaid more or less in their current forms, which our plan accomplishes.

By contrast, if the income and estate tax cuts are allowed to expire, we only need to reduce deficits by 3 percent of GDP to meet our long-term goal—stabilizing the national debt at 50 percent of GDP by 2030. In that case, we would recommend a subset of the items in Table 7-1, focusing on proposals that would be good policy regardless of the budgetary situation—energy taxes, a fee on too-big-to-fail financial institutions, and the elimination of market-distorting tax expenditures, for example. A larger portion of the higher tax revenues generated by these policies could be used in rebates back to lower- and middle-income families. Money from eliminating business tax expenditures could be used to lower corporate tax rates. A new consumption tax could be made "revenue neutral," with the proceeds used entirely to reduce individual income tax rates. A much wider range of policy options would become available. But all of this requires that the Bush tax cuts expire.

As mentioned above, there has been an abundance of deficit reduction proposals in the past few years. While our plan shares many components with other recent plans—for example, most include the elimination of at least some tax expenditures—we offer a fundamentally different path toward long-term fiscal health. Our differences with traditional liberals and conservatives are obvious. The Congressional Progressive Caucus, for example, relies much more heavily on higher tax rates: its proposed budget increases tax rates to 45 percent on income over $1 million and 49 percent for income over $1 billion, while taxing capital gains as ordinary income.[154] By contrast, we favor a top tax rate of 39.6 percent, the level set by President Clinton in 1993. The proposal of the Republican-led House Budget Committee reduces the long-term national debt by fundamentally changing the nature of Medicare, shifting the risk of rising health care costs from the government onto beneficiaries, and even cuts the top income tax rate from 35 percent (the level set by President Bush in 2001) to 25 percent.[155] As should be clear by now, we strongly oppose proposals that reduce deficits by shifting risks from the federal government onto individuals and families.

There are also clear differences between the approach laid out in this chapter and the various bipartisan proposals that have been put forward by the National Commission on Fiscal Responsibility and Reform (established by President Obama in 2010, known as "Simpson-Bowles" after its cochairs), the Bipartisan Policy Center's Debt Reduction Task Force (known as "Domenici-Rivlin" after its cochairs), the "Gang of Six" (a group of senators that created a plan during the 2011 debt ceiling standoff), or the Committee for a Responsible Federal Budget (CRFB). All of these plans reflect the same "centrist" conventional wisdom: social insurance programs—particularly Medicare—must be scaled back (though not as dramatically as in the House Budget Committee's plan) and taxes must be *cut*. For example, Simpson-Bowles dictates that federal government health care spending may not grow more than 1 percentage point faster than GDP (which is considerably slower than required by current demographic and health care trends); Domenici-Rivlin sets the same limit on growth in Medicare spending by giving beneficiaries vouchers that grow in value at a predetermined rate, regardless of actual health care inflation; and the CRFB has insisted on ending "open-ended" health care commitments.[156] At the same time, these proposals—which march under the banner of deficit reduction—all include major tax cuts. The 2001 tax cut reduced the top income tax rate to 35 percent, which will increase to 39.6 percent if the tax cut is allowed to expire. Both Simpson-Bowles and the Gang of Six set the top income tax rate somewhere between 23 and 29 percent; Domenici-Rivlin puts it at 27 percent; and the CRFB calls for lower tax rates.[157] These plans also eliminate various tax expenditures, but they still leave tax revenues far lower than they would be if the Bush tax cuts were simply allowed to expire.[158]

Our approach differs from these plans in two fundamental ways. First, we do not agree that the solution to our government's budget problems is to shift those problems onto families. The best solution for everyone is one that reduces the overall cost of health care throughout the economy. But if that cannot be achieved, plans that deal with rising costs simply by forcing the elderly and the poor to absorb them do not make the American people as a whole better off. For this reason, we do not place artificial caps on government health care spending and we do not limit the federal government's contributions to Medicare. Second, we think that now is not the time to cut taxes—and large deficits should not be used to justify deficit-

increasing tax cuts. Our preference is to let all of the Bush tax cuts expire, not to reduce income tax rates to even lower levels.

The bottom line is that our long-term budget problems can be solved without gutting our major social insurance programs or our modest safety net. We can do it the easy way, by letting the Bush tax cuts expire and adding several obvious policies that reduce deficits and make the economy run more efficiently. Or we can make the tax cuts permanent, which will require a much longer list of tax increases and spending cuts. Even in that world, we can still close the long-term budget gap while strengthening the economy and preserving the essential programs that Americans depend on. Whether we choose to do so is a question not of economics, but of politics.

CONCLUSION

A popular Government, without popular information, or the means of acquiring it, is but a Prologue to a Farce or a Tragedy; or, perhaps both. Knowledge will forever govern ignorance: And a people who mean to be their own Governors, must arm themselves with the power which knowledge gives.

—James Madison, 1822[1]

America faces a choice. At first glance, it seems like we face a boring, somewhat technical choice between various ways of dealing with budget deficits and the national debt. But how we deal with the long-term debt problem reflects a more fundamental choice of the kind of government that we want to have: what services we want it to provide, what risks we want it to protect us from, and what role we want it to play in our lives. Many people may be tempted to answer "none at all," but this is hardly a plausible answer. National defense is something that few people would be willing to forgo; more fundamentally, without government enforcement of property rights and contract law, it's not clear what kind of society could exist in the first place. Countries with minimal governments do exist; most are in the developing world, and they are hardly places of great safety, let alone prosperity.[2]

Ultimately, our choice of government implies a choice of the kind of society we want to live in. The federal government obviously does not dictate the shape of American society, which depends on the individual actions of more than 300 million people. But the government is the mechanism through which we collectively establish the rules according to which our institutions and markets evolve. Do we think that assistance to the poor should be delivered by charitable organizations rather than by government agencies? Then we should have policies that promote charitable contributions, such as the existing tax deduction. Do we think that people should have equal access to higher education regardless of their financial circumstances? Then we need educational grants and subsidized student loans (or regulations requiring schools to ensure equal opportunity). Do we want people to save more money for old age? Then we need policies that encourage retirement savings, such as tax preferences for pensions and individual retirement accounts. These are all policy choices that we expect to be made by our elected representatives in Washington. Even a decision to drastically restrict the number of choices that the government can make is a choice in favor of a certain kind of society.

We have definite opinions about the type of society that we want our children to grow up in. It should be a society in which innovation, creativity, and hard work are amply rewarded, but where people without the skills currently valued by the job market do not have to suffer hunger and homelessness. It should be a society where success can bring riches, but the opportunity to succeed is not restricted by the fortunes of birth. It should be a society where markets allocate electronic gadgets and designer handbags, but not clean air and clean water. It should be a society where people worry about whether their businesses will succeed or fail, but not about whether they will be able to afford basic health care in old age.

The government plays a crucial role in this type of society. As virtually everyone would agree, it provides the basic structures and guarantees that make a market economy possible: property rights, the rule of law, the money supply, a robust financial system, and so on. It invests in public goods that increase economic prosperity but that a free market does not produce enough of, such as transportation infrastructure, education, and basic research. It provides protection against risks that individuals and businesses cannot protect themselves against, even with the help of insurance markets. These protections take many forms: national security, ranging from the invasion of Afghanistan to the increase in aviation security after September 11, 2001; disaster relief in the wake of hurricanes, earthquakes, floods, and wildfires; monitoring of global epidemics by the Centers for Disease Control; regulations and inspection regimes to protect against toxins in our food, water, and air; the social insurance programs through which Americans protect themselves against unemployment, save for retirement, and pay for health care in old age; and safety net programs that ensure a basic minimum of food and health care for the poor. Protection from the consequences of failure is what gives people the freedom to take risks in the first place; there are so many startups in Silicon Valley because there is no stigma attached to failure. By contrast, if your only way to get decent health insurance is through your current employer, you are far less likely to quit and start a new company.

The federal government's role as the insurer of last resort was never more on display than during the financial crisis that began in 2007. At its peak, there was a real risk that the global financial system would simply stop working, with unknown but terrifying consequences for all of us. Mohamed El-Erian, chief executive of PIMCO, one of the world's leading investment firms, asked his wife to withdraw as much cash as she could from the ATM—because he didn't know if banks would open for business.[3] The Treasury Department and the Federal Reserve responded with unprecedented financial force, making trillions of dollars available to keep banks afloat at virtually any cost. In the end, the government succeeded in keeping the banks open, and instead of a second Great Depression we "only" suffered through the worst recession since World War II.

The lesson of the financial crisis should be that in today's complicated and dangerous world, government protection from extreme risks is more important than ever. Other, less dramatic changes in American society over the past few decades have also left many people more exposed to a wide variety of risks that they are ill equipped to handle on their own. The decline of traditional defined benefit pensions (which assure employees a specific level of income during retirement) has exposed more people to the risks of not saving enough and poor investment performance, making them more dependent on Social Security. The increasing cost of health care has left fifty million people uninsured and made all of us more reliant on Medicare to cover us in old age. The decline of unions has decreased job security, increasing the risk of involuntary job loss and the importance of unemployment insurance. Global competition in manufacturing and some service industries may benefit Americans overall, but makes it more likely that people will suddenly find themselves without marketable skills mid-career. In many ways, the dominance of the free market ideology—open markets and unrestrained competition above all else—has made all of us more vulnerable, as individuals, to the vicissitudes of fortune.

And yet our current large deficits—which are the direct result of a nearly catastrophic financial crisis brought on by a deregulated banking sector—are being used as a reason to dismantle the protections provided by the federal government, from environmental regulation to Medicare. Yes, government costs money. Yes, if we want to have decent social insurance programs and a basic safety net, we must be willing to pay for them. And yes, as of today, we are not paying for them: we have already run deficits for a decade, Social Security faces a moderately sized long-term deficit, and there is no plan on the books to pay for expected increases in health care costs. But the fact that we are not paying for these programs does not mean that we cannot pay for them, or that we should not pay for them. In this age of "free markets" (which are really distorted by all kinds of government guarantees and subsidies), the American middle class needs protection from extreme risks more than ever. It would be perverse to eliminate those protections because a devastating failure of those same markets has drained the government of the money to pay for them.

As we have tried to show in the previous chapter, it is possible to stabilize the national debt, preserve the fiscal space necessary to deal with future crises, and maintain our social insurance programs while also removing economic distortions and helping tackle some of our most urgent challenges. Other people will prefer different combinations of tax increases and spending cuts to bring the national debt under control, with different implications for the role of government and the way risks are spread across society. But most importantly, our long-term debt problem can be solved—without the need for drastic remedies like eliminating Medicare as an insurance program or raising tax rates to 1950s levels. With our large and growing economy and the dollar's status as the primary global reserve currency, we are unlikely anytime soon to turn into Greece, unable to find anyone willing to lend us money. Despite our massive housing bubble, we are not living through an economic contraction as severe as Ireland's. The national debt is not some monster of unfathomable proportions and appetite that will devour the U.S. economy unless we sacrifice our firstborn children to it. It is a policy problem that requires a clear vision of what kind of government we are willing to pay for and the willingness to make the choices necessary to get to that outcome.

The federal government collects tax revenue from almost all of us (when we are working) and uses that money to provide services that benefit almost all of us. So while debates about deficits and the national debt are often framed in abstract terms—what is the "right" level of taxes, for example—they are really about distributional issues: what we will do with the resources that we produce as a society. But the question is not simply about whether money should be transferred from the rich to the poor today. The most important question is how much money we should pool today to insure all of us against outcomes that we cannot foresee tomorrow. In early modern Europe, one major function of the emerging nation-state was to protect people against foreign invasion. Today, we rely on the government to protect us from a much longer list of risks, including unemployment, disability, poor health, and insufficient retirement savings.

The great deficit debate is about how much risk people should bear themselves and how much they should pool with each other via the government. We believe that we should maintain our current levels of government social insurance and risk management—especially now that the risks faced by ordinary families are only increasing because of global competition, rising health care costs, the decline of traditional pensions, and the increasing inequality generated by a winner-take-all economy. For one thing, sharing the risk of unforeseeable outcomes is only fair. Disability, unemployment, medical emergency, or a stock market crash can happen to anyone, often through no fault of her own. Is it fair for people to be forced into poverty or denied health care because of random chance?

Ours is a democratic political system, however, where public policy depends not on moral considerations, but on the decisions of elected officials who are ultimately accountable to ordinary voters. The current dysfunction of our political system, clearly visible in the

2011 debt ceiling standoff and the failure of the resulting "supercommittee," is possible in part because many Americans are confused about the federal budget, the causes of deficits, and the connection between the federal government and their own lives. These are abstract, boring topics that few people want to study in their scarce leisure time. But the stakes are particularly high. How we deal with our long-term deficits will have a fundamental impact on the nature of the social contract in America. Yet many people do not understand where their taxes go, what the government does, how it distributes resources and pools risks, and what the resulting deficits mean to them. When it comes to budgetary issues, both ordinary people and politicians in Washington are susceptible to magical thinking. This takes many forms: recipients of handouts who do not realize their benefits are provided by government social programs; tax-break beneficiaries who think the government does not help them; opinion-survey respondents who want Congress to cut spending but not to cut any actual spending programs; the persistent belief that tax cuts will pay for themselves, eliminating the need for hard choices; and the faith that since the United States has not suffered a fiscal crisis in a long time, we will be immune to such crises in the future.

Magical thinking enables politicians to avoid seriously addressing deficits and the national debt—and to punish those who try to do so. President Reagan, who made balancing the budget a central theme of his 1980 election campaign, presided over what were then the largest peacetime deficits in U.S. history. When his successor, President George H. W. Bush, agreed to raise taxes to reduce the deficit in 1990, he was widely attacked by conservatives in his own party, which contributed to his defeat two years later. President Clinton's similar decision in 1993 was one factor in his party's crushing losses in the 1994 elections. A decade later, when Vice President Dick Cheney said, "Reagan proved deficits don't matter," it probably wasn't economics he had in mind: it was politics.[4] In this political climate, there are ample rewards for talking about deficits, but not for doing much about them.

In 1812, the Democratic-Republican majority in Congress pushed for war with Great Britain yet was unwilling to raise taxes enough to pay for it. The result was a deep fiscal crisis that threatened the country's ability to defend its borders. Today, we know that an aging society and increasingly expensive health care will require higher spending by the federal government, especially given many families' meager retirement savings. So far, however, Congress has refused either to raise taxes or to scale back popular spending programs.

But at the end of the day, how we deal with our national debt will affect you, and you have the right to tell your representatives what to do about it. So the question for you is: how much risk do you want to take on? Certainly there are people—Bill Gates, Warren Buffett, the Waltons, and the Koch brothers come to mind—who can bear any amount of financial risk themselves. If you are not so lucky, are you prepared for your retirement income to depend solely on your ability to save, your investment choices, and the vicissitudes of the market? Are you ready to pay for your own health insurance in old age, no matter how much it may cost by then? Are you sure that you have the marketable skills necessary to find a new job quickly if your employer goes out of business? What would you do if you became unable to work at all? And could you pay for years of long-term care in a nursing home, either for you or for your parents?

If you are like most Americans, we suspect the answer to these questions is no, especially after a decade of stagnant median real wages was punctuated by the worst recession since the 1930s. Most Americans, we think, are made better off by programs that require insurance contributions today but provide protection against unforeseeable and unavoidable risks in the long term. The question we leave you with is this: Are you and your family willing to face these risks alone, not knowing what will happen in the future, or do you want to live in a society that will protect you from misfortunes that lie beyond your control? For this is what the debate over the national debt boils down to, and its outcome depends on you.

EPILOGUE TO THE

VINTAGE BOOKS EDITION

In August 2011, while writing this book, we were on vacation in South Florida with our families. We watched Hurricane Irene approach the Florida coastline before turning north and eventually making landfall in North Carolina. Like millions of other people, we anxiously followed the forecasts published by the National Weather Service and based on models developed by the National Hurricane Center—forecasts that families relied on when making travel plans or deciding whether or not to evacuate. That experience gave us the idea to begin chapter 4, on the role and size of the federal government, with the story of Hurricane Irene.

Late in 2012, as we write this epilogue, residents of many towns in New Jersey and New York are still digging out from under the damage caused by the devastating floods unleashed by Hurricane Sandy on October 29. The National Weather Service forecast for Sandy's path was breathtakingly accurate; the storm cruised northeast, parallel to the Atlantic coastline, before making a sharp left turn and slamming into the New Jersey coast, almost exactly as predicted. Like Irene before it, Sandy highlighted the importance of the federal government in times of crisis. In the storm's wake, New Jersey governor Chris Christie, a conservative Republican, toured the state with President Barack Obama and heaped praise on the president's response to the storm, potentially helping President Obama in the last week of a hard-fought reelection campaign.[1]

In the end, Obama defeated Republican challenger Mitt Romney on November 6 by a margin of about 3.6 percentage points in the national popular vote.[2] But to no one's surprise, the election settled none of the debates about taxes, spending, the national debt, and the federal government that prompted us to write this book. There were moments when it seemed as if the size of government, its role in society, and the place of social insurance might become central issues in the campaign. Romney selected as his running mate Representative Paul Ryan, the architect of the House Republicans' draconian plan to slash spending and convert Medicare to a voucher program while cutting taxes. In July, Obama's "you didn't build that" remark—referring to the role of public services and infrastructure, such as schools, roads, and bridges, in helping people build businesses—generated a firestorm of controversy.[3] In September, *Mother Jones* released a video of Romney at a private fundraiser claiming that "there are 47 percent who are with [Obama], who are dependent upon government, who believe that they are victims, who believe the government has a responsibility to care for them, who believe that they are entitled to health care, to food, to housing, to you name it"[4]—a clear statement of the conservative idea that America is divided into productive "makers" who pay taxes and freeloading "takers" who live off of entitlement programs.[5]

For better or for worse, however, the presidential election was not a battle between competing visions of American society and the federal government. Instead, each side focused on destroying the reputation of its opponent: The Obama campaign relentlessly portrayed Romney as an out-of-touch corporate raider who made millions by firing workers, while the Romney campaign accused the president of being clueless about the economy and having failed to restore economic growth after the financial crisis. In his final shift toward the political middle, Romney soft-pedaled the aggressive tax cuts he had championed during the Republican primary, insisting that he would not cut taxes on the rich, and steered mostly clear of his running mate's plan to restructure Medicare. Obama, for his part, insisted on letting the Bush tax cuts expire for the very rich, but generally stuck to his centrist line of balancing tax increases with spending cuts.

The outcome of the election, of course, was to reaffirm the status quo: Obama in the White House, a Democratic majority in the Senate, and a Republican majority in the House. Americans' attitudes were also essentially unchanged. According to a poll taken after the election, 79 percent of respondents were concerned about the federal budget deficit, but only 31 percent thought taxes should be raised; 71 percent favored spending cuts, but few were willing to cut Social Security, Medicare, or Medicaid.[6] Magical—and completely unrealistic—thinking is alive and well.

And so Democrats and Republicans returned from the campaign trail to again face off over taxes, spending, and debt. The scheduled expiration of the Bush tax cuts (extended with broad bipartisan support in December 2010) implied a major tax "increase," particularly on the rich, at the end of 2012. In addition, the debt ceiling compromise of August 2011, combined with the failure of the deficit reduction supercommittee, required automatic cuts to both domestic and defense spending in 2013. This combination of higher taxes and lower spending offered a unique opportunity to slash deficits and lighten the load of the national debt for decades to come—unique because it would occur automatically if Congress simply did nothing. Indeed, in chapter 7, we argued that allowing the Bush tax cuts to expire was the single biggest step we could take toward bringing our national debt under control, while reducing inequality and ensuring the revenues necessary to sustain Social Security, Medicare, and our other social insurance programs in their current form.

Instead, however, this opportunity was widely reframed as a looming catastrophe, a "fiscal cliff" over which our country might plunge. This unfortunate metaphor contained a kernel of truth: In the short term, higher taxes and lower government spending are both likely to reduce economic activity, hampering growth and increasing unemployment (although the idea that things would suddenly go bad at midnight on New Year's Eve was far-fetched). This would strain an economy that had still not recovered from the damage done by the financial crisis. At the same time, the "fiscal cliff" provided an excuse for legions of politicians, who claim to be serious about reducing deficits, to argue for lower taxes or higher spending—precisely the things that increase deficits. The specter of an economic crash made a compromise to cut taxes and increase spending seem urgently necessary. After years of complaining that Democrats and Republicans could not work together to reduce deficits, now pundits of all stripes were exhorting them to work together to *increase* deficits.

As we write this, there is guarded optimism in Washington that the two sides will reach a deal to avoid the "fiscal cliff," either at the end of 2012 or at the beginning of 2013. What would such a deal look like? The basic outline includes the following: a "down payment" on deficit reduction, meaning specific tax increases and spending cuts now; a promise to reduce deficits by even more later, with agreed-upon targets for tax revenue increases and spending reductions; procedural rules to make it easier for such a comprehensive package to pass through Congress; and a fallback plan that ensures that deficits will be reduced even if Congress fails to deliver on its promise.[7]

If this sounds familiar, it should. It's exactly what Congress and the White House did in the summer of 2011 to avoid hitting the debt ceiling, as described at the end of chapter 3. The two sides agreed on discretionary spending caps that reduced projected deficits; they created a supercommittee to work out a broader deficit reduction package, with procedures to streamline its passage; and they mandated automatic spending cuts that would kick in if the supercommittee failed, calibrated to motivate both Democrats and Republicans to reach a deal. We know what happened: the supercommittee never agreed on anything, the automatic spending cuts are scheduled to take effect, and both sides are now insisting that, because of the "fiscal cliff," they *cannot* be allowed to take effect. During the last presidential debate, President Obama even stated flatly that the scheduled cuts "will not happen."[8]

None of this should be surprising. Ronald Reagan won the presidency on a platform of reducing the federal budget deficit and proceeded to cut taxes and boost defense spending, creating what were then the largest peacetime deficits in American history. Ever since, politicians have promised to slash deficits but rarely backed words with action. There is no mystery why they behave this way. The two most significant deficit-reduction measures of the past thirty years both led to immediate punishment at the polls: George H. W. Bush's compromise with Democrats in 1990 contributed to his defeat in 1992, and Bill Clinton's 1993 budget bill was followed by a Republican landslide the following year. At the end of 2012, the fact that tax increases and spending cuts could hurt an already-fragile economy only makes the choice easier: Kick the can down the road and declare victory.

More fundamentally, the balance of power in American politics has not changed. Not only did the 2012 elections maintain the partisan status quo in Washington, but both parties stuck to their existing positions. Republicans still oppose anything that can be characterized as a tax hike, insisting that revenues can be increased while lowering tax rates. Reports of the demise of Grover Norquist and his Taxpayer Protection Pledge are probably exaggerated, since many of the right-wing donors and activists who control Republican primary politics have not softened their positions since the election.[9] President Obama still promises not to raise taxes on the middle class, while Democrats as a whole remain highly resistant to cuts in social insurance programs. Congressmen can create procedural frameworks all they want, but no amount of process can overcome the reluctance of *both* parties to reduce deficits—especially when each is convinced that holding the line will lead to victory at the polls.

Of course, we could be surprised. The president and Congress could agree on a comprehensive package of tax reforms and structural changes to entitlement programs that will significantly reduce deficits and the national debt in the long term. But we are not so sure that this would be a good thing.

Any grand bargain would probably have the following elements: Most individual tax rates would remain roughly at the levels set by the Bush tax cuts of 2001 and 2003, or would even be slightly lower; that is the price that Republicans would require in exchange for significant reductions in deductions and other tax breaks. Tax revenues would rise modestly, but would still remain much closer to the levels set by George W. Bush than those set by Bill Clinton.[10]

Social Security and Medicare would preserve their basic structure—Democrats will not agree to change Medicare into a voucher system—but with significant and far-reaching benefit cuts that go well beyond the cost-saving measures we recommended in chapter 7. Likely candidates include a change to the formula for indexing Social Security benefits (which would reduce cost-of-living adjustments for retirees), an increase in the Medicare eligibility age, higher premium contributions for well-off Medicare beneficiaries, and, most worryingly, some sort of cap on the growth rate of government health care spending.[11] There would also be significant cuts to other important safety net programs such as Medicaid and food stamps.

While such a deal would help reduce the national debt in the long term, that achievement would come at a significant cost. The biggest problem is that it would effectively lock in the low tax rates set by President Bush in 2001 and 2003, limiting the federal government's ability to raise revenues just when an aging population and rising health care costs create the urgent need for more money, not less. It would be a definitive victory for George W. Bush and for the strategy of using tax cuts to restrict the role of the federal government in society, undermining the social insurance programs that are essential to many Americans but remain poorly understood.

In discussing this book with audiences around the country, it has become strikingly clear that many voters have not really thought about how the social insurance programs they take for granted really work. We are insuring ourselves against outliving our assets and our families' ability to support us (with Social Security) and against needing a large amount of health care after we retire (with Medicare). As average life expectancy climbs and society ages, the real value of our Social Security pensions and Medicare benefits increases, so the amount that we pay in social insurance contributions should also increase—with the expectation that today's young will receive benefits in turn when they retire. Yet our political debates remain fixated on the idea that rising spending on social insurance is inherently bad, even though it simply compensates for demographic shifts and inflation.

In the abstract, it is impossible to say that lower tax and spending levels are better than higher tax and spending levels or vice-versa. It is possible, however, to say what lower taxes today imply for ordinary families tomorrow. Maintaining our comparatively low tax levels will require large and growing cutbacks in social insurance and safety net programs; as the number of retirees and the cost of health care grow, there will be less money available for each beneficiary and for other domestic spending programs. Since these programs range from modestly progressive (Social Security) to progressive (Medicare) to highly progressive (Medicaid), inequality will continue to rise. Since they provide insurance against unexpected events and unfortunate outcomes, families will take on more and more risk—in what is already an age of increasing economic insecurity.

The conventional wisdom is appealingly simple: That's all well and good, but we just can't afford it. Maintaining today's social insurance programs for decades into the future would require unprecedented levels of taxation, which would imply unacceptable distortions to our economy, for example by depressing productive investment.

In chapter 6, we explained why it makes sense for people to pool resources to protect themselves against long-term risks and why our economy can support higher tax levels in the future. More fundamentally, however, the "we can't afford it" argument is the wrong way to think about our society and our government. The federal government is a tool that we use to organize relationships among ourselves. The core question is not what percentage of our income we want to hand over to some alien entity known as the Internal Revenue Service. The core question is how we want to allocate the resources that we produce as a society: What share should be invested in public goods that make us all better off? What share should be contributed to risk-spreading programs? And what share should be consumed by individuals?

There are many reasons why the share of our resources that we devote to public investment and risk-spreading should increase over time. In a globalized economy, the opportunities for some become much larger, but the risks for almost everyone also increase. There are fewer stable jobs today, especially for people who have not finished college. Disruptive technological innovation may sound exciting, but it also means the loss of millions of middle-skilled and middle-income jobs. Information technology raises our productivity, but it has also made our society less equal and increased risk: It's ten o'clock, do you know who will have your job tomorrow?

In addition, there are fundamental economic reasons why the role of public investment should grow over time, originally described by economist William Baumol.[12] Over time, productivity increases rapidly in some industries due to technology improvements (think about automobile manufacturing) but less rapidly in others (think about classical music or, more to the point, nursing and teaching). High-productivity industries can reduce prices (think about computers and mobile phones), or at least raise prices more slowly than average. Therefore, low-productivity industries are raising prices faster than in the economy as a whole. (The point of an average is that someone must be on each side of it.) This is exactly what we are seeing in sectors such as health care and education, where productivity growth is limited by the need for human interaction and the desire to have small class sizes. And since health care and education are necessities, consuming less of them is not an option, so they become ever-larger shares of the economy.

In the United States, governments on all levels have always played a major role in education and are now paying for an increasing proportion of our growing health care bills. This is not an accident: as low-productivity services become relatively more expensive, poor people will be priced out of the market—unless the government steps in. So in our current system, as health care and education become more expensive, government spending will increase as a share of the economy. The alternative is dramatic cutbacks in public provision of vital services. Even that would not eliminate rising costs, but would shift those costs onto families—increasing inequality while reducing investment in human capital.

But this story can have a happy ending. Because productivity is growing, rapidly in some industries and slowly in others, we will be able to produce more of everything. In Baumol's words, "It is a fiscal illusion that underlies the view that consumers as a group cannot afford to pay the rising costs of education, health care, and other such services."[13] Over a period of fifty years, for example, Baumol estimates that we could produce more than three and a half times as much of everything—health care, education, and all the automobiles, computers, and other devices churned out by high-productivity sectors of the economy. This is not a secret; it results from the simple fact that, as time goes by, we get better at making stuff and providing services. According to the Congressional Budget Office, real per capita GDP—the value, adjusted for inflation and for population growth, of the goods and services we produce—will almost double over the next forty years.[14] Even taking into account the fact that the population is aging and the fact that health care is getting more expensive, we can still have more of everything.

The problem, as we have said before, is one not of economics, but of politics. We can have more of everything, but as long as education and health care are largely funded by governments, that will require higher tax levels to pay for them; if governments stop paying for these services, many people will be priced out of the market and forced to do without. We cannot avoid the basic fact that questions of taxes, spending, and deficits ultimately boil down to distributional issues—issues of who gets what. That was the case when Alexander Hamilton pushed through his plan to redeem Continental Congress debt at full face value and pay for it with tax increases; it remains the case today, in one of the richest nations on the face of the earth. We cannot deal with our national debt without deciding who will get what services and who will pay the taxes needed to fund those services.

The time for that decision will soon be at hand—if not now, then at some point in the next generation, as the United States' economic predominance wanes and it becomes an ordinary rich country. It is a decision that we should make in full consciousness of what is at stake. This should not be a game of collecting a few dollars more or less from the rich, squeezing a few dollars more or less out of Medicare, and scoring political points along the way. It should be a discussion of how we as Americans relate to each other and what kind of society we want to live in.

Unfortunately, we seem unlikely to have this discussion. Our political system shies away from big solutions, choosing haphazard, incremental measures instead. We are also stuck with the language of the early Republic, with government seen by many people as a necessary evil, and by a vocal and increasingly well-funded minority as simply evil.

Even if we don't consciously choose our common future, we will make a choice of some kind, like it or not. After nearly a year of discussing the issues in this book with many people, we have become more pessimistic about what that choice will be. We are likely to drift toward more unequal outcomes, paring back our social insurance programs while health care spending remains out of control. The end result will be to undermine our common economic future. The productivity boom that made America great was based on the principle that opportunity was open to almost everyone. People from modest backgrounds could raise capital, take risks, and become successful. The threat today is that widening disparities in income, education, and health care will close off the avenues of economic opportunity for too many people, reducing our potential as a nation.

As more and more money flows to the wealthy, could their generosity compensate for declining public investments in education, healthcare, and infrastructure? It seems unlikely. The super-rich seem more inclined to claim a larger share of national income for themselves, with several notable billionaires lining up behind the Republican Party's campaign to shrink government and, most importantly, cut taxes.[15] Although the top 0.1 percent have had a great run in recent decades, with their income share reaching record levels,[16] they have shown little willingness to help tackle our nation's serious fiscal problems. Many very successful people have made generous contributions to charities ranging from the Metropolitan Opera to the Bill & Melinda Gates Foundation. But when it comes to politics and government policy, the super-rich typically invest in lower taxes for themselves and lower spending on social insurance programs for everyone else—and many have even convinced themselves that this would be good for society as a whole.[17]

Although the media have made much of the fact that conservative groups spent millions of dollars on losing campaigns in 2012, in the long term their money has not gone to waste. The basic dynamic of American politics remains the same as we described in chapter 3: Republicans shift the debate further to the right, toward lower taxes and lower entitlement spending; Democrats struggle to hold the line. Over the decades, conservative interest groups, politicians, and media outlets have convinced much of the public that the government is too big and that even the parts that people like (such as Social Security and Medicare) are unaffordable. The idea that our existing programs can be responsibly financed, while reducing the level of government borrowing—the central idea of this book—has no natural political home.

Alexander Hamilton created one of the strongest, most innovative, and most flexible public finance schemes in the history of the world. It was able to withstand, and help the nation prevail in, even the most daunting domestic and international crises. It accommodated an incredible shift in the global role of the United States, enabling the country to bear the price of world leadership for most of the past century. It made possible the social insurance programs that make mass retirement a reality. It survived the break with gold in 1971. No one present at the Bretton Woods conference of 1944 would have thought the dollar would become more predominant, not less, once the gold link was gone.

Hamilton's system was always based on the principle that debt would be paid off, through higher taxes if necessary. For most of the past thirty years, our two major political parties have collaborated to undermine that principle, cutting taxes in good times and bad while always finding something worth spending money on—typically defense or war for Republicans and domestic programs for Democrats. The result is a growing long-term gap between the taxes that we are willing to pay and the spending that most of us rely on—a gap that could produce a fundamental shift in the relationship of the American people to each other and to the federal government.

One solution to our fiscal problems has been vigorously put forward by politicians, think tanks, and the media: cut back spending on social programs, shifting the costs and risks of old age and sickness from the federal government back onto ordinary families. There are real differences between Democrats and Republicans, but there are also important similarities: Republicans want the George W. Bush tax cuts for everyone, Democrats want them for 98 percent of everyone, and both sides want to reduce spending on social insurance programs (albeit through significantly different approaches). The question of whether marginal tax rates should rise a few percentage points for the top 2 percent of households has more ideological than policy significance. The parties probably differ most on how they would modify social insurance programs. But the fact that Democrats often feel compelled to speak the language of reform and cost savings reveals how effectively Republicans have framed the debt issue as one of profligate spending and excessive government.

There is another way to think about our government and the reasons for our growing debt. Few people living on an average Social Security benefit of $14,000 per year and relying on Medicare would describe either program as profligate. Instead, they might say that social insurance programs are a modest way to pay back retirees for a lifetime of work, or a fair way to spread risks that we all face. We know that Social Security, Medicare, and even Medicaid are popular among virtually all segments of society. If people understood the true cost of these programs, and measured it against their importance, they might very well be willing to pay more for them. But that is not a choice they have been offered. Instead, Americans have been told repeatedly that government spending is out of control and we simply cannot afford the benefits that generations of workers have come to expect. We have skipped over the discussion of what the government is and what it means to ordinary people and instead raced to the discussion of how we can balance its books.

A one-sided debate will produce the one-sided outcome that we fear: a winner-take-all society where the fortunate few reap enormous rewards and the many struggle to get by. Increasing economic inequality and political dominance by the elite can also undermine both democracy and prosperity in the long term. In the thirteenth century, Venice was one of the richest, most powerful, and most innovative city-states in Europe. That was before a small group of aristocratic families captured the city's political institutions and monopolized long-distance trade, beginning centuries of decline.[18]

Politicians of all stripes routinely claim that the United States is the greatest nation on Earth.[19] If that was ever true, there is no assurance that it will be true in the future. Self-proclaimed deficit hawks like to say that our national debt is the greatest threat to our position in the world. The national debt matters—but not because, as a country, we will someday run out of money. It matters because, if we make the wrong choices in dealing with our debt, we will become a very different, less equal, less innovative, and less vibrant society—not the land of opportunity that so many millions of people, including James's parents and Simon, crossed the seas to live in.

Simon Johnson and James Kwak
December 2012

TECHNICAL APPENDIX

Our projections for the budget balance and national debt, which we discuss in chapter 4 and later chapters, are based on the ten-year and long-term forecasts of the Congressional Budget Office. This appendix describes the adjustments to the CBO forecasts that we incorporate in our projections.

THROUGH 2021

We begin with the CBO's latest baseline forecast (as of the time of writing), published in *The Budget and Economic Outlook: An Update*, August 2011.[1] By law, the CBO's baseline forecast must follow certain rules that, many people believe, make it unrealistic. The most important rules, for our purposes, are, first, that discretionary spending in future years will grow at the rate of inflation; and, second, that current law regarding revenues and mandatory spending will remain unchanged. Because military spending is a type of discretionary spending, the first rule produces the anomalous result that spending on "overseas contingency operations"—primarily fighting in Afghanistan and Iraq—is forecast to grow at the rate of inflation over the next decade, even though our current plans are to reduce force levels and spending. For this reason, we adjust the baseline to account for the expected reduction in troop deployments, using the estimate provided by the CBO.[2] (For other discretionary spending, the general rule does not apply because future discretionary spending was subject to explicit caps by the Budget Control Act of 2011.)[3]

Because of the second rule, the CBO's baseline assumes that Congress will not act to change current law. This assumption is particularly unrealistic in cases where the law is scheduled to change but

Congress has acted repeatedly in the past to override such a change. Our projections assume that Congress will make two changes to current law that it has made multiple times in the past. First, it will continue to increase the threshold for the alternative minimum tax (AMT) along with inflation so that it does not suddenly affect a large number of middle-class households.* Second, it will protect physicians from a sudden drop in Medicare reimbursement rates.[4] For each of these changes, we adjust the baseline forecast using the CBO's estimate of its impact over the next ten years.[5]

The next major area of policy uncertainty is the 2010 tax cut, which extended the 2001 and 2003 income and estate tax cuts as well as certain provisions of the 2009 stimulus bill. The CBO's baseline forecast assumes that these tax cuts will all expire as scheduled on December 31, 2012, as dictated by current law. Because they have been extended once already, President Obama is in favor of extending most of them, and congressional Republicans are in favor of extending all of them, it seems politically unlikely that these tax cuts will all expire. One of our arguments, however, which we make in chapters 4 and 7, is that they *should* be allowed to expire. For this reason, our projections include two scenarios: one in which the tax cuts expire and one in which they do not expire. For the latter scenario, we adjust the baseline forecast using the CBO's estimate.[6] Finally, there are a number of other miscellaneous tax cuts that are scheduled to expire over the next several years. No doubt some will be extended and some will not. For simplicity, our projections assume that none of them will be extended.[7]

LONG TERM

The CBO's most recent long-term forecast was published in its *2011 Long-Term Budget Outlook* in June 2011. This forecast extends to

---

* The threshold at which the AMT applies is not itself indexed for inflation. Periodically, Congress adjusts the threshold to take inflation into account, protecting most middle-class households from having to pay the AMT. These "patches," however, are always temporary, so if one were to expire without being replaced by another, the threshold would automatically revert to its previous, lower level, immediately affecting many middle-class taxpayers.

2085, although the report focuses mainly on the period through 2035. The June 2011 long-term forecast was constructed as an extension of the then current ten-year forecast from March 2011.[8] In August, however, the Budget Control Act of 2011 was enacted, which entailed significant changes in the CBO's most recent ten-year forecast, published later that same month. For these reasons, our projections attempt to reconstruct what the CBO's long-term forecast would be today (with a few adjustments), incorporating the August ten-year forecast. In other words, our long-term projection is based on the August ten-year forecast in roughly the same way that the CBO's June long-term projection was based on the March ten-year forecast.

The CBO's *2011 Long-Term Budget Outlook* includes two scenarios: the extended-baseline scenario and the alternative fiscal scenario.[9] The extended-baseline scenario, like the ten-year baseline forecast, assumes that current law will remain largely unchanged. The alternative fiscal scenario assumes that the law will change where it is inconsistent with current policy (for example, it assumes that all expiring tax cuts will be extended indefinitely); it is similar to our ten-year projections except in the treatment of expiring tax cuts.

As above, we provide long-term projections for two scenarios: one in which the 2001–2010 tax cuts are allowed to expire and one in which they are extended indefinitely. We construct these projections the same way; the only difference is the 2021 starting point. In particular, we make the following assumptions:

- Tax revenues will grow from their 2021 level, as a percentage of GDP, at the average annual rate given by the CBO's alternative fiscal scenario in its *2009* long-term forecast.[10]
- Social Security spending will grow from its 2021 level, as a percentage of GDP, at the same rate as in the CBO's long-term forecast until it stabilizes at 6.1 percent of GDP in the early 2030s; after that point it will be identical to the CBO's long-term forecast. (Social Security spending is the same in the CBO's two scenarios.)
- Total spending on Medicare, Medicaid, the Children's Health Insurance Program, and subsidies for health insurance bought through exchanges (most government health care spending) will grow from its 2021 level, as a percentage of GDP, at the same rate as in the

CBO's alternative fiscal scenario. Spending in this scenario is higher than in the extended-baseline scenario.[11]

- Other spending, other than interest payments, will remain constant as a percentage of GDP at its 2021 level. This is a close approximation to the method followed by the CBO in both of its scenarios.[12]

- Other means of financing (changes in government accounts that affect the amount of government borrowing) will decline from 0.3 percent of GDP in 2021 to 0.1 percent in 2023.[13]

- The average effective real interest rate on federal government debt in the long term will be 2.7 percent and the average inflation rate, as measured by the Consumer Price Index, will be 2.5 percent. We project that these rates will change linearly from their 2021 values to reach their long-term values in 2031. These assumptions are very similar to those in the CBO's long-term forecast.[14]

- The average annual growth rate of real GDP will be 2.1 percent over the 2021–2035 period and 2.2 percent over the 2035–2085 period, as in the CBO's long-term forecast.[15] The GDP deflator (another measure of inflation that reflects changes in the mix of goods and services produced from year to year) will grow at 2.2 percent per year. This assumption is taken from the CBO's long-term forecast.[16]

In general, these assumptions are similar to those in the CBO's 2011 alternative fiscal scenario. The major difference is that that scenario assumes that tax revenues remain constant as a percentage of GDP from 2021.[17] We consider this an excessively conservative assumption, since it essentially states that, even in the face of rising deficits, Congress will not only refuse to increase taxes, but will actively reduce tax rates. (If the tax code were to remain exactly the same, tax revenues would grow slowly as a percentage of GDP due to rising real incomes.) We think a better assumption to use as a starting point is that Congress will simply do nothing (other than effectively indexing the alternative minimum tax), in which case tax revenues will rise slowly.

Because these are the only adjustments we make to CBO forecasts, we are incorporating the economic assumptions made by the CBO with no changes. Those assumptions may be too optimistic or too pessimistic, but we do not claim to know which one. The CBO's economic forecasts do not reflect the economic impact of higher debt levels;[18] if the national debt does increase significantly, it could have feedback effects on the economy that would increase interest rates and reduce economic growth.[19] For this reason, our scenario in which the 2001–2010 tax cuts are made permanent is probably too optimistic; in that case, while we show the national debt rising to 100 percent of GDP around 2030, feedback effects would probably cause it to reach that level even sooner. This concern is less applicable to our scenario in which the tax cuts are allowed to expire because debt levels in that scenario remain near current levels. (For the same reason, this concern is also less relevant to our "fiscal adjustment" scenarios, described below, in which we model the effect of specific reductions in the government's annual budget deficit.)

THE BUDGET CONTROL ACT OF 2011

The Budget Control Act of 2011, which ended the debt ceiling standoff of 2011, placed caps on discretionary spending through 2021 that reduced spending, relative to the CBO's previous baseline, by a total of $900 billion.[20] The CBO's August 2011 baseline, and by extension our projections, assume that those caps will be effective. This is an optimistic assumption (from a deficit reduction perspective) because Congress and the president could simply agree to lift those caps in the future.

The Budget Control Act also mandated a bipartisan congressional Joint Select Committee on Deficit Reduction (popularly known as the "supercommittee") to propose a plan to reduce deficits by at least $1.2 trillion over the next ten years. Since the CBO could not know what the supercommittee would propose, its August 2011 baseline simply spreads that $1.2 trillion in deficit reduction equally over the 2013–2021 period.[21] Our ten-year projections incorporate this CBO assumption. Our long-term projections, however, assume that whatever policies reduce deficits by $1.2 trillion over the next ten years will have no impact on later years. This is a conservative assumption, since it is highly unlikely that any set of deficit reduction policies could have a large impact through 2021 and no impact thereafter. The supercommittee's subsequent failure does not affect this analysis because, under the Budget Control Act, the $1.2 trillion of deficit reduction it was supposed to identify is simply replaced by $1.2 trillion in automatic spending cuts, mainly to discretionary programs.[22] Our projections assume that those automatic spending cuts will reduce deficits by $1.2 trillion over ten years but will have no effect in later years, which is still a conservative assumption.

In summary, it is difficult to tell what the long-term impact of the Budget Control Act will be. The two major questions are whether its discretionary spending caps will be observed by Congress and whether its automatic spending cuts will have an impact on later years,[23] and there is no way to know the answers to those questions today. Our assumptions are optimistic (lower deficits) on the first question and conservative (higher deficits) on the second question.

FISCAL ADJUSTMENTS

In chapters 6 and 7, we discuss the impact on our projections of reducing budget deficits by 3.0 percent of GDP (in the scenario where the 2001–2010 tax cuts expire on schedule) or 5.5 percent of GDP (in the scenario where the tax cuts are made permanent). In each case, it is implausible that such adjustments would be made entirely in one year, and in many cases our recommendations are for policy changes to be phased in gradually. For simplicity, however, we assume an improvement in the primary balance by 3.0 percent of GDP (or 5.5 percent) that begins in 2022 and continues in every year thereafter. This may be a conservative assumption, since our proposals could theoretically be adopted tomorrow, in which case the phase-in period could begin in 2013 or 2014 (although it would still last for several years). On the other hand, it is more likely that any major deficit reduction plan will not be adopted for several years and then will require years to phase in, so an average implementation date of 2022 seems reasonable.

Notes

ABBREVIATIONS

BEA	Bureau of Economic Analysis
CBO	Congressional Budget Office
IMF	International Monetary Fund
NBER	National Bureau of Economic Research
OECD	Organisation for Economic Co-operation and Development
OMB	Office of Management and Budget

INTRODUCTION

1. Quoted in James Surowiecki, "A Cut Too Far," *The New Yorker*, April 21, 2003.
2. James Madison, "War Message to Congress," June 1, 1812.
3. Ibid. Ironically, that same month the British repealed the Orders in Council that had been at the heart of the dispute, but word of the repeal did not reach the United States until after war had been declared.
4. Davis Rich Dewey, *Financial History of the United States*, 2nd ed. (Longmans, Green, 1903), p. 130.
5. "Naval expansion and the taxes it required during Federalist John Adams's presidency had united Republicans who had then and thereafter always resisted such initiatives as a pillar of Jeffersonian small government philosophy." David S. Heidler and Jeanne T. Heidler, *Henry Clay: The Essential American* (Random House, 2010), pp. 91–92.
6. Donald R. Hickey, *The War of 1812: A Forgotten Conflict* (University of Illinois Press, 1995), p. 50; Robert D. Hormats, *The Price of Liberty: Paying for America's Wars from the Revolution to the War on Terror* (Times Books, 2007), pp. 38–39.
7. Hickey, note 6, above, pp. 49–50; Dewey, note 4, above, p. 130. "Although a deficit was disclosed in the budget and it was generally agreed that war would take place, the proposition [to increase internal revenue taxes] was defeated." Ibid. In March, Congress voted to borrow $11 million, but the Treasury was only able to bring in $6.5 million. Congress then authorized $5 million in short-term Treasury notes—"a kind of paper money that government creditors would accept in lieu of other forms of payment." Hickey, note 6, above, pp. 49–50. The Democratic-Republican Congress did increase some taxes on overseas trade (which primarily affected the Northeast, the stronghold of the minority Federalists), but refused to increase taxes on internal commerce.

8. Hormats, note 6, above, pp. 43–44; John Steele Gordon, *Hamilton's Blessing: The Extraordinary Life and Times of Our National Debt*, revised ed. (Walker, 2010), pp. 46–48.

9. Dewey, note 4, above, p. 139.

10. Hickey, note 6, above, pp. 90–92.

11. Ibid., pp. 195–96.

12. National Park Service, "Fort Warburton," available at http://www.nps.gov/fowa/historyculture/warburton.htm. The fort was known as both Fort Warburton and Fort Washington. A later fort on the same site was and is still named Fort Washington. Ibid.

13. Ibid.; Les Standiford, *Washington Burning: How a Frenchman's Vision for Our Nation's Capital Survived Congress, the Founding Fathers, and the Invading British Army* (Three Rivers, 2009), p. 291.

14. On the Chesapeake Bay campaign, see Hickey, note 6, above, pp. 195–201; Standiford, note 13, above, pp. 222, 258–80. The burning of Washington was in part in retaliation for the Americans' burning of York (now Toronto) the previous year.

15. The Treaty of Ghent was signed in December 1814, but fighting continued into 1815 because of slow communications across the Atlantic.

16. Standiford, note 13, above, p. 281.

17. Alan Taylor, *The Civil War of 1812: American Citizens, British Subjects, Irish Rebels, & Indian Allies* (Vintage, 2011), pp. 416–17.

18. Dewey, note 4, above, pp. 119–20; Hormats, note 6, above, pp. 33–35.

19. Hormats, note 6, above, pp. 46–50.

20. Quoted in ibid., p. 39.

21. Dewey, note 4, above, pp. 139–40.

22. Unless otherwise noted, all data on government revenues, spending, deficits, and debt are from OMB, *Fiscal Year 2012 Budget of the U.S. Government: Historical Tables*, Tables 1.1, 1.2, 3.1, and 7.1. In general, when we refer to budget or debt figures for a given year, we are referring to that fiscal year. Since 1977, the federal government's fiscal year has run from October through September, so the 2010 fiscal year ended on September 30, 2010.

23. The interest rate on ten-year Treasury bonds averaged 3.3 percent in the first half of 2011; the last year that the average interest rate was so low was 1958. Federal Reserve Statistical Release H.15.

24. The Obama administration insisted that the Treasury Department would not have enough cash to meet all its obligations on August 3; some other analysts estimated that the Treasury had until August 10. Binyamin Appelbaum, "U.S. May Have Way to Cover Bills After Deadline, for Week," *The New York Times*, July 26, 2011. The probability of an actual default is disputed, but some people feared it could occur.

25. On the history of the debt ceiling, see Bruce Bartlett, "Doing Away with the Debt Ceiling," Economix (blog), *The New York Times*, August 1, 2011.

26. Republicans demanded that each $1 increase in the debt ceiling be accompanied by $1 in spending cuts over the next ten years.

27. The Tax Relief, Unemployment Insurance Reauthorization, and Job Creation Act, passed in December 2010, extended income tax cuts originally passed under President George W. Bush in 2001 and 2003, as well as some of the tax cuts contained in the 2009 economic stimulus bill, and reduced the Social

Security payroll tax by 2 percentage points. CBO, *The Budget and Economic Outlook: Fiscal Years 2011 to 2021*, January 2011, pp. 8–9.

28. See Ron Paul, "Default Now, or Suffer a More Expensive Crisis Later," Bloomberg, July 22, 2011; Lydia Saad, "U.S. Debt Ceiling Increase Remains Unpopular with Americans," Gallup, July 12, 2011. As with all polls, it's not clear what respondents really thought about the plausible policy options. Still, though, 51 percent of respondents were more concerned that "the government would raise the debt ceiling but without plans for major cuts in future spending" than that "the government would not raise the debt ceiling and a major economic crisis would result."

29. Jennifer Steinhauer, "Debt Bill Is Signed, Ending a Fractious Battle," *The New York Times*, August 2, 2011; Carl Hulse and Helene Cooper, "Obama and Leaders Reach Debt Deal," *The New York Times*, July 31, 2011.

30. On the policy changes that contributed to recent deficits and the current national debt, see chapter 3.

31. Gallatin's position actually varied over time. In December 1811, however, he "clearly demanded internal revenue taxes" to assist in wartime borrowing. Dewey, note 4, above, p. 130.

32. See Iwan Morgan, *The Age of Deficits: Presidents and Unbalanced Budgets from Jimmy Carter to George W. Bush* (University Press of Kansas, 2009), pp. 79–80.

33. Some of the 1980s deficits were a product of the 1981–1982 recession, but structural factors (government policy rather than the economic cycle) were a larger contributor, especially in the peak deficit years of 1983–1986. In 1986, for example, the economic cycle accounted for only $13 billion out of a total budget deficit of $221 billion. CBO, *Measuring the Effects of the Business Cycle on the Federal Budget: An Update*, September 1, 2009, Table 1, pp. 3–4.

34. Ron Suskind, *The Price of Loyalty: George W. Bush, the White House, and the Education of Paul O'Neill* (Simon & Schuster, 2004), p. 291.

35. David Greene, "Shaking Faith in Social Security," NPR, April 6, 2005; "Shameless Photo-Op," *The New York Times* (editorial), April 7, 2005. The Social Security trust funds exist because the payroll taxes that fund Social Security exceeded the benefits it paid out for decades. The trust fund holds special Treasury bonds—that is, promises to pay backed by the full faith and credit of the United States.

36. Privatization would have required increased outlays estimated at between $646 billion and $969 billion over the next ten years, depending on the number of people electing to participate in the individual account system. CBO, *An Analysis of the President's Budgetary Proposals for Fiscal Year 2006*, March 2005, p. 47. Individual accounts would have required additional funding amounting to more than $2 trillion in present value terms. Peter A. Diamond and Peter R. Orszag, "Reducing Benefits and Subsidizing Individual Accounts: An Analysis of the Plans Proposed by the President's Commission to Strengthen Social Security," Center on Budget and Policy Priorities and Century Foundation, June 2002. The "benefit" of privatization (for the government's finances) is that in the very long term it shifts the burden of paying for Social Security from the program itself to the individual accounts.

37. Lydia Saad, "Americans' Worries About Economy, Budget Top Other Issues," Gallup, March 21, 2011.

38. *Washington Post–ABC News poll*, April 14–17, 2011, available at http://www

.washingtonpost.com/wp-srv/politics/polls/postpoll_04172011.html, questions 14, 17. Another poll showed that Americans oppose cutting spending on every alternative except foreign aid. Frank Newport and Lydia Saad, "Americans Oppose Cuts in Education, Social Security, Defense," Gallup, January 26, 2011.

39. Social Security and Medicare percentages are for 2010. OMB, note 22, above, Table 3.2. Tax breaks are estimates for 2012. Joint Committee on Taxation, *Estimates of Federal Tax Expenditures for Fiscal Years 2010–2014*, JCS-3-10, Table 1, pp. 39, 49.

40. Suzanne Mettler, "Reconstituting the Submerged State: The Challenge of Social Policy Reform in the Obama Era," *Perspectives on Politics* (September 2010): 803–24, p. 809.

41. Suzanne Mettler, "Our Hidden Government Benefits," *The New York Times*, September 19, 2011.

42. Quoted in Philip Rucker, "Sen. DeMint of S.C. Is Voice of Opposition to Health-Care Reform," *The Washington Post*, July 28, 2009.

43. Sam Stein, "Republicans Forced to Reverse Course, Yet Again, on Medicare," *The Huffington Post*, December 8, 2009.

44. Brad DeLong, "Mark Kleiman Was Snarky Last Night: Long-Run Fiscal Crisis and the Future of America Department," *Brad DeLong: Grasping Reality with All Eight Tentacles* (blog), May 25, 2011. DeLong did not say that the two positions were substantively equivalent, however. The full quotation is: "the political lesson of the past two years is now that you win elections by denouncing the other party's plans to control Medicare spending in the long run—whether those plans are smart like the Affordable Care Act or profoundly stupid like the replacement of Medicare by RyanCare for the aged—sitting back, and waiting for the voters to reward you."

45. Technically speaking, promises to repay in one year or less are called Treasury bills, promises to repay in two through ten years are called Treasury notes, and promises to repay in more than ten years are called Treasury bonds. For convenience, we refer to all of them as Treasury bonds or simply "Treasuries" unless there is a reason to specify a particular class. The principal amount of government borrowing is not included in revenues (when the money is borrowed) or in spending (when it is paid back). Interest on government borrowing is included in spending.

46. Another way to think about it is that government spending is the inflow (the faucet), government tax revenues are the outflow (the drain), and the national debt is the stock (the water in the bathtub).

47. People tend to misunderstand the relationship between stocks and flows, primarily by applying the "correlation heuristic": the assumption that the behavior of a stock should mimic the behavior of the flows that affect it. See Matthew A. Cronin, Cleotilde Gonzalez, and John D. Sterman, "Why Don't Well-Educated Adults Understand Accumulation? A Challenge to Researchers, Educators, and Citizens," *Organizational Behavior and Human Decision Processes* 108 (2009): 116–30.

48. For details of our budgetary projections, which are based on those of the Congressional Budget Office, see chapter 4 and the Appendix.

49. Annual excess cost growth—growth in health care spending that cannot be accounted for by population growth, demographic changes, or overall eco-

nomic growth—has averaged between 1.5 percent and 2.0 percent, depending on the timeframe (2.0 percent from 1975 to 2007, 1.5 percent from 1990 to 2007 because of the shift to managed care in the 1990s). CBO, *2011 Long-Term Budget Outlook*, June 2011, p. 42. On the relative importance of aging and excess cost growth, see ibid., pp. 10–11.

50. See Simon Johnson and James Kwak, *13 Bankers: The Wall Street Takeover and the Next Financial Meltdown*, paperback ed. (Vintage, 2011), especially the Epilogue.

I. IMMORTAL CREDIT

1. Alexander Hamilton, "Report on Public Credit," January 1790, in *Reports of the Secretary of the Treasury of the United States*, vol. 1 (Blair & Rives, 1837): 3–53, p. 27.

2. Ibid., p. 31; Davis Rich Dewey, *Financial History of the United States*, 2nd ed. (Longmans, Green, 1903), p. 89. The country would miss the principal payments due in 1789, as well.

3. Dewey, note 2, above, p. 57.

4. Hamilton, note 1, above, pp. 14–15; Dewey, note 2, above, pp. 89–93.

5. Dewey, note 2, above, p. 57.

6. Hamilton, note 1, above, p. 4.

7. In April 1775–March 1776, Washington had 15,000–18,000 troops at the siege of Boston, while the British had 6,500, but that was the last time the Americans had numerical superiority until the end of the war. In New York (August 1776), Washington had 28,000, at least on paper, but the British had 32,000. In spring 1777, the colonists had a total of 8,500 troops in the field. At the time, the British had 16,000 in New York and 8,500 in Canada. The war in the South was fought with smaller forces (2,000–4,000 on the American side in various battles). In the decisive confrontation leading up to Yorktown (August–September 1781), the Americans and French had 6,000 men watching New York and another 5,000 in the South. In contrast, the British had 14,500 in New York and 7,000 in Yorktown. Craig L. Symonds, *A Battlefield Atlas of the American Revolution* (The Nautical & Aviation Publishing Company of America, 1986).

8. See Dewey, note 2, above, pp. 36–39.

9. H. W. Brands, *The First American: The Life and Times of Benjamin Franklin* (Anchor, 2002), p. 581.

10. Ron Chernow, *Washington: A Life* (Penguin, 2011), p. 366. See also Dewey, note 2, above, pp. 39–41.

11. On the timing and amount of loans, see Dewey, note 2, above, p. 47; Sidney Homer and Richard Sylla, *A History of Interest Rates*, 4th ed. (John Wiley & Sons, 2005), Table 36, p. 274.

12. See Ron Chernow, *Alexander Hamilton* (Penguin, 2005), chapters 5–7. In the late 1790s, under President John Adams, Hamilton became inspector general of the American army and subsequently second-in-command below George Washington. Douglas Ambrose, "The Life and Many Faces of Alexander Hamilton," chapter 1 in Douglas Ambrose and Robert W. T. Martin, eds., *The Many Faces of Alexander Hamilton: The Life and Legacy of America's Most Elusive Founding Father* (New York University Press, 2006).

13. Paul Kennedy, *The Rise and Fall of the Great Powers: Economic Change and Military Conflict from 1500 to 2000* (Vintage, 1989), p. 99.
14. Angus Maddison, "Historical Statistics: Statistics on World Population, GDP, and Per Capita GDP, 1–2008 A.D.," available at http://www.ggdc.net/maddison /Maddison.htm. Great Britain would eventually catch up with France early in the nineteenth century.
15. See John Brewer, *The Sinews of Power: War, Money and the English State, 1688–1783* (Harvard University Press, 1990), especially chapter 4.
16. See Kathryn Norberg, "The French Fiscal Crisis of 1788 and the Financial Origins of the Revolution of 1789," chapter 7 in Philip T. Hoffman and Kathryn Norberg, eds., *Fiscal Crises, Liberty, and Representative Government, 1450–1789* (Stanford University Press, 1994), pp. 265–66. For a comparison of tax collection practices in Great Britain and France, see Brewer, note 15, above, pp. 127–30.
17. On the importance of taxes to support increased borrowing, see Brewer, note 15, above, pp. 116, 119.
18. Steven C. A. Pincus and James A. Robinson, "What Really Happened During the Glorious Revolution?," NBER Working Paper 17206, July 2011, pp. 22–27.
19. Ibid., pp. 30–36.
20. Brewer, note 15, above, pp. 129–31. On tax levels, see ibid., pp. 89–91. More generally, Douglass North and Barry Weingast write, "What established the government's commitment to honoring its agreements . . . was that the wealth holders gained a say in each of these decisions through their representatives in Parliament." Douglass C. North and Barry R. Weingast, "Constitutions and Commitment: The Evolution of Institutions Governing Public Choice in Seventeenth-Century England," chapter 4 in Lee J. Alston, Thráinn Eggertsson, and Douglass C. North, eds., *Empirical Studies in Institutional Change* (Cambridge University Press, 1996), p. 162. North and Weingast's emphasis on legal changes implemented following the Glorious Revolution has been widely contested, but Steven Pincus and James Robinson argue that the overall institutional changes that they identified did occur. See Pincus and Robinson, note 18, above, pp. 33–34. See also Philip T. Hoffman and Kathryn Norberg, conclusion to Hoffman and Norberg, eds., note 16, above, p. 308.
21. North and Weingast, note 20, above, pp. 154–56. Over this period, the national debt grew from about 2.5 percent of GDP to about 100 percent of GDP. Great Britain built on innovations in public finance that had been developed earlier in Italy and the Netherlands. See Niall Ferguson, *The Ascent of Money: A Financial History of the World* (Penguin, 2008), pp. 71–75.
22. Brewer, note 15, above, p. 89.
23. David Stasavage, "Partisan Politics and Public Debt: The Importance of the 'Whig Supremacy' for Britain's Financial Revolution," *European Review of Economic History* 11 (2007): 123–53, pp. 125–26. Between 1688 and 1715, interest rates fluctuated depending on the balance of power between Whigs and Tories, since the latter might have wanted to cut taxes and default on the debt. Ibid., pp. 141–43. Financial elites were not a majority of the Whig Party in the early eighteenth century, but party institutions were able to ensure voting cohesion in favor of servicing the debt, particularly through taxes on land. David Stasav-

age, "Credible Commitment in Early Modern Europe: North and Weingast Revisited," *Journal of Law, Economics, & Organization* 18, no. 1 (2002): 155–86, pp. 169–71.

24. Stasavage, "Partisan Politics and Public Debt," note 23, above, p. 149.

25. Daniel Defoe, *The Complete English Tradesman*, 1725, quoted in Ian Morris, *Why the West Rules—For Now: The Patterns of History, and What They Reveal About the Future* (Farrar, Straus and Giroux, 2010), p. 486. See also Kennedy, note 13, above, pp. 79–82.

26. Richard Bonney, "France, 1494–1815," chapter 4 in Richard Bonney, ed., *The Rise of the Fiscal State in Europe, c. 1200–1815* (Oxford University Press, 1999), p. 162.

27. See ibid., p. 131.

28. Taxes could be imposed without consent, as Louis XIV did in 1710, but this did not mean that they could be reliably collected without consent because of the monarchy's dependence on tax farmers, venal officeholders, and corporate bodies. See ibid., pp. 154–55.

29. David D. Bien, "Offices, Corps, and a System of State Credit," chapter 6 in Keith Michael Baker, ed., *The French Revolution and the Creation of Modern Political Culture*, vol. 1, *The Political Culture of the Old Regime* (Pergamon, 1987), pp. 93–95.

30. Norberg, note 16, above, pp. 268–69.

31. Ibid., p. 254.

32. Stasavage, "Credible Commitment in Early Modern Europe," note 23, above, pp. 178–83.

33. Philip T. Hoffman, "Early Modern France, 1450–1700," chapter 6 in Hoffman and Norberg, eds., note 16, above, p. 252; Bonney, note 26, above, p. 135; Bien, note 29, above, p. 97.

34. Norberg, note 16, above, p. 272; Bonney, note 26, above, p. 148.

35. As of 2010, the latest year for which official figures are available. OMB, *Fiscal Year 2012 Budget of the U.S. Government: Historical Tables*, Table 3.1.

36. Norberg, note 16, above, p. 292.

37. Bonney, note 26, above, p. 148; Bien, note 29, above, p. 90.

38. Norberg, note 16, above, p. 291; Hoffman and Norberg, note 20, above, p. 300.

39. Kennedy, note 13, above, p. 80.

40. Norberg, note 16, above, pp. 295–96; Hoffman and Norberg, note 20, above, pp. 305–8.

41. Hamilton first laid out his core positions in letters between 1779 and 1781, when he was an officer in the army and an aide to General Washington. Richard Sylla, "Financial Foundations: Public Credit, the National Bank, and Securities Markets," chapter 2 in Douglas A. Irwin and Richard Sylla, eds., *Founding Choices: American Economic Policy in the 1790s* (University of Chicago Press, 2010), pp. 61–65.

42. Quoted in ibid., p. 64.

43. Hamilton, note 1, above, p. 3.

44. The $79 million estimate includes $54 million in federal government debt and $25 million in state debt. GDP was roughly $200 million; economists Louis Johnston and Samuel H. Williamson estimate nominal GDP at $187 million

in 1790 and $204 million in 1791. Louis Johnston and Samuel H. Williamson, "What Was the U.S. GDP Then?," MeasuringWorth, 2011, available at http:// www.measuringworth.com/usgdp. The equivalent figure for the United States today (including debt owed by all levels of government) is 68 percent of GDP. IMF, *Fiscal Monitor: Addressing Fiscal Challenges to Reduce Economic Risks*, September 2011, Statistical Table 8, p. 71.

45. In Albert Gallatin's first years as treasury secretary, beginning in 1801, the federal government took in about $10 million in revenue. Nicholas Dungan, *Gallatin: America's Swiss Founding Father* (New York University Press, 2010), chapter 4. The country's GDP at that time was close to $500 million, so revenue was about 2 percent of GDP. The United States could perhaps have collected more if the country's leadership had been willing to implement a fiscal system closer to that of the British. From the 1490s through 1700, the British state collected about 2 percent of national income in revenues during peacetime, but revenue in the 1700s was in the range of 6–10 percent of national income. Patrick Karl O'Brien, "Fiscal and Financial Preconditions for the Rise of British Naval Hegemony, 1485–1815," Working Paper 91/05, Department of Economic History, London School of Economics, November 2005, Figure 5, p. 13.

46. Sylla, note 41, above, p. 67.

47. Congress could assess contributions to the "common treasury, which shall be supplied by the several States, in proportion to the value of all land within each State, granted to, or surveyed for, any Person," but "the taxes for paying that proportion shall be laid and levied by the authority and direction of the legislatures of the several States, within the time agreed upon by the United States, in Congress assembled." Articles of Confederation, Article VIII. See James D. Savage, *Balanced Budgets and American Politics* (Cornell University Press, 1988), pp. 68–71. For the political context, see Merrill Jensen, *The Articles of Confederation: An Interpretation of the Social-Constitutional History of the American Revolution, 1774–1781* (University of Wisconsin Press, 1940), chapter 2.

48. John Jay, Circular Letter from Congress of the United States of America, to Their Constituents, September 13, 1779, in *Journals of the Continental Congress, 1774–1789*, vol. 15 (Government Printing Office, 1909): 1052–62, p. 1062.

49. Robert E. Wright, *One Nation Under Debt: Hamilton, Jefferson, and the History of What We Owe* (McGraw-Hill, 2008), pp. 62–69.

50. Dewey, note 2, above, p. 54. Morris was long a controversial figure who was attacked for alleged conflicts of interest. Charles Rappleye, *Robert Morris: Financier of the American Revolution* (Simon & Schuster, 2010), chapter 15. He later went bankrupt due to unsuccessful land speculations. Ibid., pp. 504–7.

51. Homer and Sylla, note 11, above, p. 274.

52. U.S. Constitution, Article I, Section 8. On the powers to impose taxes and to incur debts, see Wright, note 49, above, pp. 81–85.

53. Bernard Bailyn, *The Ideological Origins of the American Revolution*, enlarged ed. (Harvard University Press, 1992), Postscript.

54. U.S. Constitution, Article I, Section 8.

55. This position was made slightly awkward by the fact that his political ally James Madison, in Federalist 44, had argued that the means were authorized whenever the end was required. Richard Brookhiser, *James Madison* (Basic Books, 2011), p. 92.

56. Ibid., p. 62.

57. "That exigencies are to be expected to occur, in the affairs of nations, in which there will be a necessity for borrowing; That loans in times of public danger, especially from foreign war, are found an indispensable resource, even to the wealthiest of them; And that in a country which, like this, is possessed of little active wealth, or, in other words, little moneyed capital, the necessity for that resource must, in such emergencies, be proportionably urgent. And as, on the one hand, the necessity for borrowing in particular emergencies cannot be doubted, so, on the other, it is equally evident, that, to be able to borrow upon good terms, it is essential that the credit of a nation should be well established." Hamilton, note 1, above, p. 3.

58. Ibid., p. 27.

59. There is controversy over whether Hamilton intended to pay down the national debt or whether he would have preferred some debt in perpetuity. In key public statements, including his "Report on Public Credit," quoted above, Hamilton seems to have wanted to pay off the debt. Hamilton's relatively positive view of debt is one reason for the criticism he has received from across the political spectrum. Some people on the left feel that his policies unduly favored powerful rentiers (people who owned government securities) and other elites over ordinary people. See, for example, William Hogeland, *The Whiskey Rebellion: George Washington, Alexander Hamilton, and the Frontier Rebels Who Challenged America's Newfound Sovereignty* (Simon & Schuster, 2006). Some on the right think that his advocacy of public debt and relatively (for the day) expansive government powers made possible today's large, debt-financed federal government. See, for example, Thomas J. DiLorenzo, *Hamilton's Curse: How Jefferson's Arch Enemy Betrayed the American Revolution—And What It Means for Americans Today* (Crown, 2008).

60. On the terms of restructuring, see Dewey, note 2, above, pp. 94–96. The debt swap offer extended to "any of the certificates of indebtedness which the government had previously issued during the Revolutionary War and the Confederation." Ibid., p. 94. Most of these "certificates" could be exchanged at face value for the same amount of new debt, albeit under different terms. Bills of credit (the original "Continental currency"), however, were exchanged at the rate of 100 to 1. Ibid. The new debt paid a lower interest rate but was subject to only limited redemption in the short run, which made it attractive. See also Homer and Sylla, note 11, above, p. 289. Peter Garber estimates that the value of the bond exchange package was 49 cents on the dollar in November 1790 (that is, a debt reduction of 51 percent), although the precise value varied with market prices for government debt. Peter M. Garber, "Alexander Hamilton's Market-Based Debt Reduction Plan," *Carnegie-Rochester Conference Series on Public Policy* 35 (1991): 79–104, Table 9.

61. Dewey, note 2, above, p. 95.

62. Ibid., p. 105; Chernow, note 12, above, pp. 299–300. Tariffs had already been proposed before Hamilton was appointed and the Treasury Department was formally created. Madison offered the first revenue "proposition" to the House of Representatives on April 8, 1789. Dewey, note 2, above, pp. 80–84.

63. Jefferson was somewhat obsessed by and opposed to debt, perhaps in part because of debts incurred when handling the estate of his late father-in-law. See Herbert E. Sloan, *Principle and Interest: Thomas Jefferson and the Problem of Debt* (University of Virginia Press, 2001), chapter 1.

64. Quoted in ibid., p. 86.

65. Quoted in Ralph Ketcham, *James Madison: A Biography* (University of Virginia Press, 1971), p. 308. On the debate over whether the government's original creditors should be paid back (as opposed to current debt holders), see Wright, note 49, above, pp. 135–41.

66. Chernow, note 12, above, pp. 321–22.

67. Ibid., pp. 327–30. It was agreed that the capital would move first from New York to Philadelphia and then to Washington. The first move happened in 1790, the second in 1800.

68. Jefferson opposed the Bank of the United States primarily for political reasons; in particular, he feared the political and economic power the Bank might wield. We have sympathy for this political critique, but we recognize that Hamilton had the better of the economic arguments. See Simon Johnson and James Kwak, *13 Bankers: The Wall Street Takeover and the Next Financial Meltdown* (Pantheon, 2010), pp. 14–17.

69. Dewey, note 2, above, pp. 94–96.

70. Homer and Sylla, note 11, above, p. 274. For government bonds, "a price of 70 is reported for 1791, to yield 8.57%." Ibid., p. 289. For government bond yields in 1798 and 1799, see ibid., Table 38, p. 282.

71. John Steele Gordon, *Hamilton's Blessing: The Extraordinary Life and Times of Our National Debt*, revised ed. (Walker, 2010), p. 36; Bray Hammond, *Banks and Politics in America: From the Revolution to the Civil War* (Princeton University Press, 1991), chapters 4–6; Sylla, note 41, above, p. 83. For an analysis of the contribution of the financial sector to growth in the early United States, see Peter L. Rousseau and Richard Sylla, "Emerging Financial Markets and Early U.S. Growth," *Explorations in Economic History* 42 (2005): 1–26.

72. In principle, a whiskey tax, even if it is paid by whiskey producers, can be passed on to whiskey consumers, making it a consumption tax. Since demand for whiskey is often thought to be relatively inelastic, it should be relatively easy to pass on a whiskey tax. According to economic historian David O. Whitten, Hamilton's whiskey tax probably did push liquor prices upward, and the higher tariffs on imported whiskey, on balance, probably helped domestic producers. Rural farmers in the 1790s, however, may not have realized the true incidence of the whiskey tax, or they may have been more motivated by political considerations. David O. Whitten, "An Economic Inquiry into the Whiskey Rebellion of 1794," *Agricultural History* 49, no. 3 (July 1975): 491–504, pp. 499–500, 504.

73. One option would have been to simply default on the debt, which would have constituted a "tax" on people who had bought up the debt, including speculators. In some instances, arguments against paying public debts in full can be compelling, for example when those debts were incurred by a former dictator who has now been deposed. See Seema Jayachandran and Michael Kremer, "Odious Debt," April 2005, available at http://faculty.wcas.northwestern .edu/~sjv340/odious_debt.pdf.

74. See Hamilton, note 1, above, pp. 22–23.

75. For detailed histories of the Whiskey Rebellion, see Thomas P. Slaughter, *The Whiskey Rebellion: Frontier Epilogue to the American Revolution* (Oxford University Press, 1986); Hogeland, note 59, above.

76. On the democratic elements of the Whiskey Rebellion, see Wythe Holt,

"The Whiskey Rebellion of 1794: A Democratic Working-Class Insurrection," paper presented at the Georgia Workshop in Early American History and Culture, January 23, 2004, available at http://colonialseminar.uga.edu /whiskeyrebellion-6.pdf.

77. Richard H. Kohn, "The Washington Administration's Decision to Crush the Whiskey Rebellion," *Journal of American History* 59, no. 3 (December 1972): 567–84, p. 568.

78. Ibid., pp. 574–75.

79. Howard Zinn, *A People's History of the United States: 1492–Present* (Harper Perennial Modern Classics, 2005), p. 101.

80. Paul Brest, Sanford Levinson, Jack M. Balkin, Akhil Reed Amar, and Reva B. Siegel, *Processes of Constitutional Decisionmaking: Cases and Materials*, 5th ed. (Aspen, 2006), p. 102.

81. Quoted in Robert D. Hormats, *The Price of Liberty: Paying for America's Wars from the Revolution to the War on Terror* (Times Books, 2007), p. 31.

82. Quoted in ibid., p. 13.

83. On the degree of continuity between Federalist and Republican policies, see ibid., pp. 32–33.

84. On Gallatin, see Dungan, note 45, above; Raymond Walters, Jr., *Albert Gallatin: Jeffersonian Financier and Diplomat* (University of Pittsburgh Press, 1957); Edwin Gwynne Burrows, *Albert Gallatin and the Political Economy of Republicanism, 1761–1800* (Garland, 1986); Henry Adams, *The Life of Albert Gallatin* (J. B. Lippincott, 1879); John Austin Stevens, *Albert Gallatin* (Houghton, Mifflin and Company, 1899); and Henry Adams, ed., *The Writings of Albert Gallatin* (J. B. Lippincott, 1879).

85. Quoted in Adams, *The Life of Albert Gallatin*, note 84, above, p. 270.

86. Quoted in Walters, note 84, above, p. 43.

87. The claim was that Gallatin had not been a U.S. citizen for the requisite period of time. He was removed from the Senate on a party-line vote.

88. See, for example, Slaughter, note 75, above, p. 200. Gallatin later called his participation in a 1792 Pittsburgh meeting "my only political sin"—in part because the opposition movement eventually served to help the Federalists. Walters, note 84, above, p. 69.

89. On Gallatin's career in Congress, see Dungan, note 45, above, pp. 59–65. Gallatin's 1796 *Sketch of the Finances of the United States* was the most detailed assessment of American public finance to date. Adams, ed., *The Writings of Albert Gallatin*, note 84, above, vol. 3, pp. 71–207. On the differences between Hamilton's and Gallatin's positions in the 1790s, see Sylla, note 41, above, pp. 74–80.

90. Dungan, note 45, above, pp. 70–71.

91. Quoted in Hormats, note 81, above, p. 34.

92. Ibid., pp. 33–35; Dewey, note 2, above, pp. 119–20. The repeal reduced net annual revenue to the Treasury by about $600,000, of which "about five-sixths was derived from the tax on distilled liquors." Ibid.

93. Dewey, note 2, above, p. 125. Total debt was $83.0 million in 1801 and $45.2 million in 1812. There was a large increase in debt in 1804 to pay for the Louisiana Purchase, shown in these accounts as $11.2 million in "debt" and $3.7 million in "assumed claims."

94. Of the total $15 million, $2 million was paid "cash down from the surplus in the treasury," $11.25 million was raised in a loan—new "6 per cent. stock, redeemable after fifteen years in four annual installments"—and "the remainder was to be met by a temporary loan." Ibid., p. 121. (Foreign trade was booming and revenues in 1802 were higher than expected, so there was no need for a temporary loan.)

95. Brookhiser, note 55, above, chapter 9. The issue was restrictions that the French and the British had placed on American trade during the Napoleonic Wars. Napoleon offered to drop his restrictions in 1810. This was a diplomatic feint—"we commit ourselves to nothing," Napoleon said privately—but it endeared him to the Americans. Ibid., p. 186. The British, in contrast, steadfastly refused to repeal their Orders in Council restricting trade. (Ironically, the British did repeal them eventually, but the news traveled too slowly to forestall the American declaration of war. Ibid., p. 195.)

96. Walters, note 84, above, p. 254; Dewey, note 2, above, pp. 128–30; Hormats, note 81, above, pp. 37–40. On the War Hawks of the 12th Congress (1811–1813), see David S. Heidler and Jeanne T. Heidler, *Henry Clay: The Essential American* (Random House, 2010), chapter 4. Clay wanted war and eventually supported Treasury Secretary Albert Gallatin's tax proposals, but it was hard to win support from the Democratic-Republican majority.

97. Dewey, note 2, above, p. 130. In Dewey's analysis, Gallatin bears some of the fault for the failure to raise taxes before going to war; after recommending excise taxes in 1807, he backed away from them in 1808, and did not return to the proposal until late 1811. Ibid., pp. 128–30.

98. "Gallatin enumerated the advantages derived by the government from the bank, in its safe-keeping of the public deposits, in the collection of the revenues, in the transmission of public moneys, in the facilities granted to importers, and in loans that had been made to the government." Ibid., pp. 126–27. See also Walters, note 84, above, pp. 237–40.

99. Prior to the declaration of war in June 1812, "little had been accomplished either in placing the army and navy upon a possible war footing or in devising fiscal resources against the gathering crisis." Dewey, note 2, above, p. 128.

100. Ibid., pp. 123–24, 141–42.

101. Ibid., p. 133.

102. "Caught between limitations placed by Congress on the rates and prices of its loans and the reluctance of investors to buy, the Treasury was ultimately forced to accept very unfavorable terms." Homer and Sylla, note 11, above, p. 292. The yield on government debt had been below 6 percent in 1810; at the worst point it reached 9.2 percent in 1814. Bonds that had traded at a price of 104 in 1810 fell as low as 65 in 1814. Data are for the "U.S. 6s of 1790," comparing the 1810 high price with the 1814 low price. Ibid., Table 40, p. 293.

103. Hormats, note 81, above, pp. 43–44; Gordon, note 71, above, pp. 45–48.

104. Dewey, note 2, above, pp. 139–40; Hormats, note 81, above, pp. 44, 48–49. Congress imposed "specific duties upon refined sugar, carriages, licenses to distillers of spirituous liquors, sales at auction, licenses to retailers of wines, and upon notes of banks and bankers." Stevens, note 84, above, pp. 244–45.

105. Alan Taylor, *The Civil War of 1812: American Citizens, British Subjects, Irish Rebels, & Indian Allies* (Vintage, 2011), p. 416.

106. Donald R. Hickey, *The War of 1812: A Forgotten Conflict* (University of Illinois Press, 1995), pp. 197–201.

107. Ibid., p. 195.

108. The national debt was $127 million in 1815. Treasury Department, "Historical Debt Outstanding—Annual," available at http://www.treasurydirect.gov /govt/reports/pd/histdebt/histdebt.htm. GDP is estimated at $916 million, for a debt-to-GDP ratio of 14 percent. Johnston and Williamson, note 44, above.

109. Quoted in Dennis S. Ippolito, *Why Budgets Matter: Budget Policy and American Politics* (Pennsylvania State University Press, 2003), p. 48.

110. On the "balanced budget rule," see ibid., pp. 3–4. From 1792 until the War of 1812, the federal government ran an annual deficit only five times; after the war, it ran only three deficits through 1836. Gordon, note 71, above, pp. 202–4.

111. Wright, note 49, above, pp. 275–76. On the state debt crisis of the 1840s, see John Joseph Wallis, Richard E. Sylla, and Arthur Grinath III, "Sovereign Debt and Repudiation: The Emerging-Market Debt Crisis in the U.S. States, 1839–1843," NBER Working Paper 10753, September 2004.

112. Hormats, note 81, above, p. 83.

113. Colin McEvedy and Richard Jones, *Atlas of World Population History* (Penguin, 1978), p. 288; David S. Landes, *The Wealth and Poverty of Nations: Why Some Are So Rich and Some So Poor* (W. W. Norton, 1999), p. 298.

114. Gordon, note 71, above, p. 70.

115. The South did issue bonds backed by cotton, but demand for these bonds dried up because of a successful naval blockade by the North. Ferguson, note 21, above, pp. 94–96.

116. Eugene M. Lerner, "The Monetary and Fiscal Programs of the Confederate Government, 1861–1865," *Journal of Political Economy* 62 (1954): 506–22; Eugene M. Lerner, "Money, Prices, and Wages in the Confederacy, 1861–65," pp. 11–40 in Ralph Andreano, ed., *The Economic Impact of the American Civil War* (Schenkman, 1962).

117. See Thayer Watkins, "Episodes of Hyperinflation," San José State University, available at http://www.sjsu.edu/faculty/watkins/hyper.htm.

118. Hormats, note 81, above, pp. 62–74; Ippolito, note 109, above, p. 65–66; Dewey, note 2, above, p. 305. On the Civil War income tax, see Steven R. Weisman, *The Great Tax Wars: Lincoln to Wilson—The Fierce Battles over Money and Power That Transformed the Nation* (Simon & Schuster, 2002), chapter 2.

119. Hormats, note 81, above, pp. 80–82; Homer and Sylla, note 11, above, p. 304. H. W. Brands calls Cooke "America's first celebrity banker." H. W. Brands, *The Money Men: Capitalism, Democracy, and the Hundred Years' War over the American Dollar* (W. W. Norton, 2006), p. 128. On the private and public relationships between Jay Cooke and Salmon Chase during the Civil War, see Richard White, *Railroaded: The Transcontinentals and the Making of Modern America* (W. W. Norton, 2011), pp. 10–14.

120. Ippolito, note 109, above, p. 69.

121. Treasury Department, note 108, above; Johnston and Williamson, note 44, above.

122. This rate was on the "old 6s of 1848–1868," whose price fell to 86. Homer and Sylla, note 11, above, p. 303. However, the picture is complicated by the

fact that most bond issues were assumed to be payable in gold coin—so investors were both taking government credit risk and betting on gold prices. Ibid., pp. 302–3, footnote 1.

123. Ippolito, note 109, above, pp. 66–69. The greenbacks were preceded by so-called Demand Notes, which were convertible into gold coin, but only briefly; conversion was suspended in late 1861.

124. Dewey, note 2, above, p. 291.

125. One index of prices rose from 100 in 1860 to 216.8 in 1865. Ibid., p. 294.

126. The quote may be apocryphal, as there is no specific source; see Ellis Paxson Oberholtzer, *Jay Cooke: Financier of the Civil War*, vol. 1 (George W. Jacobs, 1907), p. 574.

127. Ippolito, note 109, above, pp. 74–76; Hormats, note 81, above, pp. 87–89.

128. McEvedy and Jones, note 113, above, p. 290.

129. See the calculations and comparisons in Arvind Subramanian, *Eclipse: Living in the Shadow of China's Economic Dominance* (Peterson Institute for International Economics, 2011), p. 108. On productivity improvements in nineteenth-century America, see Landes, note 113, above, chapter 19.

130. According to David Cutler and Grant Miller, "clean water was responsible for nearly half the total mortality reduction in major cities, three quarters of the infant mortality reduction, and nearly two thirds of the child mortality reduction." David Cutler and Grant Miller, "The Role of Public Health Improvements in Health Advances: The Twentieth-Century United States," *Demography* 42, no. 1 (2005): 1–22, p. 1.

131. On the campaign for workers' compensation insurance, see David A. Moss, *When All Else Fails: Government as the Ultimate Risk Manager* (Harvard University Press, 2002), chapter 6.

132. Ippolito, note 109, above, Table 3-4, p. 80.

133. This was generally true across Europe and other industrializing countries. See Vito Tanzi and Ludger Schuknecht, *Public Spending in the 20th Century: A Global Perspective* (Cambridge University Press, 2000), chapter 1. According to their estimates, general government spending (including all levels of government) in the United States amounted to 7.3 percent of GDP around 1870 and only grew to 7.5 percent of GDP in 1913. Ibid., Table 1.1, p. 6.

134. See Daron Acemoglu, Simon Johnson, and James A. Robinson, "The Colonial Origins of Comparative Development: An Empirical Investigation," *American Economic Review* 91, no. 5 (December 2001): 1369–1401; Daron Acemoglu, Simon Johnson, and James A. Robinson, "Reversal of Fortune: Geography and Institutions in the Making of the Modern World Income Distribution," *Quarterly Journal of Economics* 117, no. 4 (November 2002): 1231–94.

135. The literature on the history of Latin American development is large. See, for example, David Rock, *Argentina: 1516–1987* (University of California Press, 1987); John A. Crow, *The Epic of Latin America*, 4th ed. (University of California Press, 1992); Fernando López-Alves, *State Formation and Democracy in Latin America, 1810–1900* (Duke University Press, 2000); and Miguel Angel Centeno, *Blood and Debt: War and the Nation-State in Latin America* (Pennsylvania State University Press, 2002).

136. Barry Eichengreen and Ricardo Hausmann, "Exchange Rates and Financial Fragility," in *New Challenges for Monetary Policy: A Symposium Sponsored by the*

Federal Reserve Bank of Kansas City, Jackson Hole, Wyoming, August 26–28, 1999: 329–68.

137. OMB, note 35, above, Table 1.1.

138. Hormats, note 81, above, pp. 115–21.

139. Ibid., pp. 123–27, 132; Ippolito, note 109, above, pp. 106–8.

140. OMB, note 35, above, Table 1.1; Ippolito, note 109, above, p. 118.

141. Quoted in H. W. Brands, *Traitor to His Class: The Privileged Life and Radical Presidency of Franklin Delano Roosevelt* (Doubleday, 2008), p. 319.

142. Ibid., p. 320.

143. Max Hastings, *Inferno: The World at War, 1939–1945* (Random House, 2011), pp. 181–82.

144. OMB, note 35, above, Table 3.1.

145. David McCullough, *Truman* (Simon & Schuster, 1992), p. 291.

146. "The United States eventually provided 47 percent of the British Empire's armour, 21 percent of small arms, 38 percent of landing ships and landing craft, 18 percent of combat planes and 60 percent of transport aircraft." Hastings, note 143, above, p. 352.

147. OMB, note 35, above, Tables 1.1, 1.2; Hormats, note 81, above, pp. 163–64.

148. OMB, note 35, above, Table 2.2.

149. Ibid., Table 1.2.

150. Ibid., Table 7.1. Yields on long-term government debt stayed below 2.5 percent throughout the war. Homer and Sylla, note 11, above, Table 48. In part this was due to intervention by the Federal Reserve, but it is also generally true that confidence in government securities remained high. All of the Treasury's loan campaigns were oversubscribed. Ippolito, note 109, above, p. 151.

2. END OF GOLD

1. Nixon made this statement during the third televised presidential debate with Senator John F. Kennedy. "Kennedy Nixon Full Debate Day 3 Part 5 (1960)," YouTube, available at http://www.youtube.com/watch?v=wFqlk9f7IVs. Nixon was responding to the following question from Charles von Fremd of CBS News: "Mr. Vice President, in the past 3 years, there has been an exodus of more than $4 billion of gold from the United States, apparently for two reasons: because exports have slumped and haven't covered imports and because of increased American investments abroad. If you were president, how would you go about stopping this departure of gold from our shores?"

2. White's thesis won a prize and was published by Harvard University Press. Harry D. White, *The French International Accounts, 1880–1913* (Harvard University Press, 1933). At the end of his career, White briefly became controversial when he was accused of sharing secrets with agents of the Soviet Union and appeared before the House Un-American Activities Committee. For assessments, see R. Bruce Craig, *Treasonable Doubt: The Harry Dexter White Spy Case* (University Press of Kansas, 2004); David Rees, *Harry Dexter White: A Study in Paradox* (Coward, McCann & Geoghegan, 1973). For a spirited defense of White, see Nathan I. White, *Harry Dexter White: Loyal American* (Independent Press, 1956). The idea that White's input into designing the

international system was intended to undermine the United States is without foundation.

3. John Morton Blum, *From the Morgenthau Diaries: Years of War, 1941–1945* (Houghton Mifflin, 1967), pp. 228–29. See also Herbert Levy, *Henry Morgenthau, Jr.: The Remarkable Life of FDR's Secretary of the Treasury* (Skyhorse, 2010), p. 336; Alan H. Meltzer, *A History of the Federal Reserve, Volume 1: 1913–1951* (University of Chicago Press, 2003), p. 613.

4. White personally had many of the key insights that led to the design of the Bretton Woods system. On White's thinking, see James M. Boughton, "American in the Shadows: Harry Dexter White and the Design of the International Monetary Fund," chapter 2 in Robert Leeson, ed., *American Power and Policy* (Palgrave Macmillan, 2009); James M. Boughton, "Harry Dexter White and the International Monetary Fund," *Finance & Development* 35, no. 3 (September 1998).

5. David Graeber, *Debt: The First 5,000 Years* (Melville House, 2011), pp. 37–40. On the widespread use of credit in early modern Europe, see ibid., pp. 326–29. See also Niall Ferguson, *The Ascent of Money: A Financial History of the World* (Penguin, 2008), pp. 27–30.

6. Graeber, note 5, above, pp. 45–54.

7. In the United Kingdom, "Legal tender has a very narrow and technical meaning in the settlement of debts. It means that a debtor cannot successfully be sued for non-payment if he pays into court in legal tender. It does not mean that any ordinary transaction has to take place in legal tender or only within the amount denominated by the legislation. Both parties are free to agree to accept any form of payment whether legal tender or otherwise according to their wishes." The Royal Mint, "Legal Tender Guidelines," available at http://www.royalmint.com/Corporate/policies/legal_tender_guidelines.aspx. In the United States, under the Coinage Act of 1965, "United States coins and currency (including Federal reserve notes and circulating notes of Federal reserve banks and national banks) are legal tender for all debts, public charges, taxes, and dues. Foreign gold or silver coins are not legal tender for debts." 31 U.S.C. § 5103. According to the Treasury Department, "this statute means that all United States money as identified above are a valid and legal offer of payment for debts when tendered to a creditor. There is, however, no Federal statute mandating that a private business, a person or an organization must accept currency or coins as for payment for goods and/or services. Private businesses are free to develop their own policies on whether or not to accept cash unless there is a State law which says otherwise." Treasury Department, "Legal Tender Status," available at http://www.treasury.gov/resource-center/faqs/Currency/Pages/legal-tender.aspx.

8. Graeber, note 5, above, pp. 212–14. In ancient Mesopotamia, for example, the silver shekel was the unit of account, but silver was rarely used for actual transactions; instead, most transactions were based on credit. Ibid., pp. 38–40. In twelfth-century Europe, accounts were kept using the monetary units established by Charlemagne around 800, even though none of the coins minted under Charlemagne were still in circulation. Ibid., p. 48.

9. Jacob Goldstein and David Kestenbaum, "A Chemist Explains Why Gold Beat Out Lithium, Osmium, Einsteinium . . . ," Planet Money (blog), NPR, November 19, 2010.

10. Douglas Mudd, *All the Money in the World: The Art and History of Paper Money and Coins from Antiquity to the 21st Century* (Smithsonian, 2006), p. 136.
11. The technology that makes it possible to print money is relatively recent in the Western world. According to Douglas Mudd, Europe's "first circulating banknotes" were issued in 1661 by a Swedish bank, but "bills of credit or exchange notes with a date limitation" existed in China during the Tang dynasty in the seventh century A.D., and "Exchange Certificates without a date limitation" were issued under the Jin dynasty in 1189. Ibid., pp. 22, 29. Before the widespread use of paper money, governments could and did issue coins made out of cheap metals. The government can keep the difference between what it costs to create a piece of money and the face value of that money, which is known as seigniorage. See, for example, Akira Motomura, "The Best and Worst of Currencies: Seigniorage and Currency Policy in Spain, 1597–1650," *Journal of Economic History* 54, no. 1 (March 1994): 104–27.
12. Transactions within existing communities could be conducted using credit, but currency was more important in long-distance trade.
13. There was a mint in Massachusetts in the mid-seventeenth century, but it was shut down. Davis Rich Dewey, *Financial History of the United States*, 2nd ed. (Longmans, Green, 1903), pp. 20–21. For the primitive physical appearance of the early Massachusetts coins, see Mudd, note 10, above, p. 135.
14. "The Mexican eight reales, later renamed the peso, became the dominant silver trade coin of the world, and remained so until the late nineteenth century," primarily because Mexico produced a lot of silver. Mudd, note 10, above, p. 133. This coin was known as the Spanish dollar among foreign exchange dealers in London. "On the eve of the colonies' war of independence, Spanish silver coins were the dominant part of the coinage." Barry Eichengreen, *Exorbitant Privilege: The Rise and Fall of the Dollar and the Future of the International Monetary System* (Oxford University Press, 2011), p. 11.
15. Dewey, note 13, above, p. 19. Taxes were often paid in commodities. Using a readily produced "soft" commodity as money does not work well, as colonists discovered when they tried to use tobacco. For more details on the early monetary system in the United States, see Eichengreen, note 14, above, chapter 2.
16. See Dewey, note 13, above, chapter 1. This situation persisted through the Revolution. "Various foreign coins circulated side by side, as the English guinea, crown, and shilling; the French guinea, pistole, and crown; the Spanish pistole; and the johannes, half-johannes, and moidore; and unequal values were given in different parts of the Union to coins of the same intrinsic worth, thus affording opportunity for clipping and fraudulent change." Ibid., pp. 101–2. The gold johannes was a Portuguese coin. Eichengreen, note 14, above, p. 11.
17. Government-backed paper money was used in the Massachusetts Bay Colony from 1690. According to Douglas Mudd, this was "the first in the Western world." Mudd, note 10, above, p. 136. Thomas J. Sargent and François R. Velde review the difficult history of ensuring there is enough "small change" under commodity money systems in *The Big Problem of Small Change* (Princeton University Press, 2002).
18. In part this may have been because he hoped to get the printing contract. H. W. Brands, *The First American: The Life and Times of Benjamin Franklin* (Anchor, 2002), p. 133.

19. Ibid., p. 135. See also Walter Isaacson, *Benjamin Franklin: An American Life* (Simon & Schuster, 2003), p. 63.

20. Dewey, note 13, above, pp. 26–27. The colony put the paper money into circulation by lending between £20 and £200 to people based on the security of their property. Ibid. According to Bray Hammond, this was a standard operation in colonial America and, with a few exceptions (such as in Rhode Island), it did not involve over-issue and runaway inflation. Bray Hammond, *Banks and Politics in America: From the Revolution to the Civil War* (Princeton University Press, 1991), chapter 1. See also James D. Savage, *Balanced Budgets and American Politics* (Cornell University Press, 1988), pp. 56–66; Robert E. Wright, *One Nation Under Debt: Hamilton, Jefferson, and the History of What We Owe* (McGraw-Hill, 2008), pp. 43–45.

21. Dewey, note 13, above, pp. 29–30. Benjamin Franklin complained to the British about this issue in 1766. Ibid., p. 30.

22. Ibid., pp. 34–38. "Associated in a struggle against what was termed unlawful taxation, the colonists showed no disposition to entrust the power of taxation to a body of delegates whose authority did not rest on an organic constitution." Ibid., p. 34. Congress also passed resolutions denouncing people who would not accept its bills of credit as payment. Ibid., pp. 38–39. For an image of a 1776 "Continental Note," see Federal Reserve Bank of Minneapolis, "History of Central Banking in the United States: Currency," available at http://www.minneapolisfed.org/community_education/student/centralbankhistory/currency.cfm.

23. There are exceptions. British "consols" are a form of perpetual government debt, first issued in the eighteenth century; they have no maturity date, but they are callable (that is, the government can pay them off at any time). In general, some government debt can be redeemed at the government's discretion, but some debt can only be paid off at maturity or is subject to restrictions on redemption. Money can always be taken out of circulation at the discretion of the government.

24. Dewey, note 13, above, pp. 36, 39–41. Under the 1790 funding act, the Continental currency could be exchanged for new government debt at a ratio of 100 to 1. Ibid., p. 41.

25. These are "specie values": estimates of real purchasing power in gold or silver coin equivalents. The nominal amount of paper money created was much higher, around $240 million, but it bought less and less over time due to depreciation. Ibid., pp. 35–36.

26. Franklin made this statement after four years of war. Brands, note 18, above, p. 581.

27. Quoted in Dewey, note 13, above, p. 41. See also Mudd, note 10, above, p. 137.

28. Milton Friedman, "Bimetallism Revisited," *Journal of Economic Perspectives* 4, no. 4 (Fall 1990): 85–104, pp. 87–88. On the general use of bimetallism (silver and gold as the joint basis for a monetary system) in the eighteenth and nineteenth centuries, see Angela Redish, *Bimetallism: An Economic and Historical Analysis* (Cambridge University Press, 2000).

29. Dewey, note 13, above, p. 103. The Continental Congress had already decided in 1785–1786 that the U.S. currency should be known as the dollar and that it should be decimal; it had also specified the silver and gold value of the dollar, but almost no coin was minted. Eichengreen, note 14, above, p. 11.

30. Friedman, note 28, above, p. 88. The bimetallic standard specifically meant that both silver and gold were coined freely by the U.S. mint. "From 1837 to the Civil War, the U.S. gold dollar was defined as equal to 23.22 grains of pure gold, the silver dollar as equal to 371.25 grains of pure silver or 15.988 times as many grains of silver as of gold, rounded in common parlance to a ratio of 16 to 1." Ibid., p. 85. (A "grain" here refers to a unit of weight.) After the California gold rush, however, if you had sixteen ounces of silver, you would not want to turn it into silver dollars; instead, you would trade it for slightly more than one ounce of gold, which you could turn into slightly more gold dollars.

31. Bray Hammond argues that the United States was ahead of the United Kingdom in the sense that incorporated banks were allowed in America but not in the United Kingdom, with the exception of the Bank of England. Hammond, note 20, above, pp. 4, 65–67. The British aversion to incorporated banks was partly due to legislation that followed the collapse of the South Sea Bubble in 1720. Ibid., p. 3. Richard Sylla concludes that by 1800 the United States had more fully modernized its financial system than either of its major predecessors, the Netherlands and Great Britain. Richard Sylla, "Financial Foundations: Public Credit, the National Bank, and Securities Markets," chapter 2 in Douglas A. Irwin and Richard Sylla, eds., *Founding Choices: American Economic Policy in the 1790s* (University of Chicago Press, 2010), p. 60.

32. On the role of banks in expanding the money supply, see Ferguson, note 5, above, pp. 51–52. On early-nineteenth-century banking, see Peter Temin, *The Jacksonian Economy* (W. W. Norton, 1969), pp. 40–41. If money is defined narrowly as legal tender only, then bank notes are "near money." Bank notes were convertible into legal tender (silver or gold coin—not bullion, which is uncoined gold or silver) under well-specified conditions. As long as people were confident that this conversion could actually take place, they were happy to accept bank notes as payments. As Hamilton wrote in 1791, "the simplest and most precise idea of a bank is a deposit of coin or other property as a fund for circulating a credit upon it which is to answer the purpose of money." Quoted in Hammond, note 20, above, p. 69. This system is known as "fractional reserve banking."

33. Gold, silver, and other coins can be clipped, have their precious metal content diluted, or be debased in other ways.

34. In other words, in a gold-based "free banking" system with no central bank, money is largely created by banks. Before becoming chair of the Federal Reserve, Alan Greenspan said of such a system, "A free banking system based on gold is able to extend credit and thus to create bank notes (currency) and deposits, according to the production requirements of the economy." "Gold and Economic Freedom," chapter 6 in Ayn Rand, *Capitalism: The Unknown Ideal* (Signet, 1967).

35. Temin, note 32, above, p. 38. The bank's total assets were $82.7 million, most of which were "loans and discounts" (various kinds of credit); in addition to notes and deposits, these were balanced by $35 million in capital. Although the Second Bank of the United States had a federal charter and had some influence over the money supply, it was far from a modern central bank.

36. In 1816, John Calhoun claimed that state banks had $170 million of bank notes outstanding while holding $15 million of specie. Dewey, note 13, above, p. 149. See also the discussion of bank balance sheets in Hammond, note 20, above, pp. 78–79.

37. Privatization of the money supply had its critics. In the 1830s, for example, "At the root of people's ambivalent attitude toward insider lending was confusion about whether banks were public or private enterprises." Naomi R. Lamoreaux, *Insider Lending: Banks, Personal Connections, and Economic Development in Industrial New England* (Cambridge University Press, 1996), p. 35. "Insider lending" here refers to the practice of lending to people who are connected to directors or managers of the bank. Lamoreaux argues that this was a prevalent practice in New England during the early nineteenth century. Individual bankers did very well, in part from their ability to create money, which generated resentment. Ibid., chapter 2.

38. A bank is solvent if its assets, including loans, are worth more than its liabilities, including bank notes and deposits. Even if a bank is solvent, however, it generally cannot sell its assets instantly at their true value, so it may not be able to get its hands on enough currency (specie then, printed bills today) to pay off its liabilities in a bank run.

39. The most famous is probably the Suffolk Bank system in Boston, where one private bank monitored the convertibility of bank notes and thus the presumed liquidity and solvency of associated banks. Dewey, note 13, above, p. 155. The Suffolk Bank system was an entirely private enterprise, but it was arguably successful because it had some prototype features of a central bank: participating banks maintained balances at Suffolk and cleared the "country bank" notes they received through it. By the 1830s, "The Suffolk was in effect the central bank of New England. . . . It was regulating the extension of bank credit, supporting the country banks, on occasion tightening the curb on them, and responsibly advising them what they should do and what not." Hammond, note 20, above, p. 554; see also ibid., pp. 552, 562–63.

40. Murray N. Rothbard, *The Panic of 1819: Reactions and Policies* (Ludwig von Mises Institute, 2007). Rothbard attributes this panic to overlending by the federally chartered Second Bank of the United States. Temin, note 32, above, p. 113; Reginald Charles McGrane, *The Panic of 1837: Some Financial Problems of the Jacksonian Era* (University of Chicago Press, 1965); Clement Juglar, *A Brief History of Panics in the United States* (Cosimo Classics, 2006), p. 4; James L. Huston, *The Panic of 1857 and the Coming of the Civil War* (Louisiana State University Press, 1987); Elmus Wicker, *Banking Panics of the Gilded Age* (Cambridge University Press, 2000), p. xiii.

41. Dewey, note 13, above, pp. 145, 281.

42. Ludwig von Mises, in particular, argued that government intervention in the credit markets only causes damaging distortions such as excessive risk taking. Ludwig von Mises, *The Theory of Money and Credit* (Yale University Press, 1953). See also Murray N. Rothbard, *The Case Against the Fed* (Ludwig von Mises Institute, 2007); Richard M. Ebeling, ed., *The Austrian Theory of the Trade Cycle and Other Essays* (Ludwig von Mises Institute, 1996); Ron Paul, *End the Fed* (Grand Central, 2009).

43. Wicker, note 40, above, p. xiii. See also M. John Lubetkin, *Jay Cooke's Gamble: The Northern Pacific Railroad, the Sioux, and the Panic of 1873* (University of Oklahoma Press, 2006); Robert F. Bruner and Sean D. Carr, *The Panic of 1907: Lessons Learned from the Market's Perfect Storm* (John Wiley & Sons, 2007).

44. Walter Bagehot, *Lombard Street: A Description of the Money Market* (Book Jun-

gle, 2007). Bagehot made the key distinction between illiquid banks, which should be supported by the central bank, and insolvent banks, which should be left to fail. In practice, this turns out to be a very hard distinction to make, leaving plenty of room for interpretation. Bagehot focused on the British financial system; financial crises were common to many European countries experiencing economic development, not just the United States. See Charles P. Kindleberger, *Manias, Panics, and Crashes: A History of Financial Crises* (Basic Books, 1978).

45. See Charles Goodhart, *The Evolution of Central Banks* (MIT Press, 1988). For a modern discussion of how the Federal Reserve manages the money supply, see J. Bradford DeLong, *Macroeconomics*, updated ed. (McGraw-Hill, 2002), pp. 373–75. The Federal Reserve directly controls its own liabilities (primarily the balances in commercial banks' accounts at Federal Reserve banks), also known as "high-powered money" or the monetary base. The Federal Reserve uses reserve requirements and other tools such as buying and selling government bonds to influence the total money supply (including deposits at commercial banks).

46. Dewey, note 13, above, p. 100.

47. Ibid., pp. 278–79.

48. Ibid., pp. 321–23. On the business and culture of counterfeiting currency, see Stephen Mihm, *A Nation of Counterfeiters: Capitalists, Con Men, and the Making of the United States* (Harvard University Press, 2007).

49. Dewey, note 13, above, pp. 284–88.

50. The new treasury notes, like the bank notes they replaced, were not legal tender for all debts. They could be used to pay taxes to the government and were legal tender between national banks, which helped them gain acceptance. Ibid., pp. 326–27.

51. Ibid., pp. 325–28. "The right to make money was now the federal government's alone. A decade earlier, such an assertion—that the nation could rightly rein in 'notes not issued under its own authority'—would have been greeted with derision and unyielding opposition. But the outbreak of the war had set in motion forces that had unified the nation and coalesced support for the notes that had helped preserve it." Mihm, note 48, above, p. 359.

52. See Dewey, note 13, above, pp. 372–78; Friedman, note 28, above, p. 91. Although the monetary system was officially bimetallic until the Gold Standard Act of 1900, it was effectively on gold in 1879. Ibid., p. 88.

53. See Robert J. Barro, "Money and the Price Level Under the Gold Standard," chapter 5 in Barry Eichengreen, ed., *The Gold Standard in Theory and History* (Methuen, 1985). "The basic conclusion is that output growth—which dominates over 'technical advances' in gold production—would imply secular decline in the price level." Ibid., p. 88.

54. The fall in prices from 1869 to 1899 was likely larger in sectors like agriculture, manufacturing, and mining than in construction or building materials. See Jeffry A. Frieden, "Monetary Populism in Nineteenth-Century America: An Open Economy Interpretation," *Journal of Economic History* 57, no. 2 (June 1997): 367–95, Table 1, p. 368.

55. The amount of silver that could be coined (brought to the mint and turned into money) was limited by the Coinage Act of 1873. Dewey, note 13, above,

pp. 403–7. Proponents of free silver sought unlimited coinage. Whether or not Bryan and his supporters had a good economic argument is still being debated. See, for example, Friedman, note 28, above; Frieden, note 54, above; Marshall Gramm and Phil Gramm, "The Free Silver Movement in America: A Reinterpretation," *Journal of Economic History* 64, no. 4 (December 2004): 1108–29.

56. On the timing and size of Australian gold discoveries, see Rodney Maddock and Ian McLean, "Supply-Side Shocks: The Case of Australian Gold," *Journal of Economic History* 44, no. 4 (December 1984): 1047–67.

57. On the operation of the gold standard in detail, see Eichengreen, ed., note 53, above, especially chapters 6–8. Even during the international gold standard's heyday at the end of the nineteenth century and beginning of the twentieth century, central banks held both gold and foreign currency assets as reserves. Eichengreen, note 14, above, p. 53.

58. Ben Bernanke and Harold James, "The Gold Standard, Deflation, and Financial Crisis in the Great Depression: An International Comparison," chapter 2 in R. Glenn Hubbard, ed., *Financial Markets and Financial Crises* (University of Chicago Press, 1991), p. 37. On the motivations for restoring the gold standard, see Barry Eichengreen and Peter Temin, "The Gold Standard and the Great Depression," *Contemporary European History* 9, no. 2 (2000): 183–207. On differences between the interwar and prewar gold standard systems, see Eichengreen, ed., note 53, above, chapters 9–11.

59. See Ben S. Bernanke, "The Financial Accelerator and the Credit Channel," speech at The Credit Channel of Monetary Policy in the Twenty-first Century (conference), Federal Reserve Bank of Atlanta, Atlanta, Georgia, June 15, 2007.

60. Eichengreen and Temin, note 58, above, p. 196. Mellon is quoted in David Cannadine, *Mellon: An American Life* (Vintage, 2008), p. 402.

61. For a summary of this argument, see Bernanke and James, note 58, above, pp. 40–41.

62. Eichengreen and Temin, note 58, above, p. 200. At the time, central banks could hold U.S. dollars and U.K. pounds as reserves; as they converted them into gold, total reserve holdings by central banks fell.

63. Ibid., p. 203.

64. Barry Eichengreen, *Golden Fetters: The Gold Standard and the Great Depression, 1919–1939* (Oxford University Press, 1995), p. 328.

65. William L. Silber, "Why Did FDR's Bank Holiday Succeed?," *FRBNY Economic Policy Review*, July 2009: 19–30, pp. 21–22.

66. 48 Stat. 1, § 3. H. W. Brands, *Traitor to His Class: The Privileged Life and Radical Presidency of Franklin Delano Roosevelt* (Doubleday, 2008), pp. 327–28.

67. David M. Kennedy, *Freedom from Fear: The American People in Depression and War, 1929–1945* (Oxford University Press, 1999), p. 143.

68. 48 Stat. 31, §§ 43–45. According to Raymond Moley, then an influential presidential adviser, "The cold fact is that the inflationary movement attained such formidable strength by April 18 that Roosevelt realized that he could not block it, that he could, at most, try to direct it." Eichengreen, note 64, above, p. 331.

69. "Over the unanimous opposition of the Federal Reserve Board, Roosevelt embargoed gold exports by halting the issue of export licenses. Under the circumstances, he had little choice." Ibid., p. 332.

70. Kennedy, note 67, above, pp. 143–44.

71. Carmen M. Reinhart and Kenneth S. Rogoff, *This Time Is Different: Eight Centuries of Financial Folly* (Princeton University Press, 2009), Tables 7.2, 7.3, pp. 112–14; Alex J. Pollock, "Was There Ever a Default on U.S. Treasury Debt?," *The American Spectator*, January 21, 2009. We do not consider the 1790 restructuring itself to be an act of default, since the restructuring was voluntary. The United States had already been in default since the 1780s, however.

72. The price of gold was set at $20.67 per ounce in 1834; although greenbacks were not actually convertible into gold from the Civil War until 1879, the official price of gold remained the same. See Friedman, note 28, above, pp. 85–86.

73. Brands, note 66, above, p. 328.

74. Sidney Homer and Richard Sylla, *A History of Interest Rates*, 4th ed. (John Wiley & Sons, 2005), Tables 47–48, p. 349.

75. Bernanke and James, note 58, above, pp. 41–44; Gauti B. Eggertsson, "Great Expectations and the End of the Depression," *American Economic Review* 98, no. 4 (2008): 1476–1516.

76. Meltzer, note 3, above, p. 613.

77. Keynes argued that a gold-based system put the onus for adjustment—changes in economic policies to address external payments imbalances—on countries with current account deficits (higher imports than exports); the United Kingdom was likely to be such a country after the war. "Keynes wanted more symmetric adjustment between surplus and deficit countries. He wanted to impose financial penalties on countries that ran excessively large current account surpluses, ease the burden of adjustment on deficit countries by providing more resources to the IMF, and have the IMF run more like an international central bank with less political control exerted by the United States." Arvind Subramanian, *Eclipse: Living in the Shadow of China's Economic Dominance* (Peterson Institute for International Economics, 2011), p. 17.

78. "Sterling area" countries held a great many pounds that they were presumed likely to want to sell. Eichengreen, note 14, above, pp. 40–42. See also James M. Boughton, "Why White, Not Keynes? Inventing the Postwar International Monetary System," chapter 4 in Arie Arnon and Warren Young, eds., *The Open Economy Macromodel: Past, Present and Future* (Kluwer, 2002).

79. The United States ran a trade surplus throughout the Bretton Woods period, but this was outweighed by capital outflows.

80. See Charles P. Kindleberger, *Europe and the Dollar* (MIT Press, 1968), chapter 10.

81. In technical terms, many countries began allowing current account convertibility during the 1950s. Such convertibility is an essential requirement of membership in the IMF but was initially waived for many countries due to the "dollar shortage."

82. Paul Kennedy, *The Rise and Fall of the Great Powers: Economic Change and Military Conflict from 1500 to 2000* (Vintage, 1989), Table 42, p. 433. The postwar recovery of the West German economy is known as the "Wirtschaftswunder" (literally, economic wonder); the period following World War II is known in France as the "trente glorieuses" (literally, thirty glorious [years]).

83. Giscard d'Estaing was minister of finance in the 1960s under President Charles de Gaulle, another critic of American power. Eichengreen, note 14, above, p. 4.

Arvind Subramanian attributes the phrase "exorbitant privilege" to de Gaulle and his adviser Jacques Rueff. Subramanian, note 77, above, p. 55.

84. OMB, *Fiscal Year 2012 Budget of the U.S. Government: Historical Tables*, Tables 1.2, 7.1.

85. David G. McCullough, *Truman* (Simon & Schuster, 1992), p. 337.

86. President Harry Truman in 1947, quoted in Henry Kissinger, *Diplomacy* (Simon & Schuster, 1994), p. 453.

87. The $17 billion was a "moral commitment" by Congress, not an authorization or appropriation. Greg Behrman, *The Most Noble Adventure: The Marshall Plan and the Time When America Helped Save Europe* (Free Press, 2007), p. 165.

88. OMB, note 84, above, Table 3.1. High defense spending was due in part to the development of the American "way of war," which involved large amounts of concentrated firepower in the form of artillery and air attacks. See Robert H. Scales, Jr., *Firepower in Limited War*, rev. ed. (Presidio, 1995), chapter 1.

89. Jerry Tempalski, "Revenue Effects of Major Tax Bills," Treasury Department Office of Tax Analysis Working Paper 81, September 2006, Table 1, p. 15; Center for Tax Justice, "Top Federal Income Tax Rates Since 1913," November 2011, available at http://www.ctj.org/pdf/regcg.pdf. High marginal tax rates motivated well-paid people to develop strategies for shielding income from tax. See C. Wright Mills, *The Power Elite* (Oxford University Press, 2000), pp. 151–57.

90. "For eight years, he had steadfastly fended off those to his left who would risk the nation's private economy by ignoring deficits and spending government money at will, and those to his right who would do the same by cutting taxes and demanding unsustainable defense expenditures." Jim Newton, *Eisenhower: The White House Years* (Doubleday, 2011), p. 338. "He had come to office determined to erase the $8.2 billion budget deficit he had inherited from Truman. Steady resistance to federal spending, along with the expansion of the economy through the mid-1950s, had allowed Eisenhower to deliver surpluses in 1956 and 1957, only to have those dry up during the 1958 recession. But that recession had passed quickly, and the 1960 budget offered Ike his final opportunity to deliver the economy into safe hands. He held fast on spending and taxes, and left office with a $500 million surplus." Ibid., p. 320. On the tension between Eisenhower and Nixon over tax cuts, see G. Scott Thomas, *A New World to Be Won: John Kennedy, Richard Nixon and the Tumultuous Year of 1960* (Praeger, 2011), p. 42.

91. "American monetary liabilities to foreigners first exceeded U.S. gold reserves in 1960." Eichengreen, note 14, above, p. 50. In 1950, the United States' stock of "international reserves" (mostly gold) was $24.3 billion, while its "external liquid liabilities" (mostly central bank holdings of dollars) were $8.9 billion— a coverage ratio of 2.73. By 1959, reserves were down to $21.5 billion and external liabilities were $19.4 billion, so the coverage ratio was 1.11. Herbert G. Grubel, *The International Monetary System: Efficiency and Practical Alternatives* (Penguin, 1969), Table 2, p. 138.

92. The fear may have been exaggerated. "Why the cumulation of foreign liquid dollar claims was a problem is not clear. Of course, if U.S. gold holdings far exceeded foreign liquid dollar claims, either in private or in official hands, foreigners could not successfully directly run [on] U.S. gold reserves if the entire amount of U.S. reserves was made available to defend the parity. As liquid

claims accumulated sufficiently to exceed U.S. gold reserves, such a direct run was feasible. Nevertheless, the gulf between feasibility and profitability can be vast." Peter M. Garber, "The Collapse of the Bretton Woods Fixed Exchange Rate System," chapter 9 in Michael D. Bordo and Barry Eichengreen, eds., *A Retrospective on the Bretton Woods System: Lessons for International Monetary Reform* (University of Chicago Press, 1993), note 2, pp. 461–62. In the early 1960s, the U.S. current account was consistently in surplus. BEA, International Transactions, Table 1.

93. Quoted in Arthur M. Schlesinger, Jr., *A Thousand Days: John F. Kennedy in the White House* (Houghton Mifflin, 1965), p. 654.

94. "His administration would boost defense spending by $6 billion in 1961, surpassing Ike's final Pentagon budget by 14 percent. Kennedy seemed intent on demonstrating America's military resolve." Thomas, note 90, above, p. 295.

95. On the impact of Keynesian thinking on President Kennedy and his proposed tax cuts, including the support they received from the business community, see Robert Lekachman, *The Age of Keynes* (Random House, 1966), chapter 11.

96. Quoted in Jonathan Oberlander, *The Political Life of Medicare* (University of Chicago Press, 2003), p. 31.

97. Quoted in "Don't Let Dead Cats Stand on Your Porch," *The New York Times*, September 19, 2009.

98. Irving Fisher, "The Debt-Deflation Theory of Great Depressions," *Econometrica* 1, no. 4 (October 1933): 337–57; Ben Bernanke and Mark Gertler, "Agency Costs, Net Worth, and Business Fluctuations," *American Economic Review* 79 (1989): 14–31.

99. OMB, note 84, above, Table 7.1.

100. Olivier Jeanne has analyzed the five major periods of debt reduction in the United States. From 1791 to 1835, the national debt fell from 39.9 percent of GDP to roughly 0 percent, or 0.9 percentage points per year. From 1866 to 1916, it fell from 33.5 percent to 3.0 percent in 50 years, or 0.6 percentage points per year. From 1919 to 1930, it fell from 34.6 percent to 15.6 percent, or 1.7 percentage points per year. From 1946 to 1974, it fell from 108.7 percent to 23.9 percent, or 3.0 percentage points per year. From 1993 to 2001, it fell from 49.3 percent to 32.5 percent, or 2.1 percent per year. The average primary surplus following World War II was 1.0 percent of GDP, the second-lowest level of these five periods. The real interest rate, however, was 3.4 percentage points less than the real growth rate; in all other periods, the real interest rate was higher than the real growth rate. Olivier Jeanne, private communication, November 2011.

101. See Carmen M. Reinhart and M. Belen Sbrancia, "The Liquidation of Government Debt," NBER Working Paper 16893, March 2011. They find that, in the United States, the real interest rate averaged –3.5 percent from 1945 to 1980 and that negative real interest rates reduced the national debt by 3 percent to 4 percent of GDP per year. Ibid., pp. 38–39.

102. The higher short-term interest rates necessary to reduce gold outflows will not necessarily push up the long-term interest rates that matter more for government borrowing.

103. At the end of 1967, the U.S. had international reserves of $14.8 billion and external liquid liabilities of $33.2 billion for a coverage ratio of 0.45, the lowest since World War II. Grubel, note 91, above, Table 2, p. 138.

104. See Robert Triffin, *Gold and the Dollar Crisis* (Yale University Press, 1961), pp. 70–71.

105. As recalled by Clark Clifford, then secretary of defense, "In the midst of the growing crisis over Vietnam, a new problem broke out: a massive purchase of gold in London and international markets depleted our gold supply in a single day by almost $400 million. We still backed gold at the artificial price of thirty-five dollars per ounce, and if the international buying continued, we could see a severe weakening of the dollar." Clark Clifford with Richard Holbrooke, *Counsel to the President: A Memoir* (Random House, 1991), p. 502.

106. There were repeated rounds of negotiations, particularly with countries like Germany and Japan that had trade surpluses and were therefore continuing to accumulate gold. The United States wanted them to "revalue" (appreciate) their currencies relative to the dollar, which would reduce their exports and increase their imports. There were some revaluations but not enough to make a significant difference.

107. On the end of Bretton Woods, see Garber, note 92, above; Douglas A. Irwin, "The Nixon Shock After Forty Years: The Import Surcharge Revisited," working paper, December 9, 2011.

108. Richard Reeves, *President Nixon: Alone in the White House* (Simon & Schuster, 2001), p. 354; Paul A. Volcker and Toyoo Gyohten, *Changing Fortunes: The World's Money and the Threat to American Leadership* (Times Books, 1992), p. 77.

109. Reeves, note 108, above, p. 357.

110. Ibid., p. 363. An alternative interpretation is that President Nixon wanted to stimulate the economy and saw the Bretton Woods system as a constraint that had to be removed.

111. James Grant, "Gold at High Altitudes," *Grant's Interest Rate Observer* 29, no. 17 (September 9, 2011): 3. See also James Grant, "The Cumulative Effect of History," in *Grant's Interest Rate Observer* 29, no. 12 (June 17, 2011): 1–4.

112. Quoted in Eichengreen, note 14, above, pp. 61–62.

113. "Volatility there was in the share of dollars in foreign exchange reserves in the 1970s, but no secular decline." Ibid., p. 63.

114. This was a larger increase than that in the 1968–1974 period ($58.1 billion). Philip Armstrong, Andrew Glyn, and John Harrison, *Capitalism Since World War II: The Making and Breakup of the Great Boom* (Fontana, 1984), Tables 12.2, 16.6, pp. 298, 370. The comparison between these time periods is complicated by inflation, but the fact that there was no big shift by central banks away from dollars is not controversial.

115. Iwan Morgan, *The Age of Deficits: Presidents and Unbalanced Budgets from Jimmy Carter to George W. Bush* (University Press of Kansas, 2009), pp. 80–81.

116. OMB, note 84, above, Table 1.2. ERTA was initially projected to cost over 4 percent of GDP in its fourth year; even the Revenue Act of 1945 was only expected to cost 2.67 percent of GDP per year. Tempalski, note 89, above, Table 2, pp. 16–17.

117. OMB, note 84, above, Table 1.2. The budget deficit was 7.2 percent of GDP in 1946, which was technically in peacetime, but this was because it took time to reduce military spending after World War II.

118. "Before 1982, U.S. current account deficits were small and temporary. Deficits in some years were typically offset by surpluses in other years. Since 1982,

though, the United States has experienced large and chronic current account deficits." Craig S. Hakkio, "The U.S. Current Account: The Other Deficit," *Federal Reserve Bank of Kansas City Economic Review*, Third Quarter, 1995: 11–24, p. 12.

119. See Stephen Marris, *Deficits and the Dollar: The World Economy at Risk* (Institute for International Economics, 1985), p. 31.

120. Paul A. Volcker, testimony before the Joint Economic Committee, February 5, 1985, available at http://fraser.stlouisfed.org/historicaldocs/832/download/28426/Volcker_19850205.pdf, p. 10. See also Marris, note 119, above.

121. Morgan, note 115, above, pp. 110–12, 115–16.

122. This is in part because governments fear that the IMF will recommend inappropriate macroeconomic policies. In some instances, however, powerful elites resent IMF advice because it threatens their privileges or their hold on power. See Simon Johnson and James Kwak, *13 Bankers: The Wall Street Takeover and the Next Financial Meltdown* (Pantheon, 2010), chapter 2.

123. See Morris Goldstein and Philip Turner, *Controlling Currency Mismatches in Emerging Markets* (Institute for International Economics, 2004).

124. By the end of 2010, China held more than $1.28 trillion of U.S. Treasury securities. Elena L. Nguyen, "The International Investment Position of the United States at Yearend 2010," *Survey of Current Business*, July 2011: 113–23, Table K, p. 118. These data are for "foreign official and private holdings," but most experts think that the Chinese holdings are mostly by the official sector, primarily the central bank and other government agencies. China was the largest foreign holder of Treasuries, followed by Japan at $871.5 billion, Brazil at $184.7 billion, Russia at $169.4 billion, "OPEC Asia" at $165.8 billion, and Taiwan at $153.7 billion. Total foreign holdings of U.S. Treasury securities were over $4.3 trillion.

125. Grubel, note 91, above, Table 1, p. 136. International reserves also included "Fund positions" (credit lines that could be drawn on automatically, without conditions), which were $1.6 billion in 1948 and $6.6 billion in 1968.

126. In the 1970s, 80 percent of total central bank reserves was in dollars; this situation was little changed from the end of the Bretton Woods era. Eichengreen, note 14, above, p. 63.

127. IMF, Data Template on International Reserves and Foreign Currency Liquidity. The total for every month from March through August 2011 exceeds $7 trillion; data for later months were incomplete at time of writing. Reporting is entirely voluntary.

128. China alone has over $3 trillion in reserves. Joseph E. Gagnon, Nicholas R. Lardy, and Nicholas Borst, "The Internal Cost of China's Currency Policy," *Realtime Economic Issues Watch* (blog), Peterson Institute for International Economics, October 3, 2011. The breakdown by currency is difficult to estimate because it is a closely guarded secret in many countries. Of the reserves for which a currency breakdown is voluntarily reported to the IMF, over 60 percent was in dollars as of 2010. IMF, Currency Composition of Official Foreign Exchange Reserves. According to Federal Reserve staff estimates, dollar assets made up over 60 percent of all reserves in 2009. Linda S. Goldberg, "Is the International Role of the Dollar Changing?," *Current Issues in Economics and Finance* 16, no. 1 (January 2010), Chart 3, p. 4.

129. Treasury Department, "Monthly Statement of the Public Debt of the United

States," September 30, 2011. The $10.1 trillion figure excludes debt held by other branches of the federal government.

130. As of 2010, nonresidents held 53 percent of marketable federal government debt. IMF, *Fiscal Monitor: Addressing Fiscal Challenges to Reduce Economic Risks*, September 2011, Statistical Table 9, p. 72. As of September 2011, the Treasury Department had $9.6 trillion in marketable debt outstanding. Treasury Department, note 129, above.

131. As Stephen Cohen and Brad DeLong write, "Foreign governments and investors, mostly in Asia, have believed that macroeconomic policy and portfolio equilibrium require that they boost their holdings of dollar-denominated foreign assets to levels that two decades ago would have been regarded as absurd and unbelievable." Stephen S. Cohen and J. Bradford DeLong, *The End of Influence: What Happens When Other Countries Have the Money* (Basic Books, 2010), p. 93. On the accumulation of dollar investments by foreign countries, see ibid., chapter 5.

132. The average ten-year Treasury yield for the decade preceding the financial crisis (1998–2007) was 4.9 percent; the average for 2009–2011 was 3.1 percent; the yield at the end of 2011 was 1.9 percent. The average from April 1953 (the earliest data available from the Federal Reserve) through 2007 was 6.5 percent. Federal Reserve Statistical Release H.15.

3. DEFICITS DON'T MATTER

1. Quoted in Bob Woodward, "In His Debut in Washington's Power Struggles, Gingrich Threw a Bomb," *The Washington Post*, December 24, 2011.

2. Government Accountability Office, *Budget Policy: Prompt Action Necessary to Avert Long-Term Damage to the Economy*, OCG-92-2, June 5, 1992, pp. 1, 4.

3. Ibid., p. 6.

4. John B. Judis, "The Red Menace," *The New Republic*, October 26, 1992: 26–29, p. 26.

5. Ibid., p. 29.

6. Government revenues fell from 19.6 percent of GDP in 1981 to 17.3 percent in 1984; they grew later in the decade, but never exceeded 18.4 percent of GDP. OMB, *Fiscal Year 2012 Budget of the U.S. Government: Historical Tables*, Table 1.2.

7. Iwan Morgan, *The Age of Deficits: Presidents and Unbalanced Budgets from Jimmy Carter to George W. Bush* (University Press of Kansas, 2009), p. 153.

8. Ron Suskind, *The Price of Loyalty: George W. Bush, the White House, and the Education of Paul O'Neill* (Simon & Schuster, 2004), p. 291.

9. See Corey Robin, *The Reactionary Mind: Conservatism from Edmund Burke to Sarah Palin* (Oxford University Press, 2011), especially the Introduction and chapter 1. See also Albert O. Hirschman, *The Rhetoric of Reaction: Perversity, Futility, Jeopardy* (Belknap Press, 1991).

10. On Social Security and the business community, see Jacob Hacker, *The Divided Welfare State: The Battle over Public and Private Social Benefits in the United States* (Cambridge University Press, 2002), pp. 136–37, 140–42. The Republican Party in general became more moderate and the ideological gap between the

parties narrowed until the 1960s. Nolan McCarty, Keith T. Poole, and Howard Rosenthal, *Polarized America: The Dance of Ideology and Unequal Riches* (MIT Press, 2006), pp. 26–27.

11. Dwight D. Eisenhower, Letter to Edgar Newton Eisenhower, November 8, 1954. Quoted in Jacob S. Hacker and Paul Pierson, *Winner-Take-All Politics: How Washington Made the Rich Richer—And Turned Its Back on the Middle Class* (Simon & Schuster, 2010), p. 189. Eisenhower believed that government action was necessary to correct for the failings of the private sector. Kim Phillips-Fein, *Invisible Hands: The Making of the Conservative Movement from the New Deal to Reagan* (W. W. Norton, 2009), pp. 56–57.

12. On the history of business opposition to the New Deal, see Phillips-Fein, note 11, above.

13. See Daniel J. Balz and Ronald Brownstein, *Storming the Gates: Protest Politics and the Republican Revival* (Little, Brown, 1996), pp. 174–75.

14. Ronald Reagan, "A Time for Choosing," speech delivered on October 27, 1964, available at http://www.reagan.utexas.edu/archives/reference/timechoosing.html; Lewis F. Powell, "Attack on American Free Enterprise System," Memorandum to Eugene B. Sydnor, Jr., August 23, 1971.

15. Citizens for Tax Justice, "Top Federal Income Tax Rates Since 1913," November 2011, available at http://www.ctj.org/pdf/regcg.pdf.

16. See Daniel A. Smith, "Howard Jarvis, Populist Entrepreneur: Reevaluating the Causes of Proposition 13," *Social Science History* 23, no. 2 (Summer 1999): 173–210.

17. Phillips-Fein, note 11, above, pp. 179–83.

18. Morgan, note 7, above, p. 79; Ronald Reagan, "Reflections on the Failure of Proposition #1," *National Review*, December 7, 1973.

19. David A. Stockman, *The Triumph of Politics: How the Reagan Revolution Failed* (Harper & Row, 1986), pp. 49–50.

20. Ronald Reagan, Inaugural Address, January 20, 1981, available at http://www.reaganlibrary.com/pdf/Inaugural_Address_012081.pdf.

21. Stockman, note 19, above, pp. 53–54.

22. Ibid., p. 68; William Greider, "The Education of David Stockman," *The Atlantic*, December 1981.

23. Stockman, note 19, above, pp. 52–54.

24. Ibid., pp. 340–51.

25. Martin Feldstein, "American Economic Policy in the 1980s: A Personal View," chapter 1 in Martin Feldstein, ed., *American Economic Policy in the 1980s* (University of Chicago Press, 1994), pp. 27–29.

26. The 1981 tax cut was expected at the time to reduce revenues by $749 billion in just one year. The later tax increases were together estimated to increase revenues by $348 billion, but several of those estimates covered multiple years. (The largest tax increase, the 1983 Social Security Amendments, increased revenues by $165 billion over seven years.) Allen Schick, *The Federal Budget: Politics, Policy, Process*, 3rd ed. (Brookings Institution Press, 2007), p. 164. When enacted, the 1981 tax cut was expected to reduce revenues by an average of 2.89 percent of GDP in its first four years. All the other tax acts of the Reagan administration were together expected to increase revenues by an average of 1.94 percent of GDP in their first four years. Jerry Tempalski, "Revenue

Effects of Major Tax Bills," Treasury Department Office of Tax Analysis Working Paper 81, September 2006, Table 2, pp. 16–20.

27. The 1980s tax increases had substantial Republican support. The 1982 tax increase, for example, was supported by majorities of Republicans in both houses. Morgan, note 7, above, pp. 97–98.

28. Stockman, note 19, above, p. 376.

29. Balz and Brownstein, note 13, above, p. 117.

30. Ibid., pp. 118–26, 147.

31. Thomas Ferguson, "Legislators Never Bowl Alone: Big Money, Mass Media, and the Polarization of Congress," paper presented at the INET Conference, Bretton Woods, April 2011, p. 34; Balz and Brownstein, note 13, above, pp. 145–46.

32. In 1985–1988, Gingrich raised $1,590 million to Michel's $1,567 million; in 1989–1992, although Michel was still the party's floor leader, Gingrich raised $3,522 million to Michel's $1,353 million. Ferguson, note 31, above, Table 4. It's not clear that ideological extremism is always good for a politician's war chest, however. Nolan McCarty, Keith Poole, and Howard Rosenthal have shown that moderates generally can raise money as effectively as extremists, perhaps because those contributors interested in access to elected officials balance those contributors with ideological motivations. McCarty et al., note 10, above, chapter 5. Still, it could very well be the case that hard-line stances and controversies help ideological extremists raise money by increasing their appeal to ideologically motivated contributors. In addition, large "soft money" contributions (unlimited contributions made to organizations that are technically not affiliated with candidates) tend to come from donors with ideological motivations.

33. Balz and Brownstein, note 13, above, pp. 126–30.

34. George H. W. Bush, 1988 Republican National Convention Acceptance Address, August 18, 1988, available at http://www.americanrhetoric.com/speeches/georgehbush1988rnc.htm.

35. On the 1990 budget negotiations, see Morgan, note 7, above, pp. 137–49; Balz and Brownstein, note 13, above, pp. 130–40.

36. Quoted in Morgan, note 7, above, p. 143.

37. The renegotiated bill shifted the tax burden toward the wealthy, in particular by increasing the top income tax rate to 31 percent—an increase that was not in the original agreement. Ibid., pp. 141–47.

38. For example, the top income tax rate increased from 28 percent to 31 percent. Of the total deficit reduction, 64 percent was due to spending cuts and 36 percent to tax increases. CBO, *The 1990 Budget Agreement: An Interim Assessment*, December 1990, pp. 6–7.

39. Technically, PAYGO governed mandatory spending and taxes; discretionary spending was restricted through annual caps.

40. Schick, note 26, above, pp. 32, 81. On the PAYGO rule, see ibid., pp. 57–59.

41. Balz and Brownstein, note 13, above, pp. 77–78.

42. Quoted in ibid., p. 15.

43. Ibid., pp. 179–83.

44. See Morgan, note 7, above, pp. 163–64.

45. In January 1993, the CBO projected a 1993 deficit of $310 billion that would

fall until 1995 before rising again; the standardized-employment deficit, however, which omits the effect of economic cycles, was projected to remain flat until 1995 and rise thereafter. CBO, *The Economic and Budget Outlook: Fiscal Years 1994–1998*, January 1993, Summary Table 3, p. xvi.

46. On the January 7 meeting and the incoming Clinton administration's economic plans, see Robert E. Rubin and Jacob Weisberg, *In an Uncertain World: Tough Choices from Wall Street to Washington* (Random House, 2003), pp. 118–31; Bill Clinton, *My Life* (Alfred A. Knopf, 2004), pp. 458–63; Bob Woodward, *The Agenda: Inside the Clinton White House* (Simon & Schuster, 1994), pp. 68–82.

47. Although this was the argument at the time, it's not clear that interest rates were all that high. The average yield on ten-year Treasury notes was 7.0 percent in 1992 and had been falling since 1981. At the same time, inflation had been falling since 1982, so real interest rates were not necessarily falling. Since the early 1990s, nominal yields have generally fallen while inflation has been stable, indicating that real interest rates may have been high at the time. In any case, the consensus among economic policymakers was that interest rates were too high.

48. Rubin and Weisberg, note 46, above, p. 120. According to Rubin, Fed chair Alan Greenspan had estimated that each $10 billion in annual deficit reduction would reduce long-term interest rates by 0.1 percentage point.

49. Woodward, note 46, above, p. 73.

50. Morgan, note 7, above, pp. 171–75.

51. See ibid., p. 175.

52. After the passage of the Omnibus Budget Reconciliation Act in 1993 until the end of the Clinton presidency, real GDP grew at an average annual rate of 4.0 percent (measured from 1993 Q4 through 2000 Q4). BEA, National Income and Product Accounts, Table 1.1.1. The yield on ten-year Treasuries fell to 5.3 percent in 1998 before beginning to rise again because of the economic boom. Federal Reserve Statistical Release H.15.

53. OMB, note 6, above, Table 8.4. Anders Åslund has calculated the "peace dividend" at 2.8 percent of GDP in 1998–1999. Anders Åslund, *Building Capitalism: The Transformation of the Former Soviet Bloc* (Cambridge University Press, 2002), Table 10.1, p. 401.

54. See Morgan, note 7, above, pp. 179, 185–86.

55. One of the bills raised the debt ceiling, which the Treasury Department was on course to reach in mid-November. Treasury Secretary Robert Rubin, however, decided to borrow money from various federal trust funds, staving off default and enabling Clinton to veto the debt ceiling increase. Rubin and Weisberg, note 46, above, pp. 168–72.

56. Morgan, note 7, above, p. 188.

57. Jacob S. Hacker and Paul Pierson, *Off Center: The Republican Revolution and the Erosion of American Democracy* (Yale University Press, 2005), pp. 146–47; Ferguson, note 31, above, pp. 6–7; Eric Heberlig, Marc Hetherington, and Bruce Larson, "The Price of Leadership: Campaign Money and the Polarization of Congressional Parties," *Journal of Politics* 68, no. 4 (November 2006): 992–1005, pp. 994–95.

58. Hacker and Pierson, note 57, above, pp. 142–43.

59. Ferguson, note 31, above. Nolan McCarty, Keith Poole, and Howard Rosen-

thal show in detail that Congress has become increasingly polarized, but they argue that internal party pressure is unlikely to explain the upturn in polarization in recent decades. McCarty et al., note 10, above, pp. 54–59. Their account focuses instead on increasing income stratification: the shift of high-income groups toward the Republican Party and low-income groups toward the Democratic Party, which they attribute to the increasing importance of income on partisan affiliations. Ibid., pp. 74–76. This explanation also results in a Republican Party that is likely to focus on economic policies that benefit the wealthy, such as lower taxes and less redistribution.

60. Ferguson, note 31, above, p. 7; Ryan Grim and Arthur Delaney, "The Cash Committee: How Wall Street Wins on the Hill," *The Huffington Post*, December 29, 2009.

61. Quoted in Balz and Brownstein, note 13, above, p. 154.

62. Bruce Bartlett, " 'Starve the Beast': Origins and Development of a Budgetary Metaphor," *The Independent Review* 12, no. 1 (Summer 2007): 5–26, pp. 8–9, 11–13. The term "starve the beast" was first used by Republicans in this context in 1985. Ibid., p. 6. The empirical evidence indicates that the "starve the beast" strategy does not actually work; that is, lowering tax revenues has not resulted in lower spending, just in higher deficits. For a review, see Bruce Bartlett, "Do Tax Cuts Starve the Beast?," Bartlett's Notations (blog), *The Fiscal Times*, July 14, 2010. One theoretical possibility is that deficits just haven't been big enough to produce the pressure necessary to cut spending, but that at some point they will have the desired effect.

63. ATR was founded in 1985 to support the Reagan administration's tax reform program. See Nina J. Easton, *Gang of Five: Leaders at the Center of the Conservative Crusade* (Simon & Schuster, 2000), p. 161.

64. Robert Dreyfuss, "Grover Norquist: 'Field Marshal' of the Bush Plan," *The Nation*, May 14, 2001.

65. Drake Bennett, "Grover Norquist, the Enforcer," *Bloomberg Businessweek*, May 26, 2011.

66. Americans for Tax Reform, "Federal Taxpayer Protection Pledge Questions and Answers," available at http://www.atr.org/federal-taxpayer-protection-questions-answers-a6204.

67. Bennett, note 65, above.

68. Easton, note 63, above, p. 278.

69. Hacker and Pierson, note 11, above, pp. 209–10.

70. Balz and Brownstein, note 13, above, p. 155.

71. Susan Page, "Norquist's Power High, Profile Low," *USA Today*, June 1, 2001.

72. Catherine Rampell, "Tax Pledge May Scuttle a Deal on Deficit," *The New York Times*, November 18, 2011.

73. Easton, note 63, above, pp. 279–80, 364–65; Balz and Brownstein, note 13, above, pp. 181–82.

74. Dreyfuss, note 64, above; Page, note 71, above.

75. Quoted in Bennett, note 65, above.

76. Balz and Brownstein, note 13, above, p. 200.

77. On July 20, 2011, *The Washington Post* quoted Norquist as saying, "Not continuing a tax cut is not technically a tax increase," seemingly making it possible for pledge signers to vote for a deal that extended some but not all tax

cuts. "Out from Under the Anti-Tax Pledge," *The Washington Post* (editorial), July 20, 2011. Norquist quickly clarified that while passively allowing a tax cut to expire without a vote would not violate the pledge, voting for a plan that involved the expiration of any tax cuts would violate the pledge. Grover G. Norquist, "Read My Lips: No New Taxes," *The New York Times*, July 21, 2011.

78. Hacker and Pierson, note 57, above, chapters 4–5. For example, Representative Marge Roukema retired after surviving two primary challenges and facing a third without the support of the party leadership. Ibid., pp. 109–10.

79. Pew Research Center for the People & the Press, *Distrust, Discontent, Anger and Partisan Rancor: The People and Their Government*, April 18, 2010, p. 20. The number of Republicans with trust in government averaged more than 40 percent during the Reagan, Bush I, and Bush II administrations and less than 30 percent in the Carter, Clinton, and Obama administrations. Democratic attitudes vary within a narrower range (from 26 percent for Bush II to 34 percent for Reagan and Clinton) and display less correlation with the president's political party. Ibid., p. 4.

80. Ibid., pp. 85, 70, 64–65.

81. Ibid., p. 64.

82. Morris P. Fiorina and Samuel J. Abrams, "Political Polarization in the American Public," *Annual Review of Political Science* 11 (2008): 563–88, pp. 569–74; Ferguson, note 31, above, pp. 15–16; Hacker and Pierson, note 57, above, pp. 38–43; Lydia Saad, "In 2010, Conservatives Still Outnumber Moderates, Liberals," Gallup, June 25, 2010. Self-identified conservatives grew from 37 percent in 2008 to 42 percent in 2010; still, this is only barely higher than the 40 percent level of 2003–2004. As early as the mid-1980s, political scientists Thomas Ferguson and Joel Rogers pointed out that even the election of Ronald Reagan in 1980 and his landslide reelection in 1984 were not accompanied by any significant shift toward conservative positions among the public. Thomas Ferguson and Joel Rogers, *Right Turn: The Decline of the Democrats and the Future of American Politics* (Hill & Wang, 1986), chapter 1.

83. On opinions regarding government services and spending, see American National Election Studies, *The ANES Guide to Public Opinion and Electoral Behavior*, available at http://electionstudies.org/nesguide/nesguide.htm, Table 4A.5.

84. Richard A. Viguerie and David Franke, *America's Right Turn: How Conservatives Used New and Alternative Media to Take Power* (Bonus Books, 2004), p. 94. On the evolution of conservative direct mail, see ibid., chapters 7–8.

85. Legendary Republican strategist Karl Rove built his own career as a direct mail consultant in the 1980s and 1990s before becoming the chief political adviser to George W. Bush. James Moore and Wayne Slater, *Bush's Brain: How Karl Rove Made George W. Bush Presidential* (John Wiley & Sons, 2003), pp. 146–51.

86. On talk radio, see Balz and Brownstein, note 13, above, pp. 163–72.

87. Zev Chafets, "Late-Period Limbaugh," *The New York Times*, July 6, 2008.

88. "The Top Talk Radio Audiences," *Talkers Magazine*, updated Spring 2011, available at http://talkers.com/top-talk-radio-audiences/. After Limbaugh, the other seven (based on Spring 2011 data) were Sean Hannity, Michael Savage, Glenn Beck, Mark Levin, Dave Ramsey, Neal Boortz, and Laura Ingraham. All except Ramsey can uncontroversially be described as conservatives.

89. Jacques Steinberg, "Fox News, Media Elite," *The New York Times*, November 8, 2004; Jacques Steinberg, "Fox News Finds Its Rivals Closing In," *The New York Times*, June 28, 2008.

90. Balz and Brownstein, note 13, above, pp. 183–85.

91. Sam Howe Verhovek, "An Angry Bush Ends His Ties to Rifle Group," *The New York Times*, May 11, 1995.

92. Brody Mullins, "Chamber Ad Campaign Targets Consumer Agency," *The Wall Street Journal*, September 8, 2009.

93. Eric Lipton, Mike McIntire, and Don Van Natta, Jr., "Top Corporations Aid U.S. Chamber of Commerce Campaign," *The New York Times*, October 21, 2010.

94. According to quantitative analysis, however, the current Supreme Court is the most conservative in at least half a century. Adam Liptak, "Court Under Roberts Is Most Conservative in Decades," *The New York Times*, July 24, 2010.

95. House Budget Committee, *The Path to Prosperity: Restoring America's Promise: Fiscal Year 2012 Budget Resolution*, p. 10. The passage reads, "Mismanagement and overspending have left the nation on the brink of bankruptcy. Only recently, millions of American families saw their dreams destroyed in a financial disaster caused by misguided policies, perverse incentives, and irresponsible leadership. This crisis squandered the nation's savings and crippled its economy."

96. Fiorina and Abrams, note 82, above, p. 565; Ferguson, note 31, above, pp. 6–8. On polarization in Congress, see McCarty et al., note 10, above, especially chapter 2.

97. Lydia Saad, "Americans Still Split About Whether Their Taxes Are Too High," Gallup, April 18, 2011.

98. For details, see Morgan, note 7, above, pp. 193–97.

99. George W. Bush, 2000 Republican National Convention Acceptance Address, August 3, 2000, available at http://www.nytimes.com/library/politics/camp/080400wh-bush-speech.html.

100. Al Gore, 2000 Democratic National Convention Acceptance Address, August 17, 2000, available at http://www.washingtonpost.com/wp-srv/onpolitics/elections/goretext081700.htm. The Clinton-Gore plan to "save Social Security first" would have improved the Social Security and Medicare trust funds' balance by effectively crediting budget surpluses to the trust funds, but it would not in itself have done anything about the long-term growth in Social Security and Medicare spending. Morgan, note 7, above, p. 200.

101. *Vital Statistics of the United States, 2003, Volume 1, Natality*, Table 1-1, available at http://www.cdc.gov/nchs/data/statab/natfinal2003.annvol1_01.pdf.

102. *2011 Annual Report of the Board of Trustees of the Federal Old-Age and Survivors Insurance and Federal Disability Insurance Trust Funds*, Table V.A3, p. 90. From 1970 to 2010, life expectancy at age 65 has increased from 13.1 to 17.5 years for men and from 17.1 to 19.9 years for women.

103. *1992 Annual Report of the Board of Trustees of the Federal Old-Age and Survivors Insurance and Federal Disability Insurance Trust Funds*, pp. 21, 27.

104. CBO, *The Economic and Budget Outlook: Fiscal Years 1993–1997*, January 1992, p. 58. The actual 2002 figure was roughly 23 percent. OMB, note 6, above, Tables 13.1, 8.5, 8.7. The difference is partly due to Medicare spending reductions enacted in 1993 and 1997.

105. CBO, *The Economic and Budget Outlook: Fiscal Years 1997–2006*, May 1996, p. 69.

106. CBO, *The Long-Term Budget Outlook*, October 2000, Figure 3, p. 8, and Table 3, p. 14.

107. OMB, note 6, above, Tables 1.1, 13.1. The $312 billion surplus does not include interest paid to the Social Security trust funds by the rest of the government (to pay off previous borrowing from the trust funds); with those interest payments, the surplus was $539 billion.

108. See Daniel N. Shaviro, *Taxes, Spending, and the U.S. Government's March Toward Bankruptcy* (Cambridge University Press, 2007), p. 61.

109. It is true that the accounting rules are not particularly strict, and many pension plans are underfunded (even though they are allowed to assume relatively high future rates of return on their investments), but that is the basic concept.

110. Over the next seventy-five years (the period over which Social Security's finances are conventionally measured), the deficit was 1.89 percent of total taxable payroll. *2000 Annual Report of the Board of Trustees of the Federal Old-Age and Survivors Insurance and Disability Insurance Trust Funds*, p. 24. The Social Security trust fund annual reports did not include a present value estimate of the seventy-five-year deficit until the 2003 report. In that report, the deficit was 1.92 percent of taxable payroll and $3.5 trillion in present value terms. *2003 Annual Report of the Board of Trustees of the Federal Old-Age and Survivors Insurance and Disability Insurance Trust Funds*, p. 10.

111. In 1999, the CBO already projected Medicare spending growing from 2.4 percent of GDP to 5.8 percent in 2030, with Social Security only growing from 4.3 percent to 6.1 percent. CBO, *The Long-Term Budget Outlook: An Update*, December 14, 1999, Table 1, p. 10. Medicare is designed to draw on general revenues, so it does not have a stand-alone deficit, but higher spending requires that the program draw more money from general revenues, adding to the overall deficit.

112. Rubin and Weisberg, note 46, above, p. 164.

113. In May 2001, Senator Jim Jeffords left the Republican Party and began caucusing with the Democrats, giving them a 51–49 majority in the Senate. However, the Republicans were able to attract the few Democratic votes necessary to pass their budgetary proposals. From 2003 to 2007 the Republicans had majorities in both houses of Congress.

114. CBO, *The Budget and Economic Outlook: Fiscal Years 2002–2011*, January 2001, Table 1-1, p. 2. The projected 2010 surplus in the CBO's baseline would climb to $806 billion by May 2001. CBO, *An Analysis of the President's Budgetary Proposals for Fiscal Year 2002*, May 2001, Table 1, p. 12. In retrospect, the CBO's economic forecast was too optimistic, but it was no more optimistic than forecasts by private sector economists. In January 2001, the CBO forecast average real GDP growth of 3.0 percent for the 2001–2010 period; the Blue Chip consensus forecast (an average of private sector economists' forecasts) was for average real GDP growth of 3.3 percent. CBO, *The Budget and Economic Outlook*, January 2001, Table 2-2, p. 30.

115. Bush's tax cut proposals garnered 50–60 percent support in the abstract. Compared to using the surplus for Social Security, Medicare, or other spending priorities, however, tax cuts fared dismally in opinion polls. Polls also indi-

cated a strong preference for tax cuts targeted at "middle income Americans" rather than "across the board" tax cuts. Hacker and Pierson, note 57, above, pp. 49–53. See also Morgan, note 7, above, pp. 221–22.

116. Dreyfuss, note 64, above. For example, the Tax Relief Coalition, a group of businesses and business organizations, lobbied hard for the 2001 tax cuts, even though they affected only income and estate taxes, not corporate taxes.

117. This was the vote on the final conference report. Major congressional actions are available at http://thomas.loc.gov/cgi-bin/bdquery/z?d107:HR01836:@@@R.

118. The largest as a share of GDP was the 1981 Reagan tax cut; the second largest was the 1964 Kennedy-Johnson tax cut. In 2010, when fully phased in, EGTRRA was projected to reduce tax revenues by $176 billion, or 1.1 percent of GDP (as then projected by the CBO), making it larger than the Revenue Act of 1978. In real dollar terms, EGTRRA was the second-largest tax cut in modern history. We exclude the major tax cuts enacted as a result of the end of World War II. CBO, "Pay-As-You-Go Estimate, H.R. 1836: Economic Growth and Tax Relief Reconciliation Act of 2001," June 4, 2001; Tempalski, note 26, above, Table 2, pp. 16–20.

119. For a summary, see CBO, "Pay-As-You-Go Estimate, H.R. 1836," June 4, 2001. The estate tax repeal was phased in for 2010 only.

120. Under the "Byrd rule" in the Senate, a bill that goes through reconciliation cannot increase deficits in any year after the period specifically covered by the initial budget resolution.

121. CBO, *An Analysis of the President's Budgetary Proposals*, May 2001, p. 6. On the distributional impact of the phase-ins, see Morgan, note 7, above, p. 225.

122. CBO, "Pay-As-You-Go Estimate, H.R. 1836," June 4, 2001. The GDP estimate is from CBO, *An Analysis of the President's Budgetary Proposals for Fiscal Year 2002*, May 2001, Table 5, p. 16. Actually, it's even more complicated because some tax cuts were phased out before 2010; if those were extended to 2010 (which some eventually were), the 2010 tax cut would become even bigger.

123. Taxpayers must calculate their tax liability under both the regular income tax and the AMT and pay whichever is greater. The 2001 tax cuts, by reducing ordinary income taxes, meant that more people would have to pay the AMT. Therefore, the official assumption (based on current law) was that AMT revenues would increase, partially offsetting the reductions in the ordinary income tax. In practice, this only meant that future actions to patch the AMT would cost even more in foregone revenue than they would have otherwise. See Leonard E. Burman, William G. Gale, and Jeffrey Rohaly, "The AMT: Projections and Problems," *Tax Notes*, July 7, 2003: 105–17; Hacker and Pierson, note 57, above, pp. 61–62.

124. Morgan, note 7, above, p. 229.

125. At the time, the Center on Budget and Policy Priorities estimated that the 2001 tax cut would cost $4.1 trillion in its second decade (from 2012 through 2021), not counting additional interest on the larger national debt. Joel Friedman, Richard Kogan, and Robert Greenstein, "New Tax-Cut Law Ultimately Costs as Much as Bush Plan," Center on Budget and Policy Priorities, revised June 27, 2001.

126. CBO, *The Budget and Economic Outlook: Fiscal Years 2004–2013*, January 2003, Summary Table 1, p. xvi. The CBO was projecting surpluses to return in 2007,

but this was solely because of off-budget (Social Security trust fund) surpluses. On-budget surpluses would only return in 2012, but that assumed that the 2001 tax cut would expire.

127. Hacker and Pierson, note 57, above, pp. 53–54.

128. CBO, "Cost Estimate, H.R. 2: Jobs and Growth Tax Relief Reconciliation Act of 2003," May 23, 2003.

129. Morgan, note 7, above, p. 230.

130. Tax Policy Center, Table T08-0157, Individual Income and Estate Tax Provisions in the 2001–08 Tax Cuts with AMT Patch Extended, Distribution of Federal Tax Change by Cash Income Percentile, 2010, available at http://www .taxpolicycenter.org/numbers/displayatab.cfm?Docid=1866&DocTypeID=2. We chose the 2010 impact because this was the last year before the tax cuts were scheduled to expire; we chose the version with the extended AMT patch because the AMT has been patched.

131. Tax Policy Center, Table T08-0156, Individual Income and Estate Tax Provisions in the 2001–08 Tax Cuts with AMT Patch Extended, Distribution of Federal Tax Change by Cash Income Level, 2010, available at http://www .taxpolicycenter.org/numbers/displayatab.cfm?Docid=1865&DocTypeID=1.

132. Tax Policy Center, Table T08-0157, note 130, above.

133. 76.1 percent of all taxpaying households pay more in payroll taxes than in income taxes, including the employer share of payroll taxes. 50.6 percent of all taxpaying households pay more in payroll taxes than in income taxes when only counting the employee share of the payroll tax. These calculations are based on 2011, when the payroll tax was unusually low because of the December 2010 tax cut. Tax Policy Center, Table T11-0192, Distribution of Tax Units That Pay More in Payroll Taxes than Individual Income Taxes, by Cash Income Percentile, Current Law, 2011, available at http://www.taxpolicycenter.org/numbers /displayatab.cfm?Docid=3073&DocTypeID=2.

134. While many middle-class households have investments, a large proportion of those investments are in their houses—investments largely shielded from capital gains taxes—or in retirement savings accounts, which also enjoy tax preferences.

135. Douglas W. Elmendorf, Jason Furman, William G. Gale, and Benjamin H. Harris, "Distributional Effects of the 2001 and 2003 Tax Cuts: How Do Financing and Behavioral Responses Matter?," Brookings Institution, June 2008. The authors model the financing of the tax cuts either as an equal-dollar loss for all households or as a loss that is proportional to income; on these assumptions, either 17 percent or 22 percent of households would benefit from the tax cuts. As they say, "To be sure, if one assumes that the financing occurs entirely through spending reductions and that the foregone spending is worthless to individuals, then the standard distributional analysis applies. However, despite decades of stump speeches about unnecessary government spending, the political process has been persistently unable to identify significant outlays that voters will blithely forego." Their analysis also incorporates behavioral effects of the tax cuts, which increase the proportion of households made better off to 34 percent. Ibid., Table 5.

136. Emmanuel Saez, "Striking It Richer: The Evolution of Top Incomes in the United States (Updated with 2008 Estimates)," July 17, 2010, available at http://elsa.berkeley.edu/~saez/saez-UStopincomes-2008.pdf, Figure 2.

137. We only include fiscal years that were entirely during periods of economic expansion; we exclude FY 1991 because the economy was in recession until March 1991; we exclude FY 2001 and 2002 because the economy was in recession until November 2001, which was during the 2002 fiscal year. In addition, after correcting for the effect of the economic cycle, tax revenues still fell from 20.1 percent of GDP in 2000 to 16.5 percent in 2004; cyclically adjusted revenues ranged from 19.5 percent to 20.1 percent of GDP from 1998 through 2000, but only from 15.4 percent to 18.9 percent from 2003 through 2009. (We omit 2001 from the comparison because the first Bush tax cut took place during the 2001 fiscal year.) CBO, *Measuring the Effects of the Business Cycle on the Federal Budget: An Update*, September 1, 2009. Finally, the Bush tax cuts were not fully phased in during part of the 2001–2007 expansion; had they been fully phased in at the beginning, average revenues would have been lower.

138. George W. Bush, "What the Congress Can Do for America," *The Wall Street Journal*, January 3, 2007.

139. GDP data are from BEA, National Income and Product Accounts, Table 1.1.6. Growth is measured from the first quarter following the end of a recession to the last quarter preceding the beginning of the next recession.

140. In 2005, the CBO (then headed by a Republican appointee, Douglas Holtz-Eakin) estimated that the economic effects of a 10 percent cut in income taxes would offset between 1 percent and 22 percent of the revenue loss in the first five years; in the following five years, the economic effects might offset up to 32 percent of the revenue loss, but might also *add* 5 percent to the revenue loss. CBO, "Analyzing the Economic and Budgetary Effects of a 10 Percent Cut in Income Tax Rates," Economic and Budget Issue Brief, December 1, 2005. A paper coauthored by Gregory Mankiw, a former chair of President Bush's Council of Economic Advisers, calculates that 32.4 percent of the static revenue loss of a capital gains tax cut and 14.7 percent of the static revenue loss of a labor tax cut could be offset in present value terms (ignoring short-term Keynesian effects). N. Gregory Mankiw and Matthew Weinzierl, "Dynamic Scoring: A Back-of-the-Envelope Guide," *Journal of Public Economics* 90 (2006): 1415–33, p. 1430. An offset of 32.4 percent is a lot, but far less than 100 percent. Even then, Mankiw and Weinzierl assume that government spending falls to keep the budget in balance. Ibid., p. 1417. If instead the tax cuts are financed by additional debt, their ultimate effect can be to lower economic growth in the long term, depending on the eventual consequences of the larger debt. Eric M. Leeper and Shu-Chun Susan Yang, "Dynamic Scoring: Alternative Financing Schemes," *Journal of Public Economics* 92 (2008): 159–82, pp. 166–69.

141. The Joint Committee on Taxation estimated that a 10 percent cut in individual income tax rates would reduce economic growth in the long run if the tax cut were financed by increased borrowing. Joint Committee on Taxation, "Exploring Issues in the Development of Macroeconomic Models for Use in Tax Policy Analysis," JCX-19-06, June 16, 2006.

142. In 2007, the CBO estimated the 2010 impact of the tax cuts, including interest payments, at $269 billion. Peter R. Orszag, Letter to the Honorable John M. Spratt, Jr., July 20, 2007.

143. Through 2008, the Bush tax cuts accounted for $1.7 trillion in deficits and over $200 billion in additional interest costs. Kathy A. Ruffing and James R. Horney,

"Economic Downturn and Bush Policies Continue to Drive Large Projected Deficits," Center on Budget and Policy Priorities, May 10, 2011, p. 8. For 2009 through 2011, the CBO estimated a total impact of $729 billion, but that was before the December 2010 tax cut extension. Orszag, note 142, above. The 2010 extension added almost $200 billion to the 2011 impact of the tax cuts, not counting the new payroll tax cut and another AMT patch. CBO, "Estimate of Changes in Revenues and Direct Spending for S.A. 4753, an Amendment to H.R. 4853, the Tax Relief, Unemployment Insurance Reauthorization, and Job Creation Act of 2010," December 10, 2010.

144. An analysis by the Pew Charitable Trusts broke down the components of the increase in the 2011 national debt since the CBO's projection in January 2001. The largest factor was lower revenues due to economic changes and technical reestimates (28 percent). The second largest was the 2001/2003 tax cuts (13 percent); the December 2010 tax cuts, which largely extended the 2001/2003 tax cuts, contributed 3 percent, while other tax cuts contributed 5 percent, for a total of 21 percent attributable to tax cuts. That does not include additional interest payments because of the larger debt created by those tax cuts. (The 2009 stimulus bill, by contrast, was responsible for only 6 percent of the increase in the debt.) Pew Fiscal Analysis Initiative, *The Great Debt Shift: Drivers of Federal Debt Since 2001*, April 2011, Figure 3, p. 5.

145. Ibid.; Ruffing and Horney, note 143, above; Teresa Tritch, "How the Deficit Got This Big," *The New York Times*, July 23, 2011; Chad Stone, "What's Driving Projected Debt?," Off the Charts (blog), Center for Budget and Policy Priorities, May 20, 2011. Brian Riedl of the Heritage Foundation has argued that focusing on the Bush tax cuts is arbitrary, since the projected deficit could also be blamed on Social Security, Medicare, or other programs. Brian Riedl, "The Bush Tax Cuts and the Deficit Myth," *The Wall Street Journal*, July 13, 2010. The Bush tax cuts, however, were a policy choice made after the long-term deficits in Social Security and Medicare were clearly visible, yet without making any effort to offset the tax cuts in any way. Riedl argues that deficits must be the fault of increasing spending because tax revenues remain roughly stable at around 18 percent of GDP. But this argument ignores the fact that tax cuts—including the Bush tax cuts—are the very mechanism that keeps tax revenues from growing much higher than 18 percent of GDP for very long.

146. OMB, note 6, above, Table 1.2.

147. Defense spending grew from 3.0 percent to 4.3 percent of GDP—half of the total increase in GDP terms. Ibid., Table 8.4. As of January 2011, appropriations through 2010 were $1,104 billion, with appropriations for 2011 running at an annual rate of $159 billion. CBO, *The Budget and Economic Outlook: Fiscal Years 2011 to 2021*, January 2011, Box 3-2, p. 77. This does not include additional interest payments on the larger national debt, which came to $64 billion through 2008. Ruffing and Horney, note 143, above, p. 8. The appropriations include $126 billion for war-related activities not specifically associated with Afghanistan and Iraq. Joseph Stiglitz and Linda Bilmes have estimated the true cost of the Iraq War at over $3 trillion. Joseph E. Stiglitz and Linda J. Bilmes, *The Three Trillion Dollar War: The True Cost of the Iraq Conflict* (W. W. Norton, 2008). This figure, however, includes economic losses suffered by Americans that do not add to the government debt. See Peter Orszag, "Estimated Costs

of U.S. Operations in Iraq and Afghanistan and of Other Activities Related to the War on Terrorism," testimony before the House Budget Committee, October 24, 2007, pp. 10–14.

148. Voting information for the Authorization for Use of Military Force Against Iraq Resolution of 2002 is available at http://thomas.loc.gov/cgi-bin/bdquery/z?d107:HJ00114:@@@R.

149. Dennis S. Ippolito, *Why Budgets Matter: Budget Policy and American Politics* (Pennsylvania State University Press, 2004), p. 175.

150. Richard W. Stevenson, "Bush Unveils Plan to Cut Tax Rates and Spur Economy," *The New York Times*, January 8, 2003.

151. Elisabeth Bumiller, "White House Cuts Estimate of Cost of War with Iraq," *The New York Times*, December 31, 2002; Matthew Engel, "Cost of War Put at $200bn, but That's Nothing, Says US Adviser," *The Guardian* (London), September 16, 2002.

152. Morgan, note 7, above, p. 235.

153. Quoted in James Surowiecki, "A Cut Too Far," *The New Yorker*, April 21, 2003.

154. Nick Gillespie, "An Alliance for Freedom?," *Reason*, August-September 2008.

155. See Jonathan Oberlander, *The Political Life of Medicare* (University of Chicago Press, 2003), pp. 175–76.

156. CBO, "Estimate of Effect on Direct Spending and Revenues of Conference Agreement on H.R. 1," November 20, 2003.

157. Robert Pear, "Inquiry Confirms Top Medicare Official Threatened Actuary over Cost of Drug Benefits," *The New York Times*, July 7, 2004. The administrator, Thomas Scully, resigned after the bill passed to become a lobbyist for health care companies.

158. The seventy-five-year deficits of the three major components of Medicare, in present value terms, are: Part A (Hospital Insurance), $3.1 trillion; Part B (Medical Insurance), $13.9 trillion; and Part D (Prescription Drug Coverage), $7.5 trillion. (Part C refers to Medicare Advantage plans, which are provided by private insurers but subsidized by Medicare.) *2011 Annual Report of the Boards of Trustees of the Federal Hospital Insurance and Federal Supplementary Medical Insurance Trust Funds*, Tables III.B9, III.C15, III.C23, pp. 83, 130, 146.

159. CBO, *An Analysis of the President's Budgetary Proposals for Fiscal Year 2006*, March 2005, pp. 47–49. Participants diverting money into individual accounts would presumably receive lower guaranteed benefits when they retired. But money going into individual accounts would no longer be available to pay promised benefits to current retirees, requiring additional borrowing. The shortfall could have been reduced by lowering benefits for current retirees, but the president did not explicitly propose such a plan.

160. In 2007, Social Security ran a surplus of $81 billion, not counting interest received from the rest of the federal government. Without that surplus, the 2007 government deficit would have been $242 billion. The 2007 surplus was the sixth largest in history after 2000–2002 and 2005–2006. OMB, note 6, above, Table 13.1.

161. CBO, *The Budget and Economic Outlook: Fiscal Years 2008 to 2018*, January 2008, Summary Table 1, p. xii.

162. CBO, *The Long-Term Budget Outlook*, December 2007, Figure 1-2, p. 4.

163. Douglas W. Elmendorf, "CBO's Analysis of the Major Health Care Legislation

Enacted in March 2010," testimony before the Health Subcommittee of the
House Energy and Commerce Committee, March 30, 2011, Table 1, p. 2.

164. OMB, note 6, above, Tables 13.1 and 7.1. To calculate program deficits in any
year, we take the actual trust fund surplus or deficit and subtract any interest
received from the rest of the government and (for Medicare Parts B and D)
any transfers from general government revenues; this yields the program's true
impact on the overall federal deficit in that year. Including interest payments
from the rest of the government (but not transfers from general revenues), the
programs together ran a surplus over the same period. The $270 billion figure
does not include additional interest payments, so the true impact on the 2007
national debt is slightly larger.

165. *2011 Annual Report of the Boards of Trustees of the Federal Hospital Insurance and
Federal Supplementary Medical Insurance Trust Funds,* Table III.C19, p. 139. To
calculate the Medicare Part D deficit, we take all income except for transfers
from general revenue and subtract all expenditures.

166. Almost one-quarter of that $597 billion is due to the Medicare prescription
drug program. Ibid.

167. OMB, note 6, above, Table 7.1. Government debt as a percentage of GDP
averaged 36.7 percent from 1958 through 2007.

168. CBO, *The Budget and Economic Outlook,* January 2008, Summary Table 1,
p. xii. By law, the CBO baseline projection must follow certain rules that make it
unrealistic. Most importantly, it must assume that current law remains
unchanged; in 2007, this meant assuming that the Bush tax cuts would expire
on schedule and that the AMT would be allowed to hit middle-class households. Despite this problem, because it is constrained to follow a consistent
set of rules, the CBO baseline projection is often the best way to compare the
government's fiscal position at different points in time.

169. We recommend Simon Johnson and James Kwak, *13 Bankers: The Wall Street
Takeover and the Next Financial Meltdown* (Pantheon, 2010).

170. Job losses are changes in nonfarm employment from January 2008 through
February 2010, seasonally adjusted, from the Bureau of Labor Statistics, Current Employment Statistics Survey.

171. Unemployment data are from the Bureau of Labor Statistics, Current Population Survey.

172. BEA, National Income and Product Accounts, Table 1.1.6.

173. Revenues were 14.9 percent of GDP in 2009, the lowest since they were 14.4
percent in 1950.

174. OMB, *Fiscal Year 2012 Budget of the U.S. Government,* p. 24. The Treasury
Department estimated that future dividends paid by Fannie and Freddie would
reduce the net costs of the bailout to $73 billion. Ibid. The CBO estimated
that, including the ongoing costs of subsidies granted by Fannie and Freddie,
the total cost to the government was over $300 billion. Deborah Lucas, "The
Budgetary Cost of Fannie Mae and Freddie Mac and Options for the Future
Federal Role in the Secondary Mortgage Market," testimony to the House
Budget Committee, June 2, 2011, p. 11.

175. CBO, "Cost Estimate, H.R. 5140: Economic Stimulus Act of 2008," February 11, 2008.

176. Douglas W. Elmendorf, Letter to the Honorable Nancy Pelosi, February 13,

2009, Table 2. $288 billion is the total impact of Division B, Title I, including both direct spending (in this case, tax credits) and revenues.

177. In a *Wall Street Journal* survey, thirty-eight economists thought that the 2009 stimulus had a positive impact on economic growth and jobs; six thought it had a negative impact. Phil Izzo, "Economists Credit Fed for Alleviating Crisis," *The Wall Street Journal*, March 12, 2010. See also the private sector forecasts listed in Council of Economic Advisers, *The Economic Impact of the American Recovery and Reinvestment Act of 2009, Seventh Quarterly Report*, July 1, 2011, Table 7, p. 12.

178. CBO, *The Budget and Economic Outlook: An Update*, August 2009, Summary Table 1, p. x.

179. Federal Reserve Statistical Release H.15.

180. See Jane Mayer, "Covert Operations," *The New Yorker*, August 30, 2010; Vanessa Williamson, Theda Skocpol, and John Coggin, "The Tea Party and the Remaking of Republican Conservatism," *Perspectives on Politics* 9, no. 1 (2011): 25–43, pp. 28–30.

181. Looking at data that precede the appearance of the Tea Party, Campbell and Putnam find that the best predictors of becoming a Tea Party supporter are being a Republican and wanting religion to play a larger role in politics. Other prior predictors are being active in politics, being white, and having a "low regard for immigrants and blacks." David E. Campbell and Robert D. Putnam, "Crashing the Tea Party," *The New York Times*, August 16, 2011.

182. Nate Silver, "Poll Shows More Americans Have Unfavorable Views of Tea Party," FiveThirtyEight (blog), *The New York Times*, March 30, 2011.

183. Pew Research Center, note 79, above, p. 66.

184. Silver, note 182, above; Nate Silver, "Freshmen Republicans Push House Toward Right," FiveThirtyEight (blog), *The New York Times*, July 12, 2011.

185. On Norquist's influence in the 2011–2012 Congress, see Bennett, note 65, above.

186. CBO, "Estimate of Changes in Revenues and Direct Spending for S.A. 4753," December 10, 2010. The total fiscal impact through FY 2013 (which includes the last quarter of 2012) was $917 billion, of which $56 billion went to unemployment insurance benefits. The act was estimated to increase tax revenues slightly in later years, but those increases were contingent on certain investment incentives not being extended again.

187. See Bruce Bartlett, "Doing Away with the Debt Ceiling," Economix (blog), *The New York Times*, August 1, 2011.

188. Lori Montgomery and Paul Kane, "Obama, Congressional Leaders Gather at White House to Try to Save Debt Deal," *The Washington Post*, July 22, 2011. According to reports, Boehner agreed to $800 billion in tax increases but walked out when Obama asked for $1.2 trillion. It is important to note, however, that these tax increases were net *decreases* compared to current law because the "increases" were relative to a baseline in which all of the Bush tax cuts would be extended.

189. Carl Hulse and Jackie Calmes, "Push Intensifies for Larger Deal on Debt Impasse," *The New York Times*, July 20, 2011. Similar to the Obama-Boehner negotiations, the Gang of Six plan would have "increased" tax revenues, but only on top of a baseline that assumed the extension of the Bush tax cuts. Compared

to letting the tax cuts expire, its net effect would have been to reduce taxes by $1.5 trillion. "A Bipartisan Plan to Reduce Our Nation's Deficits," available at http://www.washingtonpost.com/r/2010–2019/WashingtonPost/2011/07/19/National-Politics/Graphics/Gang_of_Six_Document.pdf.

190. Jennifer Steinhauer and Robert Pear, "Lawmakers Aim to Stop Defense Cuts if Debt Panel Fails," *The New York Times*, November 4, 2011.

191. CBO, *Budget and Economic Outlook*, January 2011. $6.7 trillion is the CBO's baseline projection (Table 1-1, p. 2) adjusted to reflect the drawdown of troops from Iraq and Afghanistan, the continuation of Medicare reimbursement rates, and continued indexation of the alternative minimum tax (Table 1-7, pp. 22–23). $11.5 trillion also assumes the extension of all other expiring tax provisions.

192. The $900 billion in initial spending cuts were entirely in discretionary spending programs, not the major entitlement programs. The $1.2 trillion in automatic cuts do apply to Medicare (though not Social Security or Medicaid); those cuts, however, apply to provider reimbursements, not to participants' benefits.

193. Quoted in Jennifer Steinhauer, "Debt Bill Is Signed, Ending a Fractious Battle," *The New York Times*, August 2, 2011.

4. WHAT DOES THE FEDERAL GOVERNMENT DO?

1. Quoted in "The 'Misunderestimated' President?," BBC News, January 7, 2009. See also "The Best of George W. Bush," YouTube, available at http://www.youtube.com/watch?v=uO46ii3W07U ("It's a budget with a lot of line items; there's a lot of pages; there's a lot of numbers.").

2. Michael Cooper, "Hurricane Cost Seen as Ranking Among Top Ten," *The New York Times*, August 30, 2011.

3. Robert P. King, "Fed's Weather Information Could Go Dark," *The Palm Beach Post*, April 21, 2005; Timothy Noah, "Santorum's Mighty Wind," *Slate*, August 2, 2005.

4. Mike Lillis, "Cantor in Tricky Spot on Disaster Aid," *The Hill*, August 31, 2011; "Chris Christie: Send Aid Now; Cut Later," Associated Press, August 31, 2011.

5. Unless otherwise noted, all figures for 2010 and prior years are from OMB, *Fiscal Year 2012 Budget of the United States Government: Historical Tables*, Tables 1.1, 1.2, 2.1, 2.2, 2.3, 3.1, 3.2, 6.1, 7.1, 8.1, 8.4, and 8.5.

6. Frank Newport, "Americans Blame Wasteful Government Spending for Deficit," Gallup, April 29, 2011; Kaiser Family Foundation/Harvard School of Public Health, *The Public's Health Care Agenda for the 112th Congress: Chartpack*, January 2011, p. 7. The Gallup poll allowed people to say the deficit should be reduced equally through spending cuts and tax increases; 48 percent preferred mostly or only spending cuts, 37 percent preferred an equal balance, and 11 percent preferred mostly or only tax increases. The KFF/Harvard poll did not provide such an option; 57 percent preferred mainly spending cuts, 14 percent preferred mainly tax increases, and 19 percent preferred no action. It's not clear whether this is a new phenomenon or not. The American National Elec-

tion Studies longitudinal surveys do not specifically include this question. The proportion of people who think the government should reduce services and spending peaked in 1994, fell until 2000, and has been growing since; the proportion of people who think the government wastes a lot of tax money peaked in 1980, generally fell until 2002, and has been climbing rapidly since. American National Election Studies, *The ANES Guide to Public Opinion and Electoral Behavior*, Tables 4A.5, 5A.3.

7. Frank Newport and Lydia Saad, "Americans Oppose Cuts in Education, Social Security, Defense," Gallup, January 26, 2011; *Washington Post*–ABC News poll, April 14–17, 2011, available at http://www.washingtonpost.com/wp-srv/politics/polls/postpoll_04172011.html, question 17; Kaiser Family Foundation/Harvard School of Public Health, note 6, above, p. 8.

8. "American Public Vastly Overestimates Amount of U.S. Foreign Aid," WorldPublicOpinion.org, November 29, 2010. It's true that if you ask people to estimate the budgetary share of different programs separately, they are likely to overestimate them. Still, a factor of 25 is a lot. In an earlier poll, after hearing that foreign aid consumed only 1 percent of the federal budget, over 80 percent of respondents said that was too little or about right—implying that if Americans knew how little we spend on foreign aid, they wouldn't want to cut it, either. Program on International Policy Attitudes, *Americans on Foreign Aid and World Hunger: A Study of U.S. Public Attitudes*, February 2, 2001. Total "international affairs" (Function 150) spending in 2010 was $45 billion, or 1.3 percent of federal spending. Only half of this spending, however, goes to traditional economic development and humanitarian assistance; the other half is aid linked to U.S. foreign policy goals, including economic assistance for countries like Afghanistan and Iraq and programs that help our allies buy military equipment and services. Gordon Adams and Cindy Williams, *Buying National Security: How America Plans and Pays for Its Global Role and Safety at Home* (Routledge, 2010), chapters 3–4.

9. On discretionary and mandatory spending in general, see Allen Schick, *The Federal Budget: Politics, Policy, Process*, 3rd ed. (Brookings Institution Press, 2007), pp. 57–62.

10. Mandatory spending is also known as direct spending.

11. We chose 1962 because it is the first year for which OMB publishes this breakdown of total federal spending.

12. CBO, *The Budget and Economic Outlook: An Update*, August 2011, Table 1-2, pp. 4–5. This is the CBO's baseline projection, which assumes cuts to Medicare reimbursement rates that are politically unlikely to occur. See ibid., p. 25.

13. Kaiser Family Foundation/Harvard School of Public Health, note 6, above, p. 9. Even when respondents were told to assume that Congress would be reducing the deficit by cutting spending, 47 percent still said they would support no cuts in Medicaid and 39 percent would support only minor cuts. The number of Medicaid beneficiaries is expected to rise to 97 million by 2021. CBO, *The Budget and Economic Outlook: Fiscal Years 2011 to 2021*, January 2011, p. 62.

14. Averages for the 1960s cover 1962–1969 because OMB figures for this breakdown of government outlays go back only to 1962. The decade before the financial crisis is 1999–2008.

15. Defense spending averaged 3.2 percent of GDP from 1996 through 2002—the

period after the decline of defense spending following the end of the Cold War but before the invasion of Iraq.

16. Erika Bolstad and Curtis Morgan, "Budget Ax May Fall on Hurricane Hunter Planes," *Miami Herald*, September 1, 2011.

17. Employment figures exclude the Postal Service and are from December of each year (to avoid the impact of temporary Census-related hiring). Bureau of Labor Statistics, Current Employment Statistics.

18. On the history of the major government insurance programs, see Jacob S. Hacker, *The Divided Welfare State: The Battle over Public and Private Social Benefits in the United States* (Cambridge University Press, 2002).

19. David A. Moss, *When All Else Fails: Government as the Ultimate Risk Manager* (Harvard University Press, 2002).

20. In general, full Medicare eligibility requires ten years of employment in Medicare-covered employment (that is, employment for which you pay the Medicare payroll tax).

21. *2011 Annual Report of the Board of Trustees of the Federal Old-Age and Survivors Insurance and Federal Disability Insurance Trust Funds*, p. 2; *2011 Annual Report of the Boards of Trustees of the Federal Hospital Insurance and Federal Supplementary Medical Insurance Trust Funds*, p. 4.

22. The full retirement age was gradually increased beginning with people born in 1938, and is 66 for people born in 1943–1954; it will start increasing again for people born in 1955, and will reach 67 for people born in 1960 or later. John A. Svahn and Mary Ross, "Social Security Amendments of 1983: Legislative History and Summary of Provisions," *Social Security Bulletin* 46, no. 7 (July 1983): 3–48, p. 30.

23. Social Security Online, Monthly Statistical Snapshot, July 2011, Table 2.

24. Social Security and Medicare are both progressive programs on balance. Social Security combines a slightly regressive payroll tax (meaning that the poor pay a larger share of their incomes than the rich) with a significantly progressive benefit formula (meaning that the poor receive larger benefits than the rich). Medicare combines a progressive funding mechanism (a flat payroll tax, plus additional funding from general revenues) with equal benefits for all, regardless of past contributions. Whether a progressive system benefits the person in the middle of the distribution depends on the amount and shape of inequality. Today, with inequality at the highest levels of the past century, it is highly likely that median-income families are benefited by progressive tax-and-transfer policies. See Thomas Piketty and Emmanuel Saez, "Income Inequality in the United States, 1913–1998," *Quarterly Journal of Economics* 118, no. 1 (February 2003): 1–39; Emmanuel Saez, "Striking It Richer: The Evolution of Top Incomes in the United States (Updated with 2008 Estimates)," July 17, 2010, available at http://elsa.berkeley.edu/~saez/saez-UStopincomes-2008.pdf.

25. Bureau of Consumer Financial Protection Budget, Congressional Justification, available at http://www.consumerfinance.gov/wp-content/uploads/2011/02/CFPB-2012-CJ.pdf; National Endowment for the Arts, Appropriations Request for Fiscal Year 2012, February 2011, available at http://www.nea.gov/about/Budget/NEA-FY12-Appropriations-Request.pdf.

26. IMF, World Economic Outlook Database, April 2011.

27. Peter Suderman, "If You Focus on the Deficit, Then Tax Increases Are on the Table," *Reason*, April 27, 2011.

28. Bruce Bartlett, "I'd Rather Be an Unlucky Ducky," Economix (blog), *The New York Times*, September 27, 2011; Terry Miller and Kim R. Holmes, *2011 Index of Economic Freedom* (Heritage Foundation and *Wall Street Journal*, 2011), p. 6; IMF, World Economic Outlook Database, April 2011.

29. Franklin D. Roosevelt, State of the Union Address to the Congress, January 6, 1941.

30. Moss, note 19, above, pp. 154, 162–69.

31. United States Census Bureau, *Income, Poverty, and Health Insurance Coverage in the United States: 2010*, Current Population Reports P60-239, September 2011, Table 8, p. 26.

32. Moss, note 19, above.

33. See Daniel N. Shaviro, *Taxes, Spending, and the U.S. Government's March Toward Bankruptcy* (Cambridge University Press, 2007), chapter 2.

34. Tax expenditures were first identified as such by Stanley Surrey, then an official at the Treasury Department, in the 1960s. The concept of tax expenditures has been frequently criticized, most often because tax expenditures have to be measured against some "normal" tax code. Still, while there are valid disagreements over whether some provisions should count as tax expenditures (for example, is the fact that you pay capital gains tax only when you sell an asset, and not each year that it appreciates, a tax expenditure or just the normal way to administer an income tax?), most analysts agree that the concept is useful. See Leonard E. Burman, Christopher Geissler, and Eric J. Toder, "How Big Are Total Individual Income Tax Expenditures, and Who Benefits from Them?," *American Economic Review: Papers and Proceedings* 98 (2008): 79–83, p. 79.

35. Joint Committee on Taxation, *Estimates of Federal Tax Expenditures for Fiscal Years 2010–2014*, JCS-3-10, December 15, 2010, p. 39. This is the "static" revenue loss due to the tax expenditure, which does not take into account changes in behavior that would result from its elimination. The deduction for mortgage interest dates back to 1913, before federal policies to promote homeownership. Suzanne Mettler, *The Submerged State: How Invisible Government Policies Undermine American Democracy* (University of Chicago Press, 2011), p. 16. Today, however, it is routinely defended as an incentive for homeownership.

36. Donald B. Marron, "How Large Are Tax Expenditures?," *Tax Notes* (March 28, 2011): 1597; Leonard E. Burman and Marvin Phaup, "Tax Expenditures, the Size and Efficiency of Government, and Implications for Budget Reform," NBER Working Paper 17268, August 2011, pp. 6–7. The Joint Committee on Taxation does not provide a total estimate, probably because the aggregate effect of the tax expenditures differs from the sum of their individual effects because of interactions between them. An earlier analysis of tax expenditures in the individual income tax code showed that their aggregate impact was larger than the sum of their individual impacts due to interaction effects. Burman et al., note 34, above, p. 80.

37. In 2009, for example, the mortgage interest tax deduction saved families making over $100,000 a total of $53 billion ($3,800 per family); all other families saved only $24 billion ($1,100 per family). Joint Committee on Taxation, note 35, above, Table 3. In aggregate, tax expenditures account for about

11.4 percent of after-tax income for top-quintile households but only 6.8 percent of after-tax income for middle-quintile households. Burman et al., note 34, above, p. 82.

38. Whether this counts as a tax expenditure is open to debate (it depends on whether your definition of the baseline tax system allows deductions for interest expenses), but it certainly encourages companies to borrow money.

39. Mettler, note 35, above, pp. 41–43.

40. Rachel Johnson, James Nunns, Jeffrey Rohaly, Eric Toder, and Roberton Williams, "Why Some Tax Units Pay No Income Tax," Tax Policy Center, July 2011.

41. CNN Opinion Research Poll, April 9–10, 2011, available at http://i2.cdn.turner.com/cnn/2011/images/04/14/rel6f.pdf, question 19.

42. See Bruce Bartlett, "Americans Support Higher Taxes. Really," *Capital Gains and Games* (blog), June 29, 2011.

43. The 7.4 percent average is for fiscal years 2002—the first year for which large components of the 2001 tax cut were in effect—through 2010.

44. Individual income taxes averaged 8.7 percent of GDP in fiscal years 1992–2000 and 7.6 percent of GDP in fiscal years 2003–2007. We exclude fiscal years 1991, 2001, and 2002 because the economy was in recession for part of each of those years.

45. Self-employed people also pay the same payroll taxes.

46. In addition, beginning in 2013, a higher Medicare payroll tax rate will be charged on earnings above certain thresholds designed to affect high-income taxpayers.

47. The tax system as a whole remains modestly progressive, however. For example, in 2010, top-quintile households earned 53.5 percent of pre-tax income and paid 68.6 percent of federal taxes, while middle-quintile households earned 13.9 percent of pre-tax income and paid 9.8 percent of federal taxes. Tax Policy Center, Table T11-0094, Distribution of Cash Income and Federal Taxes by Filing Status and Family Type, Under Current Law, by Cash Income Percentile, 2010, available at http://www.taxpolicycenter.org/numbers/displayatab.cfm?Docid=2975&DocTypeID=7.

48. David Kocieniewski, "Where Pay for Chiefs Outstrips U.S. Taxes," *The New York Times*, August 31, 2011.

49. See David Leonhardt, "The Paradox of Corporate Taxes," *The New York Times*, February 1, 2011; David Kocieniewski, "U.S. Business Has High Tax Rates but Pays Less," *The New York Times*, May 2, 2011.

50. David Kocieniewski, "G.E.'s Strategies Let It Avoid Taxes Altogether," *The New York Times*, March 24, 2011; Jesse Drucker, "The Tax Haven That's Saving Google Billions," *Bloomberg Businessweek*, October 21, 2010.

51. This may be due in part to the fact that pass-through entities, where tax is paid only on the individual level and not on the company level, are becoming increasingly popular in the United States. The high corporate tax rate in the United States may also be inducing companies to shift their income to other countries. See Tax Policy Center, "International Taxation," in *The Tax Policy Briefing Book: A Citizens' Guide to the 2008 Election and Beyond*, available at http://www.taxpolicycenter.org/briefing-book/.

52. Over the past decade, the United States has had the eighth-lowest corporate

taxes among thirty-one OECD countries, measured as a percentage of GDP. Taxes averaged 2.5 percent of GDP over the 2000–2008 period, compared to an average of 3.5 percent for the OECD. Data are not yet available for 2009 for all countries; data are not available for the entire period for Chile and Mexico. OECD.StatExtracts, Revenue Statistics.

53. For overviews of this debate, see Alan J. Auerbach, "Who Bears the Corporate Tax? A Review of What We Know," chapter 1 in James M. Poterba, ed., *Tax Policy and the Economy*, vol. 20 (MIT Press, 2006); Rosanne Altshuler, Benjamin H. Harris, and Eric Toder, "Capital Income Taxation and Progressivity in a Global Economy," *Virginia Tax Review* 30 (2010): 355–88, pp. 360–70.

54. Again, we exclude fiscal years where the economy was in recession for part of the year. The average tax level in fiscal years 2003–2007 was 17.3 percent. The economy expanded from April 1958 to April 1960, leaving only one full fiscal year of expansion (1959), when taxes were 16.2 percent of GDP.

55. OECD.StatExtracts, Revenue Statistics. Among all OECD countries, the only ones with lower total tax rates as a percentage of GDP in 2009 were Chile and Mexico. Arguably, we pay less in taxes because we have to pay more to the private sector for health care (because the government pays for a smaller share of our health care than in comparable countries). On the other hand, however, our government pays more for health care in absolute terms than most other comparable governments. David A. Squires, "The U.S. Health System in Perspective: A Comparison of Twelve Industrialized Nations," Commonwealth Fund, Issues in International Health Policy, July 2011, Exhibit 3, p. 4.

56. In 2010, according to OECD data, the United States had the second-largest general government budget deficit (including all levels of government) as a share of GDP of thirty-two OECD countries, trailing only Ireland (and surpassing Greece). *OECD Economic Outlook No. 89*, 2011, Annex Table 27. The table does not include Chile and Mexico.

57. The Treasury has to continually redeem bonds issued in earlier years that are maturing. So if there is a deficit, the Treasury has to issue new bonds to replace the old ones and issue more new bonds to cover the deficit. The increase in debt in a given year does not exactly equal the deficit in that year because the Treasury has cash in its bank account and has balances in other accounts used by various lending programs. As with any business, the Treasury can fill a budget gap in part by drawing down its account balances, which reduces the amount of money it has to borrow. CBO, *Budget and Economic Outlook*, January 2011, pp. 19–20.

58. Since 1941, the average effective nominal interest rate paid by the government has been 4.8 percent. OMB, note 5, above, Tables 3.1, 7.1. Readers who care about economics will realize that these interest rates should be put in real (inflation-adjusted) terms. The average maturity of federal debt is about five years. "Report to the Secretary of the Treasury from the Treasury Borrowing Advisory Committee of the Securities Industry and Financial Markets Association," February 1, 2011. In 2010, inflation expectations for the next five years were about 1.4–1.8 percent, depending on the measure of inflation, meaning that the real interest rate was about 0.6–1.0 percent. CBO, *The Budget and Economic Outlook*, January 2011, Table 2-1, p. 29. In the long term, the CBO expects the real interest rate on federal debt to be about 2.7 percent in its extended-baseline scenario. CBO, *2011 Long-Term Budget Outlook*, p. 24.

59. CBO, *The Budget and Economic Outlook: An Update*, August 2011, Table 1-2, pp. 4–5. This is from the CBO's baseline projection, which is optimistic for a number of reasons.

60. There is a wide range of views on the causes of the Great Depression and the relative importance of fiscal policy. Milton Friedman and Anna Jacobson Schwartz argue that the main problem was a contraction in the supply of money. Milton Friedman and Anna Jacobson Schwartz, *A Monetary History of the United States, 1867–1960* (Princeton University Press, 1963). Ben Bernanke stresses the negative effects of bank closures. Ben S. Bernanke, *Essays on the Great Depression* (Princeton University Press, 2000). Barry Eichengreen and Peter Temin place more emphasis on the Federal Reserve's belief in the gold standard and attempts to avoid policies, like increasing the money supply, that could have caused a devaluation of the dollar. Barry Eichengreen, *Golden Fetters: The Gold Standard and the Great Depression, 1919–1939* (Oxford University Press, 1992); Peter Temin, *Lessons from the Great Depression* (MIT Press, 1989). In all of these views, however, fiscal policy did not help stimulate the economy during the early 1930s.

61. The effect of automatic stabilizers was $363 billion in 2010. CBO, *The Effect of Automatic Stabilizers on the Federal Budget*, April 2011, Table 1, p. 3.

62. The budgetary impact of the American Recovery and Reinvestment Act was $441 billion in 2010. Douglas W. Elmendorf, Letter to the Honorable Harry Reid, February 11, 2009, p. 2. Automatic stabilizers are explicitly defined to exclude the budgetary impact of legislation. See CBO, *The Effect of Automatic Stabilizers on the Federal Budget*, April 2011, p. 1.

63. For ease of understanding, in this section we discuss long-term trends and their impact on annual deficits and the national debt. An alternative way of assessing the government's long-term fiscal condition is to estimate the "fiscal gap": the difference between future revenues and spending, over a long or infinite horizon, in present value terms. On the fiscal gap and other measures of long-term budgetary balance, see Shaviro, note 33, above, chapter 5. For estimates of the current fiscal gap, see Alan J. Auerbach and William G. Gale, "Tempting Fate: The Federal Budget Outlook," Brookings Institution, June 30, 2011.

64. These rules were initially established in the Congressional Budget and Impoundment Control Act of 1974 and the Balanced Budget and Emergency Deficit Control Act of 1985. In addition, the CBO baseline projects that spending for overseas contingency operations will grow at the rate of inflation, even though current policy is for the number of troops deployed to Iraq and Afghanistan to fall. See CBO, *The Budget and Economic Outlook: An Update*, August 2011, p. 17.

65. Our adjusted baseline projection incorporates the CBO's projection of robust economic growth in the 2013–2016 period that will return the economy to its full potential by 2017. The CBO's economic forecast is not appreciably more optimistic or pessimistic than those of the Federal Reserve or private sector forecasters. Ibid., pp. 32–36.

66. A deficit of 1 percent of GDP is sustainable in the long term because average annual economic growth is likely to be significantly higher than 1 percent. A deficit of 1 percent of GDP is arguably a good thing if it is used to finance investments that increase productivity growth. See Robert Pollin, "The Case Against Deficit Hawks: Austerity Is Not a Solution: Why the Deficit Hawks

Are Wrong," *Challenge*, November-December 2010: 6–36, p. 28. Pollin targets a structural deficit of 2–3 percent of GDP on these grounds.

67. The CBO's economic forecast assumes that government policy will follow current law, including the expiration of the Bush tax cuts. CBO, *The Budget and Economic Outlook: An Update*, August 2011, p. 36. Therefore, any contractionary impact of allowing the tax cuts to expire—which could lower tax revenues and increase deficits—is already accounted for in these projections.

68. This scenario assumes that other miscellaneous tax cuts are allowed to expire. For other forecasts that assume extension of all tax cuts, see Auerbach and Gale, note 63, above; CBO, *2011 Long-Term Budget Outlook*, June 2011 (alternative fiscal scenario).

69. Per capita health care spending in the United States was $7,538 in 2008; the average for the richest fifteen countries in the OECD was $3,923 (converted on a purchasing power parity basis). Kaiser Family Foundation, "Health Care Spending in the United States and Selected OECD Countries," April 2011, available at http://www.kff.org/insurance/snapshot/OECD042111.cfm. On life expectancy, quality of care, and outcomes, see Gerard F. Anderson and Bianca K. Frogner, "Health Spending in OECD Countries: Obtaining Value per Dollar," *Health Affairs* 27, no. 6 (November-December 2008): 1718–27, Exhibit 3, p. 1723; Karen Davis, Cathy Schoen, and Kristof Stremikis, *Mirror, Mirror, on the Wall: How the Performance of the U.S. Health Care System Compares Internationally*, Commonwealth Fund, June 2010; Squires, note 55, above.

70. See, for example, Atul Gawande, "The Cost Conundrum," *The New Yorker*, June 1, 2009.

71. There is some evidence that even though higher cost sharing makes people cut back on health care, overall costs go up anyway because they end up needing more emergency care. See Atul Gawande, "The Hot Spotters," *The New Yorker*, January 24, 2011.

72. See Uwe E. Reinhardt, "Competition's Shortcomings in Curtailing Health Care Costs," Economix (blog), *The New York Times*, November 5, 2010. In general, it appears that hospitals are more concentrated than health plans and that concentration among hospitals, not concentration among health plans, is associated with higher prices. Glenn A. Melnick, Yu-Chu Shen, and Vivian Yaling Wu, "The Increased Concentration of Health Plan Markets Can Benefit Consumers Through Lower Hospital Prices," *Health Affairs* 30, no. 9 (2011): 1728–33, Exhibit 2, p. 1731.

73. Steffie Woolhandler, Terry Campbell, and David U. Himmelstein, "Costs of Health Care Administration in the United States and Canada," *The New England Journal of Medicine* 349 (2003): 768–75, Table 1, p. 771; James G. Kahn, Richard Kronick, Mary Kreger, and David N. Gans, "The Cost of Health Insurance Administration in California: Estimates for Insurers, Physicians, and Hospitals," *Health Affairs* 24, no. 6 (2005): 1629–39, Exhibit 5, p. 1637.

74. Uwe E. Reinhardt, Peter S. Hussey, and Gerard F. Anderson, "U.S. Health Care Spending in an International Context: Why Is U.S. Spending So High, and Can We Afford It?," *Health Affairs* 23, no. 3 (2004): 10–25, pp. 12–15.

75. Sheila Smith, Joseph P. Newhouse, and Mark S. Freeland, "Income, Insurance, and Technology: Why Does Health Spending Outpace Economic Growth?," *Health Affairs* 28, no. 5 (2009): 1276–84, p. 1276.

76. Changes in insurance coverage and in the costs of inputs (capital, labor, materials, and energy), by contrast, have been relatively small factors. Ibid., Exhibit 1, p. 1280. The precise impacts of income, insurance, and technology are difficult to disaggregate because rising incomes and expanding insurance coverage both contribute to increased use of new technologies.

77. OECD, Health Data 2011, Frequently Requested Data, available at http://www .oecd.org/document/16/0,3746,en_2649_37407_2085200_1_1_1_37407,00 .html. The U.S. ranked nineteenth in life expectancy in 1990 and fell to twenty-third by 2007 (the last year for which data are available for all OECD countries).

78. The CBO's long-term forecasts assume that the underlying annual rate of excess cost growth will be 1.7 percent in the early 2020s and declining thereafter; individual forecasts adjust this rate for government health care programs based on specific policy assumptions. CBO, *2011 Long-Term Budget Outlook*, June 2011, pp. 43–45.

79. Ibid., pp. 45–46. The 2035 figure includes health insurance subsidies authorized by the Affordable Care Act of 2010. The CBO's extended-baseline scenario, which conforms closely to current law, projects 2035 federal health care spending at 9.4 percent of GDP. The alternative fiscal scenario, which is intended to be more realistic, projects 2035 health care spending at 10.4 percent. Ibid., Table 1-2, p. 8.

80. CBO projections assume that the rate of health care inflation does slow down modestly over the next few decades; projections by the chief actuary for Medicare and Medicaid are slightly more pessimistic over the next twenty-five years. See ibid., pp. 42–43; Auerbach and Gale, note 63, above, pp. 11–12 and Table 3. The chief actuary's predictions are more optimistic than those of the CBO over a seventy-five-year horizon.

81. CBO, *2011 Long-Term Budget Outlook*, June 2011, pp. 10–11.

82. For Social Security's historical contribution to the budget balance, see OMB, note 5, above, Table 13.1. Social Security currently contributes to the federal deficit even though the program is still running an annual surplus. The current surplus exists only because of interest that the trust funds earn on the balances they have accumulated over the past decades. Surpluses in past years were lent to the rest of the federal government; the interest received by the trust funds comes from the rest of the federal government and therefore cannot be counted when measuring the overall government deficit (the difference between the amounts of cash flowing in and out of the government). Separately, some people argue that Social Security cannot *ever* contribute to the federal deficit because, by law, benefits must be paid out of the Social Security trust funds and therefore when those trust funds are exhausted (except for incoming payroll taxes), benefits will have to be reduced. In our opinion, even if this were to occur (which we find politically unlikely), automatic benefit cuts of 1.4 percent of GDP are no better than a deficit of 1.4 percent of GDP. A deficit gives us various options, including higher taxes, lower benefits, reductions in other spending, or more borrowing; automatic benefit cuts force us to choose one option, even if it is worse than the others.

83. *2011 Annual Report of the Board of Trustees of the Federal Old-Age and Survivors Insurance and Federal Disability Insurance Trust Funds*, pp. 114–15.

84. CBO, *2011 Long-Term Budget Outlook*, June 2011, p. 53. The Social Security trust funds are currently running an annual surplus because of the interest they earn on trust fund balances.
85. *2011 Annual Report of the Board of Trustees of the Federal Old-Age and Survivors Insurance and Federal Disability Insurance Trust Funds*, Table VI.F4, p. 187.
86. We begin with our ten-year projections, discussed above, and then extend them using the same principles applied by the CBO in its long-term budget forecasts. CBO, *2011 Long-Term Budget Outlook*, June 2011. For spending, we generally use the CBO's alternative fiscal scenario. For revenues, we assume that revenues will grow after 2021 at a rate projected by the CBO, with a different 2021 starting point depending on whether we assume the extension of the tax cuts scheduled for expiration. For more details, see the Appendix.
87. Economist James Galbraith argues that large primary deficits can be sustained indefinitely and that the CBO (and other economists) think they are unsustainable only because they overestimate the interest rate that the government will have to pay on its debts. If, as Galbraith assumes, the government pays a negative real interest rate on its debts, then the debt itself will get smaller each year, allowing for a primary deficit. James K. Galbraith, "Is the Federal Debt Unsustainable?," Levy Economics Institute of Bard College Policy Note 2011/2. For example, if the debt is 100 percent of GDP, the real interest rate is –1 percent, the primary deficit is 4 percent, and real GDP growth is 3 percent, then the debt will remain at 100 percent of GDP. Unfortunately, the federal government has historically paid a positive real interest rate on borrowing. Since 1948, the average effective real interest rate has been 1.7 percent; since 1982 (the first year after the period of high inflation at the end of the 1970s), it has been 3.7 percent. (The real interest rate is calculated using the GDP price deflator as the measure of inflation. BEA, National Income and Product Accounts, Table 1.1.4.) The CBO assumes a long-term real interest rate of 2.7 percent. CBO, *2011 Long-Term Budget Outlook*, June 2011, pp. 23–24.
88. We begin with our "optimistic" long-term projection (in which all tax cuts expire), described in note 86, above, and the Appendix. We adjust this projection by assuming that health care spending will be constant at its 2021 level indefinitely.
89. A significant number of doctors in some specialties already do not accept Medicare at all or do not accept new patients on Medicare. Julie Connelly, "Doctors Are Opting Out of Medicare," *The New York Times*, April 1, 2009.
90. CBO, *2011 Long-Term Budget Outlook*, June 2011, p. 42. Whether government-paid health care or private-paid health care has seen higher excess cost growth depends on how far back in time you look. From 1985 to 2007, excess cost growth averaged 1.4 percent per year for Medicare, 1.3 percent for Medicaid, and 1.9 percent for all other health care.
91. Ibid., p. 47.
92. CBO, *Long-Term Analysis of a Budget Proposal by Chairman Ryan*, April 5, 2011, Figure 1, p. 22. This increase is relative to projected spending on the same health care under the existing Medicare program.
93. In 2009, U.S. per capita GDP was surpassed among OECD countries only by the tiny financial haven Luxembourg and oil-rich Norway. OECD .StatExtracts, National Accounts.

94. Citizens for Tax Justice, "Top Federal Income Tax Rates Since 1913," November 2011, available at http://www.ctj.org/pdf/regcg.pdf.

95. It's more clear that poor people are helped by a high-tax/high-benefit world than that rich people are helped by a low-tax/low-benefit world. Given the problems in the individual health insurance market right now, you would have to be very rich before you would want to gamble on being able to buy health insurance after the age of sixty-five. More generally, since most people are risk-averse, insurance benefits some people above the midpoint of the income distribution (because it reduces the risk of large losses), even if it has a negative expected value in dollar terms.

96. In 207 B.C., the general Xiang Yu destroyed his boats after crossing a river and then ordered his troops to smash their cooking pots, ensuring that they could survive only by defeating the enemy. Hernán Cortés did something similar in 1519 during the conquest of Mexico.

5. WHY WORRY

1. "Memorandum from Merrill Lynch," Merrill Lynch, September 28, 2008, available at http://www.oireachtas.ie/viewdoc.asp?fn=/documents/Committees 30thDail/PAC/Reports/DocumentsReGruarantee/document3.pdf, p. 2.

2. Thomas Jefferson, Letter to William Plumer, July 21, 1816, in *The Thomas Jefferson Papers, Series 1: General Correspondence, 1651–1827*, Library of Congress. This often quoted passage continues: "We see in England the consequences of the want of it: their laborers reduced to live on a penny in the shilling of their earnings, to give up bread, and resort to oatmeal and potatoes for food; and their landowners exiling themselves to live in penury and obscurity abroad, because at home the government must have all the clear profits of their land, in fact they see the principle [*sic*] of the island transferred to the public creditors, all it's [*sic*] profits going to them for the interest of their debts."

3. On Jefferson's concept of corruption, see James D. Savage, *Balanced Budgets and American Politics* (Cornell University Press, 1988), pp. 91–97.

4. On the symbolic importance of balanced budgets and budget deficits throughout American history, see ibid., chapter 1.

5. Barack Obama, "Weekly Address: Cutting the Deficit and Creating Jobs," July 2, 2011.

6. Michelle Levi, "Boehner: Government Needs to Tighten Its Belt," Political Hotsheet (blog), CBS News, March 8, 2009.

7. Rand Paul, *The Tea Party Goes to Washington* (Center Street, 2011).

8. If the real interest rate on government debt is higher than the real growth rate and the government keeps its primary budget perfectly in balance, the debt-to-GDP ratio will grow indefinitely. If, by contrast, the real growth rate is higher than the real interest rate, then it is possible to run primary deficits indefinitely and keep the debt-to-GDP ratio stable. Historically, interest rates on Treasury debt have been slightly higher than GDP growth rates. Since 1980, the average effective (nominal) interest rate on government debt has been 6.5 percent and the average nominal GDP growth rate has been 5.8 percent. OMB, *Fiscal Year 2012 Budget of the U.S. Government: His-*

torical Tables, Tables 3.1, 7.1; BEA, National Income and Product Accounts, Table 1.1.5.

9. Taxes change incentives and therefore change people's actions from what they would be without taxes. In some instances, this can be seen as a distortion, particularly if the government has an incentive to maximize tax revenue. See, for example, Geoffrey Brennan and James M. Buchanan, *The Power to Tax: Analytic Foundations of a Fiscal Constitution* (Cambridge University Press, 2006). In other situations, so-called Pigovian taxes (after the economist Arthur Pigou) may be used to discourage activities that create negative externalities (that is, activities whose private costs are lower than their social costs, as can be the case with pollution). See William J. Baumol, "On Taxation and the Control of Externalities," *American Economic Review* 62, no. 3 (June 1972): 307–22.

10. The Treasury Department does make coins and sell those to the public, but the amount of money involved is trivial.

11. Because the Federal Reserve buys Treasury securities on the market, the demand it supplies for Treasuries can indirectly help the government finance its debt and can contribute to inflation. Still, this is significantly different from a situation where the government prints money to directly finance its operations.

12. Michael Warren, "Romney Addresses the Organized Tea Party," *The Weekly Standard*, November 4, 2011.

13. Institutional investors generally think that most companies should have some debt for at least two reasons. First, the tax code allows companies to deduct interest payments on borrowed money but not to deduct dividends paid to shareholders; this creates a financial incentive to borrow money. Second, the need to make regular interest payments is sometimes thought to discipline corporate managers, who will not have excess cash to spend on unwise, empire-building investments or on perks for themselves.

14. The "Bridge to Nowhere" was a proposed bridge to connect Ketchikan, Alaska, to Gravina Island, which had only a few residents (and an airstrip) and was served by a ferry. Congress dedicated more than $200 million to help pay for the bridge until the provision was removed due to public outrage. Instead, however, the same money was given to the state of Alaska to use as it saw fit; the state at first allocated it to the same bridge before later changing plans. Patrick J. Lyons, "The Bridge to Nowhere Gets Nowhere," *The New York Times*, September 21, 2007.

15. As discussed later in this chapter, increased government borrowing can make it harder for households and businesses to borrow money; but in a recession, fewer households and businesses want to borrow more money, reducing demand for loans, so this effect is unlikely to occur.

16. Carl Hulse, "House G.O.P. Pushes $61 Billion in Cutbacks," *The New York Times*, February 15, 2011.

17. House Budget Committee, *The Path to Prosperity: Restoring America's Promise: Fiscal Year 2012 Budget Resolution*, p. 10.

18. James Oliphant, "Opponents of Raising Debt Ceiling Risk Government Breakdown, Study Says," *Los Angeles Times*, July 14, 2011.

19. There have been various proposals to introduce bankruptcy procedures that would apply to debt issued by sovereign governments. See Anne O. Krueger,

A New Approach to Sovereign Debt Restructuring, International Monetary Fund, April 2002; Kenneth Rogoff and Jeromin Zettelmeyer, "Bankruptcy Procedures for Sovereigns: A History of Ideas, 1976–2001," *IMF Staff Papers* 49, no. 3 (2002): 470–507.

20. As discussed in chapter 2, in 1933, Congress abrogated gold indexation clauses, eliminating the rights of bondholders to be repaid in gold rather than in U.S. dollars.

21. It can also be a question of what law the government's bonds are issued under, because the government has the power to change that law. This is another reason why it is advantageous to issue bonds in your own currency and in your own domestic markets—and why investors may be more hesitant about buying bonds issued by a sovereign nation in its own currency.

22. In that case, there could still be a contractionary impact on the domestic economy if, for example, the country that defaults is dependent on exports to the countries that hold its bonds.

23. S&P downgraded Treasury debt on August 5, 2011. By August 10, the yield on ten-year Treasury bonds had fallen to 2.17 percent, the lowest level recorded by the Federal Reserve except for a few days in December 2008, at the peak of the financial crisis. Federal Reserve Statistical Release H.15.

24. For example, in July 2011, Macroeconomic Advisers (a leading consulting firm) forecast that the yield on the ten-year Treasury note would rise to 8.75 percent by 2021, due largely to deficit concerns. "The Coming Fiscal Contraction: Short-Term Pain for Long-Term Gain," *Macroadvisers* (blog), July 6, 2011.

25. During the debt ceiling crisis, some people suggested that the government could avoid default on its bonds by using incoming tax revenues to make required interest and principal payments, while not making other payments required by law or by contract. While this might temporarily forestall a default on Treasury bonds, failing to make legally required payments also counts as a default, and would have negative implications for the government's credit. Other people recommended that the president invoke the Fourteenth Amendment and order the Treasury to issue new debt in violation of the debt ceiling, or even that the Treasury create special trillion-dollar, platinum coins to fund the government. In any case, it would be best to avoid the need for such expediencies.

26. Barack Obama, "Remarks by the President at the First Meeting of the Fiscal Commission," April 27, 2010.

27. Mitt Romney, *No Apology: The Case for American Greatness* (St. Martin's, 2010), p. 166. That passage was highlighted on the "fiscal responsibility" page of his campaign website, available at http://www.mittromney.com/issues/fiscal-responsibility.

28. "U.S. Net International Investment Position at Yearend 2010," BEA press release, June 28, 2011.

29. See Alan J. Auerbach, Jagadeesh Gokhale, and Laurence J. Kotlikoff, "Generational Accounting: A Meaningful Way to Evaluate Fiscal Policy," *Journal of Economic Perspectives* 8, no. 1 (Winter 1994): 73–94. For a summary and discussion, see Daniel Shaviro, *Do Deficits Matter?* (University of Chicago Press, 1997), pp. 119–44.

30. In 1994, Auerbach, Gokhale, and Kotlikoff estimated that future generations

would have to pay lifetime net tax rates of 71 percent. Auerbach et al., note 29, above, Table 3, p. 86. In 1995, using the same approach, the CBO estimated this figure at 78 percent. CBO, *Who Pays and When? An Assessment of Generational Accounting*, November 1995, Table 1, p. 20.

31. Douglas W. Elmendorf and N. Gregory Mankiw, "Government Debt," chapter 25 in John B. Taylor and Michael Woodford, eds., *Handbook of Macroeconomics*, vol. 1 (Elsevier, 1999), p. 1624.

32. Grandchildren may also be in favor of programs that transfer money to their grandparents. When James explained how Social Security works to his five-year-old daughter, she said, "That sounds like the best program ever."

33. Real per capita disposable income (in 2005 dollars) has grown from $9,000 at the end of World War II to over $32,000 in 2011. BEA, National Income and Product Accounts, Table 7.1. This is not to say that everyone in society becomes better off, only that society as a whole becomes better off, at least materially.

34. John W. Kendrick, *Productivity Trends in the United States* (Princeton University Press, 1961), Chart 4, p. 69.

35. Even in its worst decade, the 1980s, productivity still went up by 1.4 percent per year. All productivity statistics are labor productivity (output per hour worked) in the nonfarm business sector, from the Bureau of Labor Statistics, Major Sector Productivity and Costs Index.

36. The growth rate of median household income has already slowed significantly, but that is largely because of increasing inequality. From 1990 to 2010, real median household income grew at an annual rate of 0.1 percent, while real mean household income grew at 0.6 percent per year and real per capita disposable income grew at 1.6 percent per year. Census Bureau, Historical Income Tables, Table H-6; BEA, National Income and Product Accounts, Table 7.1.

37. Real personal consumption expenditures are from 2007 Q4 to 2009 Q2. BEA, National Income and Product Accounts, Table 2.3.3. Nonfarm employment is from December 2007 to August 2009; as of the summer of 2011, total job losses were still close to seven million. Bureau of Labor Statistics, Current Employment Survey.

38. CBO, *Estimated Impact of the American Recovery and Reinvestment Act on Employment and Economic Output from April 2011 Through June 2011*, August 2011, Table 1, p. 3. The CBO estimates the impact of ARRA in 2010 Q3 at 1.4–3.6 million jobs. As of 2010 Q3, actual job losses since the beginning of the recession were still over eight million, so without ARRA total job losses would have been 9–11 million. Private sector economists' estimates also showed a positive impact of the 2009 stimulus. Menzie Chinn, "Assessing the Stimulus, One Year In: A View from the Mainstream," *Econbrowser* (blog), February 17, 2010.

39. According to Robert Rubin, then director of the National Economic Council, Greenspan projected that each $10 billion in annual deficit reduction would lower long-term interest rates by one-tenth of a percentage point. Robert E. Rubin and Jacob Weisberg, *In an Uncertain World: Tough Choices from Wall Street to Washington* (Random House, 2003), p. 120. In retrospect, it's not clear that interest rates were that high. In 1992, the average yield on ten-year Treasuries was 7.0 percent, the lowest level since 1973. Federal Reserve Statistical Release H.15. At the same time, inflation had also fallen dramatically since the 1970s

and early 1980s, so real interest rates were not particularly low. This may have been an example of how consensus policy beliefs can shift without corresponding shifts in fundamentals.

40. On the conditions under which this can hold, see "Will It Hurt? Macroeconomic Effects of Fiscal Consolidation," chapter 3 in IMF, *World Economic Outlook: Recovery, Risk, and Rebalancing*, October 2010. (The answer is yes, at least in the short term.) See also Simon Johnson, "Fiscal Contraction Hurts Economic Expansion," Economix (blog), *The New York Times*, June 23, 2011. Alberto Alesina and Silvia Ardagna have identified examples where deficit reduction had an expansionary impact on the economy. Alberto Alesina and Silvia Ardagna, "Large Changes in Fiscal Policy: Taxes Versus Spending," chapter 2 in Jeffrey R. Brown, ed., *Tax Policy and the Economy*, vol. 24 (University of Chicago Press, 2010). However, Arjun Jayadev and Mike Konczal argue that in the vast majority of those examples, either the economy was already growing strongly prior to deficit reduction, or the deficit reduction hurt growth, or both. Arjun Jayadev and Mike Konczal, "The Boom Not the Slump: The Right Time for Austerity," Roosevelt Institute working paper, August 23, 2010.

41. In 2011, through August, unemployment averaged 9.0 percent. The average for the expansionary years of 2002–2007 was 5.3 percent. The CBO estimates the long-term "natural" rate of unemployment to be 5.2 percent. CBO, *The Budget and Economic Outlook: An Update*, August 2011, p. 46.

42. Walter F. Mondale, Address Accepting the Presidential Nomination at the Democratic National Convention in San Francisco, July 19, 1984, available at http://www.presidency.ucsb.edu/ws/index.php?pid=25972#axzz1c0A8u84D.

43. The average through October was 2.9 percent. By comparison, the average ten-year Treasury yield for the decade preceding the financial crisis (1998–2007) was 4.9 percent. The average from April 1953 (the earliest data available from the Federal Reserve) through 2007 was 6.5 percent. Federal Reserve Statistical Release H.15.

44. Robert Pollin, "The Case Against Deficit Hawks: Austerity Is Not a Solution: Why the Deficit Hawks Are Wrong," *Challenge*, November-December 2010: 6–36, Table 1, p. 12. The interest rate on five-year Treasuries was 2.27 percent during the first seventeen months following the cyclical trough in 2009 compared to an average of 7.55 percent for the seventeen-month periods following previous cyclical troughs since 1970; inflation was 1.59 percent compared to 4.89 percent during previous recoveries, so the lower nominal rate is not solely due to lower inflation.

45. Stan Collender, "Bond Vigilantes Are Now Deficit Cheerleaders," *Roll Call*, August 3, 2010.

46. "The Coming Fiscal Contraction: Short-Term Pain for Long-Term Gain," *Macroadvisers* (blog), July 6, 2011. Macroeconomic Advisers acknowledged that, at the time, the bond market itself did not anticipate higher interest rates due to government budget deficits. In order to create a simulation that would show an impact of deficits on interest rates, they assumed "that investors, seeing no political progress on deficit reduction, gradually abandon their current expectations in favor of ones consistent with the baseline outcome of a persistent rise in interest rates."

47. The House budget resolution, for example, claimed that "90 percent is often

a trigger point for economic decline." House Budget Committee, note 17, above.

48. For advanced economies, they say, "The observations [from 1946 through 2009] with debt to GDP over 90 percent have median growth roughly 1 percent lower than the lower debt burden groups and mean levels of growth almost 4 percent lower. . . . Over the past two centuries, debt in excess of 90 percent has typically been associated with mean growth of 1.7 percent versus 3.7 percent when debt is low (under 30 percent of GDP), and compared with growth rates of over 3 percent for the two middle categories (debt between 30 and 90 percent of GDP)." Carmen M. Reinhart and Kenneth S. Rogoff, "Growth in a Time of Debt," *American Economic Review: Papers and Proceedings* 100, no. 2 (May 2010): 573–78, p. 575.

49. See ibid., Figure 2. The United States does show particularly poor growth when its debt exceeds 90 percent of GDP, but that is because federal government debt only exceeded 90 percent during the demobilization period after World War II, which included a short but severe recession.

50. Ibid., p. 573.

51. This is the policy recommended by Macroeconomic Advisers as well as by Peter Orszag, Laura D'Andrea Tyson, Larry Summers, and Paul Krugman. Peter Orszag, "Link U.S. Payroll Tax Holiday to Unemployment Rate," Bloomberg, June 30, 2011; Laura D'Andrea Tyson, "What's a Crisis and What Isn't," Economix (blog), *The New York Times*, July 1, 2011; Lawrence Summers, "How to Avoid a Lost Decade," *The Washington Post*, June 12, 2011; Paul Krugman, "NEC and NEC," The Conscience of a Liberal (blog), *The New York Times*, July 8, 2011.

52. Greek economic statistics are from IMF, World Economic Outlook Database, April 2011. National debt is net government debt. Greek-German spreads are available at http://www.bloomberg.com/apps/quote?ticker=.GRE GER10:IND.

53. The interest rate quoted was for ten-year government bonds. Bloomberg, L.P.

54. See, for example, Paul Krugman, "Those Elusive Bond Vigilantes," The Conscience of a Liberal (blog), *The New York Times*, April 20, 2011.

55. Such a devaluation of the dollar could take the form of rising domestic prices, a fall in the value of the dollar relative to other countries or, most likely, both. If the central bank feels pressured to print money in order to finance fiscal deficits, this may become destabilizing and damaging to economic prosperity. For example, Joseph Gagnon and Marc Hinterschweiger argue there is essentially no default risk for the United States, yet unsustainable debt levels could lead to "a drift into ever-higher inflation and interest rates, ever-lower growth or deeper recession, and eventually hyperinflation along with rapid currency depreciation." Joseph E. Gagnon and Marc Hinterschweiger, *The Global Outlook for Government Debt over the Next 25 Years: Implications for the Economy and Public Policy* (Peterson Institute for International Economics, 2011), p. 35.

56. Kelly Evans, "Jay-Z, the New Alan Greenspan," Real Time Economics (blog), *The Wall Street Journal*, November 6, 2007.

57. The same pattern occurred in the summer of 2011. Even during the rockiest days of negotiations over the debt ceiling, the yield on ten-year Treasury notes *fell*, in part because of concerns about the European sovereign debt crisis.

58. In July 2011, even when it seemed most likely that Congress might not increase the debt ceiling, ten-year Treasury yields did not go up as a result.

59. The United States' current ability to finance both its trade and government budget deficits may be due in part to the inability of emerging market countries to generate attractive financial assets for investment—which could change. See Ricardo J. Caballero, Emmanuel Farhi, and Pierre-Olivier Gourinchas, "An Equilibrium Model of 'Global Imbalances' and Low Interest Rates," *American Economic Review* 98, no. 1 (2008): 358–93.

60. Barry Eichengreen, *Exorbitant Privilege: The Rise and Fall of the Dollar and the Future of the International Monetary System* (Oxford University Press, 2011), pp. 150–52. The international economy has previously used multiple major reserve currencies; for example, both the dollar and the pound were widely held reserve currencies after World War I. Ibid., pp. 30–33. On the challenges facing the euro and the renminbi (the name for China's currency in general), see ibid., pp. 130–33, 143–45.

61. Ibid., pp. 124–26.

62. Irish economic statistics are from IMF, World Economic Outlook Database, April 2011. National debt is net government debt.

63. Michael Lewis, "When Irish Eyes Are Crying," *Vanity Fair*, March 2011.

64. See "Ireland's Banking Crisis: Timeline," *The Telegraph* (London), March 31, 2011.

65. John Murray Brown, Joshua Chaffin, and Tony Barber, "Europe Signs Up to Irish Rescue," *The Financial Times*, November 21, 2010; John McDermott, "Moody's Downgrades Ireland to Ba1 from Baa3," Alphaville (blog), *The Financial Times*, July 12, 2011.

66. See chapter 4 and the Appendix.

67. See Congressional Budget Office, *CBO's Economic Forecasting Record: 2010 Update*, July 2010. The CBO has been roughly as accurate as the Blue Chip consensus forecast, which is an average of several dozen private sector forecasts; when they miss, the CBO and the Blue Chip consensus tend to miss in the same direction. Simon Johnson is a member of the Panel of Economic Advisers of the CBO.

68. According to the Business Cycle Dating Committee of the National Bureau of Economic Research (NBER), the slowdown that began in March 2001 might not have qualified as a recession without the September 11 attacks. NBER, "The Business-Cycle Peak of March 2001," November 26, 2001, available at http://www.nber.org/cycles/november2001/.

69. See Kevin A. Hassett and R. Glenn Hubbard, *The Magic Mountain: A Guide to Defining and Using a Budget Surplus* (AEI Press, 1999), p. 12.

70. Bureau of Economic Analysis, National Income and Product Accounts, Table 1.1.6.

71. Trillions of dollars were committed as contingent liabilities; as it turned out, the government's actual direct losses on the Troubled Asset Relief Program and the bailouts of Fannie Mae and Freddie Mac were probably only in the hundreds of billions of dollars. Our assessment is that these rescue efforts were overly generous to the financial institutions that the government pulled back from the brink of collapse (and the executives who mismanaged those institutions to the brink of disaster), but we agree that it was necessary for the gov-

ernment to protect the financial system. See Simon Johnson and James Kwak, *13 Bankers: The Wall Street Takeover and the Next Financial Meltdown* (Pantheon, 2010), chapter 6.

72. The $1 trillion figure includes both the 2008 and 2009 stimulus bills.

73. For a definition and discussion of fiscal space, see Jonathan D. Ostry, Atish R. Ghosh, Jun I. Kim, and Mahvash S. Qureshi, "Fiscal Space," IMF Staff Position Note SPN/10/11, September 1, 2010.

74. James M. Boughton, "Was Suez in 1956 the First Financial Crisis of the Twenty-First Century?," *Finance and Development* 38, no. 3 (September 2001).

75. Ostry et al., note 73, above, p. 16.

76. Yields are for ten-year bonds. Data are from Bloomberg, L.P.

77. Ostry et al., note 73, above, Table 4. The probability that the United States has fiscal space exceeding 50 percent of GDP is estimated at 52–71 percent; the probability that its fiscal space exceeds 100 percent of GDP is estimated at 1–3 percent. (These figures are based on general government debt, which includes state and local government debt.) The fiscal space estimate is based on each country's *past* record of reducing deficits in response to increases in the national debt. If a country's political leaders no longer have the willingness to make similar adjustments in the future—and markets recognize this—that country will have less fiscal space than implied by its historical record.

78. As discussed above, this is the change between early 2008 and mid-2009 in the projection for the 2018 national debt; we use 2018 because it is the last year included in the CBO's ten-year forecast prior to the peak of the financial crisis.

79. For our assessment of the Dodd-Frank Act, see Simon Johnson and James Kwak, *13 Bankers: The Wall Street Takeover and the Next Financial Meltdown*, paperback ed. (Vintage, 2011), Epilogue.

80. The House Appropriations Committee report accompanying the reduction in the budget of the Securities and Exchange Commission emphasized, "With the federal debt exceeding $14 trillion, the committee is committed to reducing the cost and size of government." But the SEC is funded entirely by fees levied in the industry, and if its budget goes down, it is those fees that go down—not the federal budget deficit. James B. Stewart, "As a Watchdog Starves, Wall St. Is Tossed a Bone," *The New York Times*, July 16, 2011, p. A1.

81. The ultimate demise of the British Empire, for example, was closely linked to the financial burden of fighting World Wars I and II. On this (and much more), see Niall Ferguson, *Empire: The Rise and Demise of the British World Order and the Lessons for Global Power* (Basic Books, 2004).

82. Appropriations through 2010 were $1,104 billion. CBO, *The Budget and Economic Outlook: Fiscal Years 2011 to 2021*, January 2011, Box 3–2, p. 77. As of August 2011, the CBO's realistic projection for 2011 through 2021 was for an additional $606 billion in direct appropriations, which would bring the total to over $1.7 trillion. CBO, *The Budget and Economic Outlook: An Update*, August 2011, Table 1-8, pp. 26–27. (We take the total outlays in the baseline forecast and subtract the likely reductions due to the expected drawdown of troops.) These figures do not include the cost of interest payments on the additional debt.

83. For comparative deployment levels, see Tim Kane, "Global U.S. Troop Deployment, 1950–2005," Heritage Center for Data Analysis CDA06–02, May 24, 2006.

84. Sixty-eight million people were enrolled in Medicaid in 2010; nine million people were enrolled in CHIP in 2011. CBO, *The Budget and Economic Outlook*, January 2011, pp. 62–63.

6. ARGUING FIRST PRINCIPLES

1. Warren E. Buffett, "Stop Coddling the Super-Rich," *The New York Times*, August 14, 2011.
2. John Boehner, Address to the Economic Club of New York, May 9, 2011, available at http://www.speaker.gov/News/DocumentSingle.aspx?Document ID=240370.
3. Ezra Klein, "The Budget Deals of Reagan, Bush, Clinton and Obama, in One Chart," Ezra Klein's Wonkblog, *The Washington Post*, July 7, 2011.
4. Carl Hulse, "Long Battle on Debt Ending as Senate Set for Final Vote," *The New York Times*, August 1, 2011.
5. Carl Hulse, "Budget Talks Near Collapse as G.O.P. Leader Quits," *The New York Times*, June 23, 2011.
6. Nate Silver, "G.O.P.'s No-Tax Stance Is Outside Political Mainstream," FiveThirtyEight (blog), *The New York Times*, July 13, 2011.
7. Adam Smith, *An Inquiry into the Nature and Causes of the Wealth of Nations*, vol. 1 (Oliver D. Cooke, 1804), p. 349.
8. This book is not the place for an extended discussion of whether market forces provide more effective discipline for private companies than political forces do for politicians and regulatory agencies. Obviously, neither is perfect. In general, we think that a public company is constrained to maximize profits more tightly than, say, a regulatory agency is constrained to follow the public interest or even to conform to the preferences of a majority of the population.
9. The CBO estimates that, averaged across all workers, the former impact (substitution effect) outweighs the latter impact (income effect). It estimates a total wage elasticity of 0.129, meaning that a 10 percent increase in after-tax wages and after-tax income will cause a 1.29 percent increase in hours worked. CBO, *The Effect of Tax Changes on Labor Supply in CBO's Microsimulation Tax Model*, April 2007, p. 6.
10. In practice, this effect is small and may even be negative. Leonard E. Burman, *The Labyrinth of Capital Gains Tax Policy: A Guide for the Perplexed* (Brookings Institution Press, 1999), pp. 55–58.
11. The larger distortion in the taxed part of the economy is not compensated for by lower distortion in the untaxed part of the economy. According to basic supply and demand curves, the deadweight loss to society of a tax is proportional to the square of the amount of the tax. So if the economy is divided into two halves, A and B, a 20 percent tax on A and no tax on B will produce a greater deadweight loss than a 10 percent tax on each.
12. Jesse Drucker, "The Tax Haven That's Saving Google Billions," *Bloomberg Businessweek*, October 21, 2010.
13. Mark Zandi, an economist who has advised both Republicans and Democrats, estimated the multipliers for permanent tax cuts at 0.29–0.48, temporary tax cuts at 0.27–1.29, and spending increases at 1.36–1.73. Mark Zandi, "A Second Quick Boost from Government Could Spark Recovery," excerpts of testimony

before the House Small Business Committee, July 24, 2008, available at http://
www.economy.com/mark-zandi/documents/Small%20Business_7_24_08.pdf.
However, multipliers depend on many factors, so it is impossible to generalize
about the relative impact of tax and spending changes. For a compilation of many
estimates, see Antonio Spilimbergo, Steve Symansky, and Martin Schindler, "Fiscal Multipliers," IMF Staff Position Note SPN/09/11, May 20, 2009.

14. GDP data are from BEA, National Income and Product Accounts, Table 1.1.1.
Tax rates are from Citizens for Tax Justice, "Top Federal Income Tax Rates
Since 1913," November 2011, available at http://www.ctj.org/pdf/regcg.pdf,
and include relevant payroll taxes.

15. Emmanuel Saez, Joel Slemrod, and Seth Giertz review many empirical studies and conclude, "the best available estimates [of the long-run elasticity of
taxable income] range from 0.12 to 0.40." Emmanuel Saez, Joel Slemrod, and
Seth H. Giertz, "The Elasticity of Taxable Income with Respect to Marginal
Tax Rates: A Critical Review," August 7, 2010, available at http://elsa.berkeley
.edu/~saez/saez-slemrod-giertzJEL10round2.pdf, p. 49. The elasticity of labor
supply is close to zero for working-age men, and so taxable income responds to
changes in tax rates through other channels such as increased charitable giving,
increased tax avoidance, etc. Ibid., pp. 1–2. At the high end of the income distribution, "there is no compelling evidence to date of *real* economic responses
to tax rates"; instead, behavioral responses consist entirely of timing and avoidance. Ibid., pp. 49–50.

16. Excluding years when the top capital gains rate was exactly 25 percent (1947–
1967, covering the bulk of the postwar boom), a rate above 25 percent is
associated with GDP growth of 3.0 percent while a rate below 25 percent is
associated with GDP growth of 3.2 percent. If we include the recent recession,
average growth for years with a rate below 25 percent drops to 2.7 percent.
Capital gains rates do not significantly affect GDP growth with a lag, either.
Burman, note 10, above, p. 81.

17. Ibid., pp. 55–63.

18. An analysis by the Joint Committee on Taxation in 2005 (when both houses
of Congress were controlled by Republicans) found that reducing individual income tax rates or increasing personal exemptions would both reduce
long-term economic growth if they were not offset elsewhere in the budget.
Joint Committee on Taxation, *Macroeconomic Analysis of Various Proposals to Provide $500 Billion in Tax Relief*, JCX-4-05, March 1, 2005, p. 9. See also Eric M.
Leeper and Shu-Chun Susan Yang, "Dynamic Scoring: Alternative Financing
Schemes," *Journal of Public Economics* 92 (2008): 159–82, pp. 166–69. A recent
paper by Christina Romer and David Romer, which attempts to disentangle
tax changes from concurrent confounding factors, finds that "exogenous" tax
increases in general reduce economic output, but increasing taxes to reduce a
deficit tends to increase economic output. Christina D. Romer and David H.
Romer, "The Macroeconomic Effects of Tax Changes: Estimates Based on a
New Measure of Fiscal Shocks," *American Economic Review* 100 (June 2010):
763–801, pp. 780–87.

19. There is an immense academic literature on the capture of governmental actors
by private sector interests, with roots in political science and economics, dating
back at least to Samuel P. Huntington, "The Marasmus of the ICC: The Com-

mission, the Railroads, and the Public Interest," *Yale Law Journal* 61 (1952): 467–509; and George J. Stigler, "The Theory of Economic Regulation," *Bell Journal of Economics and Management Science* 2 (1971): 3–21. To summarize, politicians and regulators often (though not always) do what special interests want them to do, not what is in the public interest.

20. U.S. Department of Agriculture Economic Research Service, "Farm and Commodity Policy," available at http://www.ers.usda.gov/Briefing/FarmPolicy/; U.S. Energy Information Administration, *Direct Federal Financial Interventions and Subsidies in Energy in Fiscal Year 2010*, July 2011; Jim Wolf, "House Defies Veto Threat, Funds 2nd F-35 Engine," Reuters, May 27, 2010.

21. For example, benefiting more from tax expenditures does not make people more likely to regard the tax system as fair. Suzanne Mettler, *The Submerged State: How Invisible Government Policies Undermine American Democracy* (University of Chicago Press, 2011), pp. 43–44.

22. Government Accountability Office, *Opportunities to Reduce Potential Duplication in Government Programs, Save Tax Dollars, and Enhance Revenue*, GAO-11-318SP, March 2011.

23. Buffett himself has argued for significantly higher taxes on people like him. Buffett, note 1, above.

24. Frank Newport, "Americans Want New Debt Supercommittee to Compromise," Gallup, August 10, 2011.

25. *Washington Post*–ABC News poll, "Broad Opposition to Medicare Cuts Marks GOP's Risks in the Debt Debate," April 20, 2011, available at http://www.langerresearch.com/uploads/1122a2%20Debt%20Debate.pdf; Steven Thomma, "Poll: Best Way to Fight Deficits: Raise Taxes on the Rich," *McClatchy*, April 18, 2011; Jim Rutenberg and Megan Thee-Brenan, "Nation's Mood at Lowest Level in Two Years, Poll Shows," *The New York Times*, April 21, 2011; CNN/ORC Poll, conducted August 5–7, 2011, available at http://i2.cdn.turner.com/cnn/2011/images/08/09/poll.aug10.pdf.

26. John Rawls, *A Theory of Justice* (Belknap Press, 1971), p. 302.

27. In Sweden, the top wealth quintile owns 36 percent of all wealth; in the United States, the corresponding figure is 84 percent. Michael I. Norton and Dan Ariely, "Building a Better America—One Wealth Quintile at a Time," *Perspectives on Psychological Science* 6, no. 1 (2011): 9–12, p. 10. One counterargument is that people simply are not good at interpreting numerical distributions of wealth across five quintiles. In a second step, however, Norton and Ariely asked participants to estimate what the current U.S. wealth distribution is and what the ideal wealth distribution would be. In this exercise, participants overwhelmingly said that the wealth distribution should be more equal than it is today.

28. Matthew DiCarlo, "Do Americans Think Government Should Reduce Income Inequality?," *Shanker Blog*, October 24, 2011. DiCarlo cites General Social Survey data going back to the mid-1970s.

29. Peter Diamond and Emmanuel Saez, "The Case for a Progressive Tax: From Basic Research to Policy Recommendations," CESifo Working Paper 3548, August 2011, pp. 8–9.

30. House Budget Committee, *The Path to Prosperity: Restoring America's Promise: Fiscal Year 2012 Budget Resolution*, pp. 46–47; CBO, *Long-Term Analysis of a Budget Proposal by Chairman Ryan*, April 5, 2011, pp. 7–9.

31. "If I were president right now, I would go to Congress with a new system for unemployment, which would have specific accounts from which people could withdraw their own funds. And I would not put in place a continuation of the current plan." Andrew Malcolm, "The Ames Republican Debate Transcript: Everything They Said That You Missed," Top of the Ticket (blog), *The Los Angeles Times*, August 13, 2011. See also Suzy Khimm, "Romney Thinks Workers Should Pay for Their Own Unemployment Benefits," Ezra Klein's Wonkblog, *The Washington Post*, August 12, 2011.

32. According to CBO analysis, under the House Budget Committee's Medicare plan, by 2030, beneficiaries would be paying 68 percent of their health care costs in premiums and other out-of-pocket costs. CBO, *Long-Term Analysis of a Budget Proposal by Chairman Ryan*, April 5, 2011, Figure 1, p. 22.

33. The insurance company can protect itself by offering a payout in nominal terms, as in a standard life insurance policy, but then you aren't protected against inflation risk. If the insurer offers a real payout (as in health insurance, for example, where the benefit takes the form of actual health care services), then it is vulnerable to inflation risk.

34. Actually, according to the director of national intelligence, our primary security concern is "the global economic crisis and its geopolitical implications." Dennis C. Blair, *Annual Threat Assessment of the Intelligence Community for the Senate Select Committee on Intelligence*, February 12, 2009, p. 2. The first traditional national security threat identified in this report, however, was extremist terrorist groups; the next was instability in the Middle East and Southwest Asia.

35. Stockholm International Peace Research Institute, "Background Paper on SIPRI Military Expenditures Data, 2010," April 11, 2011.

36. The Special Operations Command budget is about $10 billion. Andrew Feickert and Thomas K. Livingston, *U.S. Special Operations Forces (SOF): Background and Issues for Congress*, Congressional Research Service Report for Congress, December 3, 2010. The total intelligence budget was less than $30 billion in the late 1990s, but has grown to $80 billion today. Central Intelligence Agency, FAQs, available at https://www.cia.gov/about-cia/faqs/index.html; Pam Benson, "US Spy Spending Revealed for First Time, Tops $80 Billion," CNN, October 28, 2010.

37. Gordon Adams and Cindy Williams, *Buying National Security: How America Plans and Pays for Its Global Role and Safety at Home* (Routledge, 2010), p. 1.

38. United States Census Bureau, *Income, Poverty, and Health Insurance Coverage in the United States: 2010*, Current Population Reports P60–239, September 2011, Table 8, p. 26.

39. Central Intelligence Agency, *The World Factbook*, Infant Mortality Rate, available at https://www.cia.gov/library/publications/the-world-factbook/rankorder /2091rank.html. The thirty-four countries are those identified as advanced economies by the IMF; the three countries trailing the United States are Slovakia, Estonia, and Cyprus. Overall, the United States' performance on health care quality indicators is middling to bad. Gerard F. Anderson and Bianca K. Frogner, "Health Spending in OECD Countries: Obtaining Value per Dollar," *Health Affairs* 27, no. 6 (November-December 2008): 1718–27, Exhibit 4, p. 1725. See also David A. Squires, "The U.S. Health System in Perspective: A Comparison of Twelve Industrialized Nations," Issues in International Health Policy, Commonwealth Fund, July 2011, p. 11.

40. Of the thirty-four "advanced economies" as defined by the IMF, the United States has the third highest level of disability-adjusted life years (DALYs) as measured by the World Health Organization. DALYs measure both years lost due to premature death and effective years lost to disability. World Health Organization, Global Burden of Disease, available at http://www.who.int /healthinfo/global_burden_disease/en/. Of the thirty-four advanced economies, the WHO does not provide data for Hong Kong or Taiwan; the United States ranked third of the remaining countries, surpassed only by Estonia and Slovakia. Data are age-standardized to account for different age distributions across countries.

41. Diane Geng, "GM vs. Toyota: By the Numbers," NPR, December 19, 2005.

42. See Ronald Lee and Andrew Mason, "The Price of Maturity," *Finance & Development* 48, no. 2 (June 2011): 6–11.

43. Figures are for households where the head of household is age 57–66. Jesse Bricker, Brian Bucks, Arthur Kennickell, Traci Mach, and Kevin Moore, "Surveying the Aftermath of the Storm: Changes in Family Finances from 2007 to 2009," Federal Reserve Board Finance and Economics Discussion Series Working Paper 2011–17, March 2011, Appendix Tables 2A, 2B.

44. Most elderly Americans qualify for Social Security benefits. For Social Security beneficiaries reaching retirement age in 2005, Social Security was the largest source of income for all income quintiles except the top quintile, where it was barely edged out by income from assets. Andrew G. Biggs and Glenn R. Springstead, "Alternate Measures of Replacement Rates for Social Security Benefits and Retirement Income," *Social Security Bulletin* 68, no. 2 (2008), Table 5, p. 11.

45. See IPCC, "Summary for Policymakers," in M. L. Parry, O. F. Canziani, J. P. Palutikof, P. J. van der Linden, and C. E. Hanson, eds., *Climate Change 2007: Impacts, Adaptation and Vulnerability. Contribution of Working Group II to the Fourth Assessment Report of the Intergovernmental Panel on Climate Change* (Cambridge University Press, 2007): 7–22.

46. On the social cost of carbon (the cost that is not captured by market prices), see G. W. Yohe, R. D. Lasco, Q. K. Ahmad, N. W. Arnell, S. J. Cohen, C. Hope, A. C. Janetos, and R. T. Perez, "Perspectives on Climate Change and Sustainability," chapter 20 in Parry et al., note 45, above, pp. 821–24.

47. On the costs of asthma due to pollution, see Sylvia J. Brandt, Laura Perez, Nino Künzli, Fred Lurmann, and Rob McConnell, "Costs of Childhood Asthma Due to Traffic-Related Pollution," *European Respiratory Journal* (forthcoming).

48. Note that this is different from a simple projection showing that the national debt will climb indefinitely under current policy. Today, projections show ever-climbing levels of debt, yet even thirty-year interest rates are relatively low. This implies that investors expect current policy to change.

49. Jonathan D. Ostry, Atish R. Ghosh, Jun I. Kim, and Mahvash S. Qureshi, "Fiscal Space," IMF Staff Position Note SPN/10/11, September 1, 2010, Table 3, p. 14. They estimate the level to which each country's debt naturally converges, given that country's past history of responding to changes in debt levels. The median level of general government debt varies between 50.2 percent and 62.6 percent of GDP, depending on assumptions. This corresponds to a somewhat lower level of net central government debt, the metric we generally use throughout this book.

50. These are the only four advanced economies, by the IMF's definition, whose net general government debt will exceed 100 percent of GDP in the wake of the financial crisis and recession. IMF, *World Economic Outlook Database*, April 2011.

51. OMB, *Fiscal Year 2012 Budget of the U.S. Government: Historical Tables*, Table 7.1.

52. CBO, *The Budget and Economic Outlook: An Update*, August 2011, Table 1-2, pp. 4–5.

53. The CBO, for example, projects that real economic growth will remain relatively weak through 2013 (2.6 percent in 2012, 1.7 percent in 2013). Ibid., Supplemental Material: Detailed Economic Projections, CY 2011–2021; Actual Data, 1950–2009 (xls), available at http://cbo.gov/doc.cfm?index=12316.

54. These estimates are from our projections discussed in chapter 4; for further details, see the Appendix.

55. For simplicity, our projections assume that the 3 percentage points of deficit reduction occur entirely in 2022 and apply to all years thereafter. In practice, any structural changes to the federal budget should be phased in over time. A permanent change of 3 percent of GDP, phased in during the years before and after 2022, would have roughly the same effect on the national debt.

56. A smaller reduction in annual deficits would also bring the debt below 50 percent of GDP by 2030, but the national debt would start rising quickly almost immediately thereafter. A reduction of 3 percentage points would keep the national debt below 50 percent of GDP into the 2050s.

7. WHERE DO WE GO FROM HERE?

1. "A Billion Here, a Billion There . . . ," Dirksen Center, available at http://www.dirksencenter.org/print_emd_billionhere.htm.

2. See, for example (roughly arranged from right to left): House Budget Committee, *The Path to Prosperity: Restoring America's Promise: Fiscal Year 2012 Budget Resolution*; "A Bipartisan Plan to Reduce Our Nation's Deficits," available at http://www.washingtonpost.com/r/2010–2019/WashingtonPost/2011/07/19/National-Politics/Graphics/Gang_of_Six_Document.pdf (the "Gang of Six" plan); National Commission on Fiscal Responsibility and Reform, *The Moment of Truth*, December 2010 (the "Obama fiscal commission" plan); Bipartisan Policy Center Debt Reduction Task Force, *Restoring America's Future: Reviving the Economy, Cutting Spending and Debt, and Creating a Simple, Pro-Growth Tax System*, November 2010 ("Domenici-Rivlin"); OMB, *Living Within Our Means and Investing in the Future: The President's Plan for Economic Growth and Deficit Reduction*, September 2011 (President Obama's proposal to the deficit reduction "supercommittee"); Congressional Progressive Caucus, *The People's Budget: Fiscal Year 2012*; James Crotty, "The Great Austerity War: What Caused the Deficit Crisis and Who Should Pay to Fix It?," Political Economy Research Institute Working Paper 260, June 2011.

3. This estimate is from our baseline projection introduced in chapter 4 and discussed in detail in the Appendix. In this case, the impact of extending tax cuts that would otherwise expire is based on CBO estimates from CBO, *The Budget and Economic Outlook: An Update*, August 2011, Table 1-8, pp. 26–27.

4. The personal exemption is a flat amount that all taxpayers can use to reduce

their taxable income; before 2001, it was phased out for high-income taxpayers. Taxpayers can reduce their taxable income using either the standard deduction (a flat amount) or by itemizing their actual deductions, such as mortgage interest and charitable contributions; before 2001, the amount of allowable itemized deductions was reduced for high-income taxpayers.

5. Contrary to the claims of some supporters, the Bush tax cuts did not lead to an increase in tax revenues. See the discussion in chapter 3.

6. See the discussion in chapter 3.

7. William G. Gale and Peter R. Orszag, "Economic Effects of Making the 2001 and 2003 Tax Cuts Permanent," Brookings Institution, August 2004.

8. Douglas W. Elmendorf, "The Economic Outlook and Fiscal Policy Choices," testimony before the Senate Budget Committee, September 28, 2010, pp. 29–32.

9. For example, in 2010, the CBO estimated that extending the income and estate tax cuts through 2011 would create 1 to 4 years of full-time employment per million dollars of budgetary cost through 2015. By comparison, increasing unemployment benefits would create 6 to 15 years of employment per million dollars, infrastructure investments would create 4 to 10 years, aid to states would create 3 to 9 years, and payroll tax cuts would create 4 to 11 years. Ibid., Table 1, p. 22.

10. In 2010, when Congress faced the same situation, the CBO estimated that extending some or all of the tax cuts, for two years or permanently, would reduce real GNP (gross national product) in 2020, relative to letting the tax cuts expire under then-current law. Ibid., Table 4, p. 31.

11. The Obama plan lists the ten-year cost of extending all of the income tax cuts, including indexing the alternative minimum tax for inflation, at $3.9 trillion; allowing the tax cuts to expire for high-income taxpayers and increasing the estate tax would bring in only $0.9 trillion. OMB, note 2, above, Tables S-4, S-5, pp. 58–64.

12. Grover G. Norquist, "Read My Lips: No New Taxes," *The New York Times*, July 21, 2011.

13. CBO, *The Budget and Economic Outlook: An Update*, August 2011, Supplemental Material: Expiring Tax Provisions (xls), available at http://cbo.gov/doc .cfm?index=12316. The 2021 cost of accelerated depreciation is $13.8 billion; the 2021 cost of the tax break for foreign income ("Subpart F for Active Financing Income") is $10.1 billion. No other expiring provision has a 2021 cost that exceeds $10 billion.

14. We begin with our projection for the scenario in which the income and estate tax cuts are made permanent (discussed in the Appendix) and adjust it by making all other tax cuts permanent, using the revenue estimate in CBO, *The Budget and Economic Outlook: An Update*, August 2011, Table 1-8, pp. 26–27.

15. A similar bonus depreciation provision, established in 2002, was allowed to expire at the end of 2004. Tax Policy Center, "Quick Facts: Bonus Depreciation and 100 Percent Expensing," available at http://www.taxpolicycenter.org /taxtopics/Bonus-Depreciation-and-100-Percent-Expensing.cfm. In addition, the ethanol tax credit actually did expire at the end of 2011.

16. *The 2011 Annual Report of the Board of Trustees of the Federal Old-Age and Survivors Insurance and Federal Disability Insurance Trust Funds*, Table VI.F4, pp. 187–88, intermediate scenario.

17. Ibid., p. 3. Social Security's long-term solvency is measured on a seventy-five-year horizon. The last time the system was calibrated, in 1983, Social Security had about three decades of surpluses to look forward to, so those surpluses could be balanced against deficits for the rest of the seventy-five-year period. Today, we still have those surpluses, now accumulated in the Social Security trust funds, to balance against deficits for the next few decades; after that point, however, we have deficits extending indefinitely. The CBO estimates the seventy-five-year deficit at only 1.6–2.0 percent of taxable payroll, depending on assumptions. CBO, *2011 Long-Term Budget Outlook*, June 2011, p. 54. A lower deficit means that fewer or smaller adjustments will be necessary to bring the program into balance.

18. The CBO suggests no fewer than thirty options. CBO, *Social Security Policy Options*, July 2010. For a much more detailed and thorough plan than ours, see Peter A. Diamond and Peter R. Orszag, *Saving Social Security: A Balanced Approach*, revised ed. (Brookings Institution Press, 2005).

19. *The 2011 Annual Report of the Board of Trustees of the Federal Old-Age and Survivors Insurance and Federal Disability Insurance Trust Funds*, pp. 114–15.

20. CBO, *Social Security Policy Options*, July 2010, Table 2, pp. 33–38. In this case, "taxable payroll" refers to the amount of earnings subject to the payroll tax under current law. The CBO estimates that this change would improve the program's balance by 0.2 percent of seventy-five-year GDP, which is equivalent to about 0.5–0.6 percent of seventy-five-year taxable payroll.

21. Most of the system's overall progressivity is due to the disability and survivor's insurance programs. CBO, "Is Social Security Progressive?," Economic and Budget Issue Brief, December 15, 2006. Social Security is progressive even after accounting for the fact that higher earners tend to live longer and therefore collect retirement benefits for more years.

22. CBO, *Social Security Policy Options*, July 2010, p. 31.

23. Ibid., Table 2, pp. 33–38.

24. Dawn Nuschler, Alison M. Shelton, and John J. Topoleski, *Social Security: Mandatory Coverage of New State and Local Government Employees*, Congressional Research Service Report for Congress, July 25, 2011, p. 1.

25. The Congressional Research Service estimated, using projections from 2010, that immediately expanding Social Security to cover all newly hired state and local employees would eliminate 9 percent of a total seventy-five-year funding gap of 1.92 percent of taxable payroll. Ibid., Table 2, p. 7.

26. The CBO estimates that a 1 percentage point increase in the payroll tax would reduce the seventy-five-year gap by 0.3 percent of seventy-five-year GDP. CBO, *Social Security Policy Options*, July 2010, Table 2, pp. 33–38. Combining an increase in the payroll tax rate with an increase in the taxable maximum earnings also has a small positive interaction effect.

27. Social Security Online, Monthly Statistical Snapshot, July 2011, Table 2.

28. As mentioned in chapter 6, as of 2009, only 63 percent of households that were close to retirement (head of household age 55–64) had any retirement accounts; of those households, the median value of those accounts was $86,000. Jesse Bricker, Brian Bucks, Arthur Kennickell, Traci Mach, and Kevin Moore, "Surveying the Aftermath of the Storm: Changes in Family Finances from 2007 to 2009," Federal Reserve Board Finance and Economics Discussion Series

2011–17, March 2011, available at http://www.federalreserve.gov/econresdata /scf/scf_2009p.htm, Appendix Tables 2A, 2B.

29. The four changes above would together reduce the seventy-five-year deficit by about 2.3 percent of taxable payroll.

30. For our three proposed changes other than expanding the program to newly hired state and local government employees, see CBO, *Social Security Policy Options*, July 2010, Supplemental Material: Year-by-Year Data for Changes to Social Security Finances Under Various Options with Scheduled Benefits, available at http://cbo.gov/doc.cfm?index=11580. For our fourth proposed change, see CBO, *Reducing the Deficit: Spending and Revenue Options*, March 2011, pp. 171–72.

31. After seventy-five years, the program would be running an annual deficit of about 0.3 percent of GDP. Under current law, the program deficit in 2084 is projected at 1.4 percent of GDP. Our four proposals would reduce that deficit by 1.1 percent of GDP: 0.3 percent for the payroll tax increase, 0.2 percent for raising the cap on taxable payroll, and 0.6 percent for indexing the full retirement age to longevity. Ibid. Covering all state and local government employees would have no appreciable impact by 2084.

32. United States Census Bureau, *Income, Poverty, and Health Insurance Coverage in the United States: 2010*, Current Population Reports P60–239, September 2011, Table 8, p. 26.

33. Deborah Thorne and Elizabeth Warren, "Get Sick, Go Broke," chapter 3 in Jacob S. Hacker, ed., *Health at Risk: America's Ailing Health System—And How to Heal It* (Columbia University Press, 2008), pp. 68, 73–74.

34. CBO, *The Budget and Economic Outlook: An Update*, August 2011, Table 1-4, pp. 18–19; CBO, *2011 Long-Term Budget Outlook*, June 2011, Supplemental Material: Data Underlying Scenarios and Figures, available at http://cbo.gov/ doc.cfm?index=12212 (alternative fiscal scenario).

35. Shifting costs from the government to the private sector could be good in the long run if it were to cause health care providers to deliver better services at lower costs. Our point is that limiting government health care spending in itself does not address the larger problem of high costs.

36. Gerard F. Anderson and Bianca K. Frogner, "Health Spending in OECD Countries: Obtaining Value per Dollar," *Health Affairs* 27, no. 6 (2008): 1718–27; Elliott Fisher, David Goodman, Jonathan Skinner, and Kristen Bronner, "Health Care Spending, Quality, and Outcomes: More Isn't Always Better," Dartmouth Atlas Project Topic Brief, February 27, 2009; Jonathan Skinner and Elliott S. Fisher, "Reflections on Geographic Variation in U.S. Health Care," Dartmouth Institute for Health Policy and Clinical Practice, May 12, 2010.

37. Milton C. Weinstein and Jonathan A. Skinner, "Comparative Effectiveness and Health Care Spending—Implications for Reform," *The New England Journal of Medicine* 362 (2010): 460–65, p. 463.

38. On cost savings, see R. Sean Morrison, Joan D. Penrod, J. Brian Cassel, Melissa Caust-Ellenbogen, Ann Litke, Lynn Spragens, and Diane E. Meier, "Cost Savings Associated with US Hospital Palliative Care Consultation Programs," *Archives of Internal Medicine* 168, no. 16 (2008): 1783–90; R. Sean Morrison, Jessica Dietrich, Susan Ladwig, Timothy Quill, Joseph Sacco, John Tangeman, and Diane E. Meier, "Palliative Care Consultation Teams Cut Hospital

Costs for Medicaid Beneficiaries," *Health Affairs* 30, no. 3 (2011): 454–63. On quality of life and outcomes, see Jennifer S. Temel, Joseph A. Greer, Alona Muzikansky, Emily R. Gallagher, Sonal Admane, Vicki A. Jackson, Constance M. Dahlin, Craig D. Blinderman, Juliet Jacobsen, William F. Pirl, J. Andrew Billings, and Thomas J. Lynch, "Early Palliative Care for Patients with Metastatic Non–Small-Cell Lung Cancer," *The New England Journal of Medicine* 363 (2010): 733–42; David Casarett, Amy Pickard, F. Amos Bailey, Christine Ritchie, Christian Furman, Ken Rosenfeld, Scott Shreve, Zhen Chen, and Judy A. Shea, "Do Palliative Consultations Improve Patient Outcomes?," *Journal of the American Geriatric Society* 56, no. 4 (April 2008): 593–99.

39. Commonwealth Fund, *International Profiles of Health Care Systems*, June 2010.

40. Potentially, private insurers could also administer the basic plan (in which case the federal government would pay them for each person they enroll). Theoretically, they could compete with each other by offering add-on benefits and by minimizing overhead costs. It's not clear, however, that this would be preferable to having a single administrator.

41. Under the Consolidated Omnibus Budget Reconciliation Act of 1985 (COBRA), people who leave their jobs must be allowed to buy group insurance through their former employers (for a limited period), but have to pay the entire premium themselves.

42. Lower supply, however, is currently associated with lower costs and equivalent health outcomes. Fisher et al., note 36, above, p. 2.

43. See ibid., p. 4; Atul Gawande, "The Hot Spotters," *The New Yorker*, January 24, 2011.

44. This estimate for the employer health care exclusion includes both income tax and payroll tax impacts. OMB, *Fiscal Year 2012 Budget of the U.S. Government: Analytical Perspectives*, Table 17-1, pp. 241–45.

45. While the tax exclusion increases demand for health insurance policies, the relationship between more generous policies and higher actual spending is unclear. In particular, the people who account for the most health care spending may be insensitive to marginal costs (because their care is closely directed by physicians); alternatively, if people cut back on preventive care, they may end up incurring higher costs in the end. Analysts at the Urban Institute have estimated that reducing the tax exclusion would produce a relatively small reduction in total health care spending. John Holahan, Linda J. Blumberg, Stacey McMorrow, Stephen Zuckerman, Timothy Waidmann, and Karen Stockley, "Containing the Growth of Spending in the U.S. Health System," Urban Institute Health Policy Center, October 2011, pp. 11–13. Still, eliminating the tax exclusion would certainly increase federal tax revenues.

46. Eric J. Toder, Benjamin H. Harris, and Katherine Lim, "Distributional Effects of Tax Expenditures," Tax Policy Center Research Report, July 21, 2009. Toder et al. estimate the distributional impact of the employer health plan exclusion, the deduction for self-employed health plans, and the itemized deduction for medical expenses together; the employer health plan exclusion, however, is far bigger than the other two. Eighty-five percent of people in the top income quintile have employer-sponsored health plans, compared to only 16 percent of people in the bottom quintile. Elise Gould, "Employer-Sponsored Health

Insurance Erosion Accelerates in the Recession," Economic Policy Institute Briefing Paper 283, November 16, 2010, Table 1, p. 5.

47. Ron Wyden and Robert F. Bennett, "Working Across the Aisle for Health Reform," *The Washington Post*, August 5, 2009. See also Jonathan Cohn, "Tax My Health Benefits. Please.," *The New Republic*, March 17, 2009.

48. That is, an insurer cannot refuse to renew your policy because of a change in your health status. (A policy can be rescinded if it was obtained fraudulently.) Insurers are also required to sell insurance policies to all people at the same price, except that they can adjust the price based on age, location, and whether or not you use tobacco. Kaiser Family Foundation, "Summary of New Health Reform Law," April 19, 2011.

49. Subsidies are available to families with incomes up to 400 percent of the federal poverty guidelines (about $89,000 for a family of four).

50. As mentioned above, the employer health plan exclusion currently reduces tax revenues by 1.9 percent of GDP (rising to 2.0 percent in 2016 as health care becomes more expensive). Eliminating the exclusion, however, would probably lead employers to reduce the value of their health benefits, reducing potential tax revenues; on the other hand, this would be canceled out to the extent that lower health benefits were replaced by higher wages. As employers drop their health plans, more people would buy insurance on exchanges and therefore be eligible for subsidies from the federal government. In addition, the Affordable Care Act already imposes a 40 percent excise tax, beginning in 2018, on health plans worth more than a threshold amount, with the threshold designed to grow more slowly than health care costs. By 2021, this tax is projected to bring in only 0.1 percent of GDP—a small part of the value of the employer health plan exclusion. Douglas W. Elmendorf, "CBO's Analysis of the Major Health Care Legislation Enacted in March 2010," Testimony before the Health Subcommittee of the House Energy and Commerce Committee, March 30, 2011, Table 2, p. 14.

51. See Robert Pear, "Medicaid Pays Less than Medicare for Many Prescription Drugs, U.S. Report Finds," *The New York Times*, August 15, 2011.

52. CBO, *Reducing the Deficit*, March 2011, pp. 54–55; OMB, note 2, above, Table S-5, pp. 59–64. We estimate the impact of the additional Obama administration proposals based on their projected savings in 2021; we exclude (from this calculation) proposals for greater cost sharing by beneficiaries, such as increasing Medicare premiums for high-income beneficiaries.

53. General revenues—other taxes not dedicated to Medicare—currently fund about three-quarters of Part B and five-sixths of Part D. To the extent that the Medicare funding gap is not filled by dedicated revenues, it will be filled by general revenues.

54. Premiums are currently about $100 per month, so if our proposal were currently in effect they would be about $120 per month. The revenue estimate is from CBO, *Reducing the Deficit*, March 2011, p. 51. The CBO estimates the impact of increasing premiums to 35 percent of program costs, so we divide its estimate by two.

55. Technically speaking, the payroll tax revenues fund Medicare Part A, not Parts B and D. This could create the situation where Part A is well funded, but Parts B and D require ever-increasing transfers from general revenues. Look-

ing at the federal budget as a whole, however, how money is accounted for within Medicare does not affect the size of the deficit or the national debt.

56. Centers for Medicare and Medicaid Services, "NHE Summary Including Share of GDP, CY 1960–2009," available at https://www.cms.gov/nationalhealth expend data/02_nationalhealthaccountshistorical.asp.

57. We do not recommend raising the Medicare eligibility age because, for example, raising it to 67 would simply shift the burden of health care costs for 65- and 66-year-olds onto the private sector. This is different from Social Security because Medicare is binary (you have it or you don't), while a higher normal retirement age for Social Security means that retirees can still choose to take benefits early, but those benefits will be slightly smaller.

58. CBO, *Reducing the Deficit*, March 2011, pp. 197–98. The CBO estimates a revenue increase of 0.3 percent of GDP, but that estimate assumes that the surtax on high-income households is repealed. We are not recommending repealing that surtax, so the revenues from that surtax (0.2 percent of GDP) should be added to the CBO estimate. Joint Committee on Taxation, *Estimated Revenue Effects of the Amendment in the Nature of a Substitute to H.R. 4872, as Amended, in Combination with the Revenue Effects of H.R. 3590, as Passed by the Senate, and Scheduled for Consideration by the House Committee on Rules*, JCX-17-10, March 20, 2010, p. 2.

59. Lawrence J. Korb, Laura Conley, and Alex Rothman, "A Historical Perspective on Defense Budgets," Center for American Progress, July 6, 2011; OMB, *Fiscal Year 2012 Budget of the U.S. Government: Historical Tasks*, Tables 3.1, 8.1, 8.3, 8.4; Stockholm International Peace Research Institute, "Background Paper on SIPRI Military Expenditures Data, 2010," April 11, 2011. Whether defense spending should be measured in real (inflation-adjusted) dollars or as a share of GDP is open to debate. A share of GDP is appropriate for spending categories, such as Social Security, that are affected by population growth and improvements in standards of living. It is somewhat less appropriate for categories such as defense, where the cost of protecting our country depends less on population and on rising standards of living.

60. Korb et al., note 59, above.

61. Gary Schaub, Jr., and James Forsyth, Jr., "An Arsenal We Can All Live With," *The New York Times*, May 23, 2010; Robert M. Gates, Remarks at the Navy League Sea-Air-Space Exposition, National Harbor, Maryland, May 3, 2010.

62. Lawrence Korb, "Defense Needs to Play Its Part in the Deficit Debate," *The Huffington Post*, July 28, 2011. The actual operations in Afghanistan and Iraq required additional spending on what is sometimes called "nation building," but the point here is that the military had the capability to win these wars (or at least the conventional portion of those wars) despite relatively low spending levels.

63. The administration projected $717.5 billion in budget authority for defense in 2021, or 2.9 percent of its projected GDP. OMB, *Fiscal Year 2012 Budget of the U.S. Government*, Table S-11, pp. 199–200. The CBO estimated that under the administration's budget proposal, defense outlays would be 3.1 percent of GDP in 2021. CBO, *An Analysis of the President's Budgetary Proposals for Fiscal Year 2012*, April 2011, p. 12.

64. Lawrence J. Korb, Sam Klug, and Alex Rothman, "Defense Cuts After the Debt

Deal," Center for American Progress, August 11, 2011; Sustainable Defense Task Force, *Debt, Deficits, and Defense: A Way Forward*, June 11, 2010; Tom Coburn, *Back in Black: A Deficit Reduction Plan*, July 2011, pp. 107–31. Modifying Tri-Care, the Defense Department's health care system, was recommended by the Department's *Quadrennial Review of Military Compensation* and would mainly affect retired service members who are eligible for employer-sponsored health care but elect Tri-Care instead. Sustainable Defense Task Force, *Debt, Deficits, and Defense*, p. 26.

65. Pam Benson, "US Spy Spending Revealed for First Time, Tops $80 Billion," CNN, October 28, 2010.

66. See Dana Priest and William M. Arkin, "A Hidden World, Growing Beyond Control," *The Washington Post*, July 19, 2010; Gordon Adams and Cindy Williams, *Buying National Security: How America Plans and Pays for Its Global Role and Safety at Home* (Routledge, 2010), chapter 6.

67. Gilbert E. Metcalf and David Weisbach, "The Design of a Carbon Tax," *Harvard Environmental Law Review* 33 (2009): 499–556, pp. 504–8.

68. Ibid., p. 501.

69. See G. W. Yohe, R. D. Lasco, Q. K. Ahmad, N. W. Arnell, S. J. Cohen, C. Hope, A. C. Janetos, and R. T. Perez, "Perspectives on Climate Change and Sustainability," chapter 20 in M. L. Parry, O. F. Canziani, J. P. Palutikof, P. J. van der Linden, and C. E. Hanson, eds., *Climate Change 2007: Impacts, Adaptation and Vulnerability. Contribution of Working Group II to the Fourth Assessment Report of the Intergovernmental Panel on Climate Change* (Cambridge University Press, 2007), pp. 821–24. Estimates range at least between $3 and $95 per ton of carbon dioxide. Gilbert E. Metcalf, "Designing a Carbon Tax to Reduce U.S. Greenhouse Gas Emissions," *Review of Environmental Economics and Policy* 3, no. 1 (2009): 63–83, p. 64.

70. "Summary for Policymakers," in B. Metz, O. R. Davidson, P. R. Bosch, R. Dave, and L. A. Meyer, eds., *Climate Change 2007: Mitigation. Contribution of Working Group III to the Fourth Assessment Report of the Intergovernmental Panel on Climate Change* (Cambridge University Press, 2007), p. 19. A 2007 estimate by researchers at MIT shows that the price should be set at $18 per ton of carbon dioxide and should grow at a real rate of 4 percent per year. Metcalf, note 69, above, p. 64.

71. See, for example, Metcalf, note 69, above, p. 65 ($15 in 2005 dollars, or $18 in 2015); CBO, *Reducing the Deficit*, March 2011, pp. 205–6 ($20 in 2012); Robert N. Stavins, "A Meaningful U.S. Cap-and-Trade System to Address Climate Change," *Harvard Environmental Law Review* 32 (2008): 293–371, pp. 333–34 ($18 in 2005 dollars, or $22 in 2015, in "stabilize" scenario). The CBO and Stavins proposals are for a cap-and-trade system (in which companies have to buy emissions permits, which trade on an open market), not a direct carbon tax, but the two have similar economic effects, as discussed below. Note that $20 per ton of carbon dioxide is equivalent to $73 per ton of carbon. See Metcalf, note 69, above, p. 65, note 2.

72. Twenty dollars per metric ton works out to 2 cents per kilogram of carbon dioxide; a gallon of gasoline produces 8.8 kilograms of carbon dioxide. Environmental Protection Agency, "Emission Facts: Average Carbon Dioxide Emissions Resulting from Gasoline and Diesel Fuel," EPA420-F-05-001,

February 2005. The increase in gasoline prices due to the carbon tax would be slightly offset by lower oil prices resulting from lower demand for oil. See Stavins, note 71, above, p. 334.

73. Metcalf estimates 2015 emissions of 7,050 tons of carbon dioxide equivalents with a tax of $18.40 per ton ($15 in 2005 dollars), which would yield revenues of $130 billion, or 0.7 percent of GDP. Metcalf, note 69, above, p. 66. The CBO estimates revenues beginning at 0.6 percent of GDP in 2012 and growing by 0.1 percentage point by 2021. CBO, *Reducing the Deficit*, March 2011, pp. 205–6. Stavins estimates potential revenues of $119 billion (2005 dollars) in 2015, or 0.8 percent of GDP, growing to 0.9 percent of GDP by 2020. Stavins, note 71, above, p. 336 and Table 10.

74. According to one estimate, a carbon tax would effectively cost households in the bottom income decile 3.7 percent of their income, while costing households in the top decile only 0.8 percent of their income. Metcalf and Weisbach, note 67, above, Table B, p. 513.

75. Everyone's taxes should ideally go up by the same *percentage*, not by the same number of percentage points.

76. Because many households do not pay income taxes, this would also require expansion of the earned income tax credit. People whose sole income is Social Security benefits do not benefit from the earned income tax credit, but their benefits are indexed for inflation and would automatically rise to account for higher energy costs due to a carbon tax.

77. Metcalf and Weisbach, note 67, above, p. 502, note 11; CBO, *Policy Options for Reducing CO2 Emissions*, February 2008, pp. ix–xii; Stavins, note 71, above, pp. 348–53.

78. For example, a cap would provide certainty about the total volume of emissions, but the tax rate for a direct tax could be adjusted over time to meet a given emissions target. On design features that can make these two approaches similar to each other, see Stavins, note 71, above, pp. 352–53. For another example, a cap-and-trade system is often thought to be more politically feasible because emission permits can be given (for free) to current emitters, during some initial transition period, in order to minimize their opposition to the plan. However, a similar outcome could be achieved by phasing in a carbon tax over time.

79. Ian W. H. Parry and Kenneth A. Small, "Does Britain or the United States Have the Right Gasoline Tax?," *American Economic Review* 95, no. 4 (September 2005): 1276–89, Table 1, p. 1283. Parry and Small estimate the optimal U.S. gasoline tax at $1.01 per gallon, of which only $0.05 is due to climate change effects (and therefore would be accounted for by a carbon tax), leaving $0.96 per gallon attributable to other externalities. (They estimate the social cost of carbon at only $25 per ton of carbon, or $7 per ton of carbon dioxide. Ibid., p. 1282.) Current gasoline taxes, including federal, state, and local taxes, are about $0.48 per gallon. CBO, *Reducing the Deficit*, March 2011, p. 191. Parry and Small's estimate of the optimal gasoline tax is probably too low because a higher tax would cause people to shift from heavier to lighter vehicles, reducing fatalities in traffic accidents. An additional tax of $0.27 per gallon would be necessary simply to correct for the increase in average U.S. vehicle weight since 1989, and a higher tax would be necessary to correct for all weight-related

externalities. Michael Anderson and Maximilian Auffhammer, "Pounds That Kill: The External Costs of Vehicle Weight," NBER Working Paper 17170, June 2011, pp. 27–31.

80. The CBO estimates that an increase of 25 cents per gallon would increase revenues by 0.2 percent of GDP, but that amount would decline over time because of inflation and because drivers will shift to more efficient vehicles. Indexing the gasoline tax to inflation would solve the first problem but not the second. In addition, the revenue gain from a 50-cent increase should be less than double the revenue gain from a 25-cent increase. CBO, *Reducing the Deficit*, March 2011, pp. 191–92. A tax on miles driven is preferable to an increased gasoline tax because the latter would induce some people to drive just as much, only in more efficient cars, but a mileage tax would be considerably more difficult to administer.

81. See Robert Pirog, *The Role of Federal Gasoline Excise Taxes in Public Policy*, Congressional Research Service Report for Congress, April 15, 2010, p. 6.

82. Simon Johnson and James Kwak, *13 Bankers: The Wall Street Takeover and the Next Financial Meltdown*, paperback ed. (Vintage, 2011), chapter 7.

83. See ibid., Epilogue.

84. See, for example, Anat R. Admati, Peter M. DeMarzo, Martin F. Hellwig, and Paul Pfleiderer, "Fallacies, Irrelevant Facts, and Myths in the Discussion of Capital Regulation: Why Bank Equity Is *Not* Expensive," Rock Center for Corporate Governance at Stanford University Working Paper 86, March 23, 2011.

85. See Douglas A. Shackelford, Daniel N. Shaviro, and Joel Slemrod, "Taxation and the Financial Sector," *National Tax Journal* 63 (December 2010): 781–806, pp. 798–99; IMF Staff, "A Fair and Substantial Contribution by the Financial Sector," chapter 1 in Stijn Claessens, Michael Keen, and Ceyla Pazarbasioglu, eds., *Financial Sector Taxation: The IMF's Report to the G-20 and Background Material* (IMF, 2010), pp. 11–16.

86. The proceeds from such a fee will depend on the tax rate. In early 2010, President Obama proposed a fee of 0.15 percent of total liabilities for any financial institution with more than $50 billion in assets. This fee would bring in about 0.05 percent of GDP per year. CBO, *Reducing the Deficit*, March 2011, pp. 201–2. Economists at the IMF estimate that the too-big-to-fail subsidy could be corrected for with a fee of 0.1–0.5 percent of total assets. Kenichi Ueda and Beatrice Weder di Mauro, "The Value of the Too-Big-to-Fail Subsidy to Financial Institutions," chapter 6 in Claessens et al., eds., note 85, above, p. 115. A fee levied at 0.3 percent of total liabilities, the approximate midpoint of this range, would bring in 0.1 percent of GDP each year.

87. Michael Keen, Russell Krelove, and John Norregaard, "The Financial Activities Tax," chapter 7 in Claessens et al., eds., note 85, above. Keen, Krelove, and Norregaard discuss three types of financial activities taxes; we focus on the third, which they label "FAT3." See also Shackelford et al., note 85, above, pp. 799–800; Shaviro, "Tax Reform Implications of the Risk of a U.S. Budget Catastrophe," working paper, September 1, 2011, available at http://papers .ssrn.com/sol3/papers.cfm?abstract_id=1924852, pp. 23–24.

88. See Shackelford et al., note 85, above, pp. 781–82.

89. Keen et al., note 87, above, Table 1, p. 139. Keen et al. estimate the tax base for FAT3 at 0.7 percent of GDP and for FAT2 at 2.8 percent. The difference

between FAT2 and FAT3 is that the latter only taxes profits above a higher threshold (measured as return on average equity). So the tax base for the financial activities tax will depend on where this threshold is set.

90. The role of Fannie and Freddie in the financial crisis has been debated endlessly. For our brief perspective, see Johnson and Kwak, note 82, above, pp. 144–46. For a more detailed and updated review of the debate, see David Min, "Why Wallison Is Wrong About the Genesis of the U.S. Housing Crisis," Center for American Progress, July 2011.

91. For a similar but further-reaching proposal, see John Hempton, "What to Do with Fannie and Freddie," *Bronte Capital* (blog), January 24, 2011. In 2011, the Obama administration proposed increasing the guarantee fees by 10 basis points, or 10 one-hundredths of a percentage point, and estimated that this would reduce deficits by $3.6 billion in 2020. OMB, note 2, above, pp. 21–22.

92. CBO, *Reducing the Deficit*, March 2011, pp. 28–29. The CBO estimated that fixing the loan limit at $417,000 and not adjusting it in the future would reduce the deficit by $0.5 billion in 2020; lowering the limit further would increase the amount of deficit reduction.

93. Environmental Working Group, Farm Subsidy Database, available at http://farm.ewg.org/. Farm subsidies vary from year to year based on natural and market conditions. From 2001 through 2010, they ranged from $14 billion to $24 billion.

94. U.S. Department of Agriculture Economic Research Service, "Farm and Commodity Policy," available at http://www.ers.usda.gov/Briefing/FarmPolicy/.

95. On the downstream impact of farm subsidies, see Alicia Harvie and Timothy A. Wise, "Sweetening the Pot: Implicit Subsidies to Corn Sweeteners and the U.S. Obesity Epidemic," Global Development and Environment Institute Policy Brief 09–01, Tufts University, February 2009.

96. See Timothy A. Wise, "Agricultural Dumping Under NAFTA: Estimating the Costs of U.S. Agricultural Policies to Mexican Producers," Global Development and Environment Institute Working Paper 09–08, Tufts University, December 2009.

97. Michael Grunwald, "Why the U.S. Is Also Giving Brazilians Farm Subsidies," *Time*, April 9, 2010.

98. Gilbert M. Gaul, Sarah Cohen, and Dan Morgan, "Federal Subsidies Turn Farms into Big Business," *The Washington Post*, December 21, 2006; Gilbert M. Gaul, Sarah Cohen, and Dan Morgan, "Farm Program Pays $1.3 Billion to People Who Don't Farm," *The Washington Post*, July 2, 2006.

99. President Obama in 2011 proposed a set of changes that would reduce spending by $5 billion in 2020. OMB, note 2, above, pp. 17–18. Completely eliminating all agricultural subsidies would reduce spending by about $15–20 billion in 2020.

100. CBO, *Reducing the Deficit*, March 2011, pp. 111–12. The $4 billion and $2 billion figures are for budget authority, not outlays. With capital-intensive spending projects, outlays often lag behind budget authority, although the two are generally similar in the long run.

101. Ibid., p. 110; OMB, note 2, above, pp. 22–23. The CBO and OMB estimate that higher security fees would raise about $2 billion per year by 2020. OMB estimates that higher fees for air traffic control services would raise another $1 billion.

102. Government Accountability Office, *Opportunities to Reduce Potential Duplication in Government Programs, Save Tax Dollars, and Enhance Revenue*, March 2011, GAO-11-318SP, pp. 211–13. This GAO report identifying wasteful federal government spending was mandated by the Statutory Pay-As-You-Go Act of 2010, Public Law 111–139, 124 Stat. 8, § 21.

103. Ibid., pp. 215–17.

104. OECD Programme for International Student Assessment, *PISA 2009 Results: Executive Summary* (OECD, 2010), Figure 1, p. 8. The United States ranked fourteenth in reading.

105. Sabrina Tavernise, "Soaring Poverty Casts Spotlight on 'Lost Decade,' " *The New York Times*, September 13, 2011.

106. Alisha Coleman-Jensen, Mark Nord, Margaret Andrews, and Steven Carlson, *Household Food Security in the United States in 2010*, U.S. Department of Agriculture Economic Research Service, Economic Research Report 125, September 2011, Table 1A, p. 6.

107. See notes 91, 92, and 99, above.

108. Fannie Mae, Freddie Mac, and most agricultural subsidies count as mandatory spending because they do not require annual appropriations by Congress.

109. William G. Gale and Benjamin H. Harris, "Reforming Taxes and Raising Revenue: Part of the Fiscal Solution," Brookings Institution, May 2011, pp. 12–13. $1.2 trillion is the sum of all the tax expenditures identified by OMB. Eliminating all tax expenditures would increase revenues by more or less than $1.2 trillion because of behavioral responses and interaction effects. In at least some cases, interaction effects would cause the total revenue gain to exceed the sum of the individual revenue gains. Ibid., p. 13.

110. Martin Feldstein, "The 'Tax Expenditure' Solution for Our National Debt," *The Wall Street Journal*, July 20, 2010.

111. See Daniel N. Shaviro, "1986-Style Tax Reform: A Good Idea Whose Time Has Passed," *Tax Notes* (May 23, 2011): 817–42, pp. 828–30.

112. OMB, note 44, above, Table 17-3, pp. 252–55.

113. In 2009, households making more than $100,000 saved $53 billion because of the mortgage interest deduction; all other households saved only $24 billion. Joint Committee on Taxation, *Estimates of Federal Tax Expenditures for Fiscal Years 2010–2014*, JCS-3–10, December 15, 2010, Table 3, pp. 55–60.

114. William G. Gale, Jonathan Gruber, and Seth Stephens-Davidowitz, "Encouraging Homeownership Through the Tax Code," *Tax Notes* (June 18, 2007): 1171–89, pp. 1179–81. Empirical research has shown that the deduction has no significant effect on the homeownership rate. Edward L. Glaeser and Jesse M. Shapiro, "The Benefits of the Home Mortgage Interest Deduction," in James M. Poterba, ed., *Tax Policy and the Economy*, vol. 17 (MIT Press, 2003): 37–82, pp. 76–80.

115. National Association of Realtors, "Latest Existing-Home Sales Information," press release, September 21, 2011, Local Market Data.

116. CBO, *Reducing the Deficit*, March 2011, pp. 146–47. The 0.2 percent figure is based on the projected revenue increase for 2020. The revenue increase grows to 0.3 percent of GDP over the next decade because the $400,000 cap is decreasing in real terms.

117. OMB, note 44, above, Table 17-1, Addendum: Aid to State and Local Governments.

118. Because the interest on state and local bonds is tax-exempt, their issuers can pay lower interest rates than those on corporate bonds of equivalent risk. In practice, state and local bonds pay interest rates about 25 percent lower than rates on comparable corporate bonds; this is the subsidy that is received by state and local governments. That means that anyone whose marginal tax rate is higher than 25 percent gets a tax break in addition to the subsidy to state and local governments. Michael J. Graetz and Deborah H. Schenk, *Federal Income Taxation: Principles and Policies*, 6th ed. (Foundation Press, 2008), pp. 224–25.

119. The revenue increase would take several years to phase in since the new policy would apply only to newly issued bonds. See CBO, *Reducing the Deficit*, March 2011, pp. 163–64. Note that the CBO scores the effects of replacing the tax exemption with a 15 percent subsidy. Maintaining the level of subsidy to state and local governments would probably require a larger subsidy percentage, producing correspondingly smaller revenue increases.

120. OMB, note 44, above, Table 17-1, lines 59, 172.

121. This tax expenditure currently costs $74 billion, which is almost 0.5 percent of GDP. Ibid. Eliminating it and using half the proceeds for direct subsidies would increase revenues by about 0.2 percent of GDP.

122. In 2009, the largest recipients of charitable donations were religious organizations (33 percent of all contributions) and educational organizations (13 percent). Kennard T. Wing, Katie L. Roeger, and Thomas H. Pollak, *The Nonprofit Sector in Brief: Public Charities, Giving, and Volunteering, 2010*, Urban Institute, 2010, Table 4, p. 6.

123. Frank J. Sammartino, "Options for Changing the Tax Treatment of Charitable Giving," testimony before the Senate Finance Committee, October 18, 2011, Table 1, p. 2. Alternatively, converting the donation to a 15 percent tax credit and keeping the floor at 2 percent of adjusted gross income would increase revenues by 0.2 percent of GDP while reducing total charitable contributions by less than 5 percent. Ibid.

124. This problem, among others, is caused by the realization requirement: the rule that you don't have to pay taxes on the appreciation of an asset until you sell that asset. If you own stock that gains $1,000 in value, you are now $1,000 richer, but you do not have to pay tax on that $1,000 until you sell the stock.

125. On these and other issues with capital gains taxation, see Gerald Auten, "Capital Gains Taxation," in Joseph J. Cordes, Robert D. Ebel, and Jane G. Gravelle, eds., *The Encyclopedia of Taxation and Tax Policy* (Urban Institute Press, 1999): 48–51.

126. Citizens for Tax Justice, "Top Federal Income Tax Rates Since 1913," November 2011, available at http://www.ctj.org/pdf/regcg.pdf.

127. Tax Policy Center, Table T11-0266, Tax Benefits of the Preferential Rates on Capital Gains and Qualified Dividends, Baseline: Current Law; Distribution of Federal Tax Change by Cash Income Level, 2011, available at http://www.taxpolicycenter.org/numbers/displayatab.cfm?DocID=3148. These figures are somewhat misleading because the fact of realizing capital gains in a given year itself increases household income in that year. Over the ten-year period from 1979 through 1988, however, the top 1 percent of households still received 57 percent of all capital gains, which means that they received more than 57 percent of the benefits of lower tax rates on capital

gains (because their ordinary income tax rates were higher than average). CBO, *Perspectives on the Ownership of Capital Assets and the Realization of Capital Gains*, May 1997, Table 5, p. 16.

128. Leonard E. Burman, *The Labyrinth of Capital Gains Tax Policy: A Guide for the Perplexed* (Brookings Institution Press, 1999), pp. 65–66.

129. The Tax Reform Act of 1986 set the top income tax rate—the marginal rate that applied to the highest incomes—at 28 percent and eliminated prior preferences for capital gains. A phase-out provision applying to upper-income taxpayers meant that, for certain income ranges, the marginal rate was as high as 33 percent, but once income exceeded those ranges, the marginal rate fell back to 28 percent. Joint Committee on Taxation, *General Explanation of the Tax Reform Act of 1986*, JCS-10–87, pp. 20–21, 178–79.

130. We do not attempt here to correct the many other inefficiencies in the capital gains taxation system. One additional suggestion, however, is to allow a tax credit for corporate taxes that have already been paid on profits distributed to shareholders as dividends.

131. See Burman, note 128, above, pp. 60–63. In particular, differences in capital gains tax rates across states seem to have no significant impact on capital gains.

132. Eliminating the tax preferences in the 2003 tax cut (reverting to pre-2003 rates) would increase tax revenues by $32 billion in 2016. CBO, *The Budget and Economic Outlook: An Update*, August 2011, Supplemental Material, Expiring Tax Provisions (xls), available at http://www.cbo.gov/doc.cfm?index=12316. Eliminating the tax preferences in pre-2003 law (increasing the maximum capital gains tax rate from 20 percent to 39.6 percent) would increase tax revenues by $70 billion in 2016 (static estimate). OMB, note 44, above, Table 17-1, pp. 241–45, line 71. We estimate that increasing the rate from 20 percent to 28 percent (not 39.6 percent) would increase revenues by about two-fifths of $70 billion, or $28 billion, for a total increase of $60 billion, or slightly over 0.3 percent of GDP in 2016.

133. OMB, note 44, above, Table 17-1, pp. 241–45, line 73. In 2012, $61 billion was 0.4 percent of GDP. The $61 billion OMB estimate, however, assumes a maximum capital gains tax rate of 20 percent, while our previous proposal would increase this rate to 28 percent.

134. The tax expenditure currently costs about 0.2 percent of GDP. Ibid., Table 17-1, pp. 241–45, line 61. Allowing a $100,000 exclusion reduces the potential revenue gain. Our proposed maximum rate of 28 percent, however, increases the potential revenue gain.

135. That is, the earned income tax credit reflects the judgment that the working poor should pay less income tax, or even negative income tax (to compensate for the fact that earnings from working reduce their eligibility for welfare programs), and is therefore similar to a graduated rate structure; the child tax credit reflects the judgment that families with more children should pay less income tax, and is therefore similar to personal exemptions (which are generally not thought of as a tax expenditure). See Shaviro, note 111, above, p. 823.

136. National Commission on Fiscal Responsibility and Reform, note 2, above, pp. 29–31.

137. Martin Feldstein, Daniel Feenberg, and Maya MacGuineas, "Capping Individual Tax Expenditure Benefits," *Tax Notes* (May 2, 2011): 505–9, p. 506. Their

proposal covers the employer health plan exclusion, itemized deductions, and a few tax credits; it does not include tax expenditures that encourage saving, such as the lower tax rates on capital gains and dividends.

138. Ibid., Table 1, p. 507.

139. CBO, *Reducing the Deficit*, March 2011, pp. 151–52.

140. Identifying and counting business tax breaks is a complicated endeavor. The tax expenditures listed by the OMB, added together, reduce corporate income taxes by $109 billion in 2012. OMB, note 44, above, Table 17-2, pp. 246–51. However, we exclude tax expenditures that only exist relative to the normal tax baseline, not the reference tax law baseline. For example, immediate expensing of research and experimentation expenditures (ibid., pp. 257–58) counts as a tax expenditure relative to true economic depreciation, but there is no practical way to implement true economic depreciation in the tax code. We exclude benefits to corporations that we have already discussed under the topic of individual income tax expenditures, such as the exemption for interest on state and local bonds. We include the impact of business tax breaks on individual income tax receipts.

141. One way to eliminate the tax preference for debt is to allow companies to deduct the cost of their equity capital, but that would only reduce tax revenues. One way to harmonize our international tax system with those of other countries is to exempt foreign source income, but that would also reduce tax revenues. Other solutions are also possible, but there is no a priori reason to believe that successful structural corporate tax reform would increase tax revenues.

142. BEA, National Income and Product Accounts, Table 2.1. The Federal Reserve Flow of Funds Accounts use an alternative calculation of the savings rate. That series shows the same general trend, but with more year-to-year volatility.

143. On the role of household debt in the recent credit bubble and financial crisis, see Menzie D. Chinn and Jeffry A. Frieden, *Lost Decades: The Making of America's Debt Crisis and the Long Recovery* (W. W. Norton, 2011), chapter 2; Raghuram G. Rajan, *Fault Lines: How Hidden Fractures Still Threaten the World Economy* (Princeton University Press, 2010), chapter 1.

144. See, for example, William G. Gale and Benjamin H. Harris, "A VAT for the United States: Part of the Solution," in *The VAT Reader: What a Federal Consumption Tax Would Mean for America* (Tax Analysts, 2011): 64–82, p. 68; Joseph Bankman and David A. Weisbach, "The Superiority of an Ideal Consumption Tax over an Ideal Income Tax," *Stanford Law Review* 58 (March 2006): 1413–56, p. 1422; Daniel N. Shaviro, "Replacing the Income Tax with a Progressive Consumption Tax," *Tax Notes* (April 5, 2004): 91–113, p. 92; Michael J. Graetz, "100 Million Unnecessary Returns: A Fresh Start for the U.S. Tax System," *Yale Law Journal* 112 (2002): 261–310, pp. 300–301.

145. Martin A. Sullivan, "Introduction: Getting Acquainted with VAT," in *The VAT Reader*, note 144, above: 7–14, p. 12. If an income tax and a consumption tax have the same rate, then each allows me to consume the same amount this year. If I save my money and spend it all next year, however, the income tax will leave me with less after-tax money for consumption than will the consumption tax; the income tax takes 10 percent of my wage income this year, so my interest income is 10 percent lower than under the consumption tax.

146. Kathryn James, "Exploring the Origins and Global Rise of VAT," in *The VAT Reader*, note 144, above: 15–22, p. 15.

147. Eric Toder and Joseph Rosenberg, "Effects of Imposing a Value-Added Tax to Replace Payroll Taxes or Corporate Taxes," Tax Policy Center, March 18, 2010, pp. 12–13. This estimate reflects the reduction in income and payroll taxes due to the value-added tax.

148. Jane G. Gravelle, "The Distributional Case Against a VAT," in *The VAT Reader*, note 144, above: 102–11, Table 1, p. 103. Conceptually, if you rank households by how much they consume, a value-added tax turns out to be completely proportional (flat); if you rank them by how much they earn, a VAT is regressive; if you rank people by their lifetime income, a VAT becomes less regressive (because starving college students may consume a high percentage of their income, but those people will consume a lower percentage later in life). If you think of the VAT as a tax on businesses, then some of it must be allocated to capital, which also makes it less regressive. See ibid., pp. 104–10; Gale and Harris, note 144, above, pp. 70–72.

149. Figures are for households where the head of household is age 57–66. Jesse Bricker, Brian Bucks, Arthur Kennickell, Traci Mach, and Kevin Moore, "Surveying the Aftermath of the Storm: Changes in Family Finances from 2007 to 2009," Federal Reserve Board Finance and Economics Discussion Series Working Paper 2011–17, March 2011, Appendix Tables 2A, 2B.

150. Brigitte C. Madrian and Dennis F. Shea, "The Power of Suggestion: Inertia in 401(k) Participation and Savings Behavior," *Quarterly Journal of Economics* 116 (2001): 1149–1225; James J. Choi, David Laibson, Brigitte C. Madrian, and Andrew Metrick, "For Better or for Worse: Default Effects and 401(k) Savings Behavior," chapter 3 in David Wise, ed., *Perspectives in the Economics of Aging* (University of Chicago Press, 2004); John Beshears, James J. Choi, David Laibson, and Brigitte C. Madrian, "The Importance of Default Options for Retirement Savings Outcomes: Evidence from the United States," chapter 5 in Jeffrey Brown, Jeffrey Liebman, and David A. Wise, eds., *Social Security Policy in a Changing Environment* (University of Chicago Press, 2009). For a popular summary of retirement savings behavior and default options, see Richard H. Thaler and Cass R. Sunstein, *Nudge: Improving Decisions About Health, Wealth, and Happiness* (Yale University Press, 2008), chapter 6.

151. The federal government has the power to set rules for retirement plans because it controls the tax preferences enjoyed by those plans.

152. Thaler and Sunstein, note 150, above, p. 107; David I. Laibson, Andrea Repetto, and Jeremy Tobacman, "Self-Control and Saving for Retirement," *Brookings Papers on Economic Activity* 1998, no. 1 (1998): 91–197, pp. 94–95.

153. The increase in the Social Security payroll tax does not affect the top marginal tax rate because the earnings subject to that tax will still be capped, although at a higher level. The 2001 tax cut lowered the top marginal rate by 4.6 percentage points. It is scheduled to increase by 0.9 percentage points (because of an increase in the Medicare payroll tax for high earners); our plan would increase it by another 1 percentage point. Theoretically, a value-added tax at a 5 percent rate would also reduce the incentive to work because the tax reduces the amount you can consume with the same amount of income. The marginal impact is smaller than 5 percentage points, however, since the highest-earning families consume a relatively small amount of their current income.

154. Congressional Progressive Caucus, note 2, above, p. 9.

155. House Budget Committee, note 2, above, pp. 46, 50.

156. National Commission on Fiscal Responsibility and Reform, note 2, above, pp. 41–42; Bipartisan Policy Center Debt Reduction Task Force, note 2, above, pp. 55–56; Committee for a Responsible Federal Budget, "10 Themes Emerging from the New Debt Reduction Plans," November 23, 2010, p. 5. The Gang of Six deferred unspecified health savings to later legislation, but did promise to "maintain the essential health care services that the poor and elderly rely upon." "A Bipartisan Plan to Reduce Our Nation's Deficits," note 2, above, p. 3.

157. "A Bipartisan Plan to Reduce Our Nation's Deficits," note 2, above, p. 3; National Commission on Fiscal Responsibility and Reform, note 2, above, p. 30; Bipartisan Policy Center Debt Reduction Task Force, note 2, above, p. 33; Committee for a Responsible Federal Budget, "Going Big Could Improve the Chances of Success," October 21, 2011, p. 6.

158. "A Bipartisan Plan to Reduce Our Nation's Deficits," note 2, above, p. 4 ($1.5 trillion in tax reduction over ten years, relative to current law); Bipartisan Policy Center Debt Reduction Task Force, note 2, above, p. 30 ($435 billion in tax increases over 2012–2020, relative to a baseline in which all expiring tax cuts are extended); National Commission on Fiscal Responsibility and Reform, note 2, above, p. 30 ($180 billion dedicated to deficit reduction in 2020, relative to a baseline in which all expiring tax cuts are extended); Committee for a Responsible Federal Budget, note 157, above, p. 6 ($0.8–1.2 trillion in revenue increases over ten years, relative to a baseline in which all expiring tax cuts are extended). According to the CBO, the total impact of extending all expiring tax cuts is $4.7 trillion over 2012–2020 and $800 billion in 2020. CBO, *The Budget and Economic Outlook: An Update*, August 2011, Table 1-8, pp. 26–27. So these proposals leave tax revenues only modestly higher than they would be if all expiring tax cuts were extended and far lower than they would be if those tax cuts were to expire.

CONCLUSION

1. James Madison, Letter to W. T. Barry, August 4, 1822, in Gaillard Hunt, ed., *The Writings of James Madison, Comprising His Public Papers and His Private Correspondence, Volume 9: 1819–1836* (G. P. Putnam's Sons, 1910): 103–9, p. 103. Madison was prompted to this thought by appropriations for education made by the Kentucky legislature.

2. See Bruce Bartlett, "I'd Rather Be an Unlucky Ducky," Economix (blog), *The New York Times*, September 27, 2011.

3. "When Wall Street Nearly Collapsed," CNNMoney, available at http://money.cnn.com/galleries/2009/fortune/0909/gallery.witnesses_meltdown.fortune/index.html.

4. Ron Suskind, *The Price of Loyalty: George W. Bush, the White House, and the Education of Paul O'Neill* (Simon & Schuster, 2004), p. 291.

EPILOGUE

1. President Obama was already a reasonably strong favorite to win the election before Sandy hit, however. Nate Silver. . . "Nov. 4: Did Hurricane Sandy Blow

Romney Off Course?" FiveThirtyEight (blog), *The New York Times*, November 5, 2012.

2. As of early December 2012, with not all states done counting votes. See David Wasserman, 2012 National Popular Vote Tracker, available at https://docs.google.com/spreadsheet/lv?key=0AjYj9mXElO_QdHpla01oWE1jOFZRbnhJZkZpVFNKeVE&toomany=true.

3. The complete statement was, "If you were successful, somebody along the line gave you some help. There was a great teacher somewhere in your life. Somebody helped to create this unbelievable American system that we have that allowed you to thrive. Somebody invested in roads and bridges. If you've got a business—you didn't build that. Somebody else made that happen." "Remarks by the President at a Campaign Event in Roanoke, Virginia," White House Press Release, July 13, 2012. Narrowly speaking, the controversy was over whether the word "that" referred to "business" or to the system of public services described in the previous sentences.

4. David Corn, "Secret Video: Romney Tells Millionaire Donors What He REALLY Thinks of Obama Voters," *Mother Jones*, September 17, 2012.

5. The "maker vs. taker" theory of American society was developed at conservative think tanks such as the American Enterprise Institute and propagated by, among others, the editorial page of *The Wall Street Journal*, which highlighted the "non-taxpaying class," sometimes known as "lucky duckies." Mark Schmitt, "The Theory of the Moocher Class," Next New Deal (blog), The Roosevelt Institute, September 18, 2012; "The Non-Taxpaying Class," *The Wall Street Journal* (editorial), November 20, 2002.

6. *The Economist*/YouGov Poll, November 17–19, 2012, available at http://cdn.yougov.com/cumulus_uploads/document/co13jzvbau/econTabReport.pdf.

7. See, for example, Jonathan Weisman, "Seeking Ways To Raise Taxes but Leave Tax Rate As Is," *The New York Times*, November 22, 2012.

8. Damian Paletta, "Obama Says Scheduled Cuts 'Will Not Happen,'" *The Wall Street Journal*, October 22, 2012.

9. On conservative groups' reactions to the 2012 elections, see Erik Wasson, "Conservatives Lambast Romney, Vow To Take Over Republican Party," *The Hill*, November 7, 2012; Carl Hulse, "Republicans Face Struggle over Party's Direction," *The New York Times*, November 7, 2012.

10. Recall that this is the case for all of the major bipartisan deficit reduction plans described at the end of chapter 7.

11. The Obama administration already offered to increase the Medicare eligibility age and change the indexing formula for Social Security benefits during the 2011 debt ceiling negotiations. Matt Bai, "Obama vs. Boehner: Who Killed the Debt Deal?" *The New York Times*, March 28, 2012.

12. See William J. Baumol, "Health Care, Education, and the Cost Disease: A Looming Crisis for Public Choice," *Public Choice* 77 (1993): 17–28.

13. *Ibid.*, pp. 23–24.

14. CBO, The Long-Term Budget Outlook, June 2012, Supplemental Data, Table 3, available at http://www.cbo.gov/publication/43288; analysis by the authors. Real per capita GDP grows more slowly than Baumol's estimate of total production because the latter does not take into account changes in demographic composition and because of differences in assumed productivity growth rates.

15. In the 2012 election cycle, the top five individual donors to super PACs, four of

them billionaires (Sheldon Adelson, Harold Simmons, Peter Thiel, and Robert Rowling), all contributed to conservative organizations, as did fifteen of the top twenty. Phil Hirschkorn, "Top Super PAC Donors Giving Multimillions in 2012," CBS News, September 24, 2012.

16. Anthony B. Atkinson, Thomas Piketty, and Emmanuel Saez, "Top Incomes in the Long Run of History," *Journal of Economic Literature* 49 (2011): 3–71, p. 8.

17. "They're absolutely convinced that they're not asking for special privileges for themselves. They're convinced that it just so happens that their self-interest coincides perfectly with the collective interest." Chrystia Freeland, quoted in Ezra Klein, "Romney Is Wall Street's Worst Bet Since the Bet on Subprime," Wonkblog, *The Washington Post*, November 28, 2012.

18. Daron Acemoglu and James Robinson, *Why Nations Fail: The Origins of Power, Prosperity, and Poverty* (Crown Business, 2012), chapter 6; Diego Puga and Daniel Trefler, "International Trade and Institutional Change: Medieval Venice's Response to Globalization," NBER Working Paper 18288, August 2012.

19. Barack Obama: "There is not another country on Earth that would not gladly trade places with the United States of America." Donovan Slack, "Obama: Everyone Wants To Be Us," Politico 44 (blog), *Politico*, August 8, 2012. Mitt Romney: "I believe [America] is the greatest nation in the history of the earth." Mark Halperin, "Transcript: Mitt Romney's Remarks at the Republican Jewish Coalition Forum," The Page (blog), *Time*, December 7, 2011.

TECHNICAL APPENDIX

1. CBO, *The Budget and Economic Outlook: An Update*, August 2011, Table 1-2, pp. 4–5.

2. Ibid., Table 1-8, pp. 26–27.

3. Overseas contingency operations were specifically excluded from those caps. Douglas W. Elmendorf, Letter to John A. Boehner and Harry Reid, August 1, 2011, p. 2.

4. On both changes, see CBO, *The Budget and Economic Outlook: An Update*, August 2011, p. 25.

5. Ibid., Table 1-8, pp. 26–27.

6. Ibid.

7. We think this is reasonable for several reasons. One of the largest tax breaks, a bonus depreciation provision, is similar to one that was allowed to expire in 2004 after the economy had recovered from a recession. Tax Policy Center, "Quick Facts: Bonus Depreciation and 100 Percent Expensing," available at http://www.taxpolicycenter.org/taxtopics/Bonus-Depreciation-and-100-Percent-Expensing.cfm. Another large tax break, the ethanol tax credit, was allowed to expire at the end of 2011. More generally, the current political climate should make it harder for low-profile, industry-specific tax breaks to be extended than in the past.

8. CBO, *An Analysis of the President's Budgetary Proposals for Fiscal Year 2012*, April 2011, Table 1-5, p. 14.

9. CBO, *2011 Long-Term Budget Outlook*, June 2011, pp. 2–7.

10. On the reasons why revenues grow as a share of the economy under current

law, see ibid., pp. 64–68. We use the growth rate from the 2009 alternative fiscal scenario because it assumes that the AMT is indexed for inflation but does not assume that revenues are constant as a share of GDP (the 2011 assumption). CBO, *The Long-Term Budget Outlook*, June 2009, Additional Info, available at http://cbo.gov/doc.cfm?index=10297 (see data for Figure 5-1).

11. On the differences in health care spending in the two scenarios, see CBO, *2011 Long-Term Budget Outlook*, June 2011, pp. 43–45.

12. See ibid., Table 1-1, pp. 4–5.

13. Other means of financing (OMF) reflects the difference between the cash outlays of government financing programs, such as student loans, and their budgetary cost; since most loans are paid back, the budgetary cost is just the estimated subsidy component of the loan. In a static economy, OMF should be zero, since loan repayments in any year will balance new loans advanced, except for loan losses, which are balanced by the budgetary cost. In a growing economy, OMF should be slightly positive.

14. CBO, *2011 Long-Term Budget Outlook*, June 2011, p. 24.

15. We calculate the average growth rate from the annual data in ibid., Supplemental Material: Data Underlying Scenarios and Figures (Economic Variables Underlying the Long-Term Budget Projections). The report itself specifies an average growth rate of 2.2 percent over the 2022–2085 period. Ibid., p. 25.

16. Ibid., p. 24.

17. Ibid., Table 1-1, pp. 4–5.

18. Ibid., p. 21.

19. See ibid., pp. 21–22.

20. CBO, *The Budget and Economic Outlook: An Update*, August 2011, p. 7.

21. Technically speaking, it spreads the $1.2 trillion so that the nominal dollar change in the primary balance is the same in each year from 2013 through 2021. Ibid.

22. Because the failure of the supercommittee became official as we were completing this book, we have not adjusted our projections by removing the estimated impact of the supercommittee and replacing it with the estimated impact of the automatic spending cuts. Since the total ten-year impact is the same, any change in our projections of the national debt would be minimal.

23. According to the methodology used in the CBO's long-term forecast, the automatic spending cuts would reduce discretionary spending in 2021 even further as a percentage of GDP; that reduction would become permanent under the assumption that "other spending" remains constant at its 2021 level.

Acknowledgments

This book exists because of a collaboration that extends well beyond the two authors named on its cover. It grew out of conversations with our editor, Erroll McDonald, and our agent, Rafe Sagalyn, early in 2011. They encouraged us to take on this wide-ranging project and have once again helped guide it to completion. In addition to Erroll, many other people at Pantheon, the Knopf Doubleday Publishing Group, Vintage Books, and Random House, Inc., have had a hand in turning our thoughts into words on paper: Brian Barth, Kristen Bearse, Fred Chase, Altie Karper, Lisa Montebello, Jeff Alexander, Jocelyn Miller, and no doubt others we have overlooked.

Many people helped us develop and research the ideas that are contained in this book. Daron Acemoglu, Anat Admati, Michael Ash, Anders Åslund, Bruce Bartlett, Donna Behmer, Peter Berezin, Fred Bergsten, Peter Boone, Jim Boughton, Jon Brody, Bill Cline, Gail Cohen, Jeff Connaughton, Carlo Cottarelli, Mark Cymrot, Mac Destler, Thomas Ferguson, Joe Gagnon, Rex Ghosh, Sarah Goff, Dan Immergluck, Olivier Jeanne, Rob Johnson, Nosup Kwak, David Laibson, Yair Listokin, David Moss, Marc Noland, Jonathan Ostry, Lee Price, Robert Ratner, Carmen Reinhart, Jim Robinson, Howard Rosen, Paul Rosenbaum, Matt Salomon, Otto Scharmer, Peter Siegelman, Alex Smith, Arvind Subramanian, Peter Temin, Poul Thomsen, Ted Truman, Ori Tzvieli, Steve Weisman, and John Williamson provided us with valuable feedback on our ideas or on drafts of different sections. Participants in seminars at the International Monetary Fund and the Peterson Institute for International Economics gave us the opportunity to discuss key themes of the book as we were setting them to paper. Rachael Brown, Hilary McClellan, and Jessica Murphy painstakingly checked the vast majority of the facts in the book. Matt Matera edited the citations in our endnotes. Rebecca Buckwalter-Poza, Laura Femino, Jason Glick, Amanda Lowry, and Ben Stern helped with last-minute proofreading. As this is largely a work of synthesis and interpretation, we owe a large debt to the many historians, economists, political scientists, journalists, and other researchers who have come before us, many of whom are cited in the endnotes.

Over the past year, we have been able to develop our arguments not only on our blog, *The Baseline Scenario*, but also in articles and columns in other publications. Paula Dwyer and Jim Greiff at *Bloomberg View*, Josh Mills and Kevin McKenna at *The New York Times*, Jonathan Stein and Roman Frydman at *Project Syndicate*, and Derek Thompson at *The Atlantic* made it possible for us to share our ideas with a broader audience and helped us refine our thinking and writing. Graydon Carter and Doug Stumpf gave us the valuable opportunity to outline some of our historical themes in an article in *Vanity Fair*. Peter Boone is a brilliant and generous coauthor on our blog and on many articles published elsewhere; his work with Simon on Europe and on global moral hazard has been particularly influential in shaping our ideas.

Simon enjoys the constant support of many people at both MIT Sloan School of Management and the Peterson Institute for International Economics, beginning with the incredibly hardworking Michelle Fiorenza. He benefited from all his interactions with MIT students, including participants in his Global Entrepreneurship class. The Sloan Fellows in the class of 2012 were more helpful than they can imagine, serving as a real-time sounding board in his International Economics and Macroeconomics class and his Global Markets class. Dave Schmittlein, Donna Behmer, Rob Freund, S. P. Kothari, and JoAnne Yates have allowed Simon the time, space, and support needed to develop research and take intellectual risks. Simon's co-teachers, Michellana Jester and Yasheng Huang, and everyone on the incredible G-Lab team have helped make the past year possible. Fred Bergsten, head of the Peterson Institute, continues to provide a unique environment for creative thinking and discussion. Generous funding from the Smith-Richardson Foundation and from Sir Evelyn and Lady Lynn de Rothschild through the ERANDA Foundation was again of great help, as was support on related projects from the Ford Foundation and the Institute for New Economic Thinking. Among Simon's colleagues at Peterson, Arvind Subramanian and Steve Weisman again deserve special thanks for their encouragement and willingness to share ideas; Fred Bergsten came through with particularly helpful comments at a crucial time. At MIT, Daron Acemoglu and Richard Locke are long-term co-thinkers; their influence is present even when they are not aware of it.

James was able to devote time to this book thanks to the flexibility and support of Jeremy Paul of the University of Connecticut School of Law. Lucian Bebchuk graciously gave him an institutional home at the Harvard Law School Program on Corporate Governance.

As always, we are deeply grateful for the love and support of our families. Simon thanks his parents, Ian and Cedar Johnson, and his brother, Richard Johnson, for always encouraging him to reach higher; his wife, Mary Kwak, for her love, wisdom, and patience; and his daughters, Celia and Lucie, for their unfailing good cheer and for running to greet him when he comes through the door. James thanks his parents, Nosup Kwak and Inkyung Liu, and his sister, Mary Kwak, for always supporting and encouraging him throughout his many careers; Ed and Faydine Brandt, for helping make law school and this book possible; his wife, Sylvia Brandt, for being a wonderful friend, companion, and adviser; and his children, Willow and Henry, for lighting up every day. Celia and Lucie thank Willow for a great vacation in Florida. Celia still thinks the book should have been called *Who Stole the Budget?*

Index

Page numbers in *italics* refer to figures.

348 INDEX

360 INDEX

Standiford, Les, 256n
"starve the beast," 79, 286n
Stasavage, David, 260n–1n
state government, 21–2, 32, 114, 122,
    166–7, 191, 192–3, 211–12, 323n
states' rights, 3, 21
Stavins, Robert N., 327n
Stein, Sam, 258n
Steinberg, Jacques, 288n
Steinhauer, Jennifer, 257n, 297n
Stephens-Davidowitz, Seth, 331n
"stepped-up basis," 214
Sterman, John D., 259n
Stevens, John Austin, 265n
Stevenson, Richard W., 294n
Stewart, James B., 314n
Stigler, George J., 316n–17n
Stiglitz, Joseph E., 293n
stimulus measures, 98–101, 124, 148,
    149–50, 151, 187, 189, 256n
Stockley, Karen, 324n
Stockman, David A., 72–3, 78, 283n
stock market, 52, 97–8, 121, 138, 141,
    187, 213, 232
Stone, Chad, 293n
Storm Surge Unit, 104–5
Stremikis, Kristof, 304n
structural deficits, 124–5, 142–7
student loans, 109, 137, 229, 337n
subprime mortgages, 97
Subramanian, Arvind, 268n, 277n,
    278n
subsidiaries, corporate, 120–1
subsidies, agricultural, 207–8, 209, 221,
    222, 330n, 331n
Suderman, Peter, 300n
Suez Canal crisis (1956), 158
Suffolk Bank system, 274n
Sullivan, Martin A., 334n
Summers, Lawrence, 312n
sunset provisions, 89–90
Sunstein, Cass R., 335n
"supercommittee," 102, 165, 239–40,
    338n
supplemental insurance plans, 195,
    306n
Supplemental Nutrition Assistance
    Program, 209

supply and demand, 59–60
supply-side economics, 72, 169–70
Supreme Court, U.S., 38n
Surowiecki, James, 255n, 294n
surpluses, budget, 36, 69, 76–8, 86–8,
    95–6, 126, 290n–1n, 305n, 322n
Surrey, Stanley, 300n
Suskind, Ron, 257n, 282n, 336n
Sustainable Defense Task Force, 200–1
Svahn, John A., 299n
swaps, debt, 25
Sweden, 173, 271n
Switzerland, 195
Sylla, Richard, 21–2, 259n, 261n, 264n,
    267n, 273n, 277n
Symanski, Steve, 315n–16n
Symonds, Craig L., 259n

Taliban, 200
talk shows, 82–3
Tangeman, John, 323n–4n
Tanzi, Vito, 268n
tariffs, 3–4, 24, 28–30, 35–6, 38n, 168,
    263n, 266n
Tavernise, Sabrina, 331n
"Tax Day," 100
taxes:
    agricultural, 26–7, 170, 207–8, 209,
        330n, 331n
    alternative minimum (AMT), 89, 131,
        186n, 236, 238, 290n, 291n, 295n,
        321n, 337n
    on assets, 214–15, 300n–1n, 308n,
        332n–3n
    avoidance of, 116–17, 120, 133, 166,
        169, 210–11, 213, 278n, 308n
    base for, 133, 143, 169
    on bonds, 141, 143, 211–12, 222
    brackets of, 119n, 197, 211, 216
    capital gains, 90, 169, 170, 187,
        213–15, 222–3, 300n, 332n–3n
    on carbon emissions, 178, 202, 208,
        218, 222, 327n
    on charitable contributions, 212–13,
        222, 228–9, 331n, 332n
    child credit for, 166, 187, 215, 333n
    code for, 85, 97, 116–17, 169, 171–2,
        189, 210–17, 300n, 308n, 316n

179, *182*, *183*, 204, 219, 228, 231–40, 263*n*, 264*n*, 265*n*, 279*n*, 285*n*, 295*n*–300*n*, 306*n*, 308*n*, 309*n*, 312*n*–314*n*, 319*n*
population of, 9, 12–13, 34, 36, 124–5, 127–8, 129, 130, 161, 178, 190–5, 226
savings rate in, 9, 49–50, 60, 94, 110, 117–18, 140, 143, 144*n*, 147–8, 168, 170, 174, 180, 188, 190–1, 210, 213, 215, 217–20, 221, 224, 230, 334*n*
social programs of, *see* Medicare; Social Security
stock market of, 52, 97–8, 121, 138, 141, 187, 213, 232
unemployment rate in, 13, 63, 70, 97, 98, 99, 123–4, 127, 138, 139, 147, 149, 150, 151, 156, 160–3, 174–5, 188–9, 229, 230–1, 232, 310*n*, 317*n*, 321*n*, 324*n*
universal health care, 195–6
upper class, 24, 26, 75, 90–1, 118–19, 130, 133, 163, 169–70, 172, 173–4, 187, 211, 214, 226, 286*n*, 317*n*
U.S. Chamber of Commerce, 83
utilization patterns, 177–8

vacation homes, 211
Valley Forge, 16
value-added tax (VAT), 218–19, *223*, 335*n*
Van Natta, Don, Jr., 288*n*
"veil of ignorance," 173, 174
Velde, François R., 271*n*
Verhovek, Sam Howe, 288*n*
veterans' pensions, 37
vetoes, *25*, 77–8
Vietnam War, 60, 61, 93, 160, 280*n*
Viguerie, Richard, 82, 287*n*
Virginia, 25
Volcker, Paul A., *63*, 64, 280*n*, 281*n*
von Fremd, Charles, 269*n*
voucher programs, 174–5, 199, 226
V-22 aircraft, 201

wage levels, 52, 62, 91, 119–20, 133, 140, 146, 160–1, 167, 194, 197, 217, 234, 315*n*
see also payroll taxes

Waidmann, Timothy, 324*n*
Wallis, John Joseph, 267*n*
Wall Street, 97–8
Wall Street Journal, 72, 114
Walters, Raymond, Jr., 265*n*
Wanniski, Jude, 72
warfare, 3, 4, 16–20, 30–6, 39–40, 57–8, 93, 137, 200–1, 233–4, 263*n*
War Hawks, 3, 30, 93
War of 1812, 3–7, 8, 9, 29, 30–2, 33, 35, 42, 49, 93, 233–4, 267*n*
War of the Spanish Succession, 18
Warren, Elizabeth, 323*n*
Warren, Michael, 308*n*
Washington, D.C., 4–5, 25, 31
Washington, George, 15–17, 22, 25, 26–7, 259*n*, 261*n*
Wassen, Erik, 337*n*
Wasserman, David, 337*n*
Watkins, Thayer, 253*n*
wealth, 24, 26, 75, 90–1, 118–19, 128–9, 130, 133, 163–4, 169–70, 172, 173–4, 175, 187, 203, 211, 214, 226, 286*n*, 300*n*–1*n*, 317*n*
wealth disparities, 128–9, 130, 163–4, 173–4, 175, 187, 203, 286*n*, 300*n*–1*n*, 317*n*
weapons of mass destruction, 176–7, 200
Weather Channel, 105, 115
Webster, Pelatiah, 47
Weingast, Barry R., 260*n*
Weinstein, Milton C., 323*n*
Weinzierl, Matthew, 292*n*
Weisbach, David A., 327*n*, 334*n*
Weisberg, Jacob, 271*n*, 310*n*
Weisman, Jonathan, 337*n*
Weisman, Steven R., 267*n*
welfare programs, 71, 167, 171, 179, 209
see also entitlement programs
West Virginia, 9
Whigs, 18, 260*n*
whiskey, 26–7, 28, 264*n*
Whiskey Rebellion, 26–7, 28
White, Harry Dexter, 41, 42, 55, 56, 269*n*–70*n*
White, Nathan I., 269*n*

ALSO BY SIMON JOHNSON
AND JAMES KWAK

13 BANKERS
*The Wall Street Takeover and the Next
Financial Meltdown*

In spite of its key role in creating the ruinous financial
crisis of 2008, the American banking industry has
grown bigger, more profitable, and more resistant
to regulation than ever. Anchored by six megabanks
whose assets amount to more than 60 percent of
the country's gross domestic product, this oligar-
chy proved it could first hold the global economy
hostage and then use its political muscle to fight off
meaningful reform. *13 Bankers* brilliantly charts
the rise to power of the financial sector and force-
fully argues that we must break up the big banks
if we want to avoid future financial catastrophes.
Updated, with new analysis of the government's
recent attempt to reform the banking industry, this
is a timely and expert account of our troubled political economy.

Business/Economics